"All too often books on comparative juvenile justice descend into bland description of powers and procedures. Goldson's approach is refreshingly different and innovative. Taking an historically informed inter-national and intra-national approach, this edited collection opens up a rich and detailed analysis of key contemporary thematics. Goldson skilfully brings together the insights of leading analysts from across Europe to deliver the most critically informed and perceptive work produced on European juvenile justice to date."

– **John Muncie**, *Emeritus Professor,*
The Open University

"This book offers a vital, timely and highly original analysis of juvenile justice in Europe at a time of profound changes and challenges. It is essential reading."
– **Manfred Nowak**, *Professor of International Human Rights,*
Vienna University and Independent Expert leading
the UN Global Study on Children Deprived of Liberty

JUVENILE JUSTICE IN EUROPE

At a time when Europe is witnessing major cultural, social, economic and political challenges and transformations, this book brings together leading researchers and experts to consider a range of pressing questions relating to the historical origins, contemporary manifestations and future prospects for juvenile justice. Questions considered include:

- How has the history of juvenile justice evolved across Europe and how might the past help us to understand the present and signal the future?
- What do we know about contemporary juvenile crime trends in Europe and how are nation states responding?
- Is punitivity and intolerance eclipsing child welfare and pedagogical imperatives, or is 'child-friendly justice' holding firm?
- How might we best understand both the convergent and the divergent patterning of juvenile justice in a changing and reformulating Europe?
- How is juvenile justice experienced by identifiable constituencies of children and young people both in communities and in institutions?
- What impacts are sweeping austerity measures, together with increasing mobilities and migrations, imposing?
- How can comparative juvenile justice be conceptualised and interpreted?
- What might the future hold for juvenile justice in Europe at a time of profound uncertainty and flux?

This book is essential reading for students, tutors and researchers in the fields of criminology, history, law, social policy and sociology, particularly those engaged with childhood and youth studies, human rights, comparative juvenile/youth justice, youth crime and delinquency and criminal justice policy in Europe.

Barry Goldson holds the Charles Booth Chair of Social Science at the University of Liverpool. He is also Visiting Professorial Research Fellow at the Faculty of Law, University of New South Wales, Sydney, Professorial Fellow in Social Science at Liverpool Hope University and Adjunct Professor at the School of Justice, QUT, Brisbane. He is co-chair of the European Society of Criminology Thematic Working Group on Juvenile Justice.

JUVENILE JUSTICE IN EUROPE

Past, Present and Future

Edited by Barry Goldson

Routledge
Taylor & Francis Group

LONDON AND NEW YORK

First published 2019
by Routledge
2 Park Square, Milton Park, Abingdon, Oxon OX14 4RN

and by Routledge
711 Third Avenue, New York, NY 10017

Routledge is an imprint of the Taylor & Francis Group, an informa business

British Library Cataloguing-in-Publication Data
A catalogue record for this book is available from the British Library

Library of Congress Cataloging-in-Publication Data
Names: Goldson, Barry, editor.
Title: Juvenile justice in Europe : past, present and future /
edited by Barry Goldson.
Description: Abingdon, Oxon ; New York, NY : Routledge, 2019. |
Includes bibliographical references and index.
Identifiers: LCCN 2018017294 | ISBN 9781138721319 (hardback) |
ISBN 9781138721371 (pbk.) | ISBN 9781315194493 (ebook)
Subjects: LCSH: Juvenile justice, Administration of–Europe.
Classification: LCC HV9144.A5 J88 2019 | DDC 364.36094–dc23
LC record available at https://lccn.loc.gov/2018017294

ISBN: 978-1-138-72131-9 (hbk)
ISBN: 978-1-138-72137-1 (pbk)
ISBN: 978-1-315-19449-3 (ebk)

Typeset in Bembo
by Out of House Publishing
Printed and bound by CPI Group (UK) Ltd, Croydon CR0 4YY

In memory of Alan Kurdi, whose tragic death offended justice and stained the conscience of European humanity.

CONTENTS

CONTRIBUTORS

Zoe Alker is Lecturer in Criminology, University of Liverpool, England.

Emma Bell is Professor of British Politics, Université de Savoie Mont Blanc, France.

Els Dumortier is Professor of Criminology, Vrije Universiteit Brussel, Belgium.

Barry Goldson is Professor/Charles Booth Chair of Social Science, University of Liverpool, England.

Ursula Kilkelly is Professor of Law, University College Cork, Ireland.

Tapio Lappi-Seppälä is Professor of Criminal Law and Criminology, University of Helsinki, Finland.

Ton Liefaard is Professor/UNICEF Chair in Children's Rights, Leiden University, The Netherlands.

Lesley McAra is Professor of Penology, University of Edinburgh, Scotland.

Susan McVie is Professor of Quantitative Criminology, University of Edinburgh, Scotland.

David Nelken is Professor of Comparative and Transnational Law in Context, Kings College London, England.

Maria Pisani is Lecturer in Youth and Community Studies, University of Malta, Malta.

Heather Shore is Professor of History, Leeds Beckett University, England.

Emma Watkins is a doctoral research student, University of Liverpool, England.

Colin Webster is Professor of Criminology, Leeds Beckett University, England.

ACKNOWLEDGEMENTS

The origins of this book can be traced back to various meetings of the European Society of Criminology Thematic Working Group on Juvenile Justice (ESC TWGJJ). Several, but not all, of the essays that are published in this volume began life at such meetings. I am grateful to members of the ESC TWGJJ for their friendship and collegiality and the inspiring juvenile justice scholar, Jenneke Christiaens, is deserving of particular thanks.

I am, of course, especially grateful to each of the authors and to Tom Sutton, Hannah Catterall and other colleagues at Routledge for having faith in, and realising, this collaborative project.

The respective essays develop and present some different lines of argument and understanding but, taken together, they provide a robust basis for intellectual reflection, debate and critical analysis. The reflection, debate and critical analysis is always incomplete, however, and in this sense, the book is conceived as a beginning rather than an end.

As a contributing author, and as the editor of the volume, I am hopeful that what follows will provoke further theoretical and empirical inquiry into making sense of, and making good, juvenile justice in Europe.

Barry Goldson
Liverpool, 2018

PREFACE

In 1816, the report of what was probably the first major public inquiry into 'juvenile delinquency' in any European country was published in London, England (Committee for Investigating the Alarming Increase of Juvenile Delinquency in the Metropolis, 1816). The inquiry was concerned both with the 'causes' of juvenile delinquency and, with what was perceived to be, its 'alarming increase'. The publication of the report coincided with myriad burgeoning concerns – across Europe and beyond – that centred the behaviour, public presence, conditions and treatment of identifiable groups of children and young people in the high-density urban populations of the rapidly growing industrial towns and cities. Such concerns served to inspire 'a wide range of reform initiatives that have variously, if incongruously, been interpreted as humanitarian in motive or repressive in intent' (Goldson and Muncie, 2009: xxi). The same initiatives developed and consolidated across Europe as the nineteenth century unfolded and, by the beginning of the twentieth century, recognizably 'modern' juvenile justice systems had emerged. In England, for example, the Children Act 1908 represented the legislative foundations of an institutional architecture designed specifically for the administration of juvenile justice and, as such, it reflected similar developments that were taking place elsewhere in Europe.

In 2008, exactly one hundred years following the implementation of the Children Act 1908, a global financial crisis rocked the foundations of European economies. The 'crisis' produced deep-cutting and wide-sweeping 'austerity' measures that, alongside the longer-term reformulation of welfare settlements and welfare states, have had the effect of plunging millions of Europeans into adverse social conditions. And in 2016, exactly 200 years following the publication of the first major public inquiry into 'juvenile delinquency', the United Kingdom European Union membership referendum – also known as the 'EU referendum' and the 'Brexit referendum' – returned a vote in support of the UK's departure from the European

Union. Many commentators have argued that recent patterns of migration and immigration into Europe in general, and the UK more particularly, imposed significant influence in shaping the vote to 'leave'. Whatever the motivations, however, Brexit has 'created severe tensions and strengthened exit movements elsewhere, notably in France, Italy and Denmark' (Taylor-Gooby *et al.*, 2017: 3).

In the opening two decades of the twenty-first century financial crisis, the re-drawing of welfare settlements and welfare states, Brexit – and the wider tensions that it signals – and unprecedented patterns of migration and immigration represent key transformational conditions in Europe, just as the industrial revolution characterised radical change across the nineteenth century. Equally, the same modern-day cultural, social, political and economic transformations carry multiple implications for juvenile justice in Europe, just as the industrial revolution had some two hundred years earlier.

How might the past inform the present and to what extent does the present provide a compass to the future? Fundamentally, these are the questions that are addressed in this volume by some of Europe's leading juvenile justice scholars. The book is presented in three parts – past, present and future – and taken together its constituent essays begin to unravel the continuities and changes, the convergences and divergences and the commonalities and differences that characterize juvenile justice in Europe.

Part I of the book comprises three chapters that principally engage with the past.

In Chapter 1, Els Dumortier provides a historical criminological account of the foundations of Children's Courts in Belgium and elsewhere in Europe. Dumortier argues that even though differences were clearly visible across countries/jurisdictions, certain core principles appeared to be 'common' in the conceptualisation and practice of the Children's Courts in several European countries including: an ambiguous mission; a sense of jurisdictional specificity focusing exclusively upon children and young people (both 'offenders' and those deemed to be in need of 'care'); the composition of the courts with specialised judges and 'intimate' (child-centred) procedures and settings; and, close collaboration with private (often religious) institutions and professional 'experts' (including probation officers, doctors and psychiatrists). By taking account of the major transformations of the time and the ways in which the past links to the present, the chapter serves to deepen an understanding of both the foundational principles and the contemporary practices of Children's Courts in Europe.

In Chapter 2, Heather Shore aims to 'rethink the long history of juvenile justice' by tracing key developmental milestones and critically examining cross-jurisdictional policy and practice 'transfers'. Not unlike Dumortier's essay, both continuity and change comprise pivotal reference points and Shore concludes by considering new directions for historical analyses of European juvenile justice.

In Chapter 3, Zoe Alker and Emma Watkins also engage with 'new directions' for juvenile justice scholarship by adopting an innovative integration of historical research, life-course criminology and digital methods. They note that 'the relatively recent digitisation of genealogical sources including the census, birth, marriage and death records, crime registers and newspapers means that crime historians are able to "unlock" the biographies of young offenders'. In a fascinating essay, Alker and Watkins bring the past back to life by digitising history, creating longitudinal life histories and revealing young people's experiences of both micro- and macro-processes of historical change. By 'tracing the pathways that children and young people followed into, through and out of specialist institutions', the authors extend 'aetiological accounts beyond individualized and reductionist moral discourses and place them instead within an appreciative context that integrates individual agency and complex material, social-structural, cultural, economic and political conditions'.

In Chapter 4, Ton Liefaard and Ursula Kilkelly open Part II of the book by setting out the principles of 'child-friendly justice' and exploring the interface between international human rights standards, European guidelines and contemporary juvenile justice policies and practices. The authors describe the efforts taken to consult directly with children and young people in the construction of European guidelines and consider critically both the benefits of the guidelines and their shortcomings. It is argued that the European guidelines 'underscore the significance of treating children in conflict with the law with the respect to which they are entitled'.

In Chapter 5, Lesley McAra and Susan McVie explore critically the 'shrinking' size and scope of juvenile justice systems in Europe alongside 'a phenomenon commonly referred to as the "crime drop"'. The essay is informed by robust longitudinal research – which the authors have been leading for several years – and incisive theoretical/conceptual analysis, and it points to the 'danger' of conflating 'changes in system activity with individual behavioural change'. Instead, McAra and McVie develop an analysis underpinned by what they term the 'displacement effect', the 'cultural dissonance effect', the 'concentration effect' and the 'whole-system effect'. Notwithstanding the complexities of cross-jurisdictional comparative analysis – not least 'the paucity of robust comparative data' – a strong case is made for diversion as a guiding logic for European juvenile justice policy and practice.

In Chapter 6, Tapio Lappi-Seppälä examines four European jurisdictions that are commonly thought to characterise progressive juvenile/youth justice regimes: Denmark, Finland, Norway and Sweden – the epitome of Nordic/Scandinavian 'exceptionalism' (Pratt, 2008a; Pratt 2008b). The essay addresses the complex interface between 'welfare' and 'justice' systems and it also takes account of post-juvenile justice interventions and the ways in which young adults are processed within and across the four jurisdictions.

In Chapter 7, Emma Bell shifts the analytical gaze from 'child-friendly' justice (Chapter 4), 'diversion' (Chapter 5) and progressive 'exceptionalism' (Chapter 6), to the impact of 'neoliberal austerity' on juvenile justice in Europe. Not dissimilar to other essays in the volume, Bell acknowledges the practical difficulties involved in analysing trends in juvenile justice across the European Union, but argues that the increasingly significant role played by European institutions in shaping common penal trajectories makes the study of such trends essential if we hope to better understand the drivers of penal change. In this sense, the essay focuses on macro-level trends and, particularly, the impact of neoliberal austerity in creating considerable injustices regarding children and young people across Europe.

In Chapter 8, Colin Webster maintains the focus on juvenile injustice in Europe by examining questions of 'race', ethnicity and social class. Again, the absence of comprehensive pan-European data and the attendant difficulties of engaging comparative analysis are highlighted. But Webster makes a persuasive case for taking account of the substantial over-representation of minority and migrant children and young people within conditions of persistent, long-term poverty and exclusion from education, employment or training (NEET), in order to explain the likelihood of their coming into contact with the police and juvenile justice systems across Europe. The chapter concludes that some children and young people in Europe are doubly punished for their minority/migrant status *and* for being poor.

In Chapter 9, Maria Pisani focuses more sharply on the injustices visited upon young migrants. Containment policies, the securitisation of the external borders and the use of detention are just some of the mechanisms that have been implemented and operationalized to 'manage' young migrants, including 'unaccompanied minors'. Pisani engages with the concept of 'crimmigration' and analyses critically the intersections of 'race', age and legal status in the production of poverty, social marginalisation, crime and, perhaps more significantly, criminalisation.

In Chapter 10, David Nelken concludes Part II of the volume by drawing together many of the intrinsic complexities of the comparative project. The essay opens with a general consideration of the purposes of studying juvenile justice comparatively and proceeds to discuss descriptive, explanatory and interpretative enquiries and their relation to the challenges of finding equivalence, discovering what is salient and thinking reflexively.

Chapter 11 takes the form of an extended essay that comprises Part III of the book. It is presented in two sections. The first engages with the complexities involved in reading the present. The second addresses some of the major challenges facing the future(s) of juvenile justice in Europe. The essay builds upon and extends many of the issues that earlier chapters address. It takes account of the complex nature of comparative juvenile justice at transnational/pan-European, inter-national and intra-national/sub-national levels. It also critically reviews macro-level socio-economic and political change and attempts to define the implications for the juvenile justice of tomorrow and beyond.

Taken together, the three parts and eleven chapters of the book attempt to navigate new ways of thinking about, and comprehending, juvenile justice in Europe – its historical antecedents, its contemporary manifestations and its future directions. The book deliberately avoids descriptions of country-by-country systems, socio-legal configurations, policies and practices, and instead it engages with a more thematic form of analysis. It represents an audaciously ambitious project and, as such, it is necessarily incomplete. But it also begins to define and develop the co-ordinates of a research agenda that is vital for advancing knowledge of, and intervening in, the ways in which identifiable groups of children and young people are governed through juvenile justice systems in Europe.

Barry Goldson
Liverpool, 2018

References

Committee for Investigating the Alarming Increase of Juvenile Delinquency in the Metropolis (1816) *Report of the Committee for Investigating the Alarming Increase of Juvenile Delinquency in the Metropolis*. London: J. F. Dove.

Goldson, B. and Muncie, J. (2009) 'Editor's Introduction', in B. Goldson and J. Muncie (eds.) *Youth Crime and Juvenile Justice Volume 1: The 'Youth Problem'*. London: Sage.

Pratt, J. (2008a) 'Scandinavian Exceptionalism in an Era of Penal Excess: Part I: The Nature and Roots of Scandinavian Exceptionalism', *British Journal of Criminology*, 48(2): 119–137.

Pratt, J. (2008b) 'Scandinavian Exceptionalism in an Era of Penal Excess: Part II: Does Scandinavian Exceptionalism Have a Future?' *British Journal of Criminology*, 48(3): 275–292.

Taylor-Gooby, P., Leruth, B. and Chung, H. (2017) 'The Context: How European welfare states have responded to post-industrialism, ageing populations and populist nationalism', in P. Taylor-Gooby, B. Leruth, and H. Chung, (eds) *After Austerity: Welfare State Transformation in Europe after the Great Recession*. Oxford: Oxford University Press.

PART I
Past

1

UNDER PRESSURE? THE FOUNDATIONS OF CHILDREN'S COURTS IN EUROPE

Els Dumortier

'If we can reveal that practices and beliefs have a history, then maybe we can destabilize their apparent immutability'

Bosworth, 2001: 439

Introduction: contemporary juvenile justice debates in Europe and the importance of historical perspectives

Since the 1990s many European countries have introduced reforms to their juvenile justice legislation (Junger-Tas and Decker, 2006; Muncie and Goldson, 2006 Dünkel et al., 2010; Decker and Marteache, 2017). These changes imply, to a certain extent, a departure from 'classical' juvenile justice principles that were established at the end of the nineteenth and the beginning of the twentieth centuries. Such reforms are often presented as repressive and are linked to a 'toughening up' of attitudes and demands for more robust (punitive) responses to juvenile crime and youth delinquency (Goldson, 2002; Hendrick, 2006; Muncie, 2008; Bailleau and Cartuyvels, 2010; Dumortier et al., 2012). To counter such punitive tendencies, the increased need for (the real implementation of) international children's rights standards has been advanced by several scholars (Muncie, 2008; Snacken and Dumortier, 2012; Goldson and Muncie, 2015) and, according to some, by taking account of such standards the excesses of punitiveness have been resisted in identifiable European juvenile justice systems (Dünkel, 2016). Central to such rights approaches stands the concept of broad social justice for *all children*, the need to divert as many children and young people as possible from juvenile justice systems and, at the extremes, to limit any deprivation of liberty to an intervention of last resort and for the shortest time possible (United Nations Committee on the Rights of the Child, 2007; Goldson and Muncie, 2015).

However, by focusing solely on contemporary reforms and debates, their historical antecedents, problems and 'solutions' are lost in the mists of time. In other words, by not taking history into account, contemporary debates are at risk of continuously recycling common *beliefs* pertaining to juvenile justice rather than producing *knowledge*. It is to uncover contemporary myths and beliefs about juvenile justice that a longer-term, historical European perspective is needed.

Although it is inherently hazardous to attempt to outline general trends, reforms and evolutions across national frontiers – because every jurisdiction/ country is confronted with its own particular conditions and comparative analysis is necessarily complex (Nelken, 2009) – a wider 'European perspective' can help us to deepen our understanding of the foundation of Children's Courts in different European countries. Of course, Europe is a large entity comprising 28 member states in the European Union and 47 member states in the Council of Europe. It is not, therefore, possible in a single chapter to provide a comprehensive historical account, and in this contribution the emphasis is on the origins of the children's court in Belgium. Belgium is a particularly important jurisdiction given that within international-comparative research it is often referred to as a pioneer in European juvenile justice and, to this day, it is still commonly presented as being representative of the 'welfare model' (Junger-Tas and Decker, 2006; Bateman, 2012; Tonry and Chambers, 2012, 877; Dumortier, Christiaens and Nuytiens, 2017).

Notwithstanding its significance in Europe and beyond, however, it is also clear that the course and form that juvenile justice reform took in Belgium is not completely isolated. On the contrary, several countries in Europe and beyond witnessed the rise of specialised Children's Courts at the end of the nineteenth and the beginning of the twentieth centuries (Trépanier and Rousseaux, 2018). Even though national differences were clearly present, therefore – not least due to legal and political differences between common and civil law countries – certain core principles appear to be shared in the historical conceptualisation of the 'new' Children's Courts, including: (i) an ambiguous mission of 'saving' children while also holding them to account, (ii) jurisdictional specificity (an exclusive focus on children and the exclusion of adults), (iii) the composition of the courts with specialised judges and 'intimate' (child-centred) processes, procedures and settings, and (iv) the inclusion of new collaborators working with the judge including probation officers, private (often religious) institutions and personnel and 'scientific experts' (including doctors and psychiatrists).

To understand the common elements that characterise much juvenile justice reform, we will start with a first section on the rise of the children's court in Europe in a context of major social, economic and political transformations. Our second section will then focus more sharply on the Belgian model through a diversity of sources including parliamentary sources (particularly pertaining to the Child Protection Act 1912) and judicial statistics and archives (especially relating to the Belgian Child Protection system from 1912–1965). In our conclusion and discussion we will, on the basis of this historical mapping, critically contextualise some contemporary debates that centre juvenile courts, juvenile justice and children's rights in Europe.

The emergence and development of Children's Courts in Europe: social, economic and political transformations

To comprehend the emergence and development of Children's Courts we need to take account of the challenges European societies were facing at the end of the nineteenth and beginning of the twentieth centuries. In this first section, therefore, we consider two important transformations that occurred at that time that, in turn, gave rise to two major questions (one social/structural and the other individual/moral).

The tensions between social justice and social defence

At the end of the nineteenth–beginning of the twentieth century, both Europe and the USA were confronted with the 'social question'. Ongoing processes of industrialisation and urbanisation during the nineteenth century, together with ultra-liberal politics and the absence of centralised social welfare systems, created an oppressed and highly impoverished working class who lived in miserable conditions (*'le prolétariat'*). As a consequence, many European countries witnessed the rise of 'socialist', 'communist' or 'labour' (political) movements that, together with the emerging and growing trade unions, aimed to defend the interests of the working classes; most notably, the struggle for the (universal) right to vote (Chlepner, 1972; Berger, 2006). Furthermore, sections of traditionally more conservative political parties and movements, together with the Church, also became inspired by principles of 'social justice'. In the Anglo-Saxon world, for example, a new theology of Social Christianity developed throughout the nineteenth and into the twentieth centuries (Phillips, 1996) and, in the Catholic belt of Europe, the philosophical revival of Thomas Aquinas at the end of nineteenth century, also helped to legitimise the principles of 'social justice' (Kenny, 1980; van Kersbergen, 1995).

At the end of the nineteenth and the beginning of the twentieth centuries, however, the implementation of 'social justice' was still at an embryonic stage. With regard to children and young people, key manifestations included the abolition of child labour and the obligatory education of children in many European countries (Rahikaenen, 2004). Although such steps can be taken to represent progress, they made minimal impact upon dominant modes of capitalist social ordering. The socialist and communist ideals of working towards a classless society and transforming the relations of production, distribution and exchange into 'common' entities were not shared by these early variants of 'social justice' (Chlepner, 1972). On the contrary, such 'social justice' was contingent and conditional and it was the bourgeoisie who maintained close control of the philanthropic 'patronage' for the poor by deciding who might be helped (the *deserving poor*) and who might not (the *undeserving poor*). Indeed, such ostensible expressions of 'social justice' (understood principally by reference to moral discourses) dovetailed neatly into the overarching imperative of 'social defence' or social control, a much 'tougher' response to the 'social question' and one that was principally driven by the maintenance of the status quo.

Indeed, as a reaction to the 'social question' that was framed by class struggle ('*la lutte des classes*'), 'la bourgeoisie' undertook pseudo-scientific investigations of the working classes' living conditions ('*les enquêtes sociales*') within which the 'labouring classes' (or 'perishing classes') and the 'dangerous classes' were bracketed as 'savages' to be feared, controlled and, if need be, repressed (Christiaens, 1999a). Further, backed up by the 'scientific discoveries' of early criminologists such as Lombroso (1895, 1899), Lacassagne (1913) and Ferri (1905), it was assumed that criminal acts were not the product of free choice and rational calculation (classical school) but that the root causes of crime were to be found in factors outside the control of the offender (biological or sociological positivist schools). As a consequence, the 'bankruptcy' of classical criminal law was announced by several leading scholars of the time (Cantor, 1936).

Instead of the metaphysical, philosophical and 'unscientific' concepts of 'free will' and 'guilt' drawn from the Era of Enlightenment, advocates of 'social defence' – such as the Belgian Prins (1899, 1910), the Dutchman Van Hamel (1895) and the Italian Ferri (1905) – claimed that notions of 'determinism' and 'dangerousness' should guide the state's interventions and that more fluid measures of 'social defence' were needed to complement, if not replace, classical punishment, particularly in the cases of children, young people and the mentally ill. Such (indeterminate) measures were characterised by their aims of preventing crime, of transforming adaptable and compliant 'criminals' into law-abiding citizens or, in the case of their 'incorrigible' counterparts, of neutralising them. According to Cantor (1935: 347), continental European countries and scholars were increasingly occupied with the 'theorisation' and elaboration of new *codes of social defence* (in their attempts to reconcile positivism with classicism), whereas the Anglo-Saxon world, 'in the absence of a clear penal theory', was increasingly experimenting and developing – 'from the bottom up' – new approaches in daily practice. What is absolutely clear for continental European countries is that the second half of the nineteenth century was characterised by an intensification of experiments and new measures to deal with delinquent children and young people, beggars and vagabonds (Dupont-Bouchat and Pierre, 2001).

Children of the 'lower depths'

In attempts to bolster 'social defences' and better protect society against criminality, the children of the 'lower depths' ('*les bas fonds*') received special attention. On one hand, the traditions of biological positivism presented children as more 'savage' than adults, less psychologically developed, more prone to genetic determinism and, particularly during puberty and 'adolescence', more susceptible to hormonal changes and consequent instability (Lombroso, 1899). On the other hand, socio-logical positivists, such as Ferri (1905), Lacassagne (1913) and Tarde (1890), claimed that children, and specifically working-class children, faced particular risks and were routinely exposed to bad examples amidst their miserable living conditions. Tarde (1890), for example, argued that children learn by way of imitation and growing up in neighbourhoods and families in which 'immoral practices' abounded (such as alcoholism, prostitution, violence, gambling, laziness) imposed negative effects. Equally, Adolphe Prins (1910) approached working-class children as both *unfortu-nate victims* of their own genetic inheritance, parental neglect and/or poor living conditions, and as prospective *dangerous criminals*. Accordingly, although children of '*les bas fonds*' might be excused punishment as guilty criminals (because they are unfortunate victims with no free will) they definitely had to be prevented from following a deterministic path towards adult criminality (because that would render them dangerous). In other words, working-class children were often conceptualised as miserable ('*misérable*') and 'dangerous' at one and the same time.

From the perspective of securing 'social defence' and preventing (adult) crime, therefore, 'lower class' children emerged as both a problem and, simultaneously, a key to the solution. If they could be 'corrected' in good time their path towards adult crime might be averted. This too comprised the juncture where 'social justice' and 'social defence' converged. Developments such as compulsory schooling and a broad public-health/hygiene policy (including nutrition, physical education of children, preventing and treating venereal diseases that were widespread) overlapped and intersected with initiatives to address juvenile delinquency by way of more pre-ventive and early intervention approaches engineered, not only by the Children's Courts, but also by a growing body of probation officers, foster carers and/or (pri-vate) institutions. Meanwhile, for more serious juvenile offenders, re-education took place in closed (often state-run) institutions.

Another important measure of social defence vis-à-vis working-class children (and their families) – highly promoted during the second half of the nineteenth century – was the (further) development of *parens patriae*. This doctrine, originally developed in common law countries (Bac, 1998), authorised local authorities to take responsibility for neglected, maltreated or abused children and it promoted and influenced the European-continental and civil law variant of '*la déchéance paternelle*' (or '*ontzetting/ontheffing uit de ouderlijke macht*'). By the beginning of the twentieth century many European countries introduced the possibility of with-drawing 'unfortunate' children from their 'unworthy parents' ('*les parents indignes*') and placing them in institutions or alternative families with foster carers. The prin-ciple of the 'best interest of the child' became, also in civil law, a legally accepted concept and the gateway for state intervention in what was previously perceived as an 'untouchable' domain in civil law countries until long into the nineteenth century: the 'sacred' family with the father as *pater familias* (Dupont-Bouchat, 1983; Christiaens, 1994; Van Praet, 2017). Moreover, the principle of *equity*, instead of *due process*, lay at the basis of this *parens patriae* doctrine (Bac, 1998) and it served to authorise courts to address 'with wide discretion' the problems of 'its least fortunate junior citizens' (Platt, 1974/2002: 187). In short, to 'rescue' children conventional procedural guarantees had to be overturned (Platt, 1974/2002: 188)

'Modern girls' and the city

The challenges European countries were facing at the end of the nineteenth and the beginning of the twentieth centuries were not only understood with reference to social justice and social defence. The social consequences of industrialisation and urbanisation were also commonly and explicitly interpreted as undermining society's 'morality'. Within this form of conceptual framing, not only the working classes, but especially young people and, even more specifically, girls and young women, were thought to comprise not only a 'vulnerable' but also a 'dangerous' presence in need of control, regulation and (moral) protection (Odem, 1995; De Koster, 2001; Cox, 2003). Four key manifestations are particularly noteworthy.

In the first instance, the increased attention to young people derived from mass migration from the (very) religious countryside into the developing and expanding towns and cities. This produced profound concerns amongst the upper classes and the religious power brokers and it also created tensions within the labouring classes, especially between parents and their children (De Koster, 2001). The towns and cities, with their cinemas, dance halls, malls and greater levels of social anonymity (and liberty), comprised magnets for children and young people previously accustomed to relatively sedate and conservative rural communities. The greatly expanded and largely uncontrolled leisure opportunities available to young people and the increasing draw of consumption and consumerist activities intensified adult concerns about the morality of youth (De Koster, 2001).

Second, and more specifically still, girls were deemed to be an especially vulnerable group within the context of mushrooming urbanisation, increased rural-urban migrations and the perceived diminution of 'moral' standards. The primary concern was that the 'twentieth-century modern girl' (Cox, 2003: 4) was becoming increasingly independent from her parents in tandem with greater exposure to employment, cafés, shops and other public places. With no or only limited parental or other informal control, such girls and young women were increasingly identified as being 'vulnerable' and 'at risk'. In the worst case scenarios, they were prone to seduction by men and/or to gravitating into prostitution which, as Knepper (2010: 98) observes, was rather dramatically conceived of as the 'white slave trade' in the UK and the USA, as 'traité des blanches' in France or as 'Mädchenhandel' in Germany. At the same time, however, the concept of 'female indecency' was mobilised in such a way as to present the behaviour of working-class girls and young women as a 'danger' to the moral health of society. The spread of sexual diseases, for example, was explained by reference to 'indecent' (young) women and falling pregnant outside of marriage was deemed to be a 'sin' that gravely dishonoured a young woman and her family (De Koster, 2001).

Third, by the end of the nineteenth century the question of how to react to the perceived (growing) problem of prostitution in towns and cities became a pressing political issue. Numerous campaigns against the 'white slave trade' and prostitution led to a complex and ambiguous alliance between conservative-religious movements and nascent feminist forces. Within a palpably moralistic social climate, several European countries witnessed an increase in the age of consent that was explicitly legitimated by referring to the need to protect girls' morality and honour (Odem, 1995; De Koster, 2001; Dumortier, 2006). At the same time, such increases in the age of consent served, in practice, to broaden the possibilities for Children's Courts to intervene in order to control and regulate girls' sexual behaviour (Dumortier, 2006). This in turn extended forms of institutional control whereby 'indecent girls' were held, for example, in the infamous Magdalene Asylums that – from the eighteenth century onwards – proliferated in Ireland (Finnegan, 2004) and other European countries.

Finally, the development of organised women's movements served, paradoxically, to extend the increasing regulation and control of working-class girls and young women. Together with the Suffragettes' demand for the right to vote, women were also imposing themselves more forcefully within the public sphere, and the expanding 'child protection' systems provided opportunities for women. In many countries, therefore, it was women who played the most prominent roles in promoting and implementing new 'child care' and 'child protection' systems (for example, Mary Carpenter in England and Madame Henri Carton de Wiart in Belgium). Women were also encouraged to take up roles as probation officers which, in turn, served to intensify state intervention in the control and governance of young people in general and girls and young women in particular (see later).

'America's gift to the world'[1]

In a context of major societal transformations, therefore, the foundations for new and 'modern' Children's Courts were laid across Europe and elsewhere (Bac, 1998; Rosenheim et al., 2001). International exchanges of ideas and practical initiatives pertaining to 'child care', 'child protection' and the role of Children's Courts were disseminated through a burgeoning scientific literature and via reciprocal 'field visits' made by leading figures in the European 'child saving' movement (Dumortier, 2006: 111–112). Even though European countries implemented Children's Courts at different times, with different names and with different competences and compositions, the switch from exclusively criminal to more generic Children's Courts consolidated in many (if not all) European countries (Trépanier and Rousseaux, 2018). The new courts signalled the beginning of a 'modern' era, an innovative way of responding to children and young people who were deemed 'vulnerable' or 'dangerous', or both.

The foundational principles of Children's Courts in Europe: institutional ambiguities

Although Children's Courts emerged in different ways in Europe, due to national particularities and differing legal traditions (specifically common law versus civil law traditions), some generic concepts transcended national frontiers. Four foundational principles are especially noteworthy pertaining, in turn, to: the notion of 'child saving'; the formal separation of institutional jurisdictional arrangements between adult and child; the nature of judicial powers; and, emerging networks of professional collaborators.

'Child saving': a noble mission with a punitive baseline

A 'child saving' mission underpinned the Children's Courts that emerged in the early years of the twentieth century. The mission was ambiguous, however, in that it embraced both social justice and social defence imperatives. As Platt (2002: 177) describes, 'the spirit of social justice' never stood in the way of controlling and regulating the 'criminal classes'. In Belgium, for example, the (Catholic) Minister of Justice who introduced the Children's Courts in 1912, explicitly referred to 'social justice' as a means of legitimating the new courts and their extended discretionary powers: Children's Courts would become the 'soul of patronage' and the 'illuminating centre of all protective institutions for children' (Belgian Parliamentary Debate, 1912: 375). This did not deter the Minister from also claiming that 'the new regime will in many cases bring more severity than under the actual Criminal Code' (Belgian Parliamentary Debate, 1912: 315–317). This greater severity was necessary, according to the Minister, because 'if we want to destroy or at the least combat efficiently the army of crime and the army of prostitution… it is important to dry up its source' (Belgian Parliamentary Debate, 1912: 401). The mission of 'child saving' was clearly double-edged.

Moreover, 'social justice' was conceptualised primarily as an expression of philanthropic benevolence rather than necessitating any equalisation of social ordering and/or the redistribution of power and resources. Indeed, 'social justice' in this sense must first be understood as a form of upper-class charity. It did little, if anything, to emancipate the working classes by the allocation of decent public housing, granting the right to a minimum wage, providing access to stable employment or any other measures that might serve to provide financial and material resources to working-class children and families and relieve their economically harsh situations. The misbehaviour of children was thus presented, constructed and treated principally as an expression of moral deficiency and the Children's Courts had minimal impact on material conditions. In this way, the primary approach taken by the 'new' Children's Courts heavily resembled the 'old' criminal courts with their emphasis on individual agency/responsibility and moral deficiency. The main conceptual difference between the two systems is that in the 'old' generic criminal justice system immorality was conceived as a *chosen* condition (free will), while in the new Children's Courts – framed within specialist juvenile justice systems – immorality was thought to be *socially determined* by a combination of individual fallibility and environmental conditions. The principal purpose of intervention, therefore, was the correction of '(im) morality' (Dumortier, 2006).

The similarities and continuities between generic criminal justice and specialist juvenile justice can also be illustrated by analysing the 'new' protective measures. Indeed, in many ways the new protective or re-educational ('child saving') measures resembled the old measures of repressive intervention. The placement of the child in *Benevolent Schools*, as they became known in Belgium under the provisions of the Child Protection Act 1912, actually took place in the very same institutions that were formerly known as 'youth prisons' and/or institutions that had held vagrants and beggars. In this way, the practice of detaining children in closed institutions within the Belgian 'welfare model' demonstrates an important expression of continuity. Also, 'reprimanding' the child, one of the promising new 'educative measures' provided by the Child Protection Act 1912, was actually originally introduced 20 years earlier as a *punishment* for young first-time offenders (Act on the Repression of Vagrants and Beggars, 1891–1897).

Although there are strong continuities between the generic criminal justice and the specialist juvenile justice systems in Belgium, however, there are also important differences. One of the major shifts provided by the Child Protection Act 1912 was that interventions by Children's Courts were no longer strictly and exclusively determined by the seriousness of the offence. Rather, the courts were expected to take action to 'protect' and 're-educate' children on the basis of their individual circumstances, personality and environment. These new criteria, however, were not legally defined and were left instead to the discretion of the court (Dumortier, 2012). In this way, the classical principle of *proportionality* was replaced with a much more opaque construction of discretion, flexibility and adaptability. Welfarist interventions thus became much less limited in nature, scope and length than penal sanctions and could be extended until the child reached the age of majority (21 years at the time in Belgium) or even beyond (in cases where 'social defence' imperatives demanded it). Also, the principle of equality was diminished – the same act could elicit quite different outcomes contingent on the perceived circumstances, personality and environment of the child. In earlier legislation the principles of proportionality and equality were traditionally legitimated by referring to the priorities of social defence. The Child Protection Act 1912 signalled a departure from such social defence roots: the nature, scope and length of intervention became more legitimated by referring to the 'best interests of the child'. And so it was that the ostensibly 'noble mission' of 'child saving', within the context of a specialist juvenile justice system, assumed greater controlling and punitive effects than the earlier variants of generic criminal justice.

A further reform introduced in Belgium by the Child Protection Act 1912 was the '*liberté surveillée*' (literally 'monitored liberty') provision, which imitated the Anglo-Saxon practice of probation or community supervision. The objective was to keep the child in his or her family environment if they were deemed to be morally trustworthy and the familial circumstances were considered suitable. Probation officers were required to assess such suitability before the judge determined the kind of intervention. If the option of '*liberté surveillée*' was taken, the same probation officer assumed a duty to supervise and monitor the child to ensure that her/his circumstances remained suitable. If this was deemed not to be the case, the child could be removed from her/his family and placed out of their home (even without having committed a new offence), as a 'preventative' measure.

From the inception of Children's Courts in Belgium, the ambiguities of the new 'noble mission' were firmly criticised. Several Members of Parliament questioned the extent to which the *Benevolent Schools* within the specialist juvenile justice system actually differed from the old (youth) prisons within the generic criminal justice system (Belgian Parliamentary Debate, 1912). Also Heupgen, a children's judge, wondered whether the legal changes were not 'more verbal than real' (Heupgen, 1926: 744) and claimed that 'the euphemism of the title of the Act could not remove its character' (Heupgen, 1926: 750). Moreover, as time passed, questioning the regenerative and educational merits of the 'welfare', 'care' and 'protective' logics clearly gained weight (Platt, 1977; Donzelot, 1979). Van de Kerchove (1977), for example, refers to the 'mystifying forces' of welfare language and concluded that 'welfare measures' were in essence 'repressive measures' but the emphasis on 'welfare' 'freed' the state from its constitutional duties to guarantee and administer legal rights and procedural guarantees. This form of critique has since become one of the major drivers of the call of the Children's Rights Movement for defined legal safeguards and procedural guarantees for children in order to offset excessive forms of state intervention, whether or not they are articulated and legitimised by reference to 'education', 'care', 'welfare' and/or 'protection'.

In this way, historical research reveals a long record of the ways in which juvenile justice has been, and remains, presented as a 'soft' or benign response to children but, despite attempts to keep up such appearances, the same research exposes the fact that in reality juvenile justice has never been 'non-punitive'. Researching the operational realities and effects of juvenile justice, rather than simply focusing upon its rhetorical representations is, therefore, of utmost importance (Christiaens, 2015; Trépanier and Rousseaux, forthcoming).

Adult-child separation: diversifying and expanding modes of intervention?

The second foundational principle of the new Children's Courts derives from their exclusive jurisdictional specificity: the formal separation of adult and juvenile justice. Historical-criminological research reveals how in practice this separation started in the mid-nineteenth century with the incremental removal of children from adult prisons (Christiaens, 1999b; Dupont-Bouchat, 1996; Dupont-Bouchat et al., 2001), and consolidated at the beginning of the twentieth century with the separation of children from adults in court (Dumortier, 2006). The underpinning argument was that, not unlike prisons, in court children needed to be separated from the negative influences and 'contamination' that might be imposed by contact with criminal adults. Moreover, the new mission of 'saving' and 'protecting' children demanded a specialist court presided over by a specialist judge able to administer child-centred, 'intimate' and 'confessional' justice (see below).

Not only delinquent children under 16 years of age but, taking into account the new aim of crime prevention, also 'pre-delinquent' children under 18 years of age appeared in Children's Courts. In order to judicially define such 'pre-delinquent' children, the Belgian legislator turned to the provisions of older legislation that had applied to child-beggars, vagabonds and children deemed to be beyond parental control. The Child Protection Act 1912 served to 'centralise' the appearance of children before the new children's judge instead of them having to appear in different courts and/or tribunals for different purposes (for example, before 1912, child-beggars and vagabonds typically appeared before the *Juge de Paix* (Justice of the Peace), whereas children deemed to be beyond parental control normally appeared before the *Président du Tribunal de Première Instance* (Presiding judge in the court of First Instance)). Perhaps more significantly, after the implementation of the Child Protection Act 1912 new grounds for intervention were created. In 1920, for example, truancy became a new ground for intervention and, later, the Act on the Moral Protection of Youths 1960 prohibited unaccompanied children and young people from occupying areas where drinking, dancing and gambling took place (Dumortier, 2006; Van Praet, 2017).

There was one category of children who, according to the Child Protection Act 1912, should not be sent to the Children's Court in Belgium: the neglected children of 'unworthy parents'. Such children were presented as 'real' victims and, therefore, did not belong in the Children's Court, whose aim was primarily to correct '(pre-)delinquent children'. In practice, however, neglected children often appeared in the Children's Courts. Indeed, 'unworthy parents' were left to decide by the Public Prosecutors whether they preferred to undergo the formal, public and shameful procedure of having their parental authority withdrawn by the *Tribunal de Première Instance* or whether they preferred to effectively file a case against their children before the Children's Court (Dumortier, 2012). Under the provisions of the Youth Protection Act 1965, interventions specifically regarding such neglected children or 'children in danger' formed a new and important extension of legal power. Furthermore, the same Act raised the age of criminal responsibility from 16 years to 18 years, which meant that the leeway that allowed Public Prosecutors to either prosecute 16- to 18-year-old delinquents before the *Tribunal Correctionel* or encourage parents to file a case against their 16- to 18-year-old delinquent child before the Children's Court no longer applied. At the same time, the name of the Children's Court was changed to Juvenile Court.

The widening of opportunities for intervention facilitated by the Youth Protection Act 1965 was welcomed by many commentators at the time, who believed that it represented a new 'social spirit' in the courts. Children's judges, it was argued, were finally able to move beyond old classical ideas of punishing children (Dumortier, 2012). Concerns regarding 'net-widening' were also raised, however. Heupgen – one of the only Belgian children's judges who (self-)critically commented on the new Children's Courts and their mission – was concerned that Children's Courts were becoming preoccupied increasingly with children's '*peccadilles*' (trivial juvenile misdemeanours) (Heupgen, 1931) and 'child-specific offences' (Heupgen, 1929), which meant that more and more children were entering the judicial system. Indeed, even the most fervent proponents of the Belgian child protection system started to wonder, from the interwar period onwards, whether conventional legal principles and the rule of law were being compromised in the Children's Courts (Racine, 1937). To this day, for example, holding children formally accountable for status offences continues to be criticised and condemned by the United Nations Committee on the Rights of the Child (2007). Furthermore, the mixing of children who appeared before the court as 'offenders' with those who were appearing as 'victims' of problematic familial upbringing attracted critical attention. As in 1912, the argument still continues as to whether children who have not done anything 'wrong' should face potential stigmatisation by appearing in the same courts and being treated the same way as children facing the prospect of criminal convictions.

Nevertheless, to this day, the UN Convention on the Rights of the Child (1989) and the UN Committee on the Rights of the Child (2007) still firmly promote a separate juvenile justice system for children. Notwithstanding this, in practice the institutional and jurisdictional dichotomy between adults and children means that in many countries children can be prosecuted more readily and for a wider corpus of reasons than adults; non-delinquent children often appear in juvenile courts and residential settings otherwise intended for delinquent youths; and, many children do not receive the same fundamental human and procedural rights as adults. The argument that the interests of children might be better served in a system that does not formally separate them from adults has a certain appeal. In some Scandinavian countries, such as Sweden for example, no separate youth courts exist, and delinquent children appear before adult courts without this leading, by definition, to harsher justice. On the contrary, the unified system takes into account children's age and circumstances before passing sentence (Tonry and Chambers, 2012: 882). Consequently – and from a human rights perspective – it might be posited that a single unified and humane criminal court 'for all' is preferable. At the very least, the idea of a unified humane Criminal Court 'for all' bypasses the apparently immutable dichotomy between adults (who need to be punished) and children (who need to be protected) and instead provides the basis for treating all suspects (independently of their age, sex, ethnic background etc.) in an equal, proportionate and humane way. Indeed, from a human rights perspective it remains unclear why children should not have the same procedural guarantees as adults. Conversely, why do adults not have the right to be diverted from the criminal courts for as long as possible or only ever to be placed in prison as a measure of last resort and for the shortest time?

Judicial power: enlightened despotism?

A third important foundation of the new Children's Courts was the figure of the specialised (in many countries) judge sitting alone who is able to exercise wide discretionary powers. In Belgium it has long been thought that the judge must be single seated to gain the confidence of, and initiate effective communication with, the child. A child, it is argued, will never feel comfortable before a board of judges or a bench of magistrates. The same argument is employed to legitimise more intimate 'child-centred' procedures. It is further argued that private proceedings behind closed doors are necessary to discuss delicate family issues and to shield the child from public exposure.

Generally, the rationale for the single seated judge also means that they are able to follow the child through three important phases in (Continental) legal proceedings: the preliminary (or pre-trial) phase, the judgment phase and the sentencing phase. Throughout each phase the judge enjoys wide discretionary authority as signalled above. In his *Mémoires*, the Belgian Minister of Justice who introduced the Children's Judge in Belgium, wrote that this new judge was 'established with some kind of dictatorship towards children' whose only guideline was to decide 'in the best interest of the child in front of them' (Carton de Wiart, 1948: 183). This idea strongly resembles ideologies of the so-called Enlightened Despotism of the eighteenth century: as Emperor Joseph II of Austria would have it: 'everything for the people, nothing by the people' or, in its juvenile justice guise, 'everything for the children, nothing by the children'.

In practice the presence of a single seated and powerful judge can readily lead to a culture where children's judges may not feel it necessary to wait for the second phase (judgment phase) to impose interventionist measures. On the contrary, and by reference to the logic of the 'best interest of the child', they exercise their discretion by imposing 'protective' measures during the preliminary phases (Dumortier, 2006). The Child Protection Act 1912 failed to take account of the child's procedural rights, especially during the preliminary phase (behind closed doors). Consequently, both in law and in practice, children were perceived primarily as 'objects' of the new 'protectional' system with few judicial opportunities to secure advocacy and defence. It took more than 70 years before, in 1988, Belgium was condemned by the European Court of Human Rights (Bouamar v. Belgium, 1988) for its failure to provide children with procedural safeguards including, during the preliminary phase, the right to legal assistance, the right to be heard by the judge and the right to (effectively) appeal. At the same time, the European Court also condemned Belgium for the fact that measures presented as 'protectional' nonetheless empowered the judge to place a child in an adult prison. Such traditions persist over time in key forms. Today, for example, procedural guarantees are in evidence in Belgian juvenile justice, and adult prisons have been replaced by youth detention centres but, notwithstanding this, the dominance of the pre-trial phase and the lack of due process continue to be problematic in contemporary Belgian juvenile justice practices (Dumortier et al., 2017).

The children's judge's collaborators: probation officers, scientific experts and the Church

The fourth and, for present purposes, the final foundation of the Children's Courts within the 'new' 'welfarist' paradigm pertains to the personnel who form the judge's principal collaborators. In the first place, probation officers are at hand to investigate the child's home and familial environment. These officers ('*délégués du juge de l'enfance*') further report to the judge regarding the child's (and her/his family's) cooperation and compliance with probation conditions. The almost exclusive emphasis on 'welfare' and the privileging of the child's 'best interests' serve, once again, to dilute classical procedural safeguards.

Originally probation officers were presented as 'volunteers' whose work was based on personal commitment rather than financial remuneration. Whereas judges were more or less exclusively male, 'probation officers' were normally female. Indeed, this 'motherly' figure was perceived as the perfect complement to the 'paternal' children's judge. Initially, such probation officers predominantly came from the bourgeoisie but following the Second World War and the construction of the Welfare State they 'professionalised' and started to be remunerated. Belgian judicial files provide evidence that professionalisation led to more and longer reports being prepared and presented to the courts, framed by a more neutral use of language and less explicit middle-class moralising vis-à-vis the 'working classes' (Dumortier, 2006).

In addition to probation officers, the children's judge was able to appeal to a range of 'scientific experts' including doctors, psychologists and psychiatrists to analyse the child's body and mind. The Child Protection Act 1912 statutorily introduced the 'scientific observation', diagnosis and treatment of the child in institutions (Christiaens, forthcoming). Belgian judicial files evidence increasing numbers of 'scientific observation' reports as symptomatic of a developing tendency to subject the child to scientific observation and assessment (Dumortier, 2006). Perhaps not surprisingly, the child's voice is absent, rendering them mere objects of observation. Moreover, the 'scientific' diagnosis, at least in Belgian practice, clearly took account of the services, resources and modes of intervention that were known to be available. In this way, the diagnosis seemed to reflect, above all, the available 'institutional offer' (what was currently available) rather than the genuine needs of the child. At the same time, a circularity was evident whereby 'scientific' experts were seen to legitimise the existing 'offer', given that it was seemingly compatible with the child's perceived needs (Dumortier, 2006). Furthermore, expert diagnoses normally followed the dominant scientific knowledge (or fashion) of the time leading, in Belgian practice, to very Lombrosian reports at the beginning of the twentieth century and developing towards more 'attachment'- and 'social bonding'-based reports in the 1950s and the 1960s (Dumortier, 2006). Although such reports laid claim to 'science', they also revealed, at times, a rather crude and essentialist appeal to common sense and normative prescription (Christiaens, 1999a). Homosexual boys, for example, were 'diagnosed' as needing to become more 'masculine' (Dumortier, 2006). What is also remarkable is the length of time that children were exposed to such 'scientific' observations. Even today in Belgium, pre-trial observations, often in closed institutions, tend to take three months (or more) to complete. Moreover, during this period the judicial scrutiny of practices in closed institutions holding children is significantly less stringent than it is for adults who are placed in prisons during the pre-trial phase. It is quite remarkable that very few 'official' debates exist concerning such practices. Even though the recent EU Directive (2016) – on procedural safeguards for children who are suspects or accused persons in criminal proceedings – promises to make some headway, several questions remain unanswered including, but not limited to: who decides what and who must be assessed; how such assessment should be operationalised; how long should the same assessment take to complete; in what phase of the procedure should assessment take place; what role might the child play in her/his assessment and in what circumstances, if any, might the child refuse to be assessed?

Finally, the Child Protection Act 1912 provided for a new and close collaboration between children's judges and private (in Belgium often Catholic) organisations (such as convents). This 'privatisation' of the penal complex vis-à-vis children illustrates the prevailing social policies of the time, which depended heavily on patronage and charity organised by the Catholic church and related institutions (at least in Belgium) (Dumortier, 2006). Such institutions often had a 'better' and 'softer' reputation than the state-run institutions. Moreover, the (moral) merits of Catholic education and schooling were often taken for granted. Only quite recently – together with increasing secularisation and the increasing exposure of child abuse scandals connected to the Church – has the reputation and standing of such religious institutions and practices been called into question and, indeed, seriously damaged.

Discussion and conclusions: demystifying contemporary beliefs

More than a century ago, Europe witnessed the emergence, consolidation and development of the Children's Court. A historical perspective sheds light on how, simultaneously, different countries were confronted with the same kind of pressures and addressed them via a range of similar 'solutions'. In this way, the formation of juvenile justice and the creation of Children's Courts can be seen as key responses to concerns generated by nineteenth-century modernisation – including profound transformations from agricultural/rural to industrial/urban economies and societies – that affected Europe, the USA and several other regions and countries.

In the late modern period, although some continuities are certainly evident, Children's Courts have progressed a great deal and vital discontinuities with the past are especially striking. Female children's judges are now commonplace and children's rights have been firmly anchored within the UN Convention on the Rights of the Child. The welfare of the child has become significantly more prominent and the notion of social defence has receded (at least in large part) (Goris, 2014). Social work has professionalised and scientific thinking regarding child development has advanced. Currently, however, such progress seems to be jeopardised by a politicised punitive discourse that stresses the need for 'tougher' and often more adult-like responses. Even though economic recession seems to have reduced investment in penal institutions vis-à-vis youngsters (see, for example, Goldson, 2015), a punitive and custodial approach remains immensely popular in contemporary political discourses and societal debates.

However, it would be erroneous to imagine that such punitive discourse is a peculiar feature of the contemporary period. Indeed, the concept of punishment has never been completely absent in juvenile justice even if it becomes more or less prominent at particular moments in time as the 'pendulum swings' (Ballet and Eliaerts, 1989; Dumortier and Brolet, 2003) or 'circular motions' rotate (Goldson, 2015). Moreover, punitive rhetoric is not always accompanied by (more) punitive practices and, conversely, seemingly benign non-punitive discourses that emphasise 'welfare' do not necessarily guarantee non-punitive practices. As historical research readily reveals, deeply problematic practices have claimed legitimacy even during ostensibly 'golden' welfare eras.

Other continuities are also evident through the history of juvenile justice. A single seated judge – enjoying substantial discretionary power that might be exercised at crucial junctures across the entire judicial 'pathway' taken by the child – remains in place in many countries. 'Delinquent' and 'non-delinquent' children continue to mix in juvenile courts and institutions and 'status offences' remain. Private and public organisations co-exist without any sustained and meaningful critical analysis. The centrality of social work and the 'scientific' observation and assessment of the child remains in place. In fact, the EU Directive (2016) on procedural safeguards for children conceptualises 'individual assessment' as a 'right' for each child seemingly taking little, if any, account of the fact that children may not want to be 'assessed' or that such 'assessments' may themselves be unsound, as evidenced by much historical research and practice experience.

Furthermore, the formal separation of adults and children in court remains and has been firmly anchored in an international convention specifically made 'for children', but (once more) not 'by children'. According to Cordero Arce (2015: 297), the UN Convention on the Rights of the Child is traditionally conceptualised as 'a gift' from adults to children and as it was 'drafted for children, without children' it clearly lacks legitimacy. The deeply embedded legacies of 'paternalism' and the fundamental idea that children are not yet ready to deal with 'adult rights' or 'citizenship' still lie at the heart of the UN Convention on the Rights of the Child (Cordero Arce, 2015: 297–298). From a historical long-term perspective, Cordero Arce's arguments raise the question of whether the UN Convention on the Rights of the Child is best seen as a distinctive step forward in juvenile justice history or, rather, are its central concepts and underlying priorities (such as the 'best interest of the child') above all else signifiers of continuity with historically embedded 'child protection' discourses and practices (Bernuz Beneitez and Dumortier, 2018)?

Finally, the history of juvenile justice highlights a vitally important issue. Over time, the 'usual suspects' of the juvenile justice system largely remain the same: children stemming from the poorest and most disadvantaged families and, more recently, migrants and the dispossessed. And the principal focus remains trained on individualised approaches as distinct from structural and 'societal' problems. The fact that such approaches even induce 'iatrogenic effects' (Gatti et al., 2009) and complicate the process of 'desisting from crime' (McAra and McVie, 2007) does not seem to be fully integrated in contemporary debates on the future of juvenile justice in Europe. The ever-present fear that the pendulum might swing further towards punitivity seems to incline most juvenile justice scholars to (re)defend old principles instead of searching for constructive alternatives to established systems that take account of well-known, fundamental and historically persistent failings (Dumortier and Brolet, 2003). Indeed, from a long-term historical perspective, the foundations of children's courts can be seen as anything but under pressure.

Note

1 Bac, J. (1998: 14).

References

Act on the repression of vagrants and beggars (1891) Loi du 27 novembre 1891 sur la répression du vagabondage et de la mendicité. *Pasinomie*, 439–459.

Act on the repression of vagrants and beggars (1897) Loi du 15 février 1897 modifiant la loi du 27 novembre 1891 sur la répressiondu vagabondage et de la mendicité. *Pasinomie*, 101–112.

Bac, J. (1998) *Kinderrechter in strafzaken: Evolutie en evaluatie* (Children's Judge in Criminal cases: Evolution and evaluation). Deventer: Gouda Quint.

Ballet, D. and Eliaerts, C. (1989) Pendelbewegingen in de jeugdbescherming: het voorbeeld van de Verenigde Staten (Pendulum swings in youth protection: the example of the United States). *Panopticon* (10), 402–423.

Bateman, T. (2012) Criminalising children for no good purpose: the age of criminal responsibility in England and Wales. *National Association for Youth Justice Campaign Paper.* http:// thenayj.org.uk/wpcontent/files_mf/criminalisingchildrennov12.pdf (accessed 10 August 2017).

Bailleau, F. and Cartuyvels, Y. (eds.) (2010) *The criminalisation of youth: Juvenile justice in Europe, Turkey and Canada.* Brussels: VUB-Press.

Belgian Parliamentary Debate (1912) Loi du 15 mai 1912 sur la protection de l'enfance. *Pasinomie*, 249–435.

Berger, S. (ed.) (2006) *A companion to 19th century Europe 1789–1914.* Oxford: Blackwell Publishing.

Bernuz Beneitez, M-J. and Dumortier, E. (2018) Why do children obey the law? Rethinking juvenile justice and children's rights through procedural justice. *Youth Justice* 18(1): 34–51.

Bosworth, M. (2001) The past as a foreign country? Some methodological implications of doing historical criminology. *British Journal of Criminology* (41), 431–442.

Cantor, N. (1935) Conflicts in penal theory and practice. *Journal of Criminal Law and Criminology* (26) (3), 330–350.

Cantor, N. (1936) Measures of social defense. *Cornell Law Review* (22) (1), 17–38.

Carton de Wiart, H. (1948) *Souvenirs politiques (1878–1918).* Bruxelles/Paris: Desclée De Brouwer.

Cavadino, M. and Dignan, J. (2006) *Penal systems: A comparative approach.* London Thousand Oaks and New Delhi: Sage Publications.

Chlepner, B-S. (1972) *Cent ans d'histoire sociale en Belgique.* Brussels: Editions de l'Université de Bruxelles.

Christiaens, J. (1994) Stoute kinderen achter slot en grendel. Het vaderlijk tuchtigingsrecht in de ontstaansgeschiedenis van de negentiende-eeuwe kinderbescherming. *Tijdschrift voor sociale geschiedenis* (2), 149–169.

Christiaens, J. (1999a) *De geboorte van de jeugddelinquent België (The birth of the juvenile delinquent), 1830–1930.* Brussel: VUB press.

Christiaens, J. (1999b) A history of Belgium's Child Protection Act of 1912: The redefinition of the juvenile offender and his punishment. *European Journal of Crime, Criminal Law and Criminal Justice* (7) (1), 5–21.

Christiaens, J. (2015) *It's for your own good: Researching youth justice practices.* Brussels: VUB press.

Christiaens, J. (forthcoming) Youth crime redefined: The practice of scientific observation and diagnosis within the framework of Belgian Child Protection (1913–1960). In: Trépanier J and Rousseauc X (eds.) *Youth and justice in Western states, 1815–1950: From punishment to welfare.* London/New York: Palgrave Macmillan.

Cordero Arce, M. (2015) Maturing children's rights theory: From children, with children, of children. *International Journal of Children's Rights* (23) (2): 283–331.

Cox, P. (2003) *Gender, justice and welfare: Bad girls in Britain, 1900–1950.* London/New York: Palgrave Macmillan.

Decker, S. and Marteache, N. (eds.) (2017) *International handbook of juvenile justice.* Dordrecht/New York: Springer.

De Koster, M. (2001) Weerbaar, weerspannig of crimineel? Meisjes en jonge vrouwen tussen emancipatie en delinquentie tijdens de eerste helft van de twinstigste eeuw (PhD-thesis). Bruxelles: Vrije Universiteit Brussel.

Donzelot, J. (1979) *The policing of families.* Maryland/London: The Johns Hopkins University Press.

Dumortier, E. (2006) De jeugdrechter in twijfel: Een onderzoek naar het onstaan en de praktijk van de Kinderrechter, België 1912–1965 (The juvenile judge: critical insights. A research on the birth and the practice of the Children's Judge, Belgium 1912–1965) (PhD thesis). Brussels: Vrije Universiteit Brussel.

Dumortier, E. (2012) De missie van de kinderrechter: Een onderzoek naar het ontstaan en de praktijk van de (Antwerpse) kinderrechter (België, 1912–1965) (The children's judge's mission: A study of the birth and the practices of the (Antwerp) children's judge). *Panopticon,* (33) (5), 391–414.

Dumortier, E. and Brolet, C. (2003) Waarheen met de jeugdbescherming? Over de gevreesde repressieve pendelbeweging en een fundamentele hervorming van de jeugdbescherming (The future of youth protection? On the feared repressive pendulum swings and a fundamental reform of youth protection). *Tijdschrift voor Jeugdrecht en Kinderrechten* (4) (3), 149–160.

Dumortier, E., Christiaens, J. and Nuytiens, A. (2017) Belgium In: Decker S and Marteache N (Eds.), *The international handbook of juvenile justice.* New York: Springer.

Dumortier, E., Snacken, S. Gutwirth, S., and De Hert, P. (2012) The rise of the penal state: What can human rights do about it? In: Snacken S and Dumortier E (eds.) *Resisting punitiveness in Europe? Welfare, human rights and democracy.* New York: Routledge, 107–132.

Dünkel, F. (2016) Juvenile justice and human rights: European perspectives. In: Kury H, Redo S and Shea E (eds.) *Women and children as victims and offenders. Background, prevention, reintegration.* Dordrecht/New York: Springer, 681–719.

Dünkel, F., Grzywa, J., Horsfield, P. and Pruin, I. (eds.) (2010) *Juvenile justice systems in Europe: current situation and reform developments.* Mönchengladbach: Forum Verlag Godesberg.

Dupont-Bouchat, M-S. (1983) L'intérêt de l'enfant. Approche historique. In: Gerard P, Ost F and Van De Kerckhove M, *Fonction de juger et pouvoir judiciaire. Transformations et déplacements.* Bruxelles: Publications des facultés universitaires Saint Louis, 23–54.

Dupont-Bouchat, M-S. (1996) *De la prison à l'école: Les pénitenciers pour enfants en Belgique au XIXe siècle* (1840–1914). Kortrijk-Heule (Belgium): U.G.A.

Dupont-Bouchat, M-S., Pierre, E., Fecteau, J-M., Trépanier, J., Petit, J., Schnapper, B. and Dekker, J. (2001) *Enfance et justice au XIXᵉ siècle: Essais d'histoire comparée de la protection de l'enfance 1829–1914, France, Belgique, Pays-Bas, Canada.* Paris: Presses Universitaires de France.

EU Directive (2016) 2016/800 of the European Parliament and of the Council of Ministers of 11 May 2016 on *Procedural safeguards for children who are suspects or accused persons in criminal proceedings.*

European Court of Human Rights (1988) *Bouamar v. Belgium*, 29 February 1988.

Ferri, E. (1905) *La sociologie criminelle.* Paris: Félix Alcan Editeur.

Finnegan, F. (2004) *Do penance or perish. Magdalene asylums in Ireland.* Oxford: Oxford University Press.

Gatti, U., Tremblay, R.E, and Vitaro, F. (2009) Iatrogenic effect of juvenile justice. *Journal of Child Psychology and Psychiatry* (50) (8), 991–998.

Goldson, B. (2002) New punitiveness: the politics of child incarceration. In: Muncie, J., Hughes, G. and McLaughlin, E. (eds.) *Youth justice: Critical readings.* London: Sage, 386–400.

Goldson, B. (2015) The circular motions of penal politics and the pervasive irrationalities of child imprisonment. In: Goldson B and Muncie J (eds.) *Youth crime and justice.* 2nd Edition. Los Angeles/London: Sage, 170–190.

Goldson, B. and Muncie, J. (2015) Children's human rights and youth justice with integrity. In: Goldson B and Muncie J (eds.) *Youth crime and justice.* 2nd Edition. Los Angeles/London: Sage, 227–257.

Goldson, B. and Muncie, J. (eds.) (2015b) *Youth crime and justice.* 2nd Edition. Los Angeles/London: Sage.

Goris, K. (2014) Niet delinquent, wel naar de jeugdrechter. Een onderzoek naar het problematiseren van de opvoeding en het gedrag van kinderen, ca. 1980 – heden (Not delinquent, but in youth court. A research on the problematisation of education and of behaviour of children, 1980-today) (PhD-thesis). Brussels: Vrije Universiteit Brussel.

Heupgen, P. (1926) Infractions d'enfants. *Revue de Droit Pénal et de Criminologie*, 743–751.

Heupgen, P. (1929) Juridictions des Enfants. *Revue de Droit Pénal et de Criminologie*, 1089–1092.

Heupgen, P. (1931) Déchéance de la puissance paternelle et répression. *Revue de Droit Pénal et de Criminologie*, 734–740.

Hendrick, H. (2006) Histories of youth crime and justice. In: Muncie, J. and Goldson, B. (eds.) (2006) *Comparative youth justice.* Los Angeles/London: Sage.

Judicial Archives (1912–1965) Rijksarchief Beveren, Archief van de Rechtbank van Eerste Aanleg Antwerpen, Dossiers van Rechtspleging, jaren 1912–1913, 1928, 1939, 1950, 1961.

Junger-Tas, J. and Decker, S. (eds.) (2006) *International handbook of juvenile justice.* Berlin/Dordrech/New York: Springer.

Kenny, A. (1980) *Aquino*. Oxford: Oxford University Press (Dutch version of De Morgen, 2005).

Knepper, P. (2010) *The invention of international crime: A global issue in the Making, 1881–1914*. New York: Palgrave MacMillan.

Lacassagne, A. (1913) Les transformations du droit pénal et les progrès de la médecine légale, de 1810 à 1912. *Archives de l'anthropologie criminelle*, 321–364.

Loi du 15 mai 1912 sur la protection de l'enfance (1912) *Pasinomie*, 249–435.

Lombroso, C. (1895) *L'homme criminel*. Paris: Félix Alcan.

Lombroso, C. (1899) *Le crime: Causes et remèdes*. Paris: Schleicher Frères Editeurs.

McAra, L. and McVie, S. (2007) Youth justice? The impact of system contact on patterns of desistance from offending. *European Journal of Criminology* (4) (3), 315–345.

Muncie, J. (2008) The 'punitive turn' in juvenile justice: cultures of control and rights compliance in Western Europe and the USA. *Youth Justice* 8(2): 107–121.

Muncie, J. and Goldson, B. (eds.) (2006) *Comparative youth justice*. Los Angeles/London: Sage.

Nelken, D. (2009) Comparative criminal justice: Beyond ethnocentrism and relativism. *European Journal of Criminology* (11) (4), 291–311.

Odem, M. (1995) *Delinquent daughters: Protecting and policing adolescent female sexuality in the United States, 1885–1920*. Chapel Hill: The University of North Carolina Press.

Parliamentary Debate (1912) Loi du 15 mai 1912 sur la protection de l'enfance. *Pasinomie*, 249–435.

Phillips, P. (1996) *A kingdom on earth: Anglo-American Social Christianity, 1880–1940*. Pennsylvania University Park: Pennsylvania State University Press (Penn State Press).

Platt, A. (1977) *The child savers: The invention of delinquency*. Chicago: University of Chicago Press.

Platt, A. (1974) The triumph of benevolence: the origins of the juvenile justice system in the United States. In: Quinney R (ed.) *Criminal justice in America*. Boston: Little, Brown. Republished in Muncie J, Hughes G and McLaughlin E (2004) *Youth justice: Critical readings*. London/Thousand Oaks/New Delhi: Sage Publications, 177–196.

Prins, A. (1899) *Science pénal et droit positif*. Brussel: Bruylant.

Prins, A. (1910) *La défense sociale et les transformations du droit pénal* (republished in 1986 with an introduction by Tulkens F). Genève: Editions Médecine et Hygiène.

Racine, A. (1937) Maintien ou abandon de la règle 'Nulla poena, nullum crimen, sine lege' dans les juridictions pour enfants. *Revue de droit pénal et de criminologie*, 149–165.

Rahikaenen, M. (2004) *Centuries of child labour: European experiences from the seventeenth to the twentieth century*. London: Ashgate/Routledge.

Rosenheim, M., Zimring, F., Tanenhaus, D. and Dohrn, B. (2001) *A century of juvenile justice*. Chicago: University of Chicago Press.

Sköld, J. and Swain, S. (eds.) (2015) *Apologies and the legacy of abuse of children in 'care'*. London/New York: Palgrave Macmillan.

Snacken, S. and Dumortier, E. (eds.) (2012) *Resisting punitiveness in Europe? Welfare, human rights and democracy*. New York: Routledge.

Snacken, S. and Dumortier, E. (2012) Resisting punitiveness in Europe? An introduction. In: Snacken S and Dumortier E (eds.) *Resisting punitiveness in Europe? Welfare, human rights and democracy*. New York: Routledge, 1–20.

Tarde, G. (1890) *La philosophie pénale*. Lyon/Paris: Storck/Masson.

Tonry, M. and Chambers, C. (2012) Juvenile justice cross-nationally considered. In: Feld, B. and Bishop, D. (eds.) *The Oxford handbook of juvenile crime and juvenile justice*. Oxford/New York: Oxford University Press, 871–897.

Trépanier, J. and Rousseaux, X. (eds.) (2018) *Youth and justice in Western States, 1815–1950: From punishment to welfare*. London/New York: Palgrave Macmillan.

United Nations Committee on the Rights of the Child (2007) *General Comment 10: Children's rights in juvenile justice*. New York: United Nations.

Van de Kerchove, M. (1977) Des mesures répressives aux mesures de sûreté et de protection: Réflexions sur le pouvoir mystificateur du langage. *Revue de droit pénal et de criminologie*, 245–279.

Van Hamel, G. (1895) De misdadige jeugd en de Nederlandse wet. *De Gids*, 105–142.

van Kersbergen, C. (1995) *Social capitalism: a study of Christian democracy and of the welfare state*. London/New York: Routledge.

Van Praet, S. (2017) Les sollicitations des autorités publiques par les familles pour 'conflit éducatif': Analyse de dossiers du parquet famille-jeunesse de Bruxelles, 1966–2006 (PhD-thesis). Bruxelles: Université Libre de Bruxelles.

2

BECOMING DELINQUENT? RETHINKING THE LONG HISTORY OF JUVENILE JUSTICE

Heather Shore

Introduction

In a relatively recent collection of essays about the evolution of juvenile justice – marking the centenary of the founding of the Illinois Juvenile Court in Chicago, USA in 1899 – the creation of a separate justice system for children and young people was firmly anchored to the twentieth century (Rosenheim et al., 2001). Whilst many criminology and sociology texts have paid lip service to the existence of organisations and institutions for juveniles in Western European countries and North America prior to the turn of the last century, few have given it detailed consideration (there are some exceptions of course, for example: Goldson and Muncie, 2015; Shoemaker, 2013). In most commentaries, the early history of juvenile justice has been seen in largely temporal terms, as a series of events or practices led by charitable individuals which combined to pave the way for the establishment of a 'new' system by the first decade of the twentieth century. In reality, juvenile justice systems were well established in many European countries by the late nineteenth century. Arguably, in many countries, the legislation that gave statutory effect to such reforms in the early part of the twentieth century did little more than for-malise processes and practices that had been long adopted on the ground.

This chapter will particularly consider the shared reform culture that characterised British and other European societies during this period. This was a culture of reform, practice, discourse and ideology that was shaped by prominent leaders in the European juvenile justice field. Some of the leaders formed part of a thriving network of knowledge exchange: congresses, collaborations, inspections and reciprocal visits that fuelled the circularity of debate about juvenile crime and juvenile justice in the nineteenth century. For example, the English reformer Mary Carpenter gave many papers at conferences, particularly the newly formed National Association for the Promotion of the Social Sciences (NAPSS). She also had a pivotal role in European social and educational reform networks (Hirch and Hilton, 2014: 49). A hybrid of penal reform, philanthropy and governmental interests animated an influential group of juvenile justice professionals in Europe and it was their legacy that led to the formal creation of juvenile courts in the early twentieth century. The chapter will also challenge the claim that juvenile crime was 'invented' in England in the early nineteenth century (Magarey, 1978) by showing how, in terms of institutional prescriptions, *many European countries* had made significant inroads into the care and reform of juvenile delinquents from at least the early decades of the nineteenth century.

Juvenile justice developments circa 1788–1908

In England, between 1815 and 1816, a group of men, mostly of the non-Conformist Quaker religious persuasion, collaboratively produced a report on juvenile delinquency in London: *Report of the Committee for Investigating the Causes of the Alarming Increase of Juvenile Delinquency in the Metropolis* (1816). Based on 500 interviews with juvenile offenders in London's prisons, the report has come to define a key moment in the early articulations of a juvenile justice system in England. Whilst juvenile delinquency was far from 'invented' in this period, it is clear that in Britain (and as we will see below, in Europe and North America) it was in this early part of the nineteenth century that juvenile justice systems started to evolve into their modern forms. In fact, such processes would take a century to transform into the system that was ultimately established by the Children Act 1908, which formalised many of the changes made over the previous decades. This watershed Act not only established the separate juvenile court – dealing with both criminal and welfare issues – but it also finally abolished penal custody for children below the age of 14 years. Previously, not only were children still sent to prison, but those sentenced to the Reformatory Schools also served a mandatory 10- to 14-day period of incarceration in an adult prison before they entered such Schools (Bradley, Logan and Shaw, 2009; Godfrey et al., 2017; Johnston, 2015: 150).

Over the course of the nineteenth century, the 'modern' juvenile justice system took shape. The form and structure of the system was deeply infused by tensions within Victorian reformatory rhetoric (Shore, 2008). It is important to understand that juvenile justice in this period was never simply a discussion about welfare or, indeed, penality. As a specific 'cause', it coincided with a period of growing awareness, and arguably, politicisation of what we might call the early nineteenth-century voluntary sector. As Martin Gorsky (1999: 18) suggests, the voluntary sector was deeply embedded in local urban institutional structures. The relationship between the state and forms of secular social policy was evolving at this point and the voluntary sector (which largely comprised non-Conformist activists) provided a crucial bridge in the development of juvenile justice. By the 1830s and 1840s, strategies to deal with juveniles (both in terms of rehabilitation/reform and punishment) were decisively focused on some form of penality.

Whilst ideas about the rehabilitation and reform of offenders had long been a theme of penal debates, the specific rehabilitation of the *juvenile offender* began to preoccupy reformers and penal commentators in this period (Magarey 1978; May, 1973). Rehabilitation and reform were to be located firmly within penal institutions rather than in the family – which was often seen as a source of 'corruption' – or the community. Reformatory Institutions for juvenile offenders before the mid-nineteenth century included: houses of correction; areas/wings within prisons; and the various refuges, schools and homes that were established by private groups, societies and individuals. Debate at this time primarily focused on the specific forms and functions that custodial punishment for juveniles should take. Clearly in the 1820s and 1830s, for all prisoners, the conflict between more rehabilitative/reforming and more punitive/retributive systems of custody was a key source of debate. The underpinning theme of this period was the classification and separation of different groups of prisoners (Garland, 1985: 22). Crucially, boys were to be separated from men, and incorrigible boys were to be separated from those who were deemed to be less experienced and/or less serious offenders. The main challenge in this was how to control the behaviour of children on the periphery of the criminal justice system alongside children who had already been convicted and labelled as 'criminal': the 'perishing' and the 'dangerous' juveniles respectively (Carpenter, 1851: 1–3). Consequently, there was a drive to develop an institutional architecture and a juvenile justice system that could incorporate both groups of children.

The Reformatory and Industrial Schools

The separation and categorisation of juveniles within the prison system was initially mooted through the opening decades of the nineteenth century and began to be practised – at least in theory – during the 1820s and early 1830s through the auspices of Robert Peel's Gaol Act 1823 (McConville, 1981: 248–250). In reality, the actual separation of child from adult prisoners was rather limited. As a witness to a Parliamentary Select Committee noted:

> The larger prisons, especially those in and near the metropolis, usually contain several hundred prisoners, whose periods of confinement before trial, vary from a few days to several months. It is hardly necessary to remark, that any classification, with the inadequate means provided by the Gaol Act, must be inefficacious
>
> *Report from the Select Committee on Secondary Punishments, 1832: 5*

By the 1830s it was clear that the Gaol Act was not working particularly well, and the 1835 Select Committee on Gaols and Houses of Correction recommended the establishment of a separate juvenile prison (McConville, 1981; Radzinowicz and Hood, 1990; Stack, 1979). What emerged from this was Parkhurst Prison, a former military hospital which was established exclusively as a *juvenile penitentiary* from 1838. However, according to Radzinowicz and Hood (1990: 150) up to 1841 (during what has been seen as the first phase of the Parkhurst experiment from 1838 to 1842) 'boys of bad character' were not admitted and, instead, the first boys to be sent to Parkhurst were essentially minor offenders. This practice prompted criticism and claims that the boys who were being sent to Parkhurst were arguably those least in need of such detention. The history of Parkhurst as a juvenile-specific penitentiary was relatively short-lived, however, ending in 1864 and remembered only as a failed experiment. Yet, the closure of Parkhurst – at least as a juvenile prison – should be assessed alongside the passage of the Reformatory and Industrial Schools Acts. Whilst Parkhurst was subjected to vociferous criticism, particularly in its second and third stages (from the early 1840s to the early 1850s), it also had to 'compete' with the energetic move towards the Reformatory School system.

In 1852, the Select Committee on Criminal and Destitute Children (*Report from the Select Committee on Criminal and Destitute Children*) decisively rejected the model represented by Parkhurst Prison and, through a series of discursive interactions, it shaped an alternative Reformatory School model which was given statutory effect by the passage of the first Reformatory Schools Acts (more generally known as the Youthful Offenders Act) in 1854. This was followed by the Industrial Schools Act 1857, which allowed magistrates to sentence vagrant and homeless children (the 'perishing' and potentially 'criminal') to an Industrial School. Both institutions soon proliferated and, by 1866, the Reformatory and Industrial Schools Inspectors reported that there were 65 Reformatory Schools (51 in England and 14 in Scotland) and 49 Industrial Schools (30 in England and 19 in Scotland) in December 1865 (*Report of the Inspector of Reformatory Schools of Great Britain, 9th Report*, 1866). Just over 20 years later, the Inspectors reported that there were 56 Reformatory Schools and 140 certified Industrial Schools (*Report of the Inspector of Reformatory Schools of Great Britain, 32nd Report*, 1889). Furthermore, by the eve of the First World War, as Radzinowicz and Hood (1990: 182) pointed out, additional growth was evident whilst the balance between Reformatory Schools and Industrial Schools tilted further towards the latter: 'There was a network of 208 schools, 43 Reformatories, 132 Industrial Schools, 21 day Industrial Schools and 12 Truant Schools'. The Industrial School clearly became the preferred institution for the management of juvenile offenders (the 'dangerous') or, more so, those children and young people deemed to be 'at risk' of becoming offenders (the 'perishing') (Carpenter, 1851; May, 1973: 22). Thus, the Reformatory Schools were essentially reserved for convicted offenders whilst the Industrial Schools primarily accommodated potentially delinquent and/or neglected children.

The 'categories' of children to be accommodated within Industrial Schools were broadened in 1866 to include those 'in need of care and protection', aimed particularly at children aged under 14 years but with further provisions for those aged under 12 years. As Radzinowicz and Hood (1990: 181–182) noted the number of admissions to the Industrial Schools soon accelerated: 'The number of inmates, a mere 1,668 in 1864, had jumped to 5,738 by 1868, and then by leaps and bounds to nearly 17,000 in 1881 and over 20,000 in 1885'. What is clear is that the developing system was characterised by relatively free-ranging discretion and the wording of the legislation gave significant power to the courts, particularly in respect of the youngest children (under the age of 12 years), 'who, having committed an offence punishable by imprisonment or some less punishment, ought nevertheless, in the opinion of the justices, regard being had to his age, and to the circumstances of the case, to be sent to an Industrial School' (May, 1973: 26).

Indeed, increasingly the distinction between the Industrial and the Reformatory Schools became blurred, which suggests that, by the later 1860s, magistrates were inclined to use the Industrial School for both destitute and offending children. Moreover, by the later nineteenth century local government was given a high degree of latitude in dealing with disorderly and refractory working-class children.

British juvenile justice historiography

The historiography of juvenile justice galvanised in the 1970s, emerging out of the new iterations of social history which were associated with the work of authors such as Harold Perkin (1969), Edward Thompson (1963) and Raphael Samuel (1985). Thompson, particularly, shaped a distinctive approach to the history of crime that largely privileged a 'history from below' perspective (Hay et al., 1975) and, more specifically, the early social history of *juvenile* crime and the early Victorian remodelling of juvenile justice also emerged during this period. Whilst the latter did not quite share Thompson's (1963, 1980 edn: 12) vision of rescuing ordinary people 'from the enormous condescension of posterity', it did adopt more critical and nuanced analytical approaches than had hitherto been the case. Margaret May (1973) and Susan Magarey (1978), for example, published two key articles on juvenile delinquency in Britain in the early nineteenth century, broadly influenced by the work of sociologist Anthony M. Platt and particularly his seminal book *The Child Savers: The Invention of Delinquency* (Platt, 1969). Building on an essentially Whiggish narrative of early juvenile justice, May's article examined the emergence of juvenile delinquency as a distinct legal category during a period of emergent discourses about childhood and juvenile delinquency. Meanwhile, Magarey consolidated the 'invention of the juvenile delinquent' framework with her discussion of legislative developments during the 1820s which, she persuasively argued, served to legislate the juvenile delinquent into existence.

Since the 1990s further work broadly confirmed the sequencing of key chronological developments in the evolution of juvenile justice, although it also detected an even earlier rise in the rates and patterns of juvenile prosecutions (King, 1998, 2006; King and Noel, 1993; Shore, 1999). Shore (1999: 20–21), for example, showed how in London the increased prosecution of juvenile offenders (those aged 16 years and under) could be seen from the end of the Napoleonic Wars in 1815. King (1998; 2006: 84) extended the analysis of juvenile prosecutions beyond the Metropolis by drawing on a comparative framework of juvenile offending in both urban and rural contexts. King's (2006: 84) research confirmed the dramatic rise of urban juvenile prosecutions and he noted that, by 1820–22, 'certain urban areas had experienced a veritable deluge of recorded juvenile crime'. Both King and Shore argue that the discernible increases in juvenile prosecutions (particularly in urban areas) can be explained by a combination of: changing prosecution practices; increased street policing; and, reforming zeal that focused increasingly on the removal of children from 'contaminating' environments.

Whilst the 'invention of delinquency' thesis established the timeline for the development of juvenile justice in England, the passage of the crucial mid-century legislation (signalled above) and its aftermath has been much less of a preoccupation for historians. As stated, the second half of the nineteenth century witnessed the evolution of the Reformatory and Industrial School system. Moreover, the legal apparatus to deal with juvenile offenders was increasingly honed during this period and included: the principle of separate trials for juveniles; the 'protection' of children who were identified as being vulnerable to delinquency; and, of course, separate institutional provision for juveniles. In many ways, therefore, the Children Act 1908 represented the legislative formalisation of such developments rather than any sharp and distinctive break with the past. There have, however, been some key studies of the Industrial School. Nicola Sheldon (2009, 2013), for example, has explored both the education and training experience offered to children and young people within Industrial Schools and has also examined the role of the Industrial School alongside policy and practice developments in response to truancy. Furthermore, Gillian Gear's (2013) historical work has centred the Industrial School as a 'moral institution'. Unfortunately, however, the most extensive work of these authors remains unpublished (Gear, 1999; Sheldon, 2008). Other analyses of the Industrial and Reformatory Schools in the later nineteenth century, have focused on the evolution of legislation in relation to juvenile penality (Stack, 1992, 1994).

Equally, more social and culturally informed accounts of children's experiences in the Victorian and Edwardian Reformatory institutions offer vital additions to the literature. Michelle Cale (1993) has undertaken important work on young female inmates who were deemed to be 'problematic' due to their perceived sexual precocity. Similarly, the distinct gendered experiences of young inmates is a theme that has structured many further accounts of juvenile institutions, including Linda Mahood's (1995) study of the 'child-saving' movement in Scotland and Pam Cox's (2003) work on early twentieth-century 'bad girls' in the juvenile justice system. Studies of the Irish Industrial School system (established from 1868) are also available (Rafferty and O'Sullivan, 1999). The Irish system operated independently of the British system with its own inspectorate. Moreover, whilst British Industrial Schools were characterised by an underlying secularisation, the Irish Schools (whilst funded by the State) remained within the authority of the religious orders. Moreover, an understanding (and indeed, uncovering) of the history of the Industrial Schools in nineteenth- and twentieth-century Ireland was a key part of the The Commission to Inquire into Child Abuse (2009) that ran from 2000 to 2009. In contrast, in the ongoing (since 2005) 'Independent Inquiry into Child Sexual Abuse' in England and

Wales, there is considerably less focus on Industrial and Reformatory Schools or their mid-twentieth century successors.

Notwithstanding the above studies, detailed academic analyses of individual institutions have conventionally remained scarce until the publication of the most recent work, which has adopted life-course methodologies to explore the biographies of Industrial and Reformatory School 'inmates' (Godfrey et al., 2017). Such research has been strongly influenced by criminological studies of more contemporary juvenile penal populations including the work of Glueck and Glueck (1950), for example, who tracked the lives of 500 delinquent boys in Massachusetts through the 1940s and 1950s, and the work of Sampson and Laub (2003) and Laub and Sampson (2006), who subsequently reanalysed and largely confirmed the Gluecks' findings. This more recent research design draws on historical data and innovative methodologies to gauge the long-term impacts of juvenile institutions on the biographies and life-chances of the children and young people that had been held within them (Godfrey et al., 2017).

European contexts: policy and practice transfers

Conventionally, historiography concerning developments in juvenile justice has tended to focus on the significance of particular legislative watersheds, distinctive policy milestones and the growth of proto-juvenile justice systems in the nineteenth century. Work that has considered the longer-term patterns and trajectories of the policing and control of juvenile behaviour/offending and the extent to which such developments were discernible across Europe (and beyond) is more limited. The volume edited by Cox and Shore (2002), however, explores developments in juvenile justice in France, Spain, Holland, Belgium and Norway, from the seventeenth until the twentieth century. Moreover, as the comparative study of the historical foundations of juvenile justice has started to expand, policy and practice transfers over time and between countries, regions and states become increasingly apparent. Heather Ellis (2014: 5–6), for example, argues that responses to juvenile delinquency extended *across* space rather than simply evolving *within* distinct regional and cultural places:

> Notions of juvenile delinquency, both in the West and in non-Western contexts, are constructed and understood within and through cross-cultural encounters and can only be made sense of by placing developments within a global frame.

Such work demonstrates that juvenile crime and juvenile justice were more often re-invented rather than 'invented' in the nineteenth century and that parallel developments both within and across different countries in Europe were discernible. In terms of the institutional 'care' of juveniles, however, Britain was significantly behind other countries in Europe. As Sir John Pakington MP – Chair of the Birmingham Conference on Juvenile Delinquency in 1853 – observed in relation to the provision of institutions for juveniles: 'The great exertions which had been made in almost every civilised nation of the world in this cause, with the one dark and sad exception of the land in which they lived. (Hear, hear.)' (*The Times*, 21 December 1853: 10). As noted above, it was not until the following year that the Youthful Offenders Act 1854 established the first Reformatories followed, three years later, by legislation that laid the foundations for Industrial Schools. Moreover, by the mid-nineteenth century, British 'child-savers' sought inspiration from the wider Western world in order to shape their visions of Victorian juvenile institutions.

Many prominent British reformers and commentators also visited North American penal institutions. Charles Dickens, for example, visited the Refuge for the Destitute in New York, and Sing Sing in New York State, in the 1860s. William Crawford, one of the first Inspectors of Prisons and a founding member of the 1816 Committee (*Report of the Committee for Investigating the Causes of the Alarming Increase of Juvenile Delinquency in the Metropolis*, 1816) had also toured American penitentiaries in 1833 and his findings were published as a House of Commons report in 1834 (*Report of William Crawford on the Penitentiaries of the United States*, 1834). Others focused more sharply on juvenile institutions in Europe including Sydney Turner, the chaplain of the Philanthropic Society, who made two visits to the French agricultural colony (Colonie Agricole) at Mettray (Leonards, 2002: 142) before the Philanthropic Society modelled its own Farm School in Redhill, Surrey, on Mettray. Other English juvenile justice pioneers, including Mary Carpenter and Matthew Davenport Hill, also looked to the perceived success of institutions such as Mettray in their own prescriptions for reform (Gear, 1999: 32–33). Furthermore, as Jablonka (2013: 382) notes, Mettray itself had been shaped by three major influences: Swiss farming refuges such as Neuhof and Hofwyl; the *Rauhe Haus* ('Rough House') founded in 1832 near Hamburg, Germany; and Parkhurst Prison for Boys in England. Thus, juvenile justice policy and practice across Europe, particularly in relation to institutional reform, was characterised by cross-fertilisation, shared modelling, transnational discourses and transfers not only across Europe, but also across the broader Western world.

In terms of the evolution of discrete and specialist juvenile courts and child-specific legal practices, most historians and criminologists have tended to focus on the early twentieth century as the point at which such developments were formally introduced in their respective countries. Hence, Frieder Dünkel (2016: 3) has noted that 'The history of the system of specific social control for minors in Germany dates back to the beginning of the twentieth century' and Uberto Gatti and Alfredo Verde (2016) mark the origins of the Italian juvenile justice system with the establishment of juvenile courts in 1934. More often than not, criminologists and even historians, therefore, have tended to anchor such origins stories to the twentieth century, but authors like Leonards (1990) on the Netherlands, Van Dijk, Dumortier and Eliaerts (2008) on Belgium, Christiaens (2002) on Saint-Hubert boys prison in Ghent, Dekker (1985) on the Dutch 'Mettray' and Trépanier and Tulkens (1995) on French Quebec, have each established that the evolution of parallel forms of juvenile justice in European countries and, particularly, the history of juvenile care and correctional institutions both signal active processes of policy and practice transfer and also, in many cases, predate the early twentieth century.

Juvenile justice in Europe: continuity and change

Arguably, the key paradigm deriving from historical analyses of the evolution of juvenile justice systems across many Western states is that the nature and timing of reform was broadly similar. Indeed, in Europe the evolution of separate systems to deal with young offenders followed parallel trajectories and Cox and Shore (2002: 6) have argued that common patterns can be traced that 'signified the rise of new forms of social management which required a wider reorganisation of the relationships between the state, civil institutions and citizens'. Principally, such processes encompassed: the emergence of new languages to describe delinquency; accompanying changes in the legal frameworks to respond to delinquency; the introduction and development of child specific institutions; and, the rise of new discourses about the family and state intervention, particularly in respect of families that were deemed to be 'dysfunctional' (Goldson and Jamieson, 2002: 84).

Across Europe, as in Britain, such processes had their roots in longer-term movements, reforms and historical continuities. As Paul Griffiths (2002: 33) has pointed out in his discussion of early modern youth, 'Delinquent youth can be found in all centuries'. For example, laws to respond specifically to vagrant children and child beggars were introduced in sixteenth-century Nuremberg, Germany, when the city authorities became exercised with unwanted children and the prospect of delinquent behaviour (Harrington, 2009). In seventeenth-century Stockholm, Sweden, street children were subject to various attempts to control their movement and to stop them seeking refuge in the city's buildings (Sandin, 1988). In early modern Seville, Spain, street children were placed into institutional 'care' (Tikoff, 2002; 2016). Within many early modern European cities and urban settlements, then, 'street children' were frequently perceived as a nuisance and exposed to institutional interventions that served both to remove them from the street and to 'train' them. Jonas Hanway's Marine Society in mid-eighteenth century London, for example, recruited street boys who were housed, clothed and fed, whilst they received naval training (Taylor, 1985). Juvenile delinquency then, was not simply a nineteenth-century construct. Whilst early modern, and even medieval, European societies may not have had distinct languages, institutional architectures or legal frameworks for juvenile justice, there were clearly mechanisms which problematised 'troublesome' youth and responded through courts, churches, parishes, institutions and family interventions (Hanawalt, 1993). It is important, therefore, for historians and criminologists to guard against making assumptions about the distinctively 'modern' character of juvenile justice. As Cox and Shore (2002: 6) argue, it is possible to define 'series of "moments" when delinquency was (re)created, (re)discovered and (re)invented'.

Notwithstanding the 'long' history of both continuity and change, in terms of legal frameworks the most notable European development was the introduction of the Napoleonic Code from 1804, which served to replace the patchwork of feudal laws that had previously characterised European countries. Whilst the code originated in France, it was to become the model both for European countries and developing countries outside Europe during the nineteenth century. For the treatment of juveniles, the most significant development was a new Penal Code from 1810 which contained specific provisions for legal minors and defined the age of penal majority as 16 years (Emsley, 2007). Moreover, it established a notion of 'discernement' which broadly corresponded to the English legal precedent of *doli incapax* (Cox and Shore, 2002: 7; Fishman, 2002: 13–14). Such legal frameworks became the basis for the development of juvenile justice across Europe and enshrined the principles of criminal responsibility in relation to children. In the Netherlands, for example, the *Crimineel Wetboek* – which contained some provisions pertaining to children – was introduced in 1809 but was superseded in 1811 by the Napoleonic Code (Leonards, 1990). In Germany, the French Criminal Code was enacted, and only replaced by the German Criminal Code, the *Strafgesetzbuch*, after unification in 1871 (Ruggiero and Ryan, 2013: 133). The French provisions for juveniles not only established universal principles of criminal responsibility, but also regulated punishment for children, for example, by exempting them from the death penalty and other severe punishments (Cox and Shore, 2002: 8). Whilst in other countries it took longer for such legal provisions to be instituted, the core tenets of discernement and the formalisation of a legal code to frame juvenile justice evolved from these early nineteenth-century developments.

Indeed, there was a remarkable sense of continuity in the range of formal measures which emerged to deal with youthful disorder in Europe and, from the mid-nineteenth century, the 'movement' towards juvenile justice gained momentum: the Juvenile Offenders Act 1847 in Britain; the Child Welfare Act 1896 in Norway; the Reformatory Act 1902 in Sweden; the Children Act 1908 in Britain; the Act establishing a Tribunal for Infants and Adolescents in France in 1912; the Child Welfare Act 1912, in Belgium; the Juvenile Welfare Act 1922 and the Juvenile Justice Act 1923 in Germany; and the establishment of the juvenile court in Italy in 1934. Such developments served both to explicitly define this new legal subject (the juvenile offender) and to provide duties and powers to intervene (Cox and Shore, 2002: 8; Dünkel, 2016; Gatti and Verde, 2016; Shore, 2003: 113). It is equally important to understand, however, that none of these legislative developments represented completely clean slates. Instead, as stated, the legal institutionalisation of formal juvenile justice systems in the later nineteenth and early twentieth centuries essentially formalised a set of practices which had evolved much earlier, including: discretionary practices in courtrooms, where magistrates exercised their powers in ways that took account of childhood and youth; the range of institutions which were established from the early modern period to 'rescue' and 'reform' vulnerable children; and various policy initiatives that provided for the welfare of children within the family and the community (Barron and Siebrecht, 2017; Frost, 2005; Jablonka, 2013).

What is absolutely clear, however, is that by the early twentieth century most, if not all, European countries had some form of reformatory programme which drew together charitable and philanthropic zeal and state support in the provision of institutional 'care' for both pre-delinquent and delinquent children (Cox and Shore, 2002: 11), in other words, the institutionalisation of Carpenter's distinction between the 'perishing' and the 'dangerous' (Carpenter, 1851; Shore, 1999; Whitten, 2011). The imperative to 'succour the destitute and to reform the vicious' (King, 2006: 150) consolidated in Europe over the course of the nineteenth century and underpinned a welfare-punishment nexus. Such conceptual dualism was apparent both in the children that were directed towards institutional intervention ('neglected', 'vagrant' and/or 'criminal') but also in the legitimising rationales and operational tensions that characterised institutional regimes. Should they be places of punishment or care? Should they train or reform? Should children be treated differently depending on the seriousness of their crimes? As Chris Leonards (2002) has shown, such questions shaped the debates of the penal congresses which took place in major European cities from 1846 onwards. Furthermore, from the later nineteenth century the same conference debates extended beyond an exclusive focus on institutional provision for juveniles to also embrace 'the family'. The Stockholm Congress of 1878, for example, explored the extent to which the idea of the family could be replicated in institutions. The Rome Congress in 1885 introduced a 'new' (reframed) focus on the role of parental responsibility in both the aetiology and the management of juvenile delinquency and, by 1890, the St. Petersburg Congress was demanding more powers for the court to challenge parental authority (Leonards, 2002: 112). In this way, the continuities and changes that characterised evolving juvenile justice discourses unfolded 'between and within states' (Cox and Shore, 2002: 1).

New directions in historical juvenile justice research

So where does the field develop from here? Nineteenth-century sources for the history of juvenile justice are increasingly being revealed through digitisation. For example, the digitisation of the Old Bailey,[1] the British Library Newspaper Collection and other newspapers such as *The Times*, which enable researchers to trace individual trials, shifting discursive 'voices', the processes of the Reformatory and Industrial School Acts through their various incarnations, and the public history of institutions like the Philanthropic Society and their European cousins such as Mettray. Moreover, increasingly, in the British context at least, local record offices have collaborated with commercial providers to make available, at a cost, digital versions of their records.[2] Digitisation, therefore, is enabling major new developments in historical criminology.

In this way, a project focused on juvenile offenders in Victorian reformatory institutions in the North-West of England has combined digitised records (such as the Census, newspapers, and Birth, Marriage and Death records) with archives held in the local and National Archives, to produce life-course studies of the children and young people held within the institutions (Godfrey et al., 2017). Similar life-course research has also been undertaken in Amsterdam in a project which has tracked boys originally detained in a Dutch Reform School. The Transfive study started with the collection of data relating to 198 boys who were placed in a Reform School between 1911 and 1914 (Bijleveld and Wijkman, 2009). The study has enabled researchers to explore the intergenerational dynamics of offenders from their early interactions with the criminal justice system (van de Weijer, Bijleveld and Blokland, 2014). Moreover, such projects are helping us to ask new questions about the early evolution of juvenile justice and the ways in which the measures and prescriptions that evolved in the past resonate with core aspects of modern policy and practice.

Other work, anchored in more traditionally historical frameworks, has extended the analysis of European delinquency to much less studied communities and populations. For example, Laurent Fourchard (2010) has studied the punishment of children in South Africa and Nigeria and Erin Bell (2014) has explored juvenile delinquency in Colonial Kenya, during the Mau Mau uprising. These studies enable us to continue to think about the historical developments of juvenile justice – not only in Europe but also across global contexts – as an organic and ever-evolving set of practices, lived experiences and responses to social, economic and political contingencies which every society is subject to.

Notes

1 See: www.oldbaileyonline.org.
2 The West Yorkshire Archives, for example, launched a digital version of its Reformatory School archive with Ancestry.co.uk. See: www.whodoyouthinkyouaremagazine.com/news/ancestrycouk-unveils-young-offender-records.

References

Barron, H. and Siebrecht, C. (eds) (2017) *Parenting and the State in Britain and Europe, c. 1879–1950: Raising the Nation*. Basingstoke: Palgrave Macmillan.

Bell, E. (2014) '"A most horrifying maturity in crime": Age, Gender and Juvenile Delinquency in Colonial Kenya During the Mau Mau Uprising', *Atlantic Studies*, 11(4), 473–490.

Bijleveld, C. C. J. H. and Wijkman, M. (2009) 'Intergenerational Continuity in Convictions: A Five-Generation Study', *Criminal Behavior and Mental Health*, 19(2): 142–155.

Bradley, K., Logan, A. and Shaw, S. (2009) 'Youth and Crime: Centennial Reflections on the Children Act 1908', *Crimes and Misdemeanors*, 3(2): 1–17.

Cale, M. (1993) 'Girls and the Perception of Sexual Danger in the Victorian Reformatory System', *History*, 78(253): 201–217.

Carpenter, M. (1851) *Reformatory Schools for the Perishing and Dangerous Classes and for Juvenile Offenders*. London: C. Gilpin.

Christiaens, J. (2002) 'Testing the Limits: Redefining Resistance in a Belgian Boys' Prison, 1895–1905', in Cox, P. and Shore, H. (eds), *Becoming Delinquent: European Youth, 1950–1950*. Farnham: Ashgate.

Commission to Inquire into Child Abuse Report (2009) www.childabusecommission.ie/rpt/ [Accessed 21 May 2018].

Cox, P. (2003) *Bad Girls in Britain: Gender, Justice and Welfare, 1900–1950.* Basingstoke: Palgrave Macmillan.

Cox, P. and Shore, H. (eds) (2002) *Becoming Delinquent: European Youth, 1650–1950.* Farnham, Ashgate.

De Graaf, E., Christiaens, J. and Dumortier, E. (2016) 'Children behind Belgian Bars: Rights and Resistance against the Pains of Imprisonment', in Liefaard, T. and Sloth-Nielsen, J. (eds), *The United Nations Convention on the Rights of the Child: Taking Stock after 25 Years and Looking Ahead.* Leiden: Brill.

Dekker, J. J. H. (1985) *Straffen, Redden en Opvoeden: het Ontstaan en de Ontwikkeling van de Residentiële Heropvoeding in West-Europa, 1814–1914, met Bijzondere Aandacht voor Nederlandsch Mettray.* Assen/Maastricht: van Gorcum.

Dünkel, F. (2016) 'Youth Justice in Germany', *Oxford Handbooks Online*, www.oxfordhandbooks. com/view/10.1093/oxfordhb/9780199935383.001.0001/oxfordhb-9780199935383 -e-68 [Accessed 21 May 2018].

Egmond, F. (1988) 'Children in Court: Children and Criminal Justice in the Dutch Republic', *Social and Legal Studies*, 2: 73–90.

Ellis, H. (2014) 'Introduction: Constructing Juvenile Delinquency in a Global Context', in Ellis, H. (ed.), *Juvenile Delinquency and the Limits of Western Influence, 1850–2000.* Basingstoke: Palgrave Macmillan.

Emsley, C. (2007) *Crime, Police and Penal Policy: European Experiences, 1750–1940.* Oxford: Oxford University Press.

Fishman, S. (2002) *The Battle for Children: World War II, Youth Crime, and Juvenile Justice in Twentieth-Century France.* Cambridge, MS: Harvard University Press.

Fourchard, L. (2010) 'The Making of the Juvenile Delinquent in Nigeria and South Africa, 1930–1970', *Historical Compass*, 8(2): 129–142.

Frost, N. (ed.) (2005) *Child Welfare: Major Themes in Health and Social Welfare, Vol. I, Historical Perspectives.* Abingdon: Routledge.

Garland, D. (1985) *Punishment and Welfare: A History of Penal Strategies.* London: Gower.

Gatti, U. and Verde, A. (2016) 'Juvenile Justice in Italy', *Oxford Handbooks Online*, www. oxfordhandbooks.com/view/10.1093/oxfordhb/9780199935383.001.0001/oxfordhb-9780199935383-e-66 [Accessed 21 May 2018].

Gear, G. (2013) 'Hertfordshire's Relationship with Certified Industrial Schools, 1857–1933', in Gear, G. and King, S. (eds), *A Caring County? Social Welfare in Hertfordshire from 1600.* Hatfield: University of Hertfordshire Press.

Gear, G. C. (1999) 'Industrial Schools in England, 1857–1933: Moral Hospitals or Oppressive Institutions?', unpublished PhD thesis, University of London, Institute of Education.

Glueck, S. and Glueck, E. (1950) *Unravelling Juvenile Delinquency.* New York: Commonwealth Fund.

Godfrey, B., Cox, P., Shore, H. and Alker, Z. (2017) *Young Criminal Lives: Life Course and Life Chances from 1850.* Oxford: Oxford University Press.

Goldson, B. and Jamieson, J. (2002) 'Youth Crime, the "Parenting Deficit" and State Intervention: A Contextual Critique', *Youth Justice*, 2(2): 82–99.

Goldson, B. and Muncie, J. (2015, 2nd edn) *Youth, Crime and Justice.* London: Sage.

Gorsky, M. (1999) *Patterns of Philanthropy: Charity and Society in Nineteenth-Century Bristol.* Woodbridge, Suffolk: Boydell & Brewer.

Griffiths, P. (2002) 'Juvenile Delinquency in Time', in Cox, P. and Shore, H. (eds), *Becoming Delinquent: European Youth, 1950–1950.* Farnham: Ashgate.

Hanawalt, B. A. (1993) *Growing Up in Medieval London: The Experience of Childhood in History.* Oxford: Oxford University Press.

Harrington, J. (2009) *The Unwanted Child: The Fate of Foundlings, Orphans, and Juvenile Criminals in Early Modern Germany.* Chicago: University of Chicago Press.

Hay, D., Linebaugh, P., Rule, J. G, Thompson, E. P. and Winslow, C. (1975) *Albion's Fatal Tree: Crime and Society in Eighteenth-Century England.* London: Allen Lane/Penguin.

Hirch, P. and Hilton, M. (2014) *Practical Visionaries: Women, Education and Social Progress, 1790–1930.* Abingdon: Routledge.

Independent Inquiry Into Child Sexual Abuse: www.iicsa.org.uk

Jablonka, I. (2013) 'Social Welfare in the Western World and the Rights of Children', in Fass, P. S. (ed.), *The Routledge History of Childhood in the Western World.* Abingdon: Routledge.

Johnston, H. (2015) *Crime in England, 1815–1880: Experiencing the Criminal Justice System.* London: Routledge.

King, P. and Noel, J. (1993) 'The Origins of "The Problem of Juvenile Delinquency": The Growth of Juvenile Prosecutions in London in the Late Eighteenth and Early Nineteenth Centuries', *Criminal Justice History*, 14: 17–41.

King, P. (1998) 'The Rise of Juvenile Delinquency in England, 1780–1840', *Past and Present*, 160: 116–166.

King, P. (2006) *Crime and Law in England, 1750–1840: Remaking Justice from the Margins.* Cambridge: Cambridge University Press.

Laub, J. H. and Sampson, R. J. (2006) *Shared Beginnings, Divergent Lives: Delinquent Boys to Age 70.* Boston: Harvard University Press.

Leonards, C. (1990) 'From a Marginal Institution to Institutional Marginalization: Developments in the Treatment of "Criminal" Children in the Dutch Prison System, 1833–1884', *Paedagogica Historica*, 26(2) 147–159.

Leonards, C. (1995) *De ontdekking van het onschuldige criminele kind: bestraffing en opvoeding van crimine le kinderen in jeugdgevangenis en opvoedingsgesticht 1833–1886.* Hilversum: Verloren.

Leonards, C. (2002) 'Border Crossings: Care and the "Criminal Child" in Nineteenth-Century European Penal Congresses', in Cox, P. and Shore, H. (eds) *Becoming Delinquent: European Youth, 1950–1950.* Farnham: Ashgate.

Leonards, C. (2002) 'Priceless Children? Penitentiary Congresses Debating Childhood: A Quest for Social Order in Europe, 1846–1895', in Emsley, C., Johnson, E. and Spierenburg, P. (eds) *Social Control in Europe, Vol. 2, 1800–2000.* Columbus: Ohio State University Press.

Magarey, S. (1978) 'The Invention of Juvenile Delinquency in Early Nineteenth-Century England', *Labour History* 34: 11–25, reprinted in Muncie, J., Hughes, G. and McLaughlin, E. (eds) (2002) *Youth Justice: Critical Readings.* London: Sage.

Mahood, L. (1995) *Policing Gender, Class and Family in Britain, 1800–1945.* London: UCL Press.

May, M. (1973) 'Innocence and Experience: The Evolution of the Concept of Juvenile Delinquency in the Mid-Nineteenth Century', *Victorian Studies*, 17(1): 7–29, reprinted in Muncie, J., Hughes, G. and McLaughlin, E. (eds) (2002) *Youth Justice: Critical Readings.* London: Sage.

McConville, S. (1981) *A History of English Prison Administration, vol. 1, 1750–1877.* London: Routledge and Kegan Paul.

Perkin, H. (1969) *The Origins of Modern English Society.* London: Routledge and Kegan Paul.

Platt, A. (1969) *The Child Savers: The Invention of Delinquency.* Chicago: University of Chicago Press.

Radzinowicz, L. and Hood, R. (1990) *A History of English Criminal Law and its Administration from 1750, V: The Emergence of Penal Policy.* Oxford: Oxford University Press.

Rafferty, M. and O'Sullivan, E. (1999) *Suffer the Little Children: The Inside Story of Ireland's Industrial Schools*. Dublin: New Island.

Rosenheim, M. K., Zimring, F. E., Tanenhaus, D. S. and Dohrn, B. (eds) (2001) *A Century of Juvenile Justice*. Chicago: University of Chicago Press.

Ruggiero, V. and Ryan, M. (2013) *Punishment in Europe: A Critical Anatomy of Penal Systems*. Basingstoke: Palgrave Macmillan.

Sampson, R. J. and Laub, J. H. (2003) 'Life-Course Desisters? Trajectories of Crime Among Delinquent Boys Followed to Age 70', *Criminology*, 41(3): 555–592.

Samuel, R. (1985) 'What is Social History?', *History Today*, 35(3): 34–44.

Sandin, B. (1988) 'Education, Popular Culture, and the Surveillance of the Population in Stockholm between 1600 and the 1840s', *Continuity and Change*, 3: 357–390.

Sheldon, N. (2008) 'School Attendance 1880–1939: A Study of Policy and Practice in Response to the Problem of Truancy', unpublished PhD thesis, University of Oxford.

Sheldon, N. (2009) 'The Musical Careers of the Poor: The Role of Music as a Vocational Training for Boys in British Care Institutions, 1870–1918', *History of Education*, 38(6): 747–759.

Sheldon, N. (2013) 'Something in the Place of Home': Children in Institutional Care, 1850–1918', in Goose, N. and Honeyman, K. (eds), *Childhood and Child Labour in Industrial England: Diversity and Agency, 1750–1914*. Farnham: Ashgate.

Shoemaker, D. J. (2013) *Juvenile Delinquency*. Lanham, MD: Rowman and Littlefield.

Shore, H. (1999) *Artful Dodgers: Youth and Crime in Early Nineteenth Century London*. Woodbridge, Suffolk: Boydell & Brewer.

Shore, H. (2003) '"Inventing" the Juvenile Delinquent in Nineteenth-Century Europe', in Godfrey, B. S., Emsley, C. and Dunstall, G. (eds), *Comparative Histories of Crime*. Cullompton: Willan Publishing.

Shore, H. (2008) 'Punishment, Reformation, or Welfare: Responses to "The Problem" of Juvenile Crime in Victorian and Edwardian Britain', in Johnston, H. (ed.) *Punishment and Control in Historical Perspective*. Basingstoke: Palgrave Macmillan.

Sköld, J. (2016) 'The Truth about Abuse? A Comparative Approach to Inquiry Narratives on Historical Institutional Child Abuse', *History of Education*, 45(4): 492–509.

Stack, J. A. (1979) 'Deterrence and Reformation in Early Victorian Social Policy: The Case of Parkhurst Prison, 1838–1864', *Historical Reflections*, 6: 387–404.

Stack, J. A. (1994) 'Reformatory and Industrial Schools and the Decline of Child Imprisonment in Mid-Victorian England and Wales', *History of Education*, 23(1): 59–73.

Stack, J. A. (1992) 'Children, Urbanization and the Chances of Imprisonment in Mid-Victorian England', *Criminal Justice History*, 13: 113–139.

Taylor, J. S. (1985) *Jonas Hanway, Founder of the Marine Society: Charity and Policy in Eighteenth-Century*. London: Scolar Press.

The Times, 21st December, 1853.

Thompson, E. P. (1963) *The Making of the English Working Class*. London: Victor Gollancz.

Tikoff, V. (2002) 'Before the Reformatory: A Correctional Orphanage in Old Regime Seville', in Cox, P. and Shore, H. (eds) *Becoming Delinquent: European Youth, 1950–1950*. Farnham: Ashgate.

Tikoff, V. (2016) 'Containing Risk: The Integration and Isolation of Orphanage Wards with Eighteenth-Century Seville', in Coolidge, G. E. (ed.), *The Formation of the Child in Early Modern Spain*. Abingdon: Routledge.

Trépanier, J. and Tulkens, F. (1995) *Délinquance et protection de la jeunesse: aux sources des lois belge et canadienne sur l'enfance*. Brussels: DeBoeck Université.

Van Dijk, C., Dumortier, E. and Eliaerts, C. (2008) 'Survival of the Protection Model? Competing Goals in Belgian Juvenile Justice', in Junger-Tas, J. and Decker, S. H. (eds), *International Handbook of Juvenile Justice*. New York: Springer.

van de Weijer, S. G. A., Bijleveld, C. C. J. H. and Blokland, A. A. J. (2014) 'The Intergenerational Transmission of Violent Offending', *Journal of Family Violence*, 29(2): 109–118.

Weevers, M., De Koster, M. and Bijleveld, C. (2012) '"Swept up from the streets of nowhere else to go"? The Journeys of Dutch Female Beggars and Vagrants to the Oestgeest State Labor Institution in the Late Nineteenth Century', *Journal of Social History*, 46(2): 416–429.

Whitten, M. (2011) *Nipping Crime in the Bud: How the Philanthropic Quest was put into Law*. Hook, Hampshire: Waterside Press.

3

HISTORY, LIFE-COURSE CRIMINOLOGY AND DIGITAL METHODS

New directions for conceptualising juvenile justice in Europe

Zoe Alker and Emma Watkins

Back to the future? Histories of the present

In 1816, shortly after the close of the Napoleonic Wars, the 'Committee for Investigating the Causes of the Alarming Increase of Juvenile Delinquency in the Metropolis' concluded that the main 'causes' of juvenile crime in England were the 'want of education', the 'want of suitable employment', 'the violation of the Sabbath' and 'the improper conduct of parents'. The Report continued: 'The first circumstances, which are allowed to operate in the formation of character, flow from the exercise, or neglect, of parental authority'. In addition, 'The errors of parents have done much to encourage the criminal propensities of their children… [such parents being] regardless of the welfare of their children' (Committee for Investigating the Causes of the Alarming Increase of Juvenile Delinquency in the Metropolis' 1816: 10–11).

The reform of juvenile justice across much of the nineteenth and twentieth centuries 'embodied an implicit critique of the working-class family arrangements and child rearing practices' (Clarke, 2002: 134). By the middle of the nineteenth century legislation providing for Industrial and Reformatory Schools represented the institutionalised manifestation of these concerns. The Industrial Schools Act 1861, for example, allowed for children (under the age of 14 years) to be removed from their families and detained if their parents were deemed to be unable to control them. Similarly, section 11 of the Elementary Education Act 1876 authorised School Boards to place any 'child [who] is found habitually wandering or not under proper control, or in the company of rogues, vagabonds, disorderly persons, or reputed criminals' in a Certified Industrial School or a Certified Day Industrial School. Notions of parental 'deficit' were pivotal (Goldson and Jamieson, 2002) and, as Peter King (2006: 106) observes:

> Juvenile offenders, as powerful representatives of the shape of the future and as potential mirrors of the broader state of social order, were especially likely to be seized upon as particularly dangerous manifestations of these broader

social problems, as symbols of the nascent insubordination, idleness and family degeneration of many sections of the burgeoning urban working class.

An obsession with the 'malfunctioning' urban working-class family underpinned aetiological constructions of juvenile crime and the report of the Committee into Juvenile Delinquency (1816) was part of a 'much wider explosion in public debate' which marked 'the first hesitant (and methodologically naïve) attempts to investigate the roots of criminal behavior, the ages and backgrounds of offenders and the effects of various judicial policies upon them' (King, 2006: 105).

Two hundred years later and many of the same questions persist across Europe and beyond. Why do some children, who may share the same familial background, peer networks, and neighbourhoods offend whereas others do not? What are the causes of juvenile crime? Why do some young people desist from offending when others engage in a life of recidivism? How can criminal justice agencies, policymakers and researchers prevent juvenile crime? What factors obstruct desistance and what processes contribute to desistance? Similar questions also frame research undertaken by crime historians who adopt life-course approaches to 'recover' 'criminal lives' from the eighteenth, nineteenth and early twentieth centuries and, in doing so, add a crucial historical dimension to contemporary criminological concerns (Godfrey et al., 2007; 2010; 2017).

The digitisation of historical record sets is increasingly enabling researchers to compile and compare offending trajectories and life-course histories.[1] The relatively recent digitisation of genealogical sources including the census, birth, marriage and death records, crime registers and newspapers means that crime historians are able to 'unlock' the biographies of young offenders and chart significant life-course events, processes and transitions including admission to, experience in and release from penal institutions, alongside their subsequent education, employment, housing, geographical (re)location, (re)marriage, parenthood, military conscription, re-offending, desistance and, ultimately, death. Using a combination of biographical and multivariate analysis, such research can draw upon 'cradle to grave' data to examine how juvenile justice interventions that took place over the course of the nineteenth century – including placements in Reformatory and Industrial Schools, imprisonment and transportation – were experienced by juvenile offenders and their families and the effects that such experiences imposed.

Crime historians who adopt life-course approaches typically adopt retrospective analyses of offending. As Godfrey et al. (2017: 4) explain:

> Life course criminological studies fall into two groups: prospective and retrospective. Prospective studies follow a cohort of people, usually defined by their birth year, at intervals over their lives whereas retrospective studies collate past or historic data on a given cohort.

Both retrospective and prospective studies draw upon large cohorts to create multivariate datasets to explore patterns in offending and life transitions that can help to explain the onset, continuity and/or desistance from offending. Crime historians and criminologists who engage with life-course approaches, then, centre their research around two broad but interrelated questions: first, why do some children offend when others do not, and second, what 'pathways' lead to either persistence or desistance from crime as children and young people transition into adulthood?

Arjan Blokland and Paul Nieuwbeerta (2010: 84) have encouraged historians and life-course criminologists to shape future research that involves 'comparisons between countries and historical periods'. While recent comparative criminology – including research in the juvenile/youth justice sphere – has tended to privilege contemporary inter-jurisdictional analyses, comparative *histories* of juvenile justice that cross nation state borders remain largely underdeveloped. To date, historical transnational comparative research on youth and the life course across, and between, European countries is, at best, embryonic.

This chapter aims to encourage historians and criminologists to synthesise historical and contemporary datasets to examine juvenile justice and punishment across both time and space. Gathering life histories from across Europe can provide a lens through which to examine the effects of historical, cultural, social, economic and political change upon juvenile offenders. Life-course criminology has already demonstrated the value of embedding biographies within their temporal and spatial contexts and of examining the impact of social-structural change on 'delinquent' youth. Some researchers have examined the impacts of small-scale social shifts within micro-historical contexts such as the Nilsson et al. (2013) study of young offenders in Sweden. Others have explored the effects of macro-level processes of social change including, for example, Elder's (1998) study of the impact on a cohort of young people of the Great Depression in the 1930s as the economic crisis shattered employment opportunities and produced negative legacies that extended well into adulthood. Given that swathes of Europe are currently beset by conditions of austerity, collaboration amongst European crime historians and criminologists is especially timely.

Longitudinal surveys, developmental and intergenerational analysis, life history and historical demography share a common desire to use the life course to understand change at both the personal and the collective level (Godfrey et al., 2017). As Carlsson and Sarnecki (2016: 5) note, 'Human development is dependent on social and historical conditions and processes: where and when we live impacts on how we live and how our life course unfolds'. The chapter is presented in three sections: first, we outline the contours of life-course criminological approaches, second, we review how historians have utilised the digital environment to examine criminal lives on a transnational scale and, third, we posit potential future directions for historians and criminologists of European juvenile justice.

Life-course criminology

Life-course criminologies explore the lives of 'individuals as they move through time and place, and how criminal offending changes and continues with these movements' (Carlsson and Sarnecki, 2016: 2). It follows that life-course criminologists adopt a longitudinal approach involving the creation of individual biographies of offenders as a way of exploring the relationships between patterns of offending and life-course events, processes and transitions for example: forming adult relationships, getting married, entering, leaving or being excluded from employment, entering or leaving military service and so on. Moreover, by situating individual lives within their historical, social, political, economic and cultural contexts, historians and criminologists are able to assess the ways in which life transitions impact on crime, offending and desistance.

An early and influential example of life-course criminology was Eleanor and Sheldon Glueck's study of 500 delinquent boys committed to reform schools in Massachusetts, USA in the 1930s. The study compared the offending cohort with a control group of 500 non-offending boys and explored the factors that appeared to contribute to the boys' patterns of offending or desistance (Glueck and Glueck, 1930; 1934; 1950; 1968). The Gluecks' datasets – alongside those generated by the Cambridge Somerville Youth Study, first established in 1939 and also in Massachusetts, USA – provided a foundation for further longitudinal research which followed these cohorts into old age (McCord, 1977). Several later studies drew upon much larger samples. Two American studies, the Rochester Youth Development Study followed 1000 children from New York public schools (Thornberry et al., 1998) and the Pittsburgh Youth Study followed 1,500 males up to the age of 35 (Jennings et al., 2016), while the Dunedin Longitudinal Study traced 1000 people born in early 1970s in New Zealand (Silva, 1996). These studies, and others that followed, have demonstrated the contributions that large-scale life-course and longitudinal research can make (Elder, 1998; Farrington et al., 2013; Sampson and Laub, 1993; 1997; 2003; 2006; Wolfgang et al., 1972). The capacity to identify the relationships between offending and key events, patterns, processes and transitions across multiple offenders' lives reveals the myriad of personal, structural and legal phenomena that can impinge upon, or contribute towards, repeat offending and/or desistance.

Life-course researchers commonly apply multivariate analysis to large cohorts to understand offending at both the personal/individual and the collective level. Quantitative methods are commonly applied in life-course research, but the combi-nation of quantitative and qualitative approaches enables more nuanced analyses of individual agency. Adopting a mixed methods approach Sampson and Laub (2003) followed-up the Gluecks' (1950) famous *Unravelling Juvenile Delinquency* study by applying quantitative analysis to explore generic patterns in young offenders' crim-inal careers and qualitative methods to closely analyse the individual life histories of 52 of the juveniles who featured in the Gluecks' original sample. In doing so, Sampson and Laub highlighted the vital importance of human agency: 'Indeed, they go so far as to term it the missing link in understanding both persistence and desistance, and as such human agency provides a crucial piece of the puzzle of con-tinuity and change in crime across the life course' (Carlsson and Sarnecki, 2016: 4).

While a substantial volume of life-course research has emerged out of the USA and Australasia, a significant number of studies have also been conducted in Europe (Kyvsgaard, 1998; Savolainen, 2009; Skardhamar, 2010). The *Cambridge Study in*

Delinquent Development followed the lives of 400 young male offenders from South London, England and charted their lives from primary school to late middle age, examining the impact of variables including education, peer networks, familial life, leisure patterns and socioeconomic conditions against their offending patterns (Farrington et al., 2006; 2013). Taking a longer historical timeframe, the *TransFive* project conducted in the Netherlands followed 198 young offenders who had been incarcerated in a Dutch Reform School in the 1910s (Bijleveld and Wijkman, 2009; van de Weijer, Bijleveld and Blokland, 2014), while engaging an even longer timeframe, a Swedish study tracked the lives of 320 young offenders arrested in a single town and its surrounding parishes between 1840 and 1880 (Vikström, 2011). Other Swedish studies have focused more specifically on the influence of youth gangs on pathways into crime (see, for example, Sveri, 1960). These longitudinal studies have conventionally drawn cohorts from within specific and singular geographical contexts (towns, cities, countries), but so far little has been done to collate these datasets and contribute to a transnational comparative approach. Work in this area is emerging, however, through Arjan Blokland's and Victor van der Geest's *European Development and Life Course Criminology Group* (EDLC) under the auspices of the European Society of Criminology.[2]

The life-course approach has been developed and extended by a series of crime historians based in England over the past decade. Godfrey, Cox and Farrall (2007; 2010) combined archival and digital resources to reconstruct the lives of persistent offenders who were sentenced at Crewe magistrates' courts, Cheshire, England in the nineteenth century. The two key studies *Criminal Lives* (Godfrey et al., 2007) and *Serious Offenders* (Godfrey et al., 2010) navigated historical evidence to explore the impact of Victorian criminal justice initiatives that had been introduced by legislation (including the Habitual Criminals Act 1869) to address repeat offending. Consistent with the findings of Sampson and Laub (2003; 2006), Godfrey et al. (2007; 2010) have argued that it is the informal social controls offered by personal networks, marriage, employment and relocation, rather than specific criminal justice interventions, that appear to have the greatest effect on positively addressing recidivism. As Godfrey (2016: 146) contends, the life-course approach 'forces historians to see periods of offending as unusual and secondary in the lives of most offenders' (Godfrey, 2016: 146).

Digitising history

Digitisation of historical datasets – including criminal registers, census returns, schooling and military records, alongside birth, marriage and death registers – enables crime historians to piece together the social, personal and legal dimensions of nineteenth-century offenders' lives.[3] This data facilitates the reconstruction of linked lives by collating key transition points and processes including marriage, family formation, divorce, military service, employment and housing entry and departure points, alongside records of offending, intervention, sentencing and punishment. These sources, then, make it possible to unlock the lives, family formations, and neighbourhoods of Victorian offenders and contribute to an understanding of how personal biographical events situated within socioeconomic contexts and framed by social and criminal justice policies, shape(d) the (often complex) lives of individuals.

Digitised historical datasets – including court reports, prison licences and records held by penal institutions – provide researchers with rich data. For the specific purposes of juvenile justice research, historians and criminologists are able to retrieve and examine sources from Victorian young offenders' institutions available (with some conditions and restrictions) via the National Archives in the UK.[4] The histories of young people's lived experiences within and beyond penal institutions remains largely uncovered, but historians are increasingly utilising previously untapped archives in Britain and Australia to reveal the means by which children and young people negotiated institutions including prisons, juvenile reform homes, and borstals (Rogers, 2012; Smaal, 2013).

Of course, for some time criminologists and sociologists have gathered information relating to the biographies of offenders, but the ability to create longitudinal life histories across decades, and even centuries, means that this largely untapped data can offer a crucial historical 'long-view' dimension to criminological research. As Godfrey (2016: 50) reflects: 'that this data "recovers" and pieces together the lives of the most dispossessed and criminalised in society is remarkable'. The *Criminal Lives* (2007) and *Serious Offenders* (2010) projects have inspired other crime historians to apply life-course approaches to different 'types' of offenders including women (Turner, 2011; Williams, 2016) and children and young people (Godfrey, Cox, Shore and Alker, 2017; Kilday and Nash, 2017; Rogers, 2014). More recently, the *Young Criminal Lives* project (Godfrey et al., 2017) examined the life courses of children and young people admitted to four Industrial and Reformatory Schools in northwest England between 1850 and 1920. The Project, funded by the Leverhulme Trust, gathered data on 500 individuals using a range of digitised and archival resources including: institutional records (covering their admission and discharge); census records; birth, marriage and death records; military documents; crime registers and newspapers.

In this way, the *Young Criminal Lives* study has unlocked the direct experiences of the first generations of children and young people to pass through the early juvenile justice system in England. The specific focus on childhood and youth has meant that the study has been able to address the onset of offending more directly and systematically than previous historical research. One of the major findings of the Project has been that the traceable reconviction rate among the *Young Criminal Lives* subjects was just over twenty per cent, implying that young offenders in the late nineteenth century where significantly less likely to reoffend than children and young people in conflict with the law today (Godfrey et al., 2017). Efforts to discover 'what works' or, perhaps more significantly, 'what matters' in juvenile justice continue to dominate debates amongst researchers, policymakers, juvenile justice professionals and agencies across Europe, but the 'evidence-based' emphasis rarely takes account of historical data and the lessons that history can teach. The *Young Criminal Lives* researchers explain that the lower reoffending rates uncovered by the Project can be attributed, in large part, to the impact of post-release apprenticeships and employment opportunities and have argued, in line with other historical life-course studies, that the key to desistance from crime primarily lies outside of the juvenile justice system and, rather, is rooted more in informal and 'natural' processes and stabilising 'social controls' including employment, transitioning into adult family formations/responsibilities, community engagement and reintegration and settled domiciliary arrangements (Godfrey et al., 2017).

Principally such studies have adopted a 'case study' approach and have focussed on specific towns and cities (Godfrey et al., 2007, 2010, 2017; Rogers, 2014; Turner, 2009; Williams and Godfrey, 2015). While the *Young Criminal Lives* project provided a *national* focus by sampling young offenders from towns located within the northwest of England, Derbyshire and London, historical researchers are increasingly turning to examine crime and punishment on an *international* scale. The University of Leicester's *Carceral Archipelago* project, for example, led by Professor Clare Anderson, is attempting to provide 'the first global history of penal colonies' by mapping convict flows across colonial powers including the European Empires, Russia, Latin America and Japan from circa 1415 to the 1960s.[5] With its broad temporal and spatial reach, the study is examining penality within a historical context of global expansion and the relationships between convict labour, migration and confinement across the Imperial powers engaged in transportation and colonialisation. In doing so, the study is also shifting the history of transportation beyond the immediate lens of crime and punishment to examine the broader impacts of penal colonies upon culture, economy, society and identity.

Arguably the most ambitious study for charting the life course across nations, however, is the *Digital Panopticon*, a collaboration between the Universities of Liverpool, Sheffield, Tasmania, Oxford and Sussex, with funding from the UK-based Arts and Humanities Research Council (AHRC).[6] The researchers are employing digital technologies to draw together existing and new genealogical, biometric and criminal justice datasets held by different organisations in the UK and Australia. The project is exploring the impact of different types of penal interventions and punishments on the lives of 90,000 people sentenced at the Old Bailey in London between 1790 and 1925 and is aiming to create a searchable website which will be free to use and available to the public. The research is weaving together hitherto disparate fragments of 'convict lives' and by doing so it follows individual biographical journeys from the cradle to the grave across Britain and Australia. Ultimately the resource will: allow users to search for individuals across multiple datasets; examine and compare the lives of convicts sentenced to imprisonment and transportation; investigate the effectiveness of such punishments in reducing or exacerbating offending and; interrogate and develop new research questions for understanding and exploring vast and complex bodies of social, personal and criminal justice data. The resource will provide 'biographical research on an industrial scale' (Godfrey, 2016: 150).

Early findings from the study reveal important insights for the transnational study of juvenile justice. Many children and young people were brought before the courts for behaviour typically criminalised in nineteenth-century Britain including playing pitch and toss, gambling, breaking windows, petty larceny and throwing stones. Even in its early stages, the Project's website offers a lens to the complex dynamics of childhood, youth and urban street life in the nineteenth century. Framed within a context of poverty and overcrowding in industrial towns and cities across England, working-class young people lived out their lives in increasingly 'public' ways and became more visible on the streets of rapidly growing urban centres. The Courts' willingness to criminalise and prosecute minor transgressions – such as throwing stones or playing pitch and toss – highlights the moral sensibilities and concerns over young people's public presence that were consolidating across much of Europe at the time. The Project exposes the practical effects of over-zealous forms of intervention and excessive penality. Alfred Harris, for example, was convicted of stealing '37 hooks, 15 horn whistles and 2 whip mounts' from his 'master' for which he was sentenced to 12 months imprisonment. Born in 1847, Alfred's first conviction was at age 16 years, but he was later placed on the Register of Habitual Criminals having committed a further four offences. He never married, had no children and was engaged in manual, casual and insecure labour. Seemingly the criminal justice system worked to reproduce, rather than curtail, Alfred's criminal behaviour. Earlier research undertaken by Godfrey et al. (2007; 2010) demonstrates how, for repeat (even if low-level) offenders like Alfred, the stigmatisation brought about by spells of imprisonment almost inevitably impacted negatively through the transition into adulthood and obstructed any capacity to desist from crime.

In the main, histories of juvenile justice have, from distance, focused largely upon the fears of, and policy responses to, urban youth (Cox, 2003; King, 1998; Nunn, 2015; Shore, 1999). However, the Digital Panopticon engages directly with the lived-experiences of children and young people and, by synthesizing records from the UK and Australia, the Project allows researchers to chart offenders' paths from the town or city to the courtroom and, often, to the colonies. Such narratives reveal the forces of Empire at its most unforgiving. Watkins' (2018) research traces the lives of 118 children and young people who were sentenced at the Old Bailey in London in the early nineteenth century and subsequently transported to the Australian colonies; swept up in a nascent system of labour exchange, migration and punishment. Through the meticulous documentation of life narratives, the work reveals young people's experiences of both micro and macro processes of historical change including family life, education, leisure, poverty, employment, industrialisation, urbanisation, Empire, colonialisation, migration, enforced labour, punishment and incarceration (often in the hulks of prison ships). One such case, for example, was Richard Young, born in 1827. Through nominally linking his Old Bailey records with Home Office Criminal Registers and his transportation records we can establish that he had four brothers but seems to have been orphaned. He was just 14 years of age when he was sentenced to seven years' transportation at the Old Bailey for stealing four pairs of shoes. Richard was transported directly to the Point Puer juvenile penal settlement in Port Arthur, Tasmania in 1841.

Initially such juvenile 'convicts' were assigned to adult free settlers and exposed to forced labour (Jordan, 1985: 1092). Even at the height of the demand for convict labour (1820–1830), however, children and young people were considered to have fewer skills than adult convicts and were seen to be less able to undertake strenuous physical work (Jackman, 2001: 6–7). Consequently, they were often difficult to assign and were simply kept idle in prisoner barracks. With an increasing number of juveniles financially burdening the colonial government, therefore, a solution was sought and Point Puer was established in 1833 (Slee, 2003: 5). It was the first prison of its kind in the British Empire – a separate penal institution purely for boys between the ages of nine and 18 years – and it meant that juvenile convicts were physically separated from adults. Between 1834 and 1849 some 3000 boys were detained at Point Puer and although the establishment of the institution was principally driven by pragmatic concerns, it also coincided with emerging 'ideals' in Europe in respect of obtaining juvenile rehabilitation through institutionally based retraining (Reformatory and Industrial Schools in Britain and their equivalents in many other parts of Europe) (Jackman, 2001: 7).

While Richard's case is interesting, it means little in isolation. It is through collecting and collating a series of life narratives that can be compared and contrasted that the detail of children's and young people's biographies appear and the nature of their offending and offending trajectories emerge. Indeed, by combining life courses on a large scale it is also possible to create an understanding of common social phenomena, for example, on skills and employment (Nicholas, 1988: Oxley; 1996); family-life (Maxwell-Stewart et al., 2015) or health (Kippen and McCalman, 2015) and how the same phenomena might impact upon recidivism or desistance. Furthermore, collating 'big data' in this way exposes the cruel and inhuman treatment and conditions to which children and young people were typically exposed and both humanises juvenile offenders and centres the lives of the vulnerable (McGarry and Alker, 2018: 6). As Godfrey (2016: 146) contends, the life-course approach, with its focus on the personal as well as legal experiences of offenders, 'forces historians to see periods of offending as unusual and secondary in the lives of most offenders… it emphasizes the humanity of the subject under study… and encourages a sympathetic and empathetic response'.

New directions for researching the origins and outcomes of juvenile justice in Europe

Histories of juvenile justice in Europe are few and far between which is curious given the similar trajectories of reform that characterised many countries across the nineteenth and early twentieth centuries (Cox and Shore, 2002). Such similarities are particularly evident with regard to the development of specialist institutions for the detention of children and young people. The establishment of the agricultural

Reform School in 1839 at Mettray in France formed, in many respects, a model for developments in juvenile institutions elsewhere in Europe (Christiaens, 2002; Cox and Shore, 2002; Dekker, 2005; Johnston, 2015; Radzinowicz and Hood, 1990; Trepanier, 1999). This chapter has attempted to outline some of the ways that the historical contextualisation of life-course criminology and, perhaps especially, the digitisation of historical data, can signal new directions and open up a range of possibilities for researching the origins and outcomes of juvenile justice in Europe. In doing so, we have responded, at least in part, to Blokland and Nieuwbeerta's (2010: 84) call for criminologists and historians – who engage in life-course approaches – to collate their data and compare patterns across Europe:

> Given [its] dependence on historical time and place, comparisons between countries or historical periods should become part of future efforts in life course criminology... to capitalize on the unique data position of many European countries – especially the Netherlands and the Scandinavian countries – in which detailed, individual-level life course data are available from official registers.

A more ambitious and extensive utilisation of digitised historical records can facilitate the extension of comparative life-course (youth) criminology along both its temporal and spatial dimensions.

The *Young Criminal Lives* and the *Digital Panopticon* projects provide a strong foundation upon which to build greater understanding of the origins and outcomes of juvenile justice in Europe. Tracing the pathways that children and young people followed into, through and out of specialist institutions is especially important. By extending life-course approaches and making best use of digitised data, the emerging research exposes the severe punishments and the (often inhumane) conditions and treatment endured by children and young people. It also extends aetiological accounts beyond individualised and reductionist moral discourses and places them instead within an appreciative context that integrates individual agency and complex material, social-structural, cultural, economic and political conditions. Finally, for present purposes at least, it enables an understanding of the complex intersecting relationships between the onset, continuity and/or desistance into and out of juvenile offending and key life events, patterns, processes and transitions. In this way the research implies that informal methods of social control that derive from personal and familial networks, education, training and employment opportunities, housing stability and 'normal' maturational processes are more likely to produce positive outcomes than institutional interventions and punitive impositions.

Notes

1 See, for example, the Digital Panopticon (www.digitalpanopticon.org/) and Old Bailey Online (www.oldbaileyonline.org/).
2 See: www.esc-eurocrim.org/index.php/activities/working-groups/41-edlc.

3 Websites such as *Ancestry.co.uk* and *FindMyPast.co.uk* can be used for this purpose.
4 See: www.nationalarchives.gov.uk/.
5 See: http://convictvoyages.org/about.
6 See: www.digitalpanopticon.org/.

References

Bijleveld, C. C. J. H., and Wijkman, M. (2009) 'Intergenerational Continuity in Convictions: A Five-Generation Study', *Criminal Behaviour and Mental Health*, 19(2): 142–155.

Blokland, A. A. J. and Nieuwbeerta, P. (2010) 'Life Course Criminology', in Knepper, P. and Shoham, S. G. (eds) *International Handbook of Criminology*. London: CRC Press.

Blokland, A. and Van der Geest, V. (2017) *The Routledge International Handbook of Life-Course Criminology*. Oxford: Routledge.

Carlsson, C., and Sarnecki, J. (2016) *An Introduction to Life Course Criminology*. London: Sage.

Christiaens, J. (2002) 'Testing the Limits: Redefining Resistance In a Belgian Boys Prison, 1895–1905, in Cox, P. and Shore, H. (eds) *Becoming Delinquent: British and European Youth, 1650–1950*. London: Ashgate.

Clarke, J. (2002) 'The Three Rs – Repression, Rescue, and Rehabilitation: Ideologies of Control for Working-Class Youth', in Muncie, J., Hughes, G., and McLaughlin, E. (eds) *Youth Justice: Critical Readings*. London: Sage.

Committee for Investigating the Alarming Increase of Juvenile Delinquency in the Metropolis (1816) *Report of the Committee for Investigating the Alarming Increase of Juvenile Delinquency in the Metropolis*. London: J. F. Dove.

Cox, P. (2003) *Gender, Justice and Welfare, Bad Girls in Britain: 1900–1950*. Basingstoke: Palgrave Macmillan.

Cox, P. and Shore, H. (2002) *Becoming Delinquent: British and European Youth, 1650–1950*. London: Ashgate.

Dekker, J. H. J. (2005) 'The Will to Change the Children at Risk: The Transformation of Philanthropy into Social Policy in Nineteenth-Century Western Europe', in Fecteau, J., and Janice, H. (eds) *Agency and Institutions in Social Regulation: Towards Historical Understanding of their Interaction*. Sainte Foy: Les Presses de l'Université du Quebec.

Elder, G. H. (1998) *Children of the Great Depression: 25th Anniversary Edition*. New York: Avalon Publishing.

Elder Jr, G. H. & Shanahan, M. J. (2006) 'The Life Course and Human Development', in Damon, W. and Lerner, R. M. (eds) *Handbook of Child Psychology, Volume One: Theoretical Models of Human Development* (6th edn). New York: John Wiley & Sons: 665–715.

Farrington, D. P., Coid, J. W., Harnett, L. M., Jolliffee, D., Soteriou, N., Turner, R. E. and West, D. J. (2006) *Criminal Careers up to Age 50 and Life Success up to Age 48: New Findings from the Cambridge Study in Delinquent Development*. Home Office Research, Development and Statistics Directorate (Research Study 299). London: Home Office.

Farrington, D. P., Piquero, A. R. and Jennings, W. G. (2013) *Offending from Childhood to Late Middle Age: Recent Results from the Cambridge Study in Delinquent Development*. New York: Springer.

Farrington, D. P. and Ttofi, M. M. (2015) 'Developmental and Life-Course Theories of Offending', in Morizot, J. and Kasemian, L. (eds) *The Development of Criminal and Antisocial Behaviour*. Switzerland: Springer International Publishing: 19–38.

Glueck, S. and Glueck, E. (1930) *Five Hundred Criminal Careers*. New York: Knopf.

Glueck, S. and Glueck, E. (1934) *One Thousand Juvenile Delinquents: Their Treatment by Court and Clinic*. Boston: Harvard University Press.

Glueck, S. and Glueck, E. (1950) *Unravelling Juvenile Delinquency.* New York: Commonwealth Fund.

Glueck, S. and Glueck, E. (1968) *Delinquents and Non-delinquents in Perspective.* Boston: Harvard University Press.

Godfrey, B. (2014) *Crime in England, 1880–1945: The Rough and the Criminal, the Policed and the Incarcerated.* London: Routledge.

Godfrey, B. (2016) 'Liquid Crime History: Digital Entrepreneurs and the Industrial Production of Ruined Lives' in Jacobsen, M. H. and Walklate, S. (eds) *Liquid Criminology: Doing Imaginative Criminological Research.* Oxford: Routledge.

Godfrey, B., Cox, D. and Farrall, S. (2007) *Criminal Lives. Family Life, Employment and Offending,* Clarendon Studies in Criminology. Oxford: Oxford University Press.

Godfrey, B., Cox, D. and Farrall, S. (2010) *Serious Offenders: A Historical Study of Habitual Criminals,* Clarendon Studies in Criminology. Oxford: Oxford University Press.

Godfrey, B., Cox, P., Shore, H., Alker, Z. (2017) *Young Criminal Lives,* Clarendon Studies in Criminology. Oxford: Oxford University Press.

Goldson, B. and Jamieson, J. (2002) 'Youth Crime, the "Parenting Deficit" and State Intervention: A Contextual Critique', *Youth Justice,* (2)2: 82–99.

Jackman, G. (2001) 'Get thee to Church: Hard Work, Godliness and Tourism at Australia's First Rural Reformatory', *Australasian Historical Archaeology, Special Issue: Archaeology of Confinement,* 19: 6–13.

Jennings, W. G., Loeber, R., Pardini, D. A., Piquero, A. R. and Farrington, D. P. (2016) *Offending from Childhood to Young Adulthood: Recent Results from the Pittsburgh Youth Study.* New York: Springer.

Johnston, H. (2015) *Crime in England 1815–1880: Experiencing the Criminal Justice System.* London: Routledge.

Jordan, T. E. (1985) 'Transported to Van Diemen's Land: The boys of the *Francis Charlotte* (1832) and *Lord Godrich* (1841)', *Child Development,* 56(4): 1092–1099.

Kilday, A-M. and Nash, D. (eds.) (2017) *Law, Crime and Deviance Since 1700.* London: Bloomsbury.

King, P. (1998) 'The Rise of Juvenile Delinquency in England, 1780– 1840', *Past and Present,* 160(1): 116–166.

King, P. (2006) *Crime and Law in England, 1750–1840: Remaking Justice from the Margins.* Cambridge: Cambridge University Press.

Kippen, R. and McCalman, J. (2015) 'Mortality Under and After Sentence of Male Convicts Transported to Van Diemen's Land (Tasmania), 1840–1852', *The History of the Family,* 20(3): 345–365.

Kyvsgaard, B. (1998) *Den Kriminelle Karriere.* København: Jurist og Qkonomforbundets Forlag.

Maxwell-Stewart, H., Inwood, K. and Stankovich, J. (2015) 'Prison and the Colonial Family', *The History of the Family,* 20(2): 231–448.

McCord, J. (1977) 'A Comparative View of Two Generations of Native Americans' in Meier, R. (ed.) *Theory in Criminology.* Los Angeles: Sage: 83–92.

McGarry, R. and Alker, Z. (2018), 'Biography and Autobiography in Criminological (and Victimological) Research', in Francis, P. and Davies, P. (eds) *Doing Criminological Research.* London: Sage.

Nicholas, S. (1988) *Convict Workers: Reinterpreting Australia's Past.* Cambridge: Cambridge University Press.

Nilsson, A., Bäckman, O. and Estrada, F. (2013) 'Involvement in Crime, Individual Resources and Structural Constraints: Processes of Cumulative (Dis)Advantage in a Stockholm Birth Cohort', *British Journal of Criminology,* 53: 297–318.

Nunn, C. (2015) 'Come All You Wild and Wicked Youths': Representations of Young Male Convicts in Nineteenth-Century English Broadsides', *Journal of Victorian Culture*, 20(4): 453–470.

Oxley, D. (1996) *Convict Maids: The Forced Migration of Women to Australia*. Cambridge: Cambridge University Press.

Radzinowicz, L., and Hood, R. (1990) *The Emergence of Penal Policy in Victorian and Edwardian England*. Oxford: Clarendon Press.

Rakt, M. V. D., Nieuwbeerta, P. and Graaf, N. D. D. (2008) 'Like Father, Like Son: The Relationships between Conviction Trajectories of Fathers and their Sons' *British Journal of Criminology*, 48(4): 538–556.

Rogers, H. (2012) '"Oh, What Beautiful Books!": Captivated Reading in an Early Victorian Prison', *Victorian Studies*, 55(1): 57–84.

Rogers, H. (2014) 'Kindness and Reciprocity: Liberated Prisoners and Christian Charity in Early Nineteenth-Century England', *Journal of Social History*, 47(3): 721–745.

Sampson, R. J. and Laub, J. H. (1993) *Crime in The Making: Pathways and Turning Points Through Life*. Boston: Harvard University Press.

Sampson, R. J. and Laub, J. H. (1997) 'A Life-Course Theory of Cumulative Disadvantage and the Stability of Delinquency', in Thornberry, T. (ed.) *Developmental Theories of Crime and Deviance. Advances in Criminological Theory*, vol. 7. New Brunswick: Transaction Publishers.

Sampson, R. J. and Laub, J. H. (2003) 'Life-Course Desisters? Trajectories of Crime Among Delinquent Boys Followed to Age 70', *Criminology*, 41(3): 555–592.

Sampson, R. J. and Laub, J. H. (2006) *Shared Beginnings, Divergent Lives: Delinquent Boys to Age 70*. Boston: Harvard University Press.

Savolainen J. (2009) 'Work, Family, and Criminal Desistance: Adult Social Bonds in a Nordic Welfare State', *British Journal of Criminology*, 49: 285–304.

Shore, H. (1999) *Artful Dodgers: Youth and Crime in Early Nineteenth-Century London*. Woodbridge: Boydell Press.

Skardhamar T. (2009) 'Family Dissolution and Children's Criminal Careers', *European Journal of Criminology*, 6: 203–223.

Silva, P. A. (1996) *From Child to Adult: The Dunedin Multidisciplinary Health and Development Study*. Oxford: Oxford University Press.

Slee, J. (2003) *Point Puer*, unpublished report for Port Arthur Site Management Authority, Tasmania, pp. 1–40. Available at: http://keyportarthur.org.au/extras/1056/Point%20 Puer%20article.pdf [Accessed 21 May 2018].

Smaal, Y. (2013) 'Historical Perspectives on Child Sexual Abuse, Part 1', *History Compass*, 11(9): 702–714.

Sveri, K., (1960) *Kriminalitet og Alder*. Stockholm: Almqvist & Wiksell.

Thornberry, T. P., Krohn, M. D., Lizotte, A. J. and Smith, C. A. (1998) *Taking Stock: An Overview of Findings from the Rochester Youth Development Study*. Maryland, National Criminal Justice Reference Service. Available at www.ncjrs.gov/pdffiles1/Digitization/176553NCJRS. pdf [Accessed 21 May 2018].

Trepanier, J. (1999) 'Juvenile Courts After 100 Years: Past and Present Orientations', *European Journal on Criminal Policy and Research*, 7: 303–327.

Turner, J. (2009) 'Offending Women in Stafford, 1880–1905: Punishment, Reform and Reintegration'. Unpublished PhD thesis, Keele University.

Turner, J. (2011) 'Punishing Women, 1880–1905', *Howard Journal of Criminal Justice*, 50(5): 505–515.

Van de Weijer, S., Bijleveld, C. J. H., and Blokland, A. A. J. (2014) 'Intergenerational Transmission of Violent Offending', *Journal of Family Violence*, 29(2): 109–118.

Vikström, L. (2011) 'Before and After Crime: Life-Course Analyses of Young Offenders Arrested in Nineteenth-century Northern Sweden', *Journal of Social History*, 44(3): 861–88.

Watkins, E. (2018) 'The Lives and Criminal Careers of Juvenile Offenders'. Unpublished PhD thesis, University of Liverpool.

Williams, L. (2016) *Wayward Women: Female Offending in Victorian England.* Barnsley: Pen and Sword.

Williams, L. and Godfrey, B. (2015) 'Intergenerational Offending in Liverpool and the North-west of England, 1850–1914', *The History of the Family*, 20(2): 189–203.

Wolfgang, M. E., Figlio, R. M. and Sellin, T. (1972) *Delinquency in a Birth Cohort.* Chicago: University of Chicago Press.

PART II
Present

4

CHILD-FRIENDLY JUSTICE

Past, present and future

Ton Liefaard and Ursula Kilkelly

Introduction

Child-friendly justice is now an established concept in European juvenile justice, used to articulate the extent to which children's rights are protected in judicial and other decision-making processes. The substance and language of child-friendly justice is associated with the Council of Europe's *Guidelines on Child-Friendly Justice*, a soft law instrument adopted by the Committee of Ministers in 2010. Building on international law, including the Convention on the Rights of the Child (CRC) and the case law of the European Court of Human Rights, the *Guidelines* were the first instrument to present, in a *holistic manner*, the key elements of the justice system from a children's rights perspective.[1] They are important because they set out in a practical way the obligations on states to protect children's rights in the juvenile justice system.

The aim of this chapter is to situate the *Guidelines on Child-Friendly Justice* within the context of contemporary juvenile justice. In this way, we will trace the recent history of child-friendly justice, explain the Guidelines adopted in 2010 and examine the implementation of the Guidelines with reference to recent EU studies that have sought to evaluate the extent to which child-friendly justice is observed in practice. Following the analysis of the current state of play, the chapter proceeds to assess critically the future direction of children's rights within juvenile justice and identifies some of the challenges that lie ahead.

Key principles of child-friendly justice

The *Guidelines on Child-Friendly Justice* (hereinafter: Guidelines)[2] provide the principles considered necessary to ensure that 'all rights of children' are fully respected, both in formal judicial proceedings and also in alternatives to such proceedings.[3] They deal with 'the place and role, and the views, rights and needs of the child in [judicial and alternative] proceedings'[4] and provide practical guidance for the 47 Council of Europe's Member States to 'give a place and voice to the child in justice at all stages of the procedures'.[5]

According to the Guidelines:

> '[C]hild-friendly justice' refers to justice systems which guarantee the respect and the effective implementation of all children's rights at the highest attainable level, bearing in mind the principles listed below and giving due consideration to the child's level of maturity and understanding and the circumstances of the case. It is, in particular, justice that is accessible, age appropriate, speedy, diligent, adapted to and focused on the needs and rights of the child, respecting the rights of the child including the rights to due process, to participate in and to understand the proceedings, to respect for private and family life and to integrity and dignity.[6]

The concept of child-friendly justice has developed as a result of the emergence of international and European children's rights law. Under international children's rights law, children are recognised as bearers of human rights, entitled, among other things, to participate effectively in matters affecting them, including in criminal justice proceedings. 'Effective participation' is one of the core concepts underlying the Guidelines and finds its legal basis in the child's right to be heard (art. 12 CRC) and right to a fair trial (art. 40 CRC and equivalent provision in international and regional human rights treaties, including art. 6 of the European Convention on Human Rights (ECHR)).

The European Court of Human Rights (hereinafter the European Court) has incorporated the child's right to be heard in its case law under article 8 ECHR on the protection of private and family life. Particularly in cases concerning access and custody matters, international child abduction and child protection, the Court has recognised the right to be heard as part of the assessment of the best interests of the child (Kilkelly 2015: 193–195).[7] In addition, the European Court has recognised the right to effective participation as part of the child's right to a fair trial under article 6 ECHR (Kilkelly 2015: 197), a position that was later endorsed by the UN Committee on the Rights of the Child in its 10th General Comment on 'Children's Rights and Juvenile Justice' (Kilkelly 2015: 193; United Nations, 2007). In its groundbreaking judgments T v. UK and V v. UK (i.e. the 1999 'Bulger case'), the European Court ruled, with explicit reference to article 40 of the CRC, that 'It is essential that a child charged with an offence is dealt with in a manner which takes full account of his age, level of maturity and intellectual and emotional capacities, and that steps are taken to promote his ability to understand and participate in the proceedings'.[8] The Court found that the two 11-year-old boys that stood trial for murdering a toddler, were unable to participate effectively and therefore had not received a fair trial. The court held that is was 'highly unlikely' that these boys:

would have felt sufficiently uninhibited, in the tense courtroom and under public scrutiny, to have consulted with [their lawyers] during the trial or, indeed, that, given [their] immaturity and [their] disturbed emotional state, [they] would have been capable outside the courtroom of cooperating with [their] lawyers and giving them information for the purposes of [their] defence.[9]

Later, the European Court ruled that the child's right to a fair trial does not require that s/he should 'understand or be capable of understanding every point of law or evidential detail,' but that '"effective participation" in this context presupposes... a broad understanding of the nature of the trial process and of what is at stake... including the significance of any penalty which may be imposed'.[10] In light of this, the Court also referred to the significance of the right to legal representation (see art. 6 (3) ECHR; see also art. 40 (2) CRC).[11]

The UN Committee on the Rights of the Child (hereinafter the CRC Committee) has also recognised effective participation as an essential requirement for the right to a fair trial. In its General Comment No. 10, the CRC Committee states that:

> [a] fair trial requires that the child... be able to effectively participate in the trial [and that as part of that the child] needs to comprehend the charges, and possible consequences and penalties, in order to direct the legal representative, to challenge witnesses, to provide an account of events, and to make appropriate decisions about evidence, testimony and the measure(s) to be imposed.
>
> *United Nations, 2007: para 46*

The CRC Committee also underscores the significance of acknowledging that juvenile justice proceedings 'should be conducted in an atmosphere of understanding to allow the child to participate and to express herself/himself freely'.[12] Furthermore, in its General Comment No. 12 on the child's right to be heard, the CRC Committee elaborates by providing that '[a] child cannot be heard effectively where the environment is intimidating, hostile, insensitive or inappropriate for her or his age' (United Nations 2009: para 34). Proceedings must be accessible and child-appropriate, therefore, which also means that '[p]articular attention needs to be paid to the provision and delivery of child-friendly information, adequate support for self-advocacy, appropriately trained staff, design of court rooms, [and] clothing of judges and lawyers' (United Nations, 2009: para 34). The CRC Committee also emphasises the importance of conducting court and other hearings *in camera*, aimed at enabling the child to participate, and that "[e]xceptions to this rule should be very limited, clearly outlined in national legislation and guided by the best interests of the child" (United Nations 2009: para 61). Furthermore, the CRC Committee states that accessible information is essential for effective participation. In the context of juvenile justice this means that 'every child must be informed promptly and directly about the charges against her or him in a language she or he understands, and also about the juvenile justice process and possible measures taken by the court' (United Nations, 2009: para 60).

In sum, the Guidelines build on the case law of the European Court of Human Rights and the General Comments of the CRC Committee and provide further guidance to Council of Europe's Member States on how to ensure that juvenile justice systems are child-friendly, that is: mindful of the child's right to be heard, her/his right to a fair trial and her/his related right to participate effectively. This necessarily includes: access to information; protection of private and family life; access to legal counsel and representation; avoiding undue delay; the provision of an appropriate environment in and around judicial proceedings (including after disposition); and child-specific training for professionals. Before reflecting more critically on the added value of the Guidelines, we will review the drafting of the Guidelines.

Drafting the *Guidelines on Child-Friendly Justice*: consultation with children and young people

In 2007, the European Ministers of Justice adopted Resolution No. 2 on child-friendly justice, thereby entrusting the competent bodies of the Council of Europe to prepare European Guidelines on Child-Friendly Justice. The Guidelines were drafted in close cooperation with the programme 'Building a Europe for and with Children', which made child-friendly justice one of the core pillars of the Council of Europe's Strategy on Children's Rights for 2009–2011. The drafting process was undertaken by a group of 17 specialists – set up for this precise purpose under the remit of the European Committee of Legal Co-operation (CDCJ) – comprising judges, lawyers, prosecutors, academics, psychologists, police officers, social workers and representatives of the governments of the member states. A wide range of observers, including representatives of leading international intergovernmental and non-governmental organisations such as the Children's Rights International Network (CRIN), Defence for Children International and the Children's Rights Alliance for England (CRAE) also contributed to this work. An independent scientific expert was appointed to the Committee (the former Flemish Commissioner for Children, Ms Ankie Vandekerckhove).

The drafting process took place over a period of two years during which time general principles were agreed and key issues identified. Initial discussion focused on the nature of the instrument being proposed and it is significant that there was insufficient support from States Parties to adopt the stronger of the Council of Europe's non-binding instruments – a 'Regulation' – and so the status of 'Guidelines' applied. It was accepted, as a general principle, that the Guidelines should not go beyond the standards already set out in international law and this undoubtedly limited the drafting process, while it also gave it a clear scope. Contentious issues included the age of criminal responsibility (the Guidelines simply repeat the CRC standard and disregard the standpoint of the CRC Committee) (United Nations, 2007: para 32), children deprived of their liberty (agreement was reached to include a limited section on this issue) and the question of whether judges should be required to be subjected to police vetting. The participants were unable to agree over a requirement to have proceedings involving children determined by specialist courts and thus the Guidelines are limited to recommending that Member States should further explore this principle.

It was a significant innovation of the drafting of the Guidelines – under the auspices of the Council's Children's Rights Division – that the process was informed by the views of children consulted specifically for this process. Likely to be the first instance of children participating in the international law-making process, this consultation sought to ensure that the Guidelines themselves were underpinned by a rights-based process, taking children's views and experiences of the justice system into account by means of a randomly administered survey of almost 3,800 young people from 25 Council of Europe countries. This data was enriched by a range of focus group discussions conducted with particularly vulnerable groups of children (including those in detention, refugee children and those whose relatives are in prison), and some national organisations submitted reports giving context to the consultation exercise and providing further information on the impact of the justice system on children. The consultation process was inevitably experimental, and while the data cannot be taken to be fully representative, it does provide an important insight into the experiences and perspectives of children and young people in respect of juvenile justice (Kilkelly, 2010).

About the children and young people

The respondents ranged in age from a small number of children aged 5–10 years to the majority who were aged between 11 and 17 years, about half of whom were under 15 years. An almost even number of boys and girls completed the questionnaire. The majority of children who participated in the survey had some level of contact with the justice system in either its civil (usually education or public or private family law) or its criminal (juvenile justice) context.

The views of the children and young people: information about their rights

When asked about their need for information, a very high proportion of the children and young people surveyed wanted more information about their rights. When asked who they wanted that information from, the majority chose their parents or others in a position of trust. Youth workers, and – to a lesser extent – lawyers and teachers, featured strongly. When asked where they wanted to source this information, the internet was the most popular choice, with other media – notably television – featuring strongly along with community-based services, including advertisements in health and social services offices, police stations and other public facilities. Schools were also identified as a good place to provide and promote information.

Obtaining justice

Children were asked whether they would tell someone if they were unhappy with how they were being treated. The majority said they would and parents, friends and siblings were identified overwhelmingly as the preferred confidantes. Virtually all other individuals/agencies – including official or public persons, health workers, teachers, youth/social workers, police officers and lawyers – were rarely identified, suggesting strongly that professional bodies do not always enjoy young people's trust. The two most common reasons for young people opting not to share their feelings were that they could handle the situation themselves or that they did not think that they would be believed and/or taken seriously.

Decisions made about the children and young people

Children were asked to identify what decisions had been made about them. They referred to decisions that had been made by judges, police officers or teachers in the areas of family law, including care, criminal law and education. A small majority of children reported being present when decisions had been taken about them but less than half said that they had been offered an explanation as to what would happen as a consequence of such decisions. Just over a third of the children and young people who completed the survey reported that they had been asked for their views and less than a third felt these views had been taken seriously. A third of the children and young people felt they had not been treated fairly. A significant majority reported that they had been supported through the process and about half explained that the decision had been made in a setting in which they felt safe and comfortable. When asked about what would have helped, the substantial majority of the children and young people referred to having someone who they trust to be present. Almost two thirds of the respondents said that they understood the decision made and a similar number reported that it had been explained to them. Children were asked who they would prefer to explain the decision to them and, in response, they identified a family member. Children and young people clearly valued direct explanations, preferably from the decision-maker him/herself. A large majority of children who responded considered it important to be heard, and an overwhelming number wanted to speak directly to the person making the decision, rather than having their views mediated or moderated by others.

When asked about the key principles that the Guidelines should embrace, children and young people placed particular emphasis on:

- being treated with respect;
- being listened to;

- being provided with explanations in language they understand, and
- receiving information about their rights.

Key themes

A number of key themes emerged from the analysis of the consultation with children and young people including a strong emphasis on the importance of family, a general mistrust of authority and a consistently expressed desire to be heard. The importance of family in the lives of children resonated loudly from the survey. Indeed, in every instance when children and young people were asked who they wanted to be present, who they would confide in and who they preferred to receive information and explanations from, they identified parents, siblings and friends above all others. In contrast, the survey revealed a distinct mistrust of authority on the part of the children and young people and those who expressed a view were critical of many officials – police, lawyers and others – for not treating them with respect, for failing to appreciate their particular needs as children and for not showing them empathy. As a related point, the survey made clear that children and young people want, sometimes desperately, to be heard; they want to receive information that they can understand, and they want to be supported to participate in decision-making processes that have a direct bearing on them.

Many of the concerns raised by the children and young people in the consultation found their way into the final version of the Guidelines. Although it would clearly have been preferable to have had children and young people directly involved in the drafting process, it is important that their views informed the end result, especially during the final stages of drafting.[13] Changes were made to ensure that the Guidelines responded effectively to what the children and young people had communicated about their experiences of justice and, overall, a genuine effort was made to ensure that their views were taken into account in the detail, scope and content of the Guidelines. In particular, the views of children and young people supported the extent and manner in which the Guidelines recognise the right of children to be heard, to receive information about their rights, to have access to independent representation and to participate effectively in decisions that have a direct bearing on them. The wording in all relevant sections was strengthened in these respects with reference to the outcome of the consultation process. For example, the final version of the Guidelines requires judges to respect the right of *all children* to be heard in *all matters*, and they require that the means used to facilitate such are individually tailored to each child's understanding and ability to communicate and explicitly take into account the specific circumstances of each case. The weight attached to the consultation also ensured that adequate provision was made in the Guidelines for children and young people to receive feedback on the weight attached to their views and it strengthened an emphasis on the nature of support that children should be provided with before, during and after contact with the justice system. Particular consideration was given to the role of parents and other trusted adults in accordance with the preferences that children and young people had articulated. Furthermore, the findings of the consultation provided support for the child's/young person's unequivocal right to access independent and effective complaints mechanisms at all stages of the justice system and for specialisation and comprehensive and ongoing training for all professionals who come into contact with children in the justice system. This was considered vital in order to address the lack of trust in authority that the children and young people had expressed throughout the consultation.

Critiquing the Guidelines

Before examining the (potential) impact of the Guidelines alongside the challenges concerning their implementation, we will briefly reflect on their content and their legal status (see also, Liefaard, 2016). Earlier we touched upon the drafting process in which the Member States decided that the Guidelines should not extend beyond the standards already set out in international law. Indeed, the Guidelines are rather weak at certain points or do not really add anything new. This is especially true for the minimum age of criminal responsibility – which compared to the position taken by the CRC Committee (United Nations, 2007: paras 30–35) could even be regarded as a setback – and the absence of a strong case being made for the provision of specialised courts. In addition, the references to deprivation of liberty do not really extend the reach or depth of existing international standards but simply reproduce existing provisions such as Article 37(b) and 37(c) CRC. It is nevertheless significant that the Guidelines reconfirm that the deprivation of liberty may only be used as a measure of last resort and for the shortest appropriate period of time, and that children deprived of their liberty are entitled to human rights protections, specifically in light of their vulnerability.

Indeed, the particular vulnerabilities of children in juvenile justice systems have been recognised under international children's rights law, including the case law of the European Court. It requires that children are protected against the imposition of (additional) hardship and are treated in a manner that respects their human rights and dignity. In addition, the Guidelines provide further direction on both the protection and participation that should be afforded to children and young people before, during and after judicial proceedings. With regard to children's involvement with the police, for example, the Guidelines recommend that Member States should ensure that '[w]henever a child is apprehended by the police, the child should be informed in a manner and in language that is appropriate to his or her age and level of understanding of the reason for which he or she has been taken into custody'.[14] The Guidelines also provide that children and young people in conflict with the law should be given access to a lawyer and the opportunity to contact parents or someone whom they trust.[15] Parents should in principle be informed about the arrest of their child and the reasons behind it, and they should be invited to come to the police station.[16] The Guidelines further provide that a child in police custody should not be questioned 'except in the presence of a lawyer or one of the child's parents or, if no parent is available, another person whom the child trusts'.[17] Stimulated by the case law of the European Court of Human Rights,[18] the Guidelines are also more concrete than the CRC (art. 40 (2)) and related standards such as the Beijing Rules, when it comes to access to a lawyer and the presence of a lawyer during police interrogations. At the same time, however, the Guidelines are not clear on, and are even silent on, some important issues.

First, the Guidelines refer to other forms of assistance, such as parental support, while the relevance of legal assistance for children in this particular phase of the criminal justice system should not be underestimated. The CRC Committee states that the person assisting the child 'must have sufficient knowledge and understanding of the various legal aspects of the process of juvenile justice' (United Nations, 2007: para 49). The assistance or presence of parents (or other caretakers) should be seen as a right *additional to*, rather than *instead of* or an *alternative to*, the right to legal representation. Parents have an important role to play in supporting the child emotionally and their involvement can also contribute to the effectiveness of the response to the child's offending (United Nations, 2007: paras 54–58); an approach that is in line with how important family is for children, based on the consultation of children mentioned earlier. However, this should not be taken to mean that children have to choose between parental support and the support of a lawyer.

Second, the child's right to waive legal counsel is also overlooked in the Guidelines. Although the European Court leaves open the possibility for children to waive their right to legal assistance, children have an interest in *mandatory* legal assistance, particularly in juvenile justice proceedings when the child faces police interrogation and questioning (Liefaard and Van den Brink, 2014). International consensus on this issue appears currently to be out of reach. For instance, although the European Commission's proposal for the new EU Directive originally included mandatory legal assistance, this condition did not make it into the final version of the instrument. The adopted text of the EU Directive on procedural safeguards for children in criminal proceedings (hereinafter the EU Directive)[19] leaves room for States Parties *not to provide* for legal counsel if this is regarded as disproportionate. In addition, it does not explicitly provide that legal assistance is mandatory. This appears to be at odds with article 37(d) CRC which provides for the child's right to legal *and* other appropriate assistance.

Third, the Guidelines are silent concerning the audiovisual recording of interrogations even though it is widely recognised that such practice can protect a child against ill treatment and/or infringements of her/his right to a fair trial (including her/his right to participate effectively). The EU Directive does provide for audiovisual recording, although it also leaves room for departing from such practice, for example in cases where a lawyer is present or a child is not deprived of her/his liberty.[20]

Another relevant phase of the juvenile justice system concerns the participation of children in court.[21] The Guidelines highlight the importance of the right of the child to have a lawyer in her or his own name, the right to avoid undue delay and the right to conduct proceedings in a 'child-friendly' manner, including the use of appropriate language and information. Children who are tried in court should be enabled to participate effectively, which also assumes that professionals are trained and specialist. This not only includes child-sensitivity, but also skills in how to converse with children (Rap, 2013). As far as information is concerned, the Guidelines provide that 'children should be provided with all necessary information on how to effectively use the right to be heard'.[22] The Guidelines do not elaborate on access to case files but, as stated, the right to a fair trial requires that the accused has a broad understanding of the nature of the trial process and of what is at stake[23] and that the child's lawyer has an important role to play in providing information. The Guidelines do provide that '[j]udgments and court rulings (...) should be duly reasoned and explained to [children] in language that [they] can understand'. This enables children to understand the impact of their participation on the decision-making process and it confirms the standpoint of the CRC Committee, which considers feedback to the child 'a guarantee that the views of the child are not only heard as a formality, but are taken seriously' (United Nations, 2009: para 45). Again the Guidelines leave open some critical issues, such as free legal aid (United Nations, 2007: para 49), the involvement of parents in court, which might be regarded as an important precondition of effective participation (United Nations, 2007: paras 46–54) and the right to be present during the trial.

In summary, the Guidelines provide some firm direction on the protection and participation of children and young people in contact with juvenile justice systems in Europe, although they appear, at times, to oscillate *between* the principles of protection and participation (Liefaard, 2016). A greater concern, however, is that the Guidelines are insufficiently comprehensive in crucial places. This might relate to their broad scope (covering all forms of justice proceedings), which necessitates a minimum standard that applies across civil, criminal and administrative proceedings in which children are involved. If the Guidelines had focused exclusively on juvenile justice proceedings, greater specificity would probably have been possible. Notwithstanding their limitations, however, the Guidelines serve to clarify many procedural issues, which assist States Parties in understanding and implementing key requirements of the protection *and* the effective participation of children and young people who are in conflict with the law.

Legal status of the Guidelines

A further key issue concerns the relatively weak *legal status* of the Guidelines, which raises the question of why States Parties should be concerned about their implementation, given that they are not legally binding. Yet, there are a number of reasons why Member States should take them seriously. First, they build on notions and specific provisions that can be found in legally binding instruments, in particular the UN Convention on the Rights of the Child and the case law of the European Court. Second, some of the key provisions have been incorporated into new EU legislation, which forces, at least EU Member States that are bound by this directive, to implement these within three years. Third, it is interesting to note that the European Court uses the Guidelines as a key point of reference (Liefaard, 2016: 914).[24] To date, this has only once directly affected the position of children in the juvenile justice system.[25] However, the case law on children in civil justice proceedings shows that the Guidelines form a relevant set of guidelines for the European Court when interpreting the provisions of the ECHR.

Overall, it is important that the Guidelines aim to provide a *common European standard* within the otherwise diverse context that characterises juvenile justice systems across the 47 Council of Europe Member States and can render the human rights of children and young people in conflict with the law vulnerable to violation (Goldson and Muncie 2012).

Implementing child-friendly justice

One of the interesting developments following on from the adoption of the Guidelines by the Council of Europe has been the collaboration that has emerged and consolidated with the European Union in implementing the Guidelines. In its 2011 *EU Agenda for the Rights of the Child*, the European Commission outlined several action points to help make justice systems more child-friendly, in light of the fact that it is an area 'of high practical relevance where the EU has, under the Treaties, competences to turn the rights of the child into reality by means of EU legislation' (European Commission, 2011).

In particular, the European Commission and the European Fundamental Rights Agency have undertaken and funded research to establish, in different ways, the extent to which the Guidelines on child-friendly justice have been implemented in the EU Member States. For example, the Commission commissioned a data collection study of law and policy in the 28 Member states of the European Union. Around the same time, the EU's Fundamental Rights Agency also undertook a study of the experiences and perspectives of professionals on child-friendly justice in ten EU Member States, with a focus on civil and criminal judicial proceedings, in which children participate as victims, witnesses or interested parties (EU Agency for Fundamental Rights 2015).[26] Together, these studies help to clarify the gap between the Guidelines and their implementation, while they might also help to support more effective implementation by sharing best practice between Member States and deepening consensus around the key aspects of the Guidelines. The following section addresses the contribution that the first EU study has made to our understanding of the implementation of the Guidelines in the juvenile justice sphere. The Fundamental Rights Agency study is not addressed here given that its focus centres child victims and witnesses in criminal proceedings.

Child-friendly justice: implementation in law and policy

In 2012, the European Commission carried out a study to collect data on children's involvement in criminal, civil and administrative judicial proceedings in all 28 EU Member States for the years 2008–2010 (European Commission, 2014). Although the study was very broad in scope, its findings include important information as to the progress being made in the implementation of child-friendly justice in juvenile justice proceedings. This study was summarised in a brief for policy makers (Kennan and Kilkelly, 2015) which distilled the findings from a substantial volume of data collected under a range of headings.[27] From the perspective of the criminal process and juvenile justice, serious shortcomings in securing child-friendly justice in the law and policy of EU Member States were identified in the following areas: adapting proceedings in 'child-friendly' forms; the specialisation and training of sentencers and other juvenile justice professionals; avoiding delay; access to information; facilitating the child's right to be heard; the provision of legal representation and the child's right to privacy.

In terms of the access by the child defendant to adapted ('child-friendly') proceedings, the study found that 20 EU jurisdictions have specialist juvenile or youth courts that deal with cases in the area of juvenile justice. Some of these specialist courts consist of courtrooms that are physically separated from adult courts, whereas others are ordinary courts that are adapted to the needs of children, including through the involvement of specialist judges. However, gaps exist in the remit or jurisdiction of these specialist courts, suggesting less than universal acceptance of the youth court model (Kennan and Kilkelly, 2015: 4). This is pertinent given that the Guidelines fall short of requiring the establishment of a specialist youth court to deal with child defendants, limiting provision to a recommendation that States Parties should further develop the concept of specialised courts.[28] Specialisation in other parts of the criminal/juvenile justice system (among the police, prosecution services and lawyers), was also found to be underdeveloped across Member States although there is also some good practice in the 14 Member States which were found to have established special units within their police forces to deal with child suspects/offenders and/or child victims and witnesses (Kennan and Kilkelly, 2015: 4). A small number of Member States were also found to have introduced specialisation among prosecutors and defence lawyers working with children and young people involved in criminal proceedings, including the provision of training on children's rights and needs (Kennan and Kilkelly, 2015).

Although several Member States have introduced mandatory training programmes for the key professional groups working with, or for, children within the juvenile justice system – including judges, police officers, prosecutors, defence counsel and/or social workers – such programmes are still unavailable in many jurisdictions (Kennan and Kilkelly, 2015: 25). Moreover, while continuous and ongoing training is available in some Member States for criminal/juvenile justice professionals, in most cases participation in training is voluntary and the training is provided on an *ad hoc* basis rather than as part of a structured, systematic and ongoing process of professional development (Kennan and Kilkelly 2015: 25).

While the content of the training provided to judges and prosecutors varies across countries, there is frequently an emphasis on child psychology and child welfare, in addition to the legal aspects of child-friendly justice (Kennan and Kilkelly, 2015: 26). The training that police officers receive often has a more practical orientation, focusing in particular on how to communicate with children. For example, in a number of Member States it covers child-friendly interview techniques, including the use of audiovisual equipment and in some Member States it covers aspects of child psychology, social policy, legal issues and forensic science.

In the majority of jurisdictions, there is a legal obligation to avoid undue delay in the handling of cases involving children. Most Member States have additional safeguards in place aimed at ensuring that criminal proceedings involving children are dealt with as quickly as possible. Some Member States have imposed legislative time limits on the court process, for example imposing a maximum time limit for cases involving child suspects to get to trial (Kennan and Kilkelly, 2015: 5). Only a small number of Member States provide guidance to judicial authorities on how to implement the duty to avoid undue delay in practice, however, and even when such guidance is available, it is usually general rather than specific to children (Kennan and Kilkelly, 2015: 6).

Almost all Member States have statutory provisions recognising the right of child suspects/offenders to receive information about their rights, although the scope of information provided varies across Member States (Kennan and Kilkelly 2015: 8). No states have a legislative requirement to ensure that child suspects/offenders receive information adapted to their needs, or in a child-friendly format, and in some jurisdictions, the absence of rules or procedures governing what information is to be provided, and in what form, means that practice on the ground may vary significantly (Kennan and Kilkelly 2015: 8). Although all Member States provide child suspects/offenders involved in criminal judicial proceedings with an express right to be heard, the scope of this right varies widely across Member States with conditions and exceptions applying in many cases (Kennan and Kilkelly 2015: 11). Child suspects/offenders who do not speak or understand the language of the procedure also have the right to interpretation and translation in criminal/juvenile justice proceedings in most, but surprisingly not all, Member States (Kennan and Kilkelly, 2015: 13).

A number of Member States have introduced measures to ensure that children involved in criminal judicial/juvenile justice proceedings are interviewed by the police or judicial authorities in a manner which is adapted to their needs. Such measures include providing support to prepare children for interviews; having trained officials conduct interviews; having a specialised professional (e.g. a psychologist) present at, and/or participate in, interviews; video-recording interviews; the use of child-friendly language and questions; limiting the number and length of interviews; and allowing the child to be accompanied by a person of trust (e.g. parent/guardian) (Kennan and Kilkelly, 2015: 13).

While these are positive measures that are consistent with the Guidelines, the application of these safeguards is often limited in scope or discretionary in nature. For instance, the measures are sometimes optional or conditional on the age of the child, her/his role in the proceedings and/or the type of offence (Kennan and Kilkelly, 2015: 13). According to data collected during the study, the right of child suspects to legal representation is recognised in all EU Member States and this right extends to all phases of the proceedings in the majority of jurisdictions, with some exceptions where it applies during the investigation phase only. In the majority of Member States the law imposes a legal obligation on the police (or other relevant authorities) to inform children who have been apprehended of their right to a lawyer. Child suspects are provided with defence counsel on a mandatory basis in 23 Member States although where mandatory defence exists, its application can be dependent on the seriousness of the charge and in some cases on the age of the child (Kennan and Kilkelly, 2015: 14). The right of child suspects to apply for legal aid exists in almost all Member States, but although this represents progress in the implementation of child-friendly justice, the provision of legal aid is subject to various conditions in different Member States (e.g. means test or depending on the seriousness of the charge) (Kennan and Kilkelly, 2015: 15).

Child suspects/offenders have a general right to privacy at a statutory level in all Member States (Kennan and Kilkelly, 2015: 17) although the approach adopted to hearing court proceedings in private varies widely across Member States – some permit exceptions to the rule while others decide this on a case-by-case basis (Kennan and Kilkelly, 2015: 19). Third-party access to children's criminal records is restricted in all States where this information is recorded, and most Member States automatically delete the criminal records after a specific period of time has elapsed, although the time period may depend on the type of offence, the sentence given and/or whether the child reoffended (Kennan and Kilkelly, 2015: 17).

Overall, the European Commission's study has helped to clarify the extent to which the key elements of child-friendly justice are provided for in law and policy across the EU Member States. Some good practice is clearly evident in all areas although considerable differences remain between and within Member States. The study highlights that although there is increasing provision for children's rights, in reality children and young people have few unconditional entitlements as subjects in the criminal/juvenile justice process as discretion and caveats have a diluting effect. Perhaps most significantly, the study indicates that it is the most vulnerable children who face particular obstacles in accessing justice that is child-friendly and this, combined with the mainstreaming of approaches to child-friendly justice, remain significant challenges into the future.

Analysis, conclusions, future directions and challenges

This chapter has aimed to examine the concept of child-friendly justice by means of an analysis of the drafting, content and implementation of the Guidelines on Child-Friendly Justice. In doing so, we have drawn attention to the important concept of child-friendly justice, which embraces the children's rights in the juvenile justice system. Although it is important that the Guidelines were informed by the experiences and perspectives of children and young people, their weak legal standing and limitations in terms of what they add to existing international law have perhaps served to constrain what might have otherwise been greater ambition for the Guidelines. At the same time, the focus on the procedural rights of children and young people is an important reminder that fair trial and due process matters are vital and have led to the Guidelines' appeal to regions beyond Europe.

At the same time, the Guidelines compromise areas crucial for children's fair trial rights, including the mandatory right to a lawyer and the right to be tried in specialist courts. It is significant that the more recently developed EU Directive does not support these rights either and thus, although the Guidelines reflect an emerging legal framework focused on the procedural rights of children in conflict with the law – also relevant for informal proceedings, such as diversion – consensus is not yet complete. Similarly, the failure to achieve consensus in Europe on the minimum age of criminal responsibility is a disappointment and this points to an important future area for reform.

The fact that the Guidelines are not legally binding may hamper their practical impact in Member States but there are ways in which they might also be given added effect. Their use in the European Court of Human Rights is one such way to give them 'teeth', while courts should also be encouraged strongly to implement them at national level. Just as the Guidelines have led to positive collaboration between the Council of Europe and the European Union, there is potential too for them to be given further attention by the UN treaty-monitoring bodies, especially the Committee on the Rights of the Child. Several years on from their adoption by the Committee of Ministers in 2010, there appears to be a growing sense of their importance at a practical level. Challenges in their implementation remain but now that the diversity in standing practices among many countries within the Council of Europe has at least been mapped it enables practices to be closely monitored. Overall, the Guidelines underscore the significance of treating children in conflict with the law with the respect to which they are entitled. This has the potential to ultimately contribute to juvenile justice systems that are more just and, informed by children's own demand for respect, more likely to be effective.

Notes

1 Of course, the Guidelines were not the first instrument to set out the rights of children in the justice system. These standards can be found in the range of human rights treaties and non-binding recommendations from United Nations and Council of Europe treaties dealing with the right to fair trial and deprivation of liberty.

2 Guidelines of the Committee of Ministers of the Council of Europe on Child-Friendly Justice 1, 13 (2010), available at: www.coe.int/childjustice, (accessed 15 December 2016).

3 Guidelines, supra note 2, First Part, ch. I, at para. 1.

4 Guidelines, supra note 2, First Part, ch. I at para. 3.

5 Guidelines, supra note 2, Second Part, ch. 'Structure and Content', at para. 16.

6 Guidelines, supra note 2, First Part, ch. II under. c.

7 See e.g.: ECtHR, 3 September 2015, appl. no. 10161/13 (*M & M. v. Croatia*).

8 ECtHR (GC), 16 December 1999, appl.no. 24724/94 (*T v. UK*), para. 84.

9 ECtHR (GC), 16 December 1999, appl.no. 24724/94 (*T. v. UK*), para. 88.

10 ECtHR, 15 June 2004, appl. no. 60958/00 (*S.C. v. UK*), para. 29.

11 See also ECtHR, 20 January 2009, appl. no. 70337/01 (*Güveç v. Turkey*).

12 See also: The United Nations Standard Minimum Rules for the Administration of Juvenile Justice ("The Beijing Rules") (1985): rule 14. Available at: www.ohchr.org (accessed 15 December 2016).

13 Ursula Kilkelly co-ordinated the administration of the survey and presented the analysis to the drafting committee. She was also present during finalisation of the Guidelines to ensure that the perspectives of children and young people were represented during the process.

14 Guidelines, supra note 2, First Part, ch. IV, at para. 28.

15 Ibid.

16 Guidelines, supra note 2, First Part, ch. IV, at para. 29; See also: CRC Committee 2007, supra note 14, para. 54.

17 Guidelines, supra note 2, First Part, ch. IV, at para. 30.

18 ECtHR, 27 November 2008, appl. no. 36391/02 (*Salduz v. Turkey*); ECtHR, 11 December 2008, appl. no. 4268/04 (*Panovits v. Cyprus*).

19 European Parliament legislative resolution (2016), 'on the proposal for a directive of the European Parliament and of the Council on procedural safeguards for children suspected or accused in criminal proceedings', Brussels: 2013/0408 (COD) (Adopted Text). Online. Available http://data.consilium.europa.eu/doc/document/PE-2-2016-INIT/en/pdf (accessed 15 December 2016).

20 Ibid. at para. 42, p. 17.

21 There are of course other relevant phases of the juvenile justice process such as the post-conviction phase, but it goes beyond the scope of this chapter to address them all.

22 Guidelines, supra note 2, First Part, ch. IV, at para. 48.

23 ECtHR, 9 July 2000, appl. no. 60958/00 (*S.C. v. UK*).

24 See furthermore recent case law: ECtHR (GC), 23 March 2016, appl. no. 47152/06 (*Blokhin v. Russia*), at paras. 80, 170 and 203; ECtHR, 3 September 2015, appl. no. 10161/13 (*M & M. v. Croatia*), at para. 102; ECtHR, 29 April 2014, appl. no. 60092/12 (*Z.J. v. Lithuania*), at para. 73 and 104; ECtHR, 17 July 2012, appl. no. 64791/10 (*M.D. and others v. Malta*), at para. 38.

25 ECtHR (GC) 23 March 2016, appl. no. 47152/06 (*Blokhin/Russia*), at paras. 170 and 203.

26 In 2017, the Fundamental Rights Agency published another study on child-friendly justice in which perspectives and experiences of children involved in judicial proceedings as victims, witnesses or parties in nine EU Member States are presented (EU Agency for Fundamental Rights, 2017). This study has not been included in this chapter.

27 These were: access to adapted proceedings; right to information and advice; right to be heard; right to representation; right to protection of privacy; the best interests of the child; multidisciplinary cooperation; training of professionals; monitoring mechanisms; and access to remedies.

28 Guidelines, supra note 2, First Part, ch. IV.

References

European Commission (2011) *An EU Agenda for the Rights of the Child*, COM(2011) 60 final. Brussels: European Commission.

European Commission (2014) *Summary of Contextual Overviews on Children's Involvement in Criminal Judicial Proceedings in the 28 Member States of the European Union*. Luxembourg: Publications Office for the European Union.

European Union Agency for Fundamental Rights (2015) *Child-Friendly Justice: Perspectives and Experiences of Professionals on Children's Participation in Civil and Criminal Judicial Proceedings in 10 EU Member States*. Vienna: Fundamental Rights Agency.

European Union Agency for Fundamental Rights (2017) *Child-friendly Justice: Perspectives and Experiences of Children Involved in Judicial Proceedings as Victims, Witnesses or Parties in Nine EU Member States.* Vienna: Fundamental Rights Agency.

Goldson, B. and Muncie, J. (2012) 'Towards a Global "Child friendly" Juvenile Justice?', *International Journal of Law, Crime and Justice*, 40(1): 47–64.

Kennan, N. and Kilkelly, U. (2015) *Children's Involvement in Criminal, Civil and Administrative Judicial Proceedings in the 28 Member States of the EU: Policy Brief.* Brussels: European Commission.

Kilkelly, U. (2010) *Listening to Children about Justice: Report of the Council of Europe Consultation with Children on Child-Friendly Justice.* Strasbourg: Council of Europe.

Kilkelly, U. (2015) 'The CRC in Litigation Under the ECHR', in T. Liefaard and J. E. Doek (eds) *Litigating the Rights of the Child.* Dordrecht: Springer.

Liefaard, T. (2016) 'Child-Friendly Justice: Protection and Participation of Children in the Justice System', *Temple Law Review*, 88(4): 905–927.

Liefaard, T. and Van den Brink, Y. N. (2014) 'Juveniles' Right to Counsel during Police Interrogations: An Interdisciplinary Analysis of a Youth-Specific Approach, with a Particular Focus on the Netherlands', *Erasmus Law Review*, 7(4): 206–218.

Rap, S. E. (2013) The Participation of Juvenile Defendants in the Youth Court: A Comparative Study of Juvenile Justice Procedures in Europe, PhD thesis, Utrecht: Utrecht University.

United Nations (2007) *General Comment No. 10: Children's Rights in Juvenile Justice*, UN Doc. CRC/C/GC/10, 25 April. Geneva: United Nations.

United Nations (2009) *General Comment No. 12: The Right of the Child to Be Heard*, UN Doc. CRC/C/GC/12, 20 July. Geneva: United Nations.

5

TRANSFORMATIONS IN YOUTH CRIME AND JUSTICE ACROSS EUROPE

Evidencing the case for diversion

Lesley McAra and Susan McVie

Introduction

Over the last decade, the client group of youth justice across all UK jurisdictions has been shrinking, as measured by system referrals, criminal convictions and imprisonment rates (McAra, 2017). Data from a variety of other European countries indicates that this may be part of a wider trend. For example, Eurostat data shows an average 42% fall in juvenile imprisonment rates across 30 member states.[1] This trend in youth justice sits against a background of falling recorded crime rates in many western jurisdictions since the early to mid-1990s – a phenomenon commonly referred to as the 'crime drop' (see Zimring, 2007; van Dijk et al., 2012). As crime has fallen across jurisdictions of variant architecture, ethos and policy direction, some commentators have sought to develop a universal explanation (see Farrell, 2013); however, there is as yet no widespread agreement about what caused the crime drop, and the suggestion of a 'general' drop in crime across Western Europe has been disputed (see Aebi and Linde, 2010). What is less contested is that the relationship between the crime drop and the shrinking youth justice client group is a strong one (see Farrell et al., 2015; Kim et al., 2015; Matthews and Minton, 2018), although the bulk of the research in this area has relied on analysis of official statistics such as arrest or convictions data (which are indicative of systemic activity) rather than self-reported offending data (which measures behavioural change).

History reminds us that the relationship between rates of 'crime' and trends in 'punishment' is somewhat vexed (Smith, D.J., 1999; Downes and Hansen, 2006; McAra, 2017), and it is difficult to disentangle the direction (if any) of causality. Indeed, the contraction of the youth justice client group raises important questions about *both* behavioural change and system effects. Are the observed reductions in system contact a consequence of real behavioural change, such that teenagers in general are becoming more law-abiding than their counterparts in previous decades? Or has the expansion of new technologies (including the internet, smartphones and tablets) led to a displacement of the situational contexts in which youth offending occurs and transformations in the modalities of rule breaking, such that fewer young people are 'available' for traditional forms of systemic processing? Or does the shrinking client group reflect an increased capacity within particular systems of youth justice to control the stocks and flows of young people made subject to their tutelage? And, what do the answers to these questions imply for the characteristics of the smaller numbers of young people who do become caught up in youth justice, and the longer-term impacts on their behaviour and well-being?

Drawing on findings from the Edinburgh Study of Youth Transitions and Crime,[2] we have shown that the links between youth justice (criminal conviction) and self-reported offending careers are somewhat tenuous, but that punitive and intensive forms of intervention are likely to be damaging, inhibiting the normal process of desistance from offending that occurs from the mid-teenage years onwards (McAra and McVie, 2007; McAra, 2010, 2012, 2016). On the basis of that evidence we have argued for a diversionary paradigm in the management of young people who come into conflict with the law (McAra and McVie, 2015). Significantly, the major reductions in the youth justice client group in many European jurisdictions have occurred simultaneously with renewed interest in diversion. In the UK this has been manifest in efforts to reduce the number of first-time entrants to the youth justice system within England and Wales (implemented from 2008) and the introduction of a *Whole System Approach* based on diversion in Scotland (rolled out nationally from 2011).

The aim of this chapter is to explain the changing trends in youth crime and justice in a European context and to consider what these changes mean for those young people remaining in the system. In pursing this aim we have faced a number of methodological challenges. While an in-depth cross-comparative analysis of European countries would be desirable, this has not been possible for several reasons. The biggest challenge has been the paucity of robust comparative data (both synchronic – across jurisdictions at particular time points – and diachronic – within jurisdictions over time). Where data do exist, finding easy mechanisms by which to access them is problematic and the qualifications around comparability can be extensive.[3] Systems of youth justice differ to such an extent that those measures that are available do not necessarily reflect similar stages of processing or similar decision-making criteria. The definition of 'juvenile' and the age of criminal responsibility varies so widely that data on the same age groups cannot be accessed. Recording systems and crime categories also vary in ways that prevent straightforward comparison. The most comprehensive datasets providing information about long-term trends that we have been able to access (bringing together official data, national survey data and self-report data) relate to Scotland and England/Wales. That is why we have used them as case-study jurisdictions in key sections of this chapter: we are, however, confident that the conclusions we have drawn from these case studies could reasonably be extended to our European neighbours.

In order to overcome the methodological challenges, we have brought together for the first time evidence from a range of interdisciplinary sources (including health and education data, as well as new findings from the Edinburgh Study). On the basis of these data we make the following four claims regarding the shrinking client group of youth justice systems across Europe and its impacts:

- There has not been a major reduction in youth offending – rule breaking remains a normal part of development in the teenage years, but its primary situational context has moved from the urban landscape to cyberspace, where there are far fewer 'capable guardians': the 'displacement effect'
- Institutions set up to tackle youth offending have not yet fully adapted to this transformation, and police and prosecutorial working practices are stuck in older dynamics of law enforcement: the 'cultural dissonance effect'
- A consequence is that fewer young people across most European jurisdictions (no matter the architecture or ethos) are processed through the system, but those who do become subject to its tutelage come from the most deprived and marginalised communities, and have extremely complex needs: the 'concentration effect'
- Youth justice systems – in Europe and beyond – which take a punitive approach to youth offending, or fail to address the flows of young people through the system, are far less successful (in terms of reducing the risk of reconviction) than those predicated on an integrated diversionary approach to offender management: the 'whole-system effect'.

The chapter begins with a contextual overview of evidence relating to the crime drop and its relationship to trends and policies in youth justice. This is followed by a detailed discussion of the four 'effects' identified above, using evidence from a range of sources and perspectives. We conclude with some reflections on the implications of these effects for the future of youth justice in Europe and, more particularly, how they verify the efficacy of a diversionary paradigm as an ethical and pragmatic response to youthful transgressions.

Reductions in rates of 'crime' and the European youth justice context

In this section of the chapter we overview the research evidence relating to the crime drop, highlighting the very small number of studies which have examined the contribution of young people to the observed reductions in crime. Building on this evidence, we then demonstrate how the youth justice client group across Europe has contracted in recent years and provide a critical review of the policy contexts in which this has occurred (with specific focus on our case-study jurisdictions).

The crime drop and young people: the research evidence

Over the last three decades, many countries across Europe and the western world have reported a dramatic and sustained drop in crime. First observed in New York City and then across other US cities (Zimring, 2007), recorded crime rates started to decline in the early 1990s and continued to show a distinct pattern of decline over the next 20 years (Baumer and Wolff, 2014). Remarkably similar falls in crime were subsequently witnessed across many other countries, including Canada (Ouimet, 2002), Australia and New Zealand (Mayhew, 2012; Brown, 2015). Data from the International Crime Victim Survey (ICVS) also revealed a significant crime drop across countries in Western and Central Europe from the mid-1990s (van Dijk et al. 2012), although Aebi and Linde (2010) have questioned the existence of a general crime drop across Europe because property crimes and crimes of violence have shown very different trends. In the UK, both police recorded crime data and victim survey findings demonstrate a sustained and significant fall in crime in England and Wales (ONS 2017) and Scotland (McVie, 2017) over a very similar time frame.

Various theories for the crime drop have been proposed, including: the security hypothesis proposed by Farrell et al., (2011; see also van Dijk et al., 2012), namely, that the reduction in crime is as a result of target hardening and other crime prevention initiatives; improvements in economic circumstances (Ouimet, 2002; Rosenfeld and Messner, 2009); more police officers and better policing strategies (Eck and Maguire, 2000; Levitt, 2004); increased incarceration of offenders (Spelman 2000); cultural change and increasing 'civilisation' (Tonry, 2005); diminishing drugs markets (Johnson, Golub and Dunlap, 2000; Levitt, 2004); political and socioeconomic change and the development of black markets and new lines of transporting illegal commodities (Aebi and Linde, 2012); and several US-specific theories, such as better gun control policies (Duggan, 2001), reductions in lead in petrol (Reyes, 2007) and the legalisation of abortion (Donohue and Levitt, 2001). However, there is as yet no specific theory that identifies young people as a primary driver of the crime drop.

Only a small number of crime drop studies have examined the role of age as a factor, and there has been no systematic examination of the extent to which reductions in crime may be accounted for by young people. However, the studies that do exist consistently show that during the period of the crime drop (from the early to mid-1990s onwards) there was a large fall in arrests and convictions amongst young people. For example, Farrell et al. (2015) found that US arrest rates for property crime and various forms of violence reduced significantly amongst those in adolescence and early adulthood. There were also modest declines in arrest rates amongst those up to age 40; however, the arrest rates for those aged over 40 increased markedly. Also using US data, Kim et al. (2015) found evidence of a sharp fall in arrests amongst those aged 16 to 20 years in the early years of the crime drop. Both studies concluded that the decline in arrest rates did not reflect a universal reduction in recorded crime across different age groups but was disproportionately influenced by declining crime amongst younger people.

European studies are rare; however, Estrada et al. (2016) used Swedish register data to analyse gender and socioeconomic effects on youth conviction rates over the period of the crime drop. Focusing on three cohorts (born in 1965, 1975 and 1985) they found that the prevalence of conviction declined sharply amongst young men for property crime, although it increased modestly for young women, while prevalence of conviction for violence increased for both young men and women. However, the overall trends masked large discrepancies between those from different socioeconomic backgrounds. The biggest declines in conviction were observed amongst those from the highest income group, while those in the lowest income group saw a sizeable increase in risk of conviction. This was true for both violence and property crime, and applied to both men and women, although the risk was especially high amongst young men. This study did not examine differences across age groups; however, it does indicate that the mechanisms for explaining change in youth conviction rates may differ for men and women, and that socioeconomic factors may have played a critical role in these changes.

Matthews and Minton (2018) examined changes in the age pattern of convictions between 1989 and 2014 using data from the Scottish Offenders Index. They revealed a substantial decline in the conviction rate for both men and women up to their mid-twenties, but also an increased rate of conviction for those in their late twenties to mid-forties. Most notably, they observed three distinct periods of change. From 1989 to 2000, there was a decline in rates of conviction for men under 25, but no change for older men or for women; from 2001 to 2006, there was no change in the conviction rates for young men or women, but an increase for those aged mid-20s to early 40s; while from 2007 to 2011, there was a rapid decline in conviction for men and, especially, women under the age of 20, but stable conviction rates for those aged 30 and above. This study is important because the periods of change in conviction bear a marked similarity to key eras of change in Scottish justice policy – suggesting that any theory of the crime drop needs to take account of both policy impact and behavioural change – a point to which we will return later in the chapter.

The shrinking client group of European youth justice systems

Extending significantly the research evidence just presented, we have found a considerable decline in youth crime rates across many European countries as measured by official administrative data.

Table 5.1 summarises data from 10 countries during the early part of the twenty-first century. As noted earlier, there is little consistency in terms of the type of data available (which ranges from crimes to offenders, raw numbers to rates, and suspects to those arrested or convicted), the age group for which data are available (which is as low as ten and as high as 21), the period of decline (which starts as early as 1995 and ends as late as 2015) and the extent of the decline (which ranges from 16% in Austria to 70% in Denmark). Nevertheless, these data demonstrate a marked and sustained reduction in the numbers of young people being caught up in European youth justice systems, especially from the mid-2000s onwards.

TABLE 5.1 Comparative data on youth justice system contact across 10 European countries

Country (source)	Data type	Age group	Period of decline	Extent of decline
Austria (Bruckmuller, 2017)	Rate per 100,000 registered juvenile suspects (identified as alleged offenders based on suspicion by the police)	Age 14–17	2008–2014	18%
		Age 18–21	2004–2014	16%
	Number of convictions	Age 14–17	2004–2014	37%
		Age 18–21	2005–2014	34%
Belgium (Dumortier et al., 2017)	Youth justice cases reported to the public prosecutor office	Not stated	2010–2014	~25%★
Denmark (Storgaard, 2017)	Number of suspicions or charges by the police	Age 10–17	2006–2015	54%
		Age 10–14	2006–2015	70%
		Age 15–17	2006–2015	46%
Germany (Dunkel and Heinz, 2017)	Rate per 100,000 population of police registered suspects of crimes	Age 14–17	2007–2014	~29%★
		Age 18–20	2005–2014	~19%★
Eire (Seymour, 2017)	Number of offences committed by children	Age 10–17	2011–2013	25%
Poland (Stando-Kawecka, 2017)	Number of juvenile crimes recorded by the police	Age 13–17	2011–2013	~30%★
	Number of juvenile suspects recorded by the police	Age 13–17	2007–2013	~55%★
Slovenia (Filipcic and Plesnicar, 2017)	Number of juvenile offenders involved in criminal activities registered by the police	Age 14–18	2004–2014	45%
	Number of criminal offenses committed by juvenile offenders registered by the police	Age 14–18	2004–2014	43%
Spain (Fernandez-Molina et al., 2017)	Rate of police arrest per 1000 population	Age 14–17	2004–2014	40%
Sweden (Sarnecki, 2017)	Rate of conviction per 1000 population	Age 15–17	1995–2005	~50%★
Switzerland (Pruin et al., 2017)	Number of police registered cases charged with violations against the Criminal Code	Age 10–14	2009–2013	45%
		Age 15–17	2009–2014	37%
	Number of convicted minors	Age 10–13	2006–2013	52%
		Age 14–15	2006–2012	43%
		Age 16–17	2006–2014	38%

★ Extent of decline has been estimated because exact data were not provided. The period of decline reflects a continuous drop in juvenile justice contact from the highest and lowest levels within the data provided.

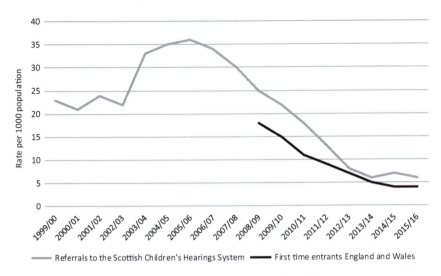

FIGURE 5.1 Rate per capita of offence referrals (Scotland) and first-time entrants (England/Wales)

Sources: Scottish Children's Reporter Administration statistics and population data from the National Records of Scotland; Youth Justice Board Statistics and Annual Population Data for England and Wales

These trends are also evident in our two case-study jurisdictions. The following figures highlight a range of key measures of youth justice activity for England/Wales and Scotland. The data are expressed as rates per capita to take account of changes in the population of young people over time.[4] Although the data presented are not always directly comparable, because of architectural differences between the systems,[5] the overall direction of travel is the same. Starting with entry into the system, the number of first-time entrants to youth justice in England/Wales declined by 78% between 2008/09 and between 2015/16 (Figure 5.1).[6] Slightly longer-term trend data are available for Scotland, and show that between 2005/06 and 2013/14 there was an 83% fall in offence referrals to the Children's Reporter (Figure 5.1).[7] Turning to court convictions for young people, there were similar reductions in both jurisdictions. The rate of conviction for 16–17-year-olds in Scotland fell by 77% between 2006/07 and 2013/14, while in England/Wales conviction rates for children aged 10–17 declined by 67% between 2008 and 2013 (Figures 5.2a and 5.2b, respectively). And finally, there were major reductions in custody rates for young people. The rate of custody in England and Wales (for 10–17-year-olds) fell by 44% from 2008 to 2015, and in Scotland there was a 60% drop in custody rates for 16–17-year-olds between 2009 and 2013 (Figure 5.3).[8] These trends demonstrate not only the reduced 'stock' (absolute numbers of entrants) of young people entering the youth justice system, but the subsequent impact on the diminishing 'flow' through the system (from arrests, to convictions, to imprisonment).

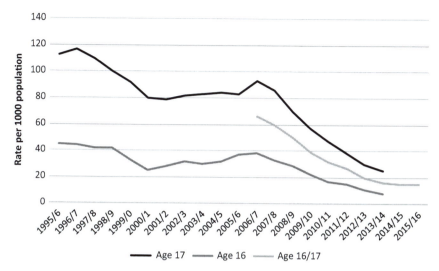

FIGURE 5.2A Rate of convictions per 1000 population, age 16 and 17 (Scotland)
Source: Criminal Proceedings in the Scottish Courts, Statistical Bulletins

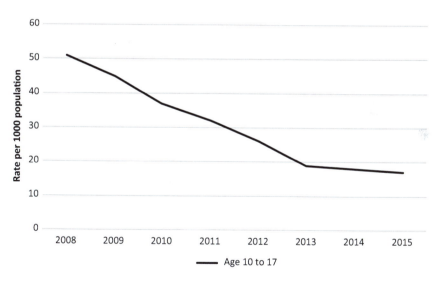

FIGURE 5.2B Rate of convictions per 1000 of the population, age 10–17 (England and Wales)
Source: Youth Justice Board Statistics

The policy contexts of system contraction

As was noted, the commonalities across western jurisdictions regarding reductions in crime rates have led some commentators to search for a universal rather than a system-specific explanation of change. Importantly, there has been little exploration

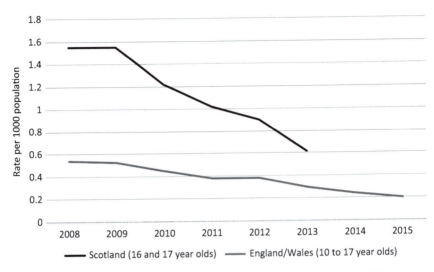

FIGURE 5.3 Rate of detention in secure accommodation or custody per 10000 population, age 16 and 17 (Scotland) and age 10–17 (England and Wales)

Source: Scottish Prison Statistics; Youth Justice Board Statistics. Rates calculated using national population data

of the policy contexts in which these trends have occurred, especially with regard to youth justice. Our review of European youth justice systems, however, reveals that the contraction in their client group has often coincided with the consolidation of, or renewed commitment to, diversion as an integral component of policy. Diversion as a policy is, of course, associated with active efforts to reduce the numbers of people processed by systems and, although it can take many forms, jurisdictions that embrace it would be expected to show a shrinking client group.

Examples of youth justice jurisdictions (re-)embracing diversion include Belgium from 2006 (Dumortier et al., 2017), Eire from 2001 (Seymour, 2017), Spain from 2000 (Molina et al., 2017) and Germany from as far back as 1990 (Dunkel and Heinz, 2017). However, the correspondence between an increased emphasis on diversion and reductions in system activity is particularly marked in our two case-study jurisdictions. Even so, the histories of the ways in which diversion has been interwoven in policy have differed between England/Wales and Scotland and current approaches involve a range of disparate practices. We summarise the developments in these two jurisdictions below.

(i) England[9]

Within England, a systems management approach to diversion was first embraced during the 1980s. This was a practitioner-led initiative which aimed to address both the stock and flow of young people through the system: underscored by 'a sense of how decisions made at one point in the system could have repercussions at another' (Smith, 2010: 126). Systems management was abandoned in the early 1990s by a (Conservative) government which embraced a mantra of 'prison works', led by a Prime Minister whose response to youth crime was to 'understand less' and 'condemn more' (McAra, 2011). It was also largely overlooked in the late 1990s/ early 2000s following the Blairite New Labour 'revolution' in youth justice, which re-emphasised 'toughness' but within the confines of a youth justice architecture whose principal statutory aim was to prevent offending by young people: an architecture which resulted in increased levels of tutelage over young people and their families (Goldson, 2010; McAra, 2017).

A major change occurred in 2008, with the publication of the Youth Crime Action Plan which aimed to reduce the number of first-time entrants to the youth justice system below the age of 18 by one fifth by 2020. This was accompanied by a strategy of 'non-negotiable' support and targeted interventions for high-risk families whose children were identified as being most likely to become prolific offenders. While these more recent developments can be regarded as an attempt to reduce the 'stock' of young people coming into the system, rather less effort has been expended on 'flow'. The subsequent years of both the Conservative/Liberal Democrat (2010–15) and Conservative government (from 2015), have seen a more qualified commitment to any particular ethos. This includes tropes such as 'payment by results', the 'rehabilitation revolution', and the 'educational secure estate' coming to the fore but as yet not completely followed through, in a context where youth justice has largely fallen off the electoral agenda, supplanted by more pressing constitutional issues (see McAra, 2017).

(ii)   Scotland

Within Scotland, diversion first became a major part of the youth justice narrative in the early 1960s, with the publication of the Kilbrandon Report (1964) and its ambition to import a minimal intervention approach into a new framework for juvenile justice. A new tribunal system of youth justice, known as the Children's Hearings System, was explicitly aimed at avoiding the criminalisation and stigmatisation of young people within an educational model of care (implemented via the Social Work [Scotland] Act 1968). In the immediate post-devolutionary period (from 1999 to 2007), Labour/Liberal Democratic coalition governments took a far more punitive (and less robustly evidenced) approach to matters of youth crime than the earlier 'Kilbrandon years'. They grafted onto Scotland's traditionally welfarist model of justice a complex and competing admixture of rationales, including actuarialism, just deserts and restoration, and took steps to 'fast-track' persistent offenders into the system (McAra, 2017). Characterised by penal expansionism and attempts to build social solidarity by means of a punitive and exclusionary dynamic, the 'fast-track years' (especially from 2003 to 2005) formed the antithesis of the Kilbrandon aims.

The expansionist experiment ended abruptly in the final years of the Labour/ Liberal Democrat years (2006–07), as the fast track system and other associated programmes were ineffective in tackling persistent offending. This penal lacuna was marked by the beginnings of a new narrative predicated on early intervention: one which came to fruition only in the subsequent Scottish National Party (SNP) government years (from 2007 onwards, 'the progressive era'). Indeed, the SNP immediately abandoned previous targets and placed greater emphasis on developing research-led logic models to inform policy and practice. This included drawing on Edinburgh Study findings to inform the diversionary imperatives of a new Whole System Approach (WSA) to youth justice (rolled out nationally, after successful pilot, from 2011). The stated ambition of WSA is to divert young people who come into conflict with the law away from formal measures wherever possible, using a set of interventions calibrated carefully to the level of risk posed and, crucially, proportionate to the needs of the young person: and thus tackling both stocks and flows (see Scottish Government, 2015).

Final reflections on crime reduction and policy

In this contextual section we have shown how youth justice activity across Europe has mirrored the broader trends in crime rates identified in the international research. But we have also demonstrated that the reductions in the youth justice client group have occurred over a period in which diversionary policies have been foregrounded in many jurisdictions. At face value, the Scottish data presented is strongly suggestive of policy period effects (reinforcing the findings of Matthews and Minton 2018), with the fluctuating trends in referrals and convictions corresponding with variant policy eras (namely reductions during the Kilbrandon years, increases during the 'fast track' years, followed by significant reductions in the more 'progressive era' of diversion).

However, as we will demonstrate, policy change is only part of the story. Indeed, the key to understanding reductions in youth justice activity lies in a greater understanding of the 'four effects' outlined earlier (and their cumulative impact on young people); and it is to a more detailed consideration of these that the chapter now turns.

The displacement effect

In this section we present evidence that there may have been a decline in some traditional modes of youth offending but that changing patterns of leisure activity, facilitated by the technological revolution, have opened up new opportunities and spaces for youthful transgression. As such, there has been a displacement of offending over time from the physical to the virtual world where there are fewer 'capable guardians', and this may account, in part, for the shrinking client group of youth justice.

Reductions in traditional modes of street-based offending

Various newspaper reports across Europe have heralded a decline in youth offending.[10] However, finding evidence to support the argument that there has been a real drop in youth crime underpinned by fundamental behavioural change is problematic. Official data, such as that presented in Table 5.1, shows a decline in young people being dealt with by the system, but not an actual drop in offending. For that we need well-validated measures of self-reported offending from repeated cross-sectional studies and, unfortunately, these are few and far between. One valuable resource is the International Self-Report Delinquency (ISRD) Study which has been conducted over three waves (in 1999, 2006 and 2015) covering countries from across Europe, Africa, Asia, North America and Latin America. This may well reveal an overall drop in youth crime (early findings from Spain suggest so, Fernando-Molina et al., 2017); however at the time of writing, the overview report from the most recent wave, which included 26 European countries, has not yet been published.

Looking at our case-study jurisdictions, we found tentative, albeit not conclusive, evidence that some forms of youth offending have declined in England/Wales and Scotland. Data from the Offending Crime and Justice Survey suggests that there was a reduction in the rate of youth offending in England and Wales in the mid-2000s. Hales et al. (2009) found that 12–13-year-olds born between 1992 and 1996 were less likely to report vandalising property than similar aged children born between 1989 and 1991; although, there were insufficient sweeps of this survey to demonstrate any long-term trend. Meanwhile, the Health Behaviours in School-Age Children (HBSC) Study which was carried out in 2002, 2006 and 2010 found a significant fall in violent behaviour in 19 out of 30 European and North American countries, including the UK. Studying the involvement of 11-, 13- and 15- year-olds in physical fighting, Pickett et al. (2013) observed that the standardised rate of violence per 100 children within the UK declined significantly from 13.2 in 2002 to 10.6 in 2010. Again however, the snapshot nature of this study does not allow us to determine whether this is part of a long-term trend or merely a fluctuating pattern, and the figures were not disaggregated for the different constituent parts of the UK.

An alternative way of determining whether there has been a change in behaviour amongst young people is to elicit the views of those who are victimised. The UK crime surveys, for example, routinely ask all victims of crime whether they were able to say something about the person or people who committed the crime. If so, the victim is asked to estimate the age of the offender(s). Figure 5.4 shows how victim perceptions of the age of offenders have changed since 1992 in England and Wales. There was a clear shift during the last decade, with victims being less likely to report that the offender was under the age of 24, and an increase in the perception that the offender was aged 25 or over, especially since 2010/11. Of course, this trend could well be a function of the changing nature of crimes for which one or more of the offenders are observed, however, it is interesting that data from the crime surveys in Scotland (shown in Figure 5.5) shows a remarkably similar picture (although comparable data are not available for all years).

The UK crime surveys also collect useful information on people's perceptions of certain types of problems in their local areas, including forms of anti-social

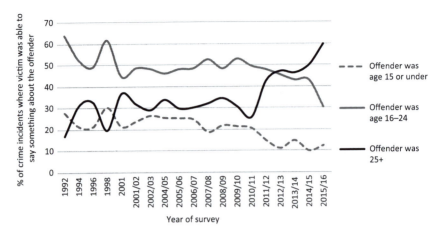

FIGURE 5.4 Change in the age of offenders (as reported by victims) in England and Wales, 1992–2015/16

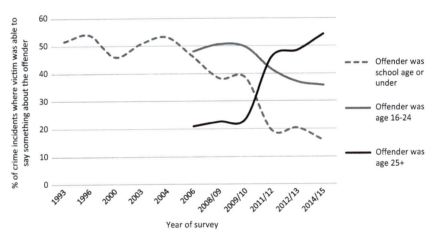

FIGURE 5.5 Change in the age of offenders (as reported by victims) in Scotland, 1993–2014/15

behaviour that are typically associated with children and young people. The Crime Survey for England and Wales shows a fall of 43% in respondents reporting that teenagers were hanging around on the streets and causing a big or fairly big problem in their local area between 2004/5 and 2014/15, while the percentage of people reporting a high level of anti-social behaviour in their neighbourhoods fell by 35% over the same period (ONS, 2015). The Scottish Crime and Justice Survey includes similar questions, although trend data is only available from 2008/09 to 2014/15. Nevertheless, over that period there was a 48% reduction in Scottish respondents reporting that violence between groups of individuals or gangs was a very or fairly common problem in their local area, and a 26% decline in people behaving in an anti-social manner (Scottish Government, 2016a). Thus, while there is limited self-report evidence from young people about their behaviour, public perceptions are certainly consistent in their view that street-based youth offending has reduced within the last decade.

There are also compelling long-term trend data on other associated 'risky behaviours'. For example, the Scottish Schools Adolescent Lifestyle and Substance Use Survey (SALSUS) shows an ongoing reduction from 2002 to 2013 amongst 13 and 15 year old boys and girls in both alcohol consumption and drug use, and an even longer-term decline in smoking (Scottish Government, 2016b, 2016c). Similar survey data for children aged 11 to 15 in England show an almost identical pattern (Fuller and Hawkins, 2013), and indeed the HBSC surveys indicate an average decline in smoking and drinking prevalence across European countries between 2002 and 2010.[11] There have also been declines in other forms of 'psychosocial disorders' for young people, such as suicide rates. Data published by the Scottish Public Health Observatory show that suicide rates amongst 15–24-year-olds in Scotland fell by 64% between 2000 and 2014. While data available from the Office for National Statistics suggest that suicide rates amongst 15–24-year-olds in England and Wales reduced by about half from 1998 to 2008, although the trend has increased slightly since then. Again, data from many other European countries shows a fall in suicide rates between 1995 and 2010, with an average decline of 31% (Eurostat, 2012).

So, although the evidence on youth offending is limited, if we look to a wider range of sources about change in public perceptions of youth behaviour and broader aspects of health and wellbeing there are strong indications of a positive change in youth lifestyles, certainly within the last decade and possibly over a longer time frame. Given the co-dependency of youth offending behaviour with a range of other problematic behaviours (see Rutter and Smith, 1995), it is highly plausible that young people's engagement in offending may have simply declined. However, given the stability of the age-crime curve over time (see Farrington, 1986; Loeber and Farrington, 2014) it is just as plausible that young people's propensity to offend has not diminished but has simply been displaced to a range of activities that are neither being captured by our existing measures of crime nor by the youth justice system itself.

Transformations in the situational context of offending

The argument for a potential displacement effect points to the rapid expansion in young people's use of electronic devices and time spent on the internet, and whether this has impacted on the propensity and capacity of young people to commit more traditional forms of youth crime. Or, as the *Washington Post* recently put it in response to a Danish study that showed falling youth crime rates, 'Why are European kids committing fewer crimes? They're too busy on their phones' (22 February 2017). But is there evidence to support the hypothesis that children are simply spending too much time on electronic gadgets to find the time to get involved in offending? Or is it the case that they have simply transferred their propensity to offend from on-street to online offending?

There is no doubt that the amount of time spent by young people on phones, computers and tablets has increased exponentially across Europe. A recent report showed that internet access had risen from 55% of all households across 28 EU countries in 2007 to 81% in 2014, and it was even higher in households with dependent children (Eurostat, 2015). Moreover, the HBSC study points to a worrying increase in 'screen-time behaviour' across 30 countries, especially amongst boys (Bucksch et al., 2016). In the UK, 93% of young people reported daily internet use, clearly demonstrating that online activities represent a way of life for contemporary British youth. There are, of course, many purposeful uses such as seeking information for education, taking part in civic activities (such as voting or consultations) and contacting public organisations. But by far the greatest use is for social activities, including messaging people and visiting social-networking sites. A survey commissioned by the UK Safer Internet Centre (2015) found that three quarters of 11–16-year-olds were regular YouTube and Facebook users, and a quarter used six or more social network and messaging apps every week. By definition, more leisure time spent engaging in indoor online activities means less time for doing outdoor activities, which for many young people in prior decades would have included hanging around in public places, exposing themselves to potentially risky situations and getting involved in delinquent behaviours.

So, exactly how prevalent is online offending, or 'cybercrime' as it is more commonly known? Comparable data for Europe generally are not available; however, a new set of 'experimental statistics' published from the 2016 Crime Survey for England and Wales suggests that online fraud is now the most common form of victimisation in the country (ONS, 2017). The survey tested a range of questions, covering experience of bank and credit card fraud, non-investment fraud, computer viruses, and email and social-media hacking, and found that the public experienced an estimated 5.6m cybercrimes in the year prior to interview, which accounted for almost half of all crimes committed. Unfortunately, the CSEW statistics cannot tell us who commits such crimes and whether this has become the preferred mode of offending by young people.

There are a number of reports on young people's experiences of crime online, either as offenders or victims, although many of them are small-scale, unsystematic studies or based on largely anecdotal evidence, which suggests a significant need for further research in this area. Studies of 'serious' forms of online offending behaviour are rare. Exceptions include a recent NSPCC report on children and young people who display harmful sexual behaviour online (Belton and Hollis, 2016), which estimated that between 3% and 15% of online offences involving indecent images of children were committed by children and young people, and that some were involved in online grooming and sexual solicitation of other children and young people. An interesting point to note from this report was that most young people who offended online had not engaged in offline sexual offending.

In addition, the National Crime Agency's National Cyber Crime Unit (NCCU) has declared that young people are increasingly becoming involved in cybercrime through an illegal pathway that typically starts with cheating on computer games and leads to more significant forms of behaviour including hacking systems, minor forms of financial gain and, finally, serious cybercrime (CREST 2015). The NCCU notes that those at risk may be as young as 12 years, are likely to be deeply interested in technology and spend a large part of their lives online – again, it appears very few of them are engaged in offline offending.

Most of the academic literature on online offending focuses on cyberbullying, which takes many forms including 'flaming' (sending angry or rude messages to a private space online), harassment, cyberstalking, social exclusion and sexting (Li, 2008, Mitchell et al., 2012). There is no single agreed definition of cyberbullying at a European level, most EU member states lack specific data on cyberbullying and its prevalence and the forms it takes vary widely from study to study; however, there are indications that North-East European countries have the highest rates of online risk while Western and Southern European countries have the lowest risk (European Parliament, 2016). A UK-wide study of 4,500 11–16-year-olds by Beatbullying (Cross et al., 2012) found that 28% had been targeted by some form of cyberbullying, while 17% admitting to cyberbullying others. Another national survey of 1,500 13–18-year-olds (conducted by the UK Safer Internet Centre 2016) found that 25% of respondents had experienced online 'hate crime' (because of gender, sexual orientation, race, religion, disability or transgender identity), of whom a quarter reported that it happened to them all or most of the time. While a much smaller study in the West of England (Katz and Lovelace, 2011) found that 48% of all respondents between ages 10 and 16+ had experienced one or more forms of online bullying (including threatening messages and nasty comments), which rose to 62% amongst 14- and 15-year-olds. Experts suggest that online forms of bullying have not replaced offline experiences – indeed they should be treated as discrete phenomena (Dempsey et al., 2009). However, evidence suggests that for young people who are vulnerable offline, their experiences may well be exacerbated online (Haddon and Livingstone, 2014).

A number of recent studies suggest that the most common form of online offending amongst young people is 'low-level' behaviour such as illegal downloading of films or music. A study of 12–15-year-olds in England and Scotland found that a third of children in both countries reported illegally downloading films, media or music (Herlitz et al., 2016a, 2016b). What is more, the prevalence of this form of offending was far higher than for other more 'traditional' types of youth offending, including group fighting, theft, graffiti and shoplifting. This phenomenon has been replicated in surveys in other European countries; for example, online downloading was reported by just under half of children in a German survey (Gorgen, Taefi and Kraus, 2013) and around three quarters of children surveyed in Belgium (Christiaens and Evenepoel, 2013). In Spain, the ISRD study showed a downward trend in most forms of offending behaviour between 2006 and 2015 but an increase in the prevalence of illegal downloading from 65% to 80% (Fernandez-Molina et al., 2017).

Similarly, an EU child online safety project found that 75% of children aged 12 to 16 had downloaded pirated material (Davidson et al., 2017).

In sum, while there is still a lack of evidence about the changing profile of youth offending, we must allow for the strong possibility that the ease with which some forms of online crime can be carried out, and the lack of obvious surveillance or policing, opens up opportunities for those who have the propensity to engage in deviant acts to do so with minimal risk of sanction or exposure. Historically, the age-crime curve would suggest that those most at risk of such propensity are teenagers and young adults. Therefore, we must be cautious about claiming that apparent declines in street-based forms of offending (measured through traditional means) are evidence of a trend towards *increasing lawfulness* amongst young people, as suggested by the author of a study for the Danish Crime Prevention Council Study which showed a decline over time in theft, violence and vandalism amongst 14–15-year-olds (Balvig, 2007). Rather, what the patterns observed above may indicate, is that the transformations in the situational contexts of leisure and of associated crime opportunities, mean that fewer young people are available for traditional modes of street-based policing: and it is to the implications of the displacement effect for policing practices and system activity more generally that the next section turns.

The cultural dissonance and concentration effects

In this section of the chapter we show how the institutions which play a key role in tackling youth offending have not fully adapted to the displacement effects described above. Indeed, there is strong evidence from a range of sources, which indicates that police and prosecutorial practices are stuck in older dynamics of law enforcement focused on young people from the most deprived neighbourhoods and family backgrounds – a phenomenon which we have termed the cultural dissonance effect. This cultural dissonance effect, in combination with the displacement effect, has resulted in a youth justice client group smaller in scope than hitherto but more intensively vulnerable and challenging – a 'concentration effect'. Here, we present new analysis of Scottish data on police stop and search as well as recent findings from the Edinburgh Study of Youth Transitions and Crime on the working cultures of agencies. Similar datasets that would allow this issue to be addressed are not available more widely across Europe, and the Edinburgh Study in particular is one of the very few European studies of its kind to combine extensive longitudinal self-report data with linked administrative records.

Police Stop and Search Data

The rate at which young people are stopped and searched by the police is a good indicator of youth justice activity and, more importantly, provides useful insights into who becomes policed. In earlier work, we observed that the cultural practices of Scottish policing were such that they tended to focus on the 'usual suspects', who were disproportionately from deprived backgrounds (McAra and McVie,

2005). Since 2015, there has been major transformation in the use of stop and search in Scotland following concerns about the widespread use of the tactic and, in particular, the hugely disproportionate targeting of consensual searches against children and young people (Murray, 2014; HMICS, 2015). Unique data released by Police Scotland shows that stop and search is now rarely used for those aged under 12, and the rate of searches amongst teenagers has declined considerably. Nevertheless, 19% of all searches conducted in 2016 involved a young person aged between 12 and 17 even though they only represent 6% of the population. Furthermore, the detection rates for this group were lower than for any other age group. In fact, only 20% of searches involving a young person under the age of 18 recovered any illegal item, compared with 31% for those aged 18 to 20 and 34% for those aged 21 to 25.

No information is collected on the social background of individuals stopped by the police, but it is possible to examine the socio-demographic characteristics of the areas in which most searches take place. Figure 5.6 shows the rate of searches per 1000 population for young people aged 12 to 17 during 2016 according to the deprivation quintile of the area in which the search was conducted.[12] It shows that the rate of search increased according to level of area deprivation, with rates for 12–17-year-olds in the 20% most deprived areas of Scotland being twice as high as for those in the least deprived quintile. In other words, while it is not possible to say whether young people from the *most deprived households* are currently more likely to be stopped and searched (although our earlier research showed that they were), it is certainly the case that young people who frequent public places in the *most deprived neighbourhoods* are at substantially increased likelihood of being stopped and searched.

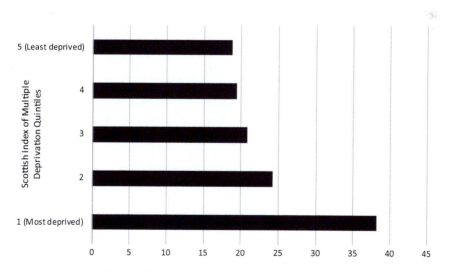

FIGURE 5.6 Rate of stop and search per 1000 12–17-year-olds in Scottish Multimember Ward areas, categorised into SIMD quintiles (2016)

The Edinburgh Study

Turning then to evidence from the Edinburgh Study: a core aim was to track pathways into and out of crime for a cohort of 4,300 young people who started secondary school in the City of Edinburgh in 1998. Importantly, these young people grew to adulthood in the post-devolutionary era, and thus lived through each of the policy eras in youth justice described earlier in the chapter: the 'Kilbrandon years' (pre 1999); the 'fast-track years' (2000–2006); and the 'progressive policy era' (from 2007 onwards). In past work, we showed how the working cultures of both the police and the Children's Reporter resulted in a recycling of the usual suspects – mostly boys from socially deprived backgrounds – during the teenage years (McAra and McVie, 2005, 2007). In following up the cohort to age 24, we now present strong evidence of continuity in institutional cultural practices, such that earlier involvement with agencies of justice continues to predict later police and prosecutorial decision-making even though the offending behaviour of the person has diminished in seriousness and persistence. Indeed, once identified as a usual suspect the 'master-status' of offender cannot be readily shrugged off.

Importantly, there appears to be a degree of inertia with regard to such cultural practices that is at odds with the dynamics of policy transformation – in sum, policy and practice do not readily align (McAra, 2016). Thus, at age 11 (during the 'Kilbrandon years'), those who had been warned or charged by the police in the previous year had almost eight times greater odds of being warned and charged again, even when the analysis controlled for the young person's involvement in serious offending. Similarly, those from low socioeconomic status households had over twice the odds of being warned and charged than their more affluent counterparts. At age 15 (during the 'fast-track years') the same dynamic was found, with odds ratios of 10 and 1.4 respectively for previous warning and charges and low socioeconomic status; and similarly at age 22 (during the progressive phase of policy), those who had been warned or charged in the previous year had around ten times greater odds of being warned or charged during the current year and young men from low socioeconomic households had over three and a half times greater odds of being warned or charged, again even when controlling for involvement in serious offending (McAra, 2016). Thus, regardless of the predominant justice paradigm operating at any particular point in time, those who are *already* in the system (especially those from poorer backgrounds) experience this cultural dissonance effect.

Impacts of cultural dissonance

The long-term consequence of the continuities in cultural practices described above is a concentration effect with regard to the young people who do get caught up in the youth justice system. Although the above data relate only to Scotland, both the Youth Justice Board in England/Wales and the Scottish Prisons Inspectorate have noted that institutions are now dealing with a smaller population but one with greater concentrations of complex needs, including challenging behaviours, extensive histories of trauma and abuse and mental health issues (see Youth Justice Board, 2016b, HMIP, 2016). A particular concern has been the continued over-representation of black, Asian and minority ethnic young people in the English/Welsh youth justice system and, in both jurisdictions, the high concentrations of children who have early histories of care (Prison Reform Trust, 2013, Scottish Prison Service, 2015). For example, in England/Wales looked-after children make up 30% of boys and 44% of girls in custody, in a context where fewer than 1% of children overall are in care. Similarly, in Scotland research has found that 33% of young people in custody have care histories (see Broderick and Carnie, 2015), in contrast to just over 1% of the general population of children (Scottish Government, 2017). European data in this area are limited; however, Estrada et al., (2016) also pointed to a strong socioeconomic concentration effect in the changing rates of conviction in their Swedish study.

Given these cultural dissonance and concentration effects, how then have they affected the capacity of youth justice systems to support vulnerable young people and transform their behaviour? What, indeed, is the impact of these twin effects on the young people who become the focus of the institutional gaze?

The whole-system effect?

In this final section of the chapter we demonstrate how integrated diversionary policies (focused on stocks *and* flows) may be more effective in the shorter term in reducing the risks of reconviction for young people caught up in the system. However, we also argue that without challenging the cultural dissonance effect and tackling the vulnerabilities associated with the concentration effect, there is a danger of longer-term recycling of the most needy of the usual suspect population. Indeed, without properly developing and resourcing a holistic and contextualised approach to young people in conflict with the law (a whole-system effect), reductions in the client group of youth justice systems may not be sustainable over the longer term.

In developing these arguments, we foreground data from our case-study jurisdictions, in particular reconviction data from both England/Wales and Scotland, and evidence from the Edinburgh Study on outcomes of intervention.[13]

Patterns of reconviction

Both England/Wales and Scotland track the criminal conviction histories of cohorts of young people who have had youth justice system contact. Some caution is required in comparing trends given that the data is generated in a slightly different way in each jurisdiction (note too that published data from England and Wales cannot be disaggregated). In keeping with the rates of criminal convictions highlighted earlier in the chapter, the numbers of young people in the tracked cohorts in both jurisdictions have been reducing dramatically over the past decade or so. However, there are major differences in the relative 'success' between Scotland

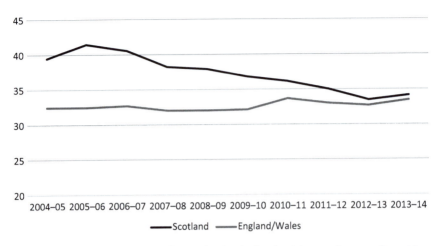

FIGURE 5.7 Reconviction Rates for Under 21s in Scotland (rates relate mostly to 16–20-year-olds) and England Wales (includes 10- to 20-year-olds)

Source: Ministry of Justice and Scottish Government Statistics

and England/Wales in terms of reducing reconviction rates of those caught up in the system. The most recently published data (see Figure 5.7) indicates that reconviction rates in Scotland for young people (aged under 21) have declined since the mid-2000s by around 16% (Scottish Government, 2015b). In contrast reconviction rates in England/Wales have been relatively stable over the same time frame, with a more recent rise of some 3% (Ministry of Justice, 2016).

Again the longer-term trends for Scotland are suggestive of the policy period effects outlined above: with relative stability during the Kilbrandon years; followed by a sharp rise in reconviction rates during the fast-track (more punitive) years, when the police and criminal justice system more generally was urged to react swiftly and firmly to youthful transgressions; and then a reduction as fast-tracking was abandoned, followed by a more progressive set of policies from 2007 including an integrated approach to diversion. Within England/Wales, by contrast, the rise in reconviction rates has occurred during a period in which diversion has been grafted onto a system, but which more recently has had no strongly overarching ethos (McAra, 2017). These findings would indicate that integrated and whole-systems approaches (tackling both stocks *and* flows of young people coming through the system) may be more effective in tackling reoffending than systems which lay greater emphasis on first-time entrants (i.e. controlling the stocks more than the flows).

Interestingly, there has been a short-term rise since 2013/14 in reconviction within Scotland and it will be important to track whether this is a statistical blip or the beginning of a longer-term trend. A reducing and then stabilising trend might, however, be expected in a context where the majority of less serious offenders are gradually diverted away from the system or diverted into community rather custodial disposals, leaving a smaller and potentially more recalcitrant group of young people presenting with complex needs (as per the concentration effect described above). The cultural dissonance effect means that the police will consistently focus their activity in deprived neighbourhoods and on the usual suspects, constantly recycling them into the system – a stigmatising dynamic which our earlier research has shown is likely to compromise the young person's capacity to desist from offending (McAra and McVie, 2007).

Edinburgh Study findings on long-term impacts

The most recent analysis of Edinburgh Study data takes the above contentions one-step further: highlighting the lagged effects of punitive/fast-track interventions and the extremely poor longer-term outcomes for those who become the 'property' of systems.

Within Scotland, the peak age of conviction has gradually been rising over time (from age 18 to 20 in the early 2000s to the late twenties today, see Matthews and Minton, 2018), as have reconvictions amongst the older cohorts tracked by the Scottish Government (those aged over 30). The Edinburgh Study cohort, now in their early thirties, is part of this recent history, an age group that (as noted above) was subject to the punitive turn and fast track years of youth justice in Scotland over their early to mid-teenage years. For those caught up in the system from their early years, this has resulted in very long-term recycling. As evidence we present the subsequent conviction histories and experience of imprisonment for two sets of groups matched using quasi-experimental analysis (Table 5.2).

First, we compare a group of young people at age 12 with early referrals to youth justice with a matched group of 'controls' with no history of such contact; and second, we compare a group of young people who were referred on offence grounds at age 14 and made subject to compulsory measure of supervision with a matched control group who had no such referrals. The groups were created using propensity score matching to ensure that the characteristics of the young people were as similar as possible, other than that one group had experience of system

TABLE 5.2 Edinburgh Study Data on longer-term impacts of intervention

	Pattern of Chronic Conviction by age 22	Experience of custody by age 24
Early referral to hearings	36	42
Sig.	.014	.002
Matched Controls	18	9
Supervision at age 14	47	31
Sig.	.000	.000
Matched Controls	6	0

contact/intervention and the other did not (see McAra and McVie, 2007 and McAra, 2016 for further details).

As can be seen in Table 5.2, those with early referrals to juvenile justice by age 12 were significantly more likely than their matched counterparts to have a pattern of chronic conviction by age 22 (that is convictions in every year from age 16), with 42% ending up in custody by age 24 as opposed to 9% of the controls. Similarly, those who had experience of supervision in the system at age 14 were significantly more likely to be chronic convictees by age 22 and a third had experience of custody by age 24 as contrasted with none of the controls.

Importantly, we know that young people with chronic system contact are from the most deprived backgrounds but also that system contact exacerbates deprivation (McAra and McVie, 2015a). Indeed we have shown that the odds of not being in education, training or employment at age 18 are greatly elevated by early experience of system contact, even when controlling for school experience and other factors strongly linked to unemployment risk (McAra, 2016), and that poverty itself is a strong predictor of later involvement in violence (McAra and McVie, 2015b).

Taken together, the lessons from the Edinburgh Study are in favour of a maximum diversion approach to both youth and adult criminal justice, but also demonstrate that headline policy change does not always result in transformations in the working practices of youth justice institutions. Without a truly functioning whole system approach, integrated into a wider set of social justice and economic responses to poverty, the reductions in reconviction rates in Scotland are not sustainable over the longer term and the rise in reconvictions in England/Wales will not be remedial.

Conclusions

Against the backdrop of reducing crime rates internationally, this chapter has highlighted the ways in which the shrinking youth client group across many European jurisdictions has coincided with a renewed policy emphasis on diversion. However, the evidence suggests that policy alone has not led to the transformations in the numbers of young people being processed in each system. Indeed the client group of youth justice has been significantly shaped by: displacement effects which have transposed much anti-social behaviour from the physical to the virtual world and thereby radically reduced the population available for policing; cultural dissonance effects which mean that the police are continuing to focus most of their activity on the much reduced street-based crime of the urban poor; and, concomitant, concentration effects such that the youngsters sucked deepest into the system form a smaller but highly vulnerable group.

An integrated system of diversion (focusing on controls of both the stocks and flows of young people processed by the system), as implemented in Scotland, may be more effective (in terms of reducing reconviction rates) over the shorter term. However, the evidence suggests that systems management by itself is unlikely to sustain reductions in the numbers of young people being reconvicted over the longer term, without major changes in the cultural practices of the police and greater efforts to transform the conditions in which the most vulnerable young people live.

In approaching this chapter, we have been forcibly reminded of the many gaps that still exist in terms of data coverage and the challenges posed by data quality and comparability across many western systems of justice. Without good data and a rigorous approach to analysis which examines underlying transformations in youth lifestyles (as we have attempted here), there is a danger that commentators will continue to conflate changes in system activity with individual behavioural change. Fundamentally in evidencing the case for a whole system approach to diversion, we strongly urge policymakers and practitioners as well as theorists of the crime drop to be appropriately reflexive with regard to the shifting patterns and loci of youthful transgressions and the dynamics of institutional praxis. By overlooking the four effects outlined in this chapter, youth justice systems will always and every-where be set up to fail.

Notes

1 See Table 23 from Eurostat Crime and Criminal Justice Statistics, May 2016. http:// ec.europa.eu/eurostat/statistics-explained/index.php/Crime_and_criminal_justice_ statistics#Source_data_for_tables_and_figures_.28MS_Excel.29.

2 The Edinburgh Study has been funded by grants from the Economic and Social Research Council (R000237157; R000239150), the Scottish Government and the Nuffield Foundation. Further details on the aims, methods and impacts of the Edinburgh Study can be found here: www.law.ed.ac.uk/research/making_a_difference/esytc.

3 For example, the 2014 *European Sourcebook of Crime and Criminal Justice Statistics* only provides useful comparable trend data for minors on prosecutions (for a few countries only) and prison population data, and provides extensive health warnings on definitional issues.

4 While the UK does have an aging population and the number of young people in the gen-eral population has correspondingly reduced, this does not in itself explain the shrinking client group of youth justice. When statistics on youth justice activity are expressed as a rate per 1000 population rather than a raw number, the real reductions are both marked and sustained.

5 A court-based system of justice in England/Wales covering young people aged 10 to 17 and a lay-tribunal model in Scotland, covering young people referred on care and protec-tion grounds from birth up to age 15 and those referred on offence grounds from age 8 to 15, with the vast majority of 16- and 17-year- old offenders being dealt with in the adult courts (McAra 2010).

6 First-time entrants are defined as those receiving their first substantive 'outcome' – repri-mand, final warning, with or without intervention, or court disposal for those sent direct to court without a reprimand or final warning. As discussed below, the number of first-time entrants was officially designated as a target for youth justice in England/Wales from 2008 only.

7 The Reporter is the official who investigates referrals and determines if there is a prima facie case that at least one of the grounds for referral to a children's hearing has been met and that the child is in need of compulsory measures of care.

8 Prisons data for this age group were not available in Scotland for 2014 and 2015.
9 Although youth justice statistics for England and Wales cannot be disaggregated, it should
be noted that since devolution Wales has followed a somewhat divergent trajectory from
that of England. Indeed, the Welsh Assembly has attempted creatively to use the powers at
its disposal over children's services, health, education and housing, to implement a child's
rights ethos into youth justice – in a context where youth justice itself was not devolved
(McAra 2017).
10 *The Telegraph* (9 April 2017) Violent video games 'reduce crime'; *The Local* (23 January
2017) Danish youth crime at all-time low as kids choose being online over causing
trouble; Swissinfo.ch (7 December 2015) Youth violence on the decline in Switzerland;
The Independent (16 May 2014) Who should get credit for declining youth crime?
Young people of course; *Dutch Daily News* (3 March 2013) Youth crime decreases in the
Netherlands.
11 The HBSC survey data for 2010 and 2014 show a fall in the percentage of 15-year-
olds who reported drinking at least once a week. (www.euro.who.int/__data/assets/
pdf_file/0017/303470/HBSC-No.7-factsheet_Alcohol.pdf?ua=1) or smoking at least
once a week (www.euro.who.int/__data/assets/pdf_file/0016/303532/HBSC-No.7_
factsheet_Tobacco.pdf).
12 The rates of search per 1000 population for 12–17-year-olds were calculated for 324
Multimember Wards in Scotland using data from Police Scotland. The 2016 Scottish Index
of Multiple Deprivation (SIMD) rankings were averaged within each Multimember
Ward, and then the Multimember Wards were grouped into SIMD quintiles. There
are 352 Multimember Wards in Scotland, but no searches of 12–17-year-olds were
conducted in 28 of them during 2016.
13 Recidivism rates across Europe more generally are notoriously difficult to compare since
many countries do not publish relevant data and, amongst those that do, there is significant variation in how recidivism is defined and reported (see Fazel and Wolf 2015).

References

Aebi, M. and Linde, A. (2010) 'Is there a crime drop in western Europe?' *European Journal on Criminal Policy and Research*, 16(4): 251–277.
Aebi, M.F. and Linde, A. (2012) Crime trends in Western Europe according to official statis-
tics from 1990 to 2007. In J. Van Dijk, A. Tseloni and G. Farrell (Eds) *The international crime drop*. Basingstoke: Palgrave Macmillan.
Balvig, F. (2007) *Youth survey: why young people's lawfulness in Denmark is spreading*. Glostrup:
The Danish Crime Prevention Council. www.dkr.dk/media/8252/uk_youth-survey.pdf
[Accessed 3 March 2017].
Bateman, T. (2012a) 'Youth justice news', *Youth Justice*, 12(2): 144– 55.
Bateman, T. (2012b) 'Who pulled the plug? Towards an explanation of the fall in child impris-
onment in England and Wales', *Youth Justice*, 12(1): 36–52.
Baumer, E.P. and Wolff, K.T. (2014) 'Evaluating contemporary crime drop(s) in America,
New York City, and many other places', *Justice Quarterly*, 31(1): 5–38, DOI: 10.1080/
07418825.2012.742127.
Belton, E. and Hollis, V. (2016) *A review of the research on children and young people who display harmful sexual behaviour online*. London: NSPCC Evaluation Department.
www.nspcc.org.uk/globalassets/documents/research-reports/review-children-young-
people-harmful-sexual-behaviour-online.pdf [Accessed 14 May 2018].
Broderick, R. and Carnie, J. (2015) *Prisoners who have been in care as 'looked after children', 15th Survey Bulletin*. Edinburgh: Scottish Prison Service.

Brown, R. (2015) *Explaining the property crime drop: The offender perspective.* Trends and issues in crime and criminal justice no. 495. Canberra: Australian Institute of Criminology.

Bruckmuller, K. (2017) Austria. In S.H. Decker and N. Marteache (Eds) *International handbook of juvenile justice* (2nd edn). Switzerland: Springer.

Bucksch, J., Sigmundova, D., Hamrik, Z., Troped, P.J., Melkevik, O., Ahluwalia N., Borraccino, A., Tynjala, J., Kalman, M. and Inchley, J. (2016) 'International trends in adolescent screen-time behaviours from 2002 to 2010', *Journal of Adolescent Health,* 58(4): 417–425. OI.org/10.1016/j.jadohealth.2015.11.014.

Butts, J.A. (2000) *Youth crime drop.* Research report: Urban Institute Justice Policy Center. www.urban.org/sites/default/files/publication/62721/410246-Youth-Crime-Drop. PDF [Accessed 14 May 2018].

Christiaens, J. and Evenepoel, A. (2013) Exploring the youth crime prevention field in Belgium: experts' and youngsters' views. In T. Gorgen, B. Kraus, A. Taefi, J.J.B Beneitez, J. Christiaens, G. Mesko, H. Perista and O. Toth (Eds) *Youth deviance and youth violence: Findings from a European study on juvenile delinquency and its prevention.* Munster: YouPrev. www.youprev.eu/pdf/YouPrev_InternationalReport.pdf [Accessed 14 May 2018].

Crest (2015) *Identify, intervene, inspire: helping young people to pursue careers in cyber security, not cyber crime.* London: National Crime Agency. www.nationalcrimeagency.gov.uk/publications/758-crest-helping-young-people-to-pursue-careers-in-cyber-security-not-cyber-crime/file [Accessed 14 May 2018].

Cross, E.J., Piggin, R., Douglas, T. and Volkaenal-Flatt, J. (2012) *Virtual violence II: progress and challenges in the fight against cyberbullying.* London: Beatbullying.

Davidson, J., DeMarco, J., Bifulco, A., Bogaerts, S., Caretti, V., Aiken, M., Cheevers, C., Corbari, E., Scally, M., Schilder, J., Schimmenti, A. and Puccia, A. (2017) *Enhancing police and industry practice: EU child online safety project.* London: Middlesex University.

Donohue, J. and Levitt, S. (2001) 'The impact of legalised abortion on crime', *Quarterly Journal of Economics,* 116(2): 279–420.

Downes, D. and Hansen, K. (2006) Welfare and punishment in comparative perspective. In S. Armstrong, and L. McAra (Eds) *Perspectives on punishment: the contours of control.* Oxford: Oxford University Press, 133–154.

Duggan, M. (2001) 'More guns, more crime', *Journal of Political Economy,* 109(5): 1086–1114.

Dunkel, F. and Heinz, W. (2017) Germany. In S.H. Decker and N. Marteache (Eds) *International handbook of juvenile justice* (2nd edn). Switzerland: Springer.

Dumortier, E., Christiaens, J. and Nuytiens, A. (2017) Belgium. In S.H. Decker and N. Marteache (Eds) *International handbook of juvenile justice* (2nd edn). Switzerland: Springer.

Eck, J.E. and Maguire, E.R. (2000) Have changes in policing reduced violent crime? In A. Blumstein and J. Wallman (Eds) *The crime drop in America.* New York: Cambridge University Press.

Estrada, F., Backman, O. and Nilsson, A. (2016) 'The darker side of equality? The declining gender gap in crime: historical trends and an enhanced analysis of staggered birth cohorts,' *British Journal of Criminology,* 56(6): 1272–1290. DOI: https://doi.org/10.1093/bjc/azv114.

European Parliament (2016) *Cyberbullying among young people.* Study for the LIBE Committee. www.europarl.europa.eu/RegData/etudes/STUD/2016/571367/IPOL_STU(2016)571367_EN.pdf [Accessed 14 May 2018].

Eurostat (2012) Health at a glance: Europe 2012. Suicide statistics. www.oecd-ilibrary.org/sites/9789264183896-en/01/07/index.html?contentType=&itemId=%2Fcontent%2Fchapter%2F9789264183896-10-en&mimeType=text%2Fhtml&containerItemId=%2Fcontent%2Fserial%2F23056088&accessItemIds= [Accessed 15 April 2017].

Eurostat (2016) *Crime and criminal justice statistics.* http://ec.europa.eu/eurostat/statistics-explained/index.php/Crime_and_criminal_justice_statistics#Source_data_for_tables_and_figures_.28MS_Excel.29 [Accessed 27 February 2017].

Eurostat (2015) *Being young in Europe today – digital world.* http://ec.europa.eu/eurostat/statistics-explained/index.php/Being_young_in_Europe_today_-_digital_world#Youth_online:_a_way_of_life. [Accessed 3 March 2017].

Farrell, G. (2013) 'Five tests for a theory of the crime drop', *Crime Science*, 2(5), 1–8.

Farrell, G., Tseloni, A., Mailley, J. and Tilley, N. (2011) 'The crime drop and the security hypothesis', *Journal of Research in Crime and Delinquency*, 48(2): 147–175.

Farrell, G., Laycock, G. and Tilley, N. (2015) 'Debuts and legacies: the crime drop and the role of adolescence-limited and persistent offenders', *Crime Science*, 4(16): 1–10.

Farrington, D.P. (1986) 'Age and crime', *Crime and justice: a review of research*, 7: 189–250.

Farrington, D.P., Piquero, A.R. and Jennings, W.G. (2013) *Offending from childhood to late middle age: recent results from the Cambridge study in delinquent development.* New York: Springer.

Fazel, S. and Wolf, A. (2015) 'A systematic review of criminal recidivism rates worldwide: current difficulties and recommendations for best practice', *PLOS ONE*, 10(6). doi: 10.1371/journal.pone.0130390

Fernandez-Molina, E., Beneitez, M.J.B. and Bartolome-Gutierrez, R. (2017) Spain. In S.H. Decker and N. Marteache (Eds) *International handbook of juvenile justice* (2nd edn). Switzerland: Springer.

Filipcic, K. and Plesnicar, M.M. (2017) Slovenia. In S.H. Decker and N. Marteache (Eds) *International handbook of juvenile justice* (2nd edn). Switzerland: Springer.

Fuller, E. and Hawkins, V. (2013) *Smoking, drinking and drug use among young people in England in 2013.* London: National Centre for Social Research.

Goldson, B. (2010) 'The sleep of (criminological) reason: knowledge-policy rupture and New Labour's youth justice legacy', *Criminology and Criminal Justice*, 10(2): 155–178.

Gorgen, T., Taefi, A. and Kraus, B. (2013) On nets and how to knot them: juveniles and experts on delinquency and prevention in Germany. In T. Gorgen, B. Kraus, A. Taefi, J.J.B. Beneitez, J. Christiaens, G. Mesko, H. Perista and O. Toth (Eds) *Youth deviance and youth violence: findings from a European study on juvenile delinquency and its prevention.* Munster: YouPrev. www.youprev.eu/pdf/YouPrev_InternationalReport.pdf [Accessed 14 May 2018].

Haddon, L. and Livingstone, S. (2014) The relationship between offline and online risks. In C. von Feilitzen, and J. Stenersen (Eds.) *Young people, media and health: risks and rights.* The Clearinghouse Yearbook 2014. Goteborg: Nordicom.

Hales, J., Nevill, C., Pudney, S. and Tipping, S. (2009) *Longitudinal analysis of the offending, crime and justice survey 2003–06.* Research Report 19. London: Home Office. www.gov.uk/government/uploads/system/uploads/attachment_data/file/116611/horr19-report.pdf [Accessed 14 May 2018].

Herlitz, L., McVie, S., Hough, M. and Murray, K. (2016a) *Understanding and preventing youth crime in England: key findings.* Booklet produced for Schools.

Herlitz, L., McVie, S., Hough, M. and Murray, K. (2016b) *Understanding and preventing youth crime in Scotland: key findings.* Booklet produced for Schools.

HM Inspectorate of Constabulary Scotland (2015) *Audit and assurance review of stop and search: phase 1.* Edinburgh: HM Inspectorate of Constabulary in Scotland.

HM Inspectorate for Prisons in Scotland (2016) Longitudinal inspection of HMYOI www.prisonsinspectoratescotland.gov.uk/publications/longitudinal-inspection-hmyoi-polmont-19-21-april-2016 [Accessed 14 May 2018].

Johnson, B., Golub, A. and Dunlap, E. (2001) The rise and decline of hard drugs, drug markets, and violence in inner city New York. In A. Blumstein and J. Wallman (Eds) *The crime drop in America*. New York: Cambridge University Press.

Kim, J., Bushway, S., and Tsao, H-S. (2015) 'Identifying classes of explanations for crime drop: period and cohort effects for New York state', *Journal of Quantitative Criminology*, 32(3): 357–375.

Levitt, S. (2004) 'Understanding why crime fell in the 1990's: four factors that explain the decline and six that do not', *Journal of Economic Perspectives*, 18(1): 163–190.

Li, Q. (2008) 'Cyberbullying in high schools: A study of students' behaviours and beliefs about this new phenomenon', *Journal of Aggression, Maltreatment and Trauma*, 19(4): 372–392. DOI.org/10.1080/10926771003788979.

Loeber, R. and Farrington, D.P. (2014) Age- crime curve. In G. Bruinsma and D. Weisburd (Eds) *Encyclopedia of criminology and criminal justice*. New York: Springer.

Matthews, B. and Minton, J. (2018) 'The age-crime curve and the crime drop in Scotland', *European Journal of Criminology*, 15(3): 296–320.

Mayhew, P. (2012) The case of Australia and New Zealand. In J. Van Dijk, A. Tseloni and G. Farrell (Eds) *The international crime drop*. Basingstoke: Palgrave Macmillan.

McAra, L. (2010) Models of youth justice. In D. Smith (Ed) *A new response to youth crime*. Cullompton: Willan Publishing.

McAra, L. (2011) The impact of multi-level governance on crime control and punishment. In A. Crawford (Eds) *International and comparative criminal justice and urban governance*. Cambridge: Cambridge University Press.

McAra, L. (2016) 'Can criminologists change the world? Critical reflections on the politics, performance and effects of criminal justice', *British Journal of Criminology*, advance access: doi: 10.1093/bjc/azw015.

McAra, L. (2017) Youth justice. In A. Liebling, S. Maruna, and L. McAra, (Eds) *The Oxford handbook of criminology* (6th edn). Oxford: Oxford University Press.

McAra, L. and McVie, S. (2005) 'The usual suspects? Street-life, young offenders and the police', *Criminal Justice*, 5(1): 5–36.

McAra, L. and McVie, S. (2007) 'Youth justice? The impact of system contact on patterns of desistance from offending', *European Journal of Criminology*, 4(3): 315–345.

McAra, L. and McVie, S. (2010) 'Youth crime and justice: key messages from the Edinburgh study of youth transitions and crime', *Criminology and Criminal Justice*, 10(2): 179–209.

McAra, L. and McVie, S. (2012) 'Negotiated order: towards a theory of pathways into and out of offending', *Criminology and Criminal Justice*, 12(4): 347–376.

McAra, L. and McVie, S. (2015a) The case for diversion and minimum necessary intervention. In B. Goldson and J. Muncie (Eds) *Youth crime and justice* (2nd edn). London: Sage.

McAra, L. and McVie, S. (2015b) 'The reproduction of poverty', *Criminal Justice Matters*, 3(3) (November): 4–5.

McVie, S. (2017) Social order: crime and justice in Scotland. In D. McCrone (ed.) *The new sociology of Scotland*. London: Sage.

Ministry of Justice (2016) *Proven reoffending statistics quarterly bulletin January to December 2014, England and Wales*. London: Ministry of Justice www.gov.uk/government/uploads/system/uploads/attachment_data/file/563185/proven-reoffending-2014.pdf [Accessed 14 May 2018].

Mitchell, K.J., Finkelhor, D., Jones, L.M. and Wolek, J. (2012) 'Prevalence and characteristics of youth sexting: a national study', *Paediatrics*, 129(1):13–20. doi: 10.1542/peds.2011-1730.

Morgan N. (2014) *The heroin epidemic of the 1980's and 1990's and its effect on crime trends – then and now: technical report*. London: Home Office.

Murray, K. (2014) *Stop and search in Scotland: an evaluation of police practice*. SCCJR Report 01/2014. Glasgow: Scottish Centre for Crime and Justice Research.

Newburn., T., (1997) Youth, Crime and Justice. In M. Maguire, R. Morgan, R. Reiner (Eds) *The Oxford handbook of criminology* (2nd edn). Oxford: Clarendon Press, pp. 613–660.

ONS (2015) Crime in England and Wales: Year ending March 2015. www.ons.gov.uk/peoplepopulationandcommunity/crimeandjustice/bulletins/crimeinenglandandwales/2015-07-16#anti-social-behaviour [Accessed 24th March 2017].

ONS (2017) Crime in England and Wales: Year ending Sept 2016. www.ons.gov.uk/peoplepopulationandcommunity/crimeandjustice/bulletins/crimeinenglandandwales/yearendingsept2016 [Accessed 3rd March 2017].

Ouimet, M. (2002) 'Explaining the American and Canadian crime "drop" in the 1990s', *Canadian Journal of Criminology*, 44: 33–50.

Pickett, W. et al. (2013) 'Trends and socioeconomic correlates of adolescent physical fighting in 30 countries', *Paediatrics*, 131(1): 18–26.

Pearson, G. (1983) *Hooligan: a history of respectable fears*. London: MacMillan.

Prison Reform Trust (2013) *Prison: the facts – Bromley Briefings*. London: Prison Reform Trust. www.prisonreformtrust.org.uk/Portals/0/Documents/Prisonthefacts.pdf [Accessed 14 May 2018].

Pruin, I., Aebersold, P. and Weber, J. (2017). Switzerland. In S.H. Decker and N. Marteache (Eds) *International handbook of juvenile Justice* (2nd edn). Switzerland: Springer.

Reyes, J.W. (2007) Environmental policy as social policy? The impact of childhood lead on exposure on crime. National Bureau of Economic Research Working Paper Series: Working paper 13097. Cambridge, MA: NBER. www3.amherst.edu/~jwreyes/papers/LeadCrime.pdf [Accessed 14 May 2018].

Rosenfeld, R. and Messner, S.F. (2009) 'The crime drop in comparative perspective: the impact of the economy and imprisonment on American and European burglary rates', *British Journal of Sociology*, 60(3): 445–471. DOI: 10.1111/j.1468-4446.2009.01251.x.

Rutter, M. and Smith, D.J. (1995) *Psychosocial disorders in young people: time trends and their causes*. Chichester: Wiley.

Sampson, R.J. (2015) 'Crime and the life course in a changing world: Insights from Chicago and implications for global criminology', *Asian Criminology*, 10(4): 277–286.

Sarnecki, J. (2017) Sweden. In S.H. Decker and N. Marteache (Eds) *International handbook of juvenile justice* (2nd edn). Switzerland: Springer.

Scottish Government (2008) *Preventing offending by young people: a framework for action*, www.gov.scot/Resource/Doc/228013/0061713.pdf [Accessed 14 May 2018].

Scottish Government (2015) *Preventing offending: getting it right for children and young people*, www.gov.scot/Resource/0047/00479251.pdf [Accessed 14 May 2018].

Scottish Government (2016a) *Scottish crime and justice survey 2014/15: main findings*. Edinburgh: Scottish Government National Statistics Publication. www.gov.scot/Resource/0049/00496532.pdf

Scottish Government (2016b) *Scottish schools adolescent lifestyle and substance use survey (SALSUS 2015: alcohol summary report)*. www.gov.scot/Resource/0050/00508267.pdf [Accessed 14 May 2018].

Scottish Government (2016c) *Scottish schools adolescent lifestyle and substance use Survey (SALSUS 2015: drugs summary report)*. www.gov.scot/Resource/0050/00508297.pdf [Accessed 14 May 2018].

Scottish Government (2017) *Children's social work statistics Scotland 2015/16*, www.gov.scot/publications/2017/03/6791 [Accessed 14 May 2018].

Seymour, M. (2017) Ireland. In S.H. Decker and N. Marteache (Eds) *International handbook of juvenile justice* (2nd edn). Switzerland: Springer.

Smith, D. (2010) 'Out of care 30 years on', *Criminology and Criminal Justice*, 10 (2): 119–135

Smith, D.J. (1999) 'Less crime without more punishment', *Edinburgh Law Review*, 3 (3): 1–20

Spelman, W. (2000) The limited importance of prison expansion. In A. Blumstein and J. Wallman (Eds) *The crime drop in America*. New York: Cambridge University Press.

Stando-Kawecka, B. (2017) Poland. In S.H. Decker and N. Marteache (Eds) *International handbook of juvenile justice* (2nd edn). Switzerland: Springer.

Storgaard, A. (2017) Denmark. In S.H. Decker and N. Marteache (Eds) *International handbook of juvenile justice* (2nd edn). Switzerland: Springer.

Tonry, M. (2005) 'Why are Europe's crime rates falling?', *Criminology in Europe: Newsletter of the European Society of Criminology*, 4 (2): 1, 3–11.

Tremblay, R.E. and Nagin, D.S. (2005) The developmental origins of physical aggression in humans. In R.E. Tremblay, W.H. Hartup and J. Archer (Eds) *Developmental origins of aggression*. New York: Guilford Press, pp. 83–106.

UK Safer Internet Centre (2016) *Power of image: a report into the influence of images and videos in young people's digital lives*. Report by the UK Safer Internet Centre.

Van Dijk, J., Tseloni, A. and Farrell, G. (2012) *The international crime drop*. Basingstoke: Palgrave Macmillan.

Wikstrom, P-O.H. and Butterworth, D.A. (2006) *Adolescent crime: individual differences and lifestyles*. Cullompton: Willan Publishing.

Youth Justice Board (2016) Youth Justice Board for England and Wales business plan 2016/17. London: YJB. www.gov.uk/ government/ uploads/ system/ uploads/ attachment_ data/ file/ 567003/ yjb- business- plan- 2016-17.pdf [Accessed 14 May 2018].

Zimring, F.E. (2007) *The great American crime decline*. Oxford: Oxford University Press.

6

YOUTH JUSTICE AND YOUTH SANCTIONS IN FOUR NORDIC STATES

Denmark, Finland, Norway and Sweden

Tapio Lappi-Seppälä

Introduction

Youth justice in the Nordic countries (Denmark, Finland, Iceland, Norway and Sweden) is based on a division of labour between child protection and criminal justice. All offenders under the age of 15 years are dealt with only by the child welfare authorities. Young offenders aged 15 to 17 years are dealt with by both the child welfare system and the system of criminal justice. Young adults aged 18 to 20 are dealt with by the criminal justice authorities (and to some extent the child welfare system by providing aftercare).

The functioning of these two systems is based on fundamentally different principles. The principal criterion for all child welfare interventions is the best interests of the child. The welfare system consists of a wide variety of open-care measures, as well as institutional interventions. All interventions are designed to be supportive and criminal acts have little or no formal role in determining the nature of such interventions. Child welfare operates under the social services system.

The criminal justice system, on the other hand, makes little distinction between offenders of different ages. All offenders from the age of 15 years are sentenced in accordance with the same Criminal Code. Strictly speaking, there is no separate juvenile criminal system in the sense in which this concept is usually understood in most other legal systems. There are no Juvenile Courts. Also, the number of specific penalties only applicable to juveniles has been quite limited, albeit growing in number over the past few years.

Nordic youth justice must be seen in the framework of the Nordic Welfare State. It is an integral element of a wider system of universal social services which the state provides to *all* people as an entitlement. It follows that *all* children are covered by this system. Youth justice falls under the child welfare system, but the reach of the child welfare system extends well beyond problems related to youth crime and embraces all elements relevant to the well-being and safe development of the child.

This chapter aims to provide an overview of the reform and implementation of youth sanctions in four selected Nordic states: Denmark, Finland, Norway and Sweden. It sketches major historical phases in the development of the Nordic youth justice model together with a review of law reforms from the 1990s onwards. This is followed by an overview of contemporary sanctions and an analysis of recent sentencing trends and current sentencing practices.[1]

The welfare-based foundations of Nordic youth justice

The foundations for the Nordic model of youth justice were laid down at the turn of the twentieth century when the Nordic countries introduced child protection legislation which granted municipal authorities the right to intervene because of children's behaviour. The first child protection law was passed in Norway in 1896 (*vergårdsloven*) and other Nordic countries followed the model in the early 1900s. Reforms were carried out in 'packages' both in child protection legislation and in criminal law. Children aged below 15 years were dealt with under the child welfare system. Children aged 15–17 years were provided with specific arrangements of non-prosecution and waiver of sentence, which allowed prosecutors to drop charges and the courts to waive the imposition of penalties and to transfer cases to the social welfare authorities. These practices expanded during the 1930s and 1940s, especially in Sweden. In 1952 Sweden adopted a specific sanction, 'transfer to social welfare authorities', with the result than over 70% of all 'offenders' below the age of 18 years were not prosecuted and were instead referred to the social welfare system (Anttila, 1952: 40, Strahl et al., 1955: 265). Other Nordic countries developed similar practices – albeit on a smaller scale – regarding non-prosecution and waiver of sentence.

Other measures targeted especially (but not exclusively) at young offenders included *conditional* imprisonment and suspended sentences, introduced in Norway in 1894, in Denmark in 1904, in Sweden in 1905 and in Finland in 1918.[2] Conditional imprisonment became a major community sanction for juveniles in Denmark, Finland, Norway and Sweden, whereby custodial detention was suspended while children and young people were referred for child welfare interventions by way of transfer orders to 'social care' (*samhällsvård*), organized by the child welfare authorities. Subsequently this sanction evolved into an independent probation-type sanction in the 1965 Criminal Code (*skyddstilsyn*) (see Nordlöf, 2005: 199–200).

Non-prosecution and immediate transfer to child welfare authorities were usually reserved for minor offences, whereas middle-rank offences were typically dealt with by way of conditional and suspended sentences. But more serious offences – and offenders aged 18 years and above – were often still sentenced to adult prisons. This practice came under increasing criticism during the 1920s and 1930s, as models for specific youth prisons started to emerge in continental Europe and England. Finland established a specialist youth prison in 1927 for offenders aged

15–17 years by simply converting a former Reformatory School into a prison. Norway established a 'work-school' for young offenders aged 18–23 years in 1928 (see NOU, 2008: 15–16) and, in 1965, the 'work-school' was transformed into a youth prison (only to be abolished ten years later, see below). In practice Denmark acted as the Nordic forerunner in the development of the specialist youth prison, enacting a new Criminal Code in 1930, although the substantial majority of prisoners were aged 18 years or older while offenders below the age of 18 years were primarily dealt with by social welfare authorities.

Sweden followed the Danish example by passing a new Act on youth prison in 1935 targeted at 18–20-year-olds who could not be treated within the social welfare system. For offenders below the age of 18 years Sweden had already established 'compulsory treatment' in 1902, a penalty imposed under criminal law. During the 1930s and 1940s, however, 'compulsory treatment' was slowly replaced by 'protective treatment' – to be provided by child welfare authorities – and it was finally abolished in 1947, when children aged 15–17 years were ordered to attend 'juvenile treatment schools' operating under the child welfare authorities. Finland enacted a full-scale reform of juvenile justice in 1940 informed by the reforms of the child welfare system in 1936. Prosecutors and the courts were granted extensive rights to waive penal measures to transfer cases for child welfare interventions.

Turning away from institutionalisation and indeterminate sanctions in the 1960s

'Treatment' ideologies prevailed in the Nordic states from the 1930/40s until the late 1960s. Such positions were strongest in the more affluent countries of Sweden and Denmark and weakest in Finland, which had suffered from several wars and socioeconomic and political crises during the first half of the twentieth century.[3] In the 1960s circumstances started to change. The Nordic states experienced heated debates on both the legitimacy and the effects of involuntary 'treatment' in institutions, both penal and otherwise. The relatively widespread use of confinement and compulsory treatment in various institutions (including healthcare and the treatment of alcoholics) was criticized for compromising human rights and for being ineffective. Critical research findings on the negative effects of treatment shifted political priorities from custodial sanctions to community alternatives and to open-care measures.

The 1960/70s witnessed radical reforms in the field of social policy, alcohol policy, healthcare, child welfare and criminal justice policy. Treatment in reformatory schools started to receive increasing public criticism (in Finland) in the mid-1960s. The debates had visible and immediate impact on a range of social practices and, in juvenile justice and child welfare the number of children and young people placed in youth prisons and residential care establishments started to decline from 1966 onwards. In Denmark, for example, up until the mid-1960s youth prison had enjoyed significant support, despite evidence of high recidivism rates (Greve, 1996: 159). Even by the mid-1960s there were well over 400 juveniles in youth prison, corresponding to around 13% of the total Danish prison population (see Betaenkning, 1972/667: 114). But as optimism regarding treatment started to wither away during the 1960s, criticism of institutionalization and indeterminate sanctions, including youth prison, grew stronger. By 1971 the number of juvenile prisoners had fallen to approximately 200 and, in 1973, Denmark completely abolished youth prison together with other forms of indeterminate sanctions. Similarly, in Norway the youth prison, newly established in 1965, was criticized from the outset for excessive severity and for its breach of the proportionality principle (see NOU, 2008/15: 17–18). In 1974, the whole juvenile code was repealed and provisions for youth prison were abolished on the grounds of ineffectiveness (high reoffending rates) and lack of legal safeguards. Similar action was taken in Finland in 1976 and in Sweden in 1979. Overall, a critique of prolonging prison terms on ostensibly 'rehabilitative' grounds gathered momentum and such practices were deemed false and unfounded (SOU, 1977/83: 77–79; Nordlöf, 2005: 195–196).

The abolition of youth prisons in the Nordic states principally reflected doubts about the overall effectiveness of *any form* of custodial 'treatment', alongside an underlying critical attitude towards indeterminate sentences. The main point was that the goal of rehabilitation did not justify the use of custodial sanctions – not to mention prolonged confinement on such grounds – and, besides, the assumptions and hopes about the rehabilitative effects of institutional treatment were either overly optimistic or totally false. The practical results of such reforms varied in each Nordic state, depending on previous conventions, practices and conditions. Finland, for example, with a long history of overuse of imprisonment, witnessed substantial prison reduction and engaged a decisive long-term strategy of decarceration. Its results were visible in a dramatic fall in the use of imprisonment in general, and juvenile imprisonment in particular, from the mid-1960s onwards (Lappi-Seppälä, 2009). Figure 6.1 illustrates the downward trends in the number of juvenile prisoners from 1975 to 2015, both in real terms (numbers) and as a proportion (%) of the total prison population. In the age group 15–17 years, the number of prisoners fell from 120 in 1975 to 5–10 from the mid-1990s onwards or, in proportionate terms,

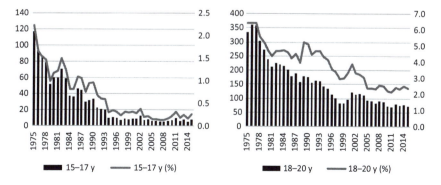

FIGURE 6.1 Prisoners aged 15–17 years and 18–20 years in Finland, 1975–2015

from over 2% of the total prison population to approximately 0.2%. Similarly, the number of young adults (aged 18–20 years) declined from over 350 in 1975 to below 100 for most of the period from the late 1990s onwards, falling to approximately 60 in 2015 (from over 6% of the total prison population to approximately 2.5% over the same period).

Nordic youth justice reforms from the 1990s

The decline of the 'rehabilitative ideal' – and the emerging penal neo-classicism (which arose especially in Finland) – did not entail increasing penal severity in the Nordic states. In the USA and the UK, the post-rehabilitative period was characterized by disciplined penal practices, increased control and, eventually, dramatically growing imprisonment rates. In Finland, the outcome was very much the opposite. The new Finnish sanction ideology – 'humane neo-classicism' – stressed the general requirement of humanizing the sanction system, as well as upholding respect for legal safeguards. The legacy of the 1960s liberal critique expressed itself by way of bolstering an appreciation for legal safeguards and energizing an inherently critical approach towards the use of imprisonment in general, and especially the penal detention of children and young people.

Youth justice reform in Nordic states after the turn of the 1960s has been consistent in its efforts to reduce the use of unconditional prison sentences for children and young people. This overarching trend is visible in several reforms. Each Nordic state has established legal barriers to the use of unconditional prison sentences. In the late 1980s, for example, both Sweden and Finland included provisions in their Criminal Codes that served to restrict the courts powers to impose unconditional prison sentences for offenders below the age of 18 years. Such powers were reserved exclusively for 'special' or 'extraordinary' cases. Similar provisions were integrated into the Norwegian Code in 2005.[4] Denmark, however, lacks the corresponding restriction. Other reforms have introduced community alternatives designed to replace prison sentences while, at the same time, in the limited number of cases where penal detention applies, 'ordinary' prison sentences have been substituted by more refined and specialist custodial penalties. The following provides an overview of some of the major reforms in each of the four Nordic states under consideration.

Developing new community alternatives

Finland 1994: An additional step between conditional and unconditional prison sentences. In 1994 Finland started an experiment with a new non-residential juvenile penalty (made permanent in 2004). The main aim of the reform was to provide an intermediate step between conditional and unconditional prison sentences, and thereby to delay the transition between community sentences and prison sentences. The target group for the reform were offenders with previous conditional sentences and who thereby were at greatest risk of next being sentenced to an unconditional prison sentence. The sanction required clearly-defined social and re-integrative goals and enforcement was arranged in cooperation with the Social Welfare Board. The order is defined by programmes developed by the Probation Service and the social welfare authorities. At the point of implementation, the estimated scope of nationwide application was around 300 cases each year. However, the first year following implementation approximately only 100 penalties in five district courts were imposed after which time the numbers declined incrementally until they reached the present level of around five to ten cases each year. The 'failure' of this sanction is sometimes associated with the strict requirement of issuing this sentence only for high-risk cases, either because there are very few such cases or, such high-risk cases as there are, are deemed to be too demanding/serious for such a penalty. Another, perhaps more plausible explanation, is that juveniles otherwise suitable for this sanction are usually already engaged with the Child Welfare system – possibly even placed in child welfare institutions – and in such cases, there is little, if anything, that juvenile punishment can add, at least from a rehabilitative point of view.

Denmark 1998: Smarter (and quicker) sanctions in the form of juvenile contracts. In 1998 Denmark introduced a specific Youth Contract as a special condition attached to the withdrawal of charges (non-prosecution). The aim was/is to introduce a quicker and more proportionate response for children and young people who had no substantial criminal record. The sanction includes a signed contract between the parties (offender, parents, social services and the police) for activities to be taken during the period of, usually, one year. On the offenders' part the contract includes a standard condition of not re-offending within the agreed time and obligations to participate in certain activities, for instance to complete school and to engage with a social training programme. If the juvenile fulfils the conditions of the contract within the specified time, the charge is deleted from his or her criminal record one year after the contract was signed (Egge, 2004; Storgaard, 2013). Shortly after the introduction of the Youth Contract the number of contracts issued varied between 200–250 per year but, from 2007 the number fell below 100 and it currently stands at about 20–30.

Norway 2002: Community service (punishment) for juveniles. Norway started experimenting with community service in 1984 (after Denmark in 1981). In 1991 community service became a permanent part of the general sanction system to be used instead of short-term prison sentences. In 2002 community service was renamed 'community punishment' as part of a wider reform of criminal justice (Andenæs, 2004: 411). In the younger age groups, the new sanction was aimed at the replacement, not only of prison sentences, but also previously used combinations of conditional imprisonment with supervision. Subsequently the Norwegian legislator has on several occasions stressed the aim to increase the use of community punishment as a replacement for both prison sentences and unsupervised conditional imprisonment (see for example Ot.prp. nr. 5 2000–2001: 126).

Sweden 2007: Providing social services under the criminal justice framework. Up until 2007 the main sanction for children and young people aged 15–17 years in Sweden was transfer to the Social Welfare Board. The system had been criticized for its lack of transparency, proportionality and consistency. It was also deemed that child welfare was receiving clients who in reality were not in need of the kind of support and treatment that the services could provide. To overcome these difficulties, the transfer order was divided into two separate sanctions in 2007. *Youth Care* is a court order for offenders under the age of 21 years that obliges the Social Welfare Board to take actions that promote the young offender's future social development and re-integration. *Youth Service* consists of unpaid work for 20–150 hours and attendance in programmes of employment or education. It is mainly targeted at offenders below the age of 18 years. Taken together the 2007 reforms had the effect of increasing the number of imposed youth sanctions in the age group 15–17 years from 2,775 in 2006 to 4,216 in 2008. This increase was accompanied by a corresponding *reduction* in the number of fines from 6,350 in 2006 to 5,516 in 2008 which was a principal aim of the reforms.

Creating alternatives to (conventional forms of) custody

A second set of reforms concerned more direct initiatives to replace conventional prison sentences with other alternatives for children and young people.

Denmark 1973 and 2001: Serving the sentence in an alternative manner. Denmark adopted in 1973 a system of 'serving a sentence in an alternative manner'. This entailed the opportunity to apply the custodial sentence outside prison: in hospital, family care or in an appropriate alternative institution if the 'prisoner' needed special treatment. This option gained wider application in the course of the 1990s, after Denmark ratified the UN Convention on the Rights of the Child in 1991 (Kyvsgaard, 2004: 372). Since 2001 all convicted offenders under the age of 18 years have been required to serve their 'prison' sentences in an alternative manner, unless special reasons, such as the perceived 'dangerousness' of the young offender, require otherwise (ibid). These sentences are usually served either in secure child welfare institutions or in specific 'pensions' (boarding houses). The latter are small units administered by the Department of Corrections. In addition, there is one prison with 80 cells dedicated for young men up to the age of 23 years and women of all ages (Storgaard, 2009).

In 2001 Denmark also introduced a new half-residential Youth Sanction. This reform was triggered by a sequence of serious offences committed by young offenders (Kyvsgaard, 2004: 373; Storgaard, 2009: 382). The sanction is designed for juveniles with a more substantial criminal career. It is imposed by the courts but administered by the social welfare authorities. The sanction consists of three phases which when combined last for two years in total. Following a period in secure accommodation the offender is placed in an open residential institution. Both the secure and open forms of accommodation are managed by the Social Welfare System. The sanction is designed to be used instead of prison sentences for offenders below the age of 18 years at the time the offence was committed. Even if the sanction is not defined as imprisonment, however, the restrictions on liberty and the powers of the institution staff are, especially in secure accommodation, not unlike those of a prison (Storgaard, 2009). Moreover, during the first years of implementation the annual number of youth sanctions gravitated around 100 sentences, three times more than the drafters anticipated (Vestergaard, 2004: 74). Secure confinement normally extended to two months (in over 70% of cases), and placements in open units extended for at least six months.

The Youth Sanction combines punishment (criminal justice) with treatment (health and welfare). It has received severe scholarly criticism due to its lack of consistency, predictability and proportionality. It has been characterized as a 'punishment in disguise' (Storgaard, 2009: 387–390) and the critique derives from concerns that were first expressed in the1960s: the criminal justice system should not make unfounded and unrealistic promises; punishment should be predictable and proportionate; the controlling (punitive) and rehabilitative (welfare and treatment) functions of intervention should be separate and applied in ways that are demonstrably appropriate, legitimate and effective.

Sweden 1999: Replacing imprisonment with Secure Youth Care. If Denmark addressed the obligations required to comply with the United Nations Convention on the Rights of the Child (particularly the separation of juveniles from adult prisoners) by placing juveniles sentenced to prison in small hostels, the Swedish response was to introduce, in 1999, a new sanction called Secure Youth Care.[5] Secure Youth Care is enforced not by the prison administration, but by the Swedish National Board of Institutional Care (*States institutionsstyrelse*, abbreviated SIS).[6] Secure Youth Care can be used only in cases where the young offender would have otherwise been sentenced to prison. The enforcement of Secure Youth Care takes place in juvenile homes designed to provide involuntary treatment. Six homes, with a total capacity of 68 places, receive juveniles sentenced to Secure Youth Care. The enforcement of Secure Youth Care starts in a closed unit and, in the course of time, the juvenile is moved into a more open environment.

Secure Youth Care has also received criticism. The aim of the 1999 reform was neither to increase nor to decrease the use of custodial sentences for young offenders. During the drafting stage, it was assumed that there would be a need for about ten places. Shortly after implementation, however, the annual number of sentences reached over 100, a clear sign of net-widening. Not only had the number of custodial sentences increased but the sentences had also become longer. A comparison between 1990–1998 and 1999–2000 indicates that the average length of sentences for offenders aged between 15–17 years increased from 6.6 to 9.2 months (including both 'pure' prison sentences and combinations of probation and imprisonment). Indeed, critics pointed out that Secure Youth Care increased the number of imposed custodial sentences from the previous level of around 30–40 prison sentences to over 100 (Kühlhorn, 2002: 56). Since the peak years, however, the number of sentences has more recently fallen back to around 40 per year.[7] But the separation of punishment under the criminal law and treatment under the child welfare authorities has become more blurred by the fact that juveniles placed under Secure Youth Care may also be placed under involuntary care after the completion of their sentence, should there be 'a clear need to continue the treatment' in order to provide for the perceived well-being and health of the juveniles (see Care of Young Persons Special Provisions

Act 3.2 §, 1990: 52). Thus, in practice the final outcome resembles the indeterminate juvenile sentences that were abolished in the 1970s.

Norway 2014: Replacing youth imprisonment with restorative justice and social work. In 2014 Norway enacted two new specific sanctions for offenders aged 15–17 years: 'Juvenile punishment' (*Ungdomsstraff*) and 'Juvenile follow-up' (*Ungdomsoppfølging*) (Penal Code section 37 and section 52a; criminal procedure section 71a). The stated aim of the reforms was to reduce the use of prison sentences for offenders below the age of 18 years and also to address the criticism that Norway had received from the European Committee for the Prevention of Torture and Inhuman and Degrading Treatment or Punishment (CPT) in 2011 for placing children (those under the age of 18 years) in prisons. 'Juvenile punishment' is to be used for serious offences (with a maximum penalty of three years or more), or in cases of recidivism (for less serious offences). Consent of the offender is required, and the court fixes the length of sentence (from six months to two years). 'Juvenile follow-up' is a more lenient sanction that may be attached as a requirement for conditional imprisonment or a conditional fine.

Both 'Juvenile punishment' and 'Juvenile follow-up' sanctions are underpinned by restorative principles and enforcement powers are given to the Conflict-Counsels. The content of the sanction is decided in a mediation meeting with a large number of actors including representatives from schools, child welfare and healthcare agencies and the local municipality, alongside the police and the probation service. The first part of the meeting consists of a regular mediation process, following the rules confirmed in the Mediation Act. During the latter part of the meeting, a specific youth plan is drafted to guide the enforcement. The plan includes a variety of measures aimed to give the young offender firmer frames for his/her life. As described in the preparatory works, the aim was to replace the 'physical walls of the prison with social walls' of the community. No data is available pertaining to the extent to which the sanctions have been able to replace prison sentences. However, the latest annual reports from prison services indicate that young people below the age of 18 years have practically disappeared from Norwegian prisons as the figures in Table 6.1 illustrate (Kriminalomsorgen, 2015: 39).

Critics, on the other hand, have directed attention to the wide and uncontrolled discretion of the Conflict-Counsels in designing the contents of the sanctions, as well as the fact that by giving his/her consent to the sanction the offender loses his/her right to appeal against the court's decision (Holmboe, 2016a).

TABLE 6.1 Children (aged below 18 years) admitted to prisons in Norway 2007–2015

	2007	*2008*	*2009*	*2010*	*2011*	*2012*	*2013*	*2014*	*2015*
Remanded	44	45	74	45	53	46	27	26	24
Sentenced	11	20	14	19	5	5	0	1	0
Total	55	65	88	64	58	51	27	27	24

An overview of contemporary non-custodial sanctions in the Nordic states

The overview of contemporary sanctions is divided into two compartments: out-of-court measures and court-imposed sanctions.

Out-of-court sanctions

Summary fines. In each of the Nordic states under consideration, summary fines are imposed both by the police and by prosecutors. The police normally issue summary fines for minor traffic offences. Prosecutors tend to impose summary fines in cases when the offence – if taken to court – would likely be dealt with by the imposition of a fine (at most). Prosecutor's fines are imposed as day-fines in Finland, as day-fines or fixed fines in Sweden and as fixed fines in Denmark and Norway.

Diversion and non-prosecution. The same Nordic states provide opportunities for diversion both at the level of pre-investigation (non-reporting or warning by the police) and, arguably more significantly, at the level of prosecution (non-prosecution). Non-prosecution[8] appears in both conditional and unconditional form. Conditional non-prosecution – which is commonly used in Norway – carries conditions which must be met, otherwise the case might be taken to court (rendering it similar to a suspended sentence). In Denmark both conditional and unconditional forms of non-prosecution are applied, whereas in Sweden and Finland, non-prosecution decisions are exclusively unconditional. Under the legality principle (applied in Finland and Sweden but not in Denmark and Norway) non-prosecution is possible only for reasons defined by law. The main grounds relate to the petty nature of the offence and the young age of the offender (under the age of 18 years). Non-prosecution can also be based on reasons of equity or criminal policy expediency.

Mediation. In 1981, Norway was the first Nordic state to experiment with mediation. Finland followed suit in 1983, Sweden in 1987 and Denmark in 1998. Norway was also the first country to expand the system nationwide by passing a law on mediation in 1991 (the Act on 'Conflict Counsels'), followed by the other states: Sweden in 2002; Finland in 2006 and Denmark in 2010.[9] Mediation has the most 'official role' in Norway, where it serves to divert cases automatically from the criminal justice system. In the other countries, the processing of the case is left to the discretion of the prosecutor. In Finland and Sweden, establishing an agreement or settlement between the offender and the victim provides possible grounds for non-prosecution or waiving or mitigating punishment by the court. In Denmark, the role and the practical relevance of mediation has remained more restricted. Mediation is normally co-ordinated by social welfare authorities and is based on voluntary work in all four states. Participation in mediation is necessarily voluntary for all parties involved.

Mediation gained widespread implementation in Finland and Norway in the 1990s. Today the annual number of offenders attending mediation comes close to 12,000 in Finland and around 8,000 in Norway. The number of juveniles aged

15–17 years attending mediation hovers at around 3,000 per year in both countries, while the annual number of offenders in that age group sentenced in criminal courts (traffic offences excluded) stands at around 7,500. In other words, the annual number of juveniles aged 15–17 years attending mediation comprises about 30–40% of all criminal justice disposals in that age group. The clear majority of cases involve either minor property offences or minor forms of assault. Since the enactment of national mediation laws, the number of referrals has increased also in Sweden but less so in Denmark (Lappi-Seppälä and Storgaard, 2015).

Court-ordered sanctions

Court ordered sanctions can further be divided into *general sanctions* (applicable to all offenders) and *specific sanctions* (limited to children and young people below the age of 18 years and, in some cases, to young people aged 18–20 years).[10] General sanctions include:

- Fines
- Conditional imprisonment and suspended sentences
- Community service
- Probation and treatment orders
- Electronic monitoring

Specific sanctions include:

- Juvenile Punishment (in Finland)
- Youth Care and Youth Service (in Sweden)
- Juvenile Punishment and Juvenile Follow-up (in Norway)

Fines. Fines are the most commonly used penalty in all Nordic states. Denmark, Finland and Sweden (but not Norway) impose fines as day-fines (a system first adopted in the 1920s and 1930s). The day-fine system aims to ensure proportionality of the fine for offenders of different income levels. The *number* of day-fines is determined on the basis of the seriousness of the offence while the *amount* of a day-fine depends upon the individual financial circumstances of the offender. Such fines are normally applied as sole principal sanctions although they can also be combined with other alternatives, most often with conditional sentences but sometimes also with unconditional imprisonment (see below). Attitudes towards fines as penalties for juveniles vary across the Nordic states under consideration. Norwegian and Swedish legislators, in particular, have taken a very critical view towards the use of fines for children and young people. In Norway, the legislature proposed to replace fines with more 'purposeful' (*hensiktsmessige*) sanctions, such as conditional non-prosecution and mediation (see Prop 135 2010/11: 90–91) and in Sweden one of the core aims of the youth justice reforms in 2007 was to reduce the use of fines.

Conditional imprisonment and suspended sentences. The lower end of the community punishments consists of conditional imprisonment or suspended sentences. In Finland, the court imposes the sentence but postpones its enforcement contingent upon the probation period, whereas in Sweden the court postpones the pronouncement of the sentence to allow for the probation period. In Denmark and Norway both options are in use although the postponement of enforcement (conditional imprisonment/sentence) is more common. Conditional imprisonment can also be combined with supervision, fines, community service or – in Denmark and Norway – prison. In Denmark and Norway, the sentence may also be attached with different conditions, such as obliging the offender to participate in rehabilitative programmes or mediation, to pay compensation to the victim or to report regularly to the police. In Sweden, the suspended sentence can be combined with fines or with community service.

Community service. Community service appears in different forms across the Nordic states. In Finland and Norway community service comprises an independent sanction (although in 2001 Norway renamed community service 'community punishment'). In Denmark and Sweden community service is attached either to conditional imprisonment or to a probation order. In Finland, long (over one year) conditional prison sentences may be combined with a short (20–60 hour) community service order. In Denmark community service can also be combined with fines and unconditional imprisonment. In addition, community service may be attached with separate conditions concerning residence, school attendance or work. The maximum number of community service hours varies from 240 (Finland) to 420 (Norway).

Probation and treatment orders. Sweden is the only Scandinavian country with a separate probation type of sanction. *Probation* ('protective supervision', *skyddstilsyn*) means a period of three years in which the sentenced person is supervised during the first year. Probation may be used alone (simple probation) or attached to fines or a short prison sentence (14 days to three months). It may also be combined with a treatment order and with community service. *Contract treatment (kontraktsvård)* is targeted primarily at long-term substance misusers when there is a demonstrable link between the misuse of substances and offending. A contract is made between the court and the offender regarding the nature of treatment that can last between six months and two years. Part of the treatment takes place in an institution although treatment is always voluntary (but, in reality, the choice is limited to either complying with the treatment contract or going to prison).

Electronic monitoring. During the 2000s all four Nordic states included electronic monitoring as a part of sanctions systems and sentence enforcement, both in front-door (prior-to-prison custody) and back-door (post-prison custody) versions. Each of the countries apply electronic monitoring as a condition of extended early release from prison. Electronic monitoring may also be used as a replacement for prison sentences. Models in front door-version applications vary. In Sweden, Norway and Denmark, prison sentences are converted to electronic monitoring by the decisions of enforcement authorities. In Finland, the decision is taken by the courts, following the model used in connection with community service. In all countries, electronic monitoring is designed to replace short-term prison sentences, usually below six months.

Finland – Juvenile Punishment. The Finnish juvenile punishment is a 4–12-month long community sanction comparable in severity to conditional imprisonment for offenders under the age of 18 years at the time of the offence. The length of the sanction is determined by the court, whereas the detailed content is set by the Probation Service. Violations of the enforcement plan can lead to reprimands or to the case being returned to the court by the prosecutor. In such cases, the court may elect to extend the period of supervision, convert the sentence into fines or conditional imprisonment or, in more serious cases, to impose a sentence of unconditional imprisonment.

Sweden – Youth Care and Youth Service. Youth Care is a court order applied to offenders below the age of 21 years. It obliges the Social Welfare Board to take actions that promote the young offender's future social development and reintegration. It may include both voluntary and/or involuntary treatment. Youth Care can replace a prison sentence up to one year. Youth Service is targeted mainly at offenders between the ages 15 and 17 years. It consists of unpaid work for 20–150 hours plus engagement in programmes of employment or education. Youth Service and Youth Care are deemed to represent the same level of sentence severity and are contingent upon the perceived need for treatment. Youth Care is reserved for offenders who are deemed to need treatment and programme work. The upper limit for the use of Youth Service as a replacement for imprisonment is approximately 6 months (Borgeke, 2008: 405–409).

Norway – Juvenile Punishment and Juvenile Follow-up. In Norway community punishment is a hybrid sentence containing elements drawn from conventional forms of community service and supervision orders. The new Juvenile Punishment, however, is an interesting and seemingly unique combination of restorative justice and traditional social work designed as an alternative to prison sentences or, in some cases, instead of community punishment. As discussed earlier, Juvenile Follow-up' is a more lenient sanction that may be attached as a requirement for conditional imprisonment or a conditional fine.

Current trends in Nordic sentencing practices

We can now turn to an analysis of sentencing practices in three different respects: first, sentencing trends regarding children and young people aged 15–17 years over the period 2005–2014/16; second, the use of different custodial sanctions over a longer period in relation to the same age group of children and young people; third, a cross-sectional comparative analysis of present practices in respect of all sanctions.

The graphs reveal declining trends in juvenile sanctions in each of the Nordic states over the decade from 2005,[11] although specific country profiles show some differences. For example, Finland imposes more fines than any of its neighbours

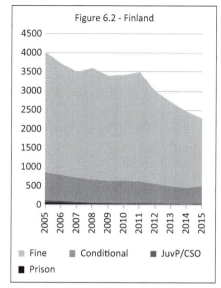

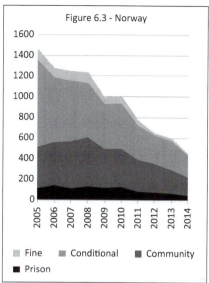

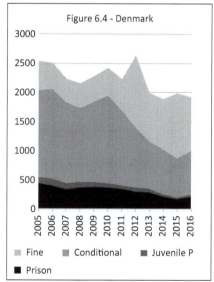

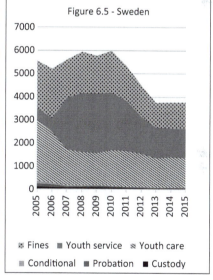

FIGURES 6.2–6.5 Sentencing trends 2005–2014/16 – offenders aged 15–17 years (absolute numbers)

whereas Norway makes minimal use of financial sanctions. Another major difference relates to the use of unconditional imprisonment. While this option is barely visible in the Finnish and the Swedish graphs, it is significantly more prevalent in the Danish and Norwegian states (although still conspicuously low compared to many other jurisdictions in Europe).

Figure 6.6 displays trends in the absolute numbers (n) of imposed prison sentences on 15–17-year-olds over the period 1990–2016 and Figure 6.7 illustrates corresponding trends in respect of custodial sanctions as a proportion (%) of all sentences imposed by the courts.[12]

The longest data series available are from Finland and Denmark. Trends from the early 1990s to the mid-2000s point in opposite directions. Finland reduced the number of imposed prison sentences from 350 to around 50, whereas Denmark quintupled the number of prison sentences from little over 100 in 1990 to 550 in 2006 (almost tripling in a period of just a few years in the early 2000s). The major explanation for this is the overall increase in the number of convicted juveniles in Denmark. This is also reflected in the increased use of community sanctions (from 800 to 1500) in the same period but the increase in the number of juvenile convictions imposed its most dramatic effect in terms of the rise in unconditional prison sentences. Also, the share of prison sentences as a proportion of all court-imposed sanctions increased from 14% in 2000 to 22% in 2005 in Denmark, a trend that might be accounted for by changing sentencing practices pertaining to violent and property offences.[13]

Since 2005, however, the absolute numbers of prison sentences imposed on 15–17-year-olds have displayed a *downward trend* in all four countries. After increases in the period 2000–2006, Denmark more than halved the number of prison sentences. Similar declines in absolute numbers are also visible in Finland, Norway and Sweden, even if relative shares (as a percentage of all court convictions) have remained more stable (especially in Norway).

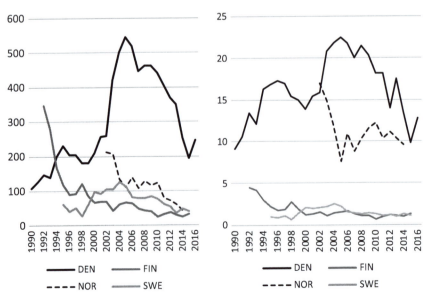

FIGURES 6.6–6.7 Custodial sanctions 1990–2016: offenders aged 15–17 years – absolute numbers (n) and custodial sanctions as a proportion (%) of all sentences

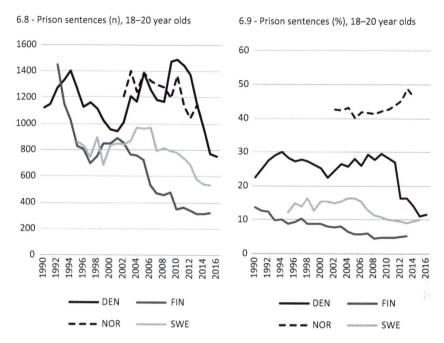

6.8 - Prison sentences (n), 18–20 year olds

6.9 - Prison sentences (%), 18–20 year olds

FIGURES 6.8–6.9 Custodial sanctions 1990–2016: offenders aged 18–20 years – absolute numbers (n) and custodial sanctions as a proportion (%) of all sentences

Not dissimilar to the patterning of prison sentences for children and young people aged 15–17 years, declining trends in prison sentences for young people aged 18–20 years are evident in all countries in recent years (see Figures 6.8–6.9). This is most dramatic in Finland where the number of prison sentences for young people aged 18–20 years decreased from over 1400 in 1990, to approximately 800 in the early 2000s to little over 300 in 2015. Although absolute numbers of prison sentences have dipped in Norway – from a high of approximately 1400 in 2002, to a low of approximately 900 in 2014 – custodial sanctions as a proportion (%) of all sentences imposed by the courts have essentially remained stable notwithstanding an increase in the period 2012–14.

Comparing sanctioning practices across Nordic states 2014–16: offenders aged 15–17 years and 18–20 years

To produce exact comparisons between the Nordic states, the figures need to be calculated relative to the population in each age group. The following provides a cross-sectional overview of the use of different pre-court sanctioning practices pertaining to the age groups 15–17 years and 18–20 years over the period 2014–2016.[14]

Out-of-court sanctions: Non-prosecutions and summary fines

Minor offences are dealt with by non-prosecution and summary fines. Table 6.2 displays the number of non-prosecutions and prosecutorial summary fines relative

TABLE 6.2 Non-prosecutions and summary fines (per 100,000 population in each age group): offenders aged 15–17 years and 18–20 years (2014–16)

	Denmark 2016	Finland 2015	Norway 2014	Sweden 2015
15–17 years (all court disposals)	**(911)**	**(1187)**	**(240)**	**(987)**
Non-prosecution	68	453	862	838
Summary fines (prosecutor imposed)	1171	4489	363	468
18–20 years (all court disposals)	**(3324)**	**(3038)**	**(1093)**	**(1332)**
Non-prosecution	110	317	305	364
Summary fines (prosecutor imposed)	5152	8489	4463	941

to age groups 15–17 years and 18–20 years (with the total number of all court disposals for each age group presented in brackets). The data are presented relative to 100,000 population in each age group.

Non-prosecution has the widest application in the age group 15–17 years in Norway and Sweden (800+ cases relative to 100,000 population). Finland (453 cases), deploys non-prosecution just over half as often as Norway and Sweden, whereas non-prosecution is used significantly less often in Denmark (68 cases). In the 18–20 years age group practices in Finland, Norway and Sweden are very similar and, again, Denmark is something of an outlier.

Differences between the countries in respect of the use of fines are more marked, especially in the age group 15–17years. Finland imposes many more fines compared to the other Nordic states. Similar, although less acute, differences are also visible in the age group 18–20 years.

Notwithstanding such differences, however, the substantial majority of juvenile (15–17 years) cases are dealt with by way of summary proceedings in each of the countries evidencing a notable emphasis on diversionary policies and practices.

Court-ordered sanctions (alternatives to prison)

To simplify the comparative analysis for present purposes, court-ordered sanctions are grouped into four categories:

- 'Prison' includes all *conditional* prison sentences (and combinations) including 'Youth Sanction' (Denmark) and 'Secure Youth Care' (Sweden).
- 'Community' includes all combinations with community service (except those with prison), including 'Juvenile Punishment' in Finland and 'Youth Service' and 'Youth Care' in Sweden.
- 'Conditional' includes simple conditional sentences, as well as those attached with fines and/or supervision, suspended sentences, and probation (in Sweden).
- 'Fines' includes only court-imposed fines and excludes prosecutor-imposed (summary) fines.

The data are presented relative to 100,000 population in each age group (penalty rates) and as percentages (penalty shares) of all court disposals (see Figures 6.10–6.13).

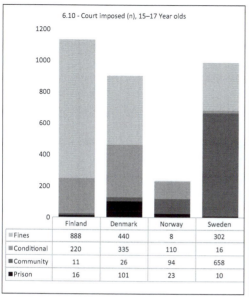
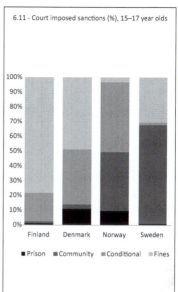

	Finland	Denmark	Norway	Sweden
Fines	888	440	8	302
Conditional	220	335	110	16
Community	11	26	94	658
Prison	16	101	23	10

FIGURES 6.10–6.11 Court-imposed sanctions (alternatives to prison): offenders aged 15–17 years – absolute numbers (n – per 100,000 population) and as a proportion (%) of all sentences (2014–16)

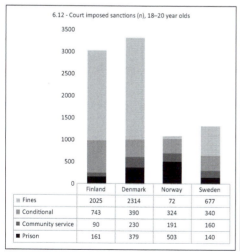
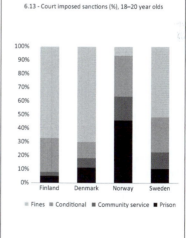

	Finland	Denmark	Norway	Sweden
Fines	2025	2314	72	677
Conditional	743	390	324	340
Community service	90	230	191	160
Prison	161	379	503	140

FIGURES 6.12–6.13 Court-imposed sanctions (alternatives to prison): offenders aged 18–20 years – absolute numbers (n – per 100,000 population) and as a proportion (%) of all sentences (2014–16)

Over the period 2014–16, court-ordered fines are the standard sanctions for offenders aged 15–17 years in both Finland and Denmark, accounting for 78% and 48% of all sentences respectively. In Sweden fines are used in just under one in three cases (30%), whereas Norway makes minimal use of this sanction.

Not unlike sentencing practices concerning children and young people ages 15–17 years, for offenders aged 18–20 years court-imposed fines are the most commonly applied sanction in Finland and Denmark and, to a substantial but lesser extent, Sweden. Again, financial penalties are imposed significantly less often in Norway. penalty in the 18–20 age group in Finland, Denmark and Sweden (from 50% to around 70%).

Custodial sanctions

Combining both age groups, both Denmark and Norway impose substantially more prison sentences than Finland and Sweden. This is most likely accounted for by the tendency in the former countries to impose very short-term prison sentences.[15] When compared with other European jurisdictions, however, the Nordic states are exceptionally parsimonious in respect of custodial sentencing – especially the penal detention of juveniles (aged 15–17 years) – although account should also be taken of children and young people who have their liberty restricted in 'child care' establishments (Lappi-Seppälä, 2011: 243–254).

TABLE 6.3 Custodial sanctions: offenders aged 15–17 years★ and 18–20 years★ – absolute numbers (n – per 100,000 population) (2014–16)

	Denmark	Finland	Norway	Sweden
Offenders aged 15–17 years				
Custodial sanctions (totals)	**101**	**16**	**22**	**11**
Imprisonment	45	16	14	1
Combinations	34	..	8	0
Juvenile Punishment/Secure Youth Care	17	..	..	10
Offenders aged 18–20 years				
Custodial sanctions (totals)	**379**	**161**	**503**	**140**
Imprisonment	268	161	278	123
Combinations	101	..	225	14
Juvenile Punishment/Secure Youth Care	0	..	..	3
All custodial sanctions (15–20 years)	**480**	**177**	**525**	**151**

★ In Denmark, Finland and Norway ages apply to the point at which the offence was committed, in Sweden ages apply to the point at which the sentence was imposed.

Concluding remarks

The Nordic states under consideration here have been exceptionally successful in their determination to restrict the use of imprisonment for children and young people. At any given time, the number of juvenile prisoners has fallen from the higher levels of the 1960s to close to zero today. Sanctions that are applied to juveniles in criminal proceedings principally comprise either out-of-court non-prosecutions and summary fines, or social-work oriented community-based interventions centred around support, treatment, supervision, education and training. In these senses, the Nordic states share a progressive orientation to juvenile justice.

On closer inspection, however, some differences between the countries become evident. Even after considering the substantial reduction in the number of custodial sentences imposed on children and young people in recent years, Denmark continues to detain more 15–17 years than her neighbours. Equally, although Norway has reduced the number of prison sentences imposed on young people aged 15–17 years, imprisonment is significantly more conspicuous in the 18–20 years age group (as is also the case in Denmark). But such patterning must be understood and interpreted in a wider inter-jurisdictional context within which practices in all the Nordic countries remain progressive and where the penal detention of children and young people continues to be the lowest in Europe.

Each of the Nordic states considered here, continues to follow the dualistic models adopted in the early 1900s in which a division of labour pertains between child welfare and juvenile justice, albeit with some modifications. There are, of course, differences in emphasis. The co-operation between child welfare and juvenile justice has traditionally been strongest in Sweden where 'custodial' sentences for 'offenders' aged 15–17 years are normally served in secure child welfare institutions (as is mostly also the case in Denmark), and where community supervision (alternatives) is operationalized by social services. Finland (and partly Norway), on the other hand, is more consistent in its efforts to separate 'punishment' and 'treatment' and child welfare institutions have no role in the execution of sanctions imposed via the juvenile justice system. Both approaches have their advantages as well as their problems. Removing welfare-based and/or rehabilitative elements from juvenile justice – should that ever have been the intention – runs counter to the social welfare state ideology itself that is so deeply embedded across the Nordic states. On the other hand, including child welfare agencies (especially residential institutions) in the enforcement of juvenile justice sanctions runs the risk of net-widening and, ultimately, increased reliance on (closed) institutional interventions. Institutions that claim to uphold 'the best interests of the child' are harder to resist: thresholds for imposing 'custodial' sanctions in institutions that are ostensibly designed to provide 'socio pedagogic treatment' may well be lower than those that obtain in the case of more conventional penal detention. The question of trans-institutionalisation – spanning juvenile justice, child welfare, education and health – merits closer attention.

So, while the progressive nature of Nordic juvenile justice is noteworthy, there is a clear need for a research agenda that approaches 'welfare' institutions from a critical perspective – in the 'spirit of the 1960s' – with an emphasis on legal security, procedural justice, children's rights and the underpinning principle of minimum necessary intervention. The foundational critique of 'treatment' ideology persists: 'welfare' and 'care' may well convert to 'punishment', especially seen through the eyes of children and young people themselves. Beyond questions of principle, actual effect-analyses – comparing outcomes between different child welfare interventions and traditional juvenile justice responses – are also largely missing in this complex and contested field (Vinnerljung and Sallnäs, 2008).

Notes

1 The chapter is informed by some of my earlier work (see Lappi-Seppälä, 2011; 2015) but it is substantially extended and revised to include up-to-date statistical information and to take account of recent legislative changes. I am grateful for the comments received from Anette Storgaard and Michael Tärnfalk.

2 Sentences of imprisonment of no more than two years can be imposed as a *conditional sentence* in cases where there are no reasons – such as previous offences – that require the court to impose an *unconditional* sentence of penal detention. When the custodial sentence is conditional, the enforcement of the punishment is postponed for a probationary period of at least one year and at most three years. A supplementary fine may also be imposed in tandem with conditional imprisonment and, if the probationary period is over one year long, community service may also be imposed. *Unconditional* imprisonment refers to a sentence served in prison.

3 For more detailed accounts of the historical events that influenced and redirected penal development in Finland from 1918 to 1945 see Lappi-Seppälä, 2009 and von Hofer and Lappi-Seppälä, 2013.

4 Backup for these reforms was received from the United Nations Convention on the Rights of the Child. See Article 37b '… The arrest, detention or imprisonment of a child … shall be used only as a measure of last resort and for the shortest appropriate period of time', and Article 37c '… every child deprived of liberty shall be separated from adults unless it is considered in the child's best interest not to do so…'.

5 Secure Youth Care Act 1998: 603.

6 SIS is responsible for the administration of all involuntary treatment provided in institutional settings, including the treatment of children placed in secure facilities. For more information, see www.stat-inst.se/om-webbplatsen/other-languages/the-swedish-national-board-of-institutional-care/.

7 Enforcement arrangements also raised some concern. Like in Denmark, some juvenile institutions hold both children who are serving a criminal sentence (punishment) and those who are placed for other reasons (health and welfare). This has raised questions about whether this mixing creates additional tensions given that those serving a sentence know beforehand when they are to be released, while those placed in the same institutions for other reasons often live in a state of uncertainty. However, interviews with children and young people imply that this is not a major problem. The majority of the children and young people interviewed would have preferred a determinate placement but they did not wish to change their position with those sentenced to Secure Youth Care, because of the more strict restrictions related to visits and furloughs (Palm, 2003).

8 Non-prosecution refers here to a deliberate decision to drop the charge even if there is a known offender and his/her guilt has been established, as distinct from not prosecuting due to the lack of evidence (or for other procedural reasons).

9 On the development of mediation in the Nordic countries, see the country reports in Dünkel *et al.*, 2015.

10 National youth sanctions that apply in Norway are discussed in more detail in Holmboe, 2016b. For more detailed discussion of youth sanctions that apply in Denmark, see Kyvsgaard, 2004 and Storgaard, 2013, for those that apply in Sweden, see Borgeke and Månsson, 2007; Sarnecki and Estrada, 2006 and Tärnfalk, 2007 and for those that apply in Finland, see Marttunen, 2008.

11 Similar patterns also apply to patterns of recorded and self-reported crime. For Denmark, for example, see Justitsministeriets Forskningskontor, September 2016, 'Kriminalitet og alder Udviklingen i strafferetlige afgørelser 2006–2015'.

12 Percentage shares are included in order to control for possible effects of the overall decline in the number of juvenile convictions.

13 See Justitsministeriets Forskningsenhed Marts 2006, Udviklingen i strenge straffe til unge lovovertrædere 1990–2004 http://justitsministeriet.dk/sites/default/files/media/ Arbejdsomraader/Forskning/Forskningsrapporter/2006/udviklingen_i_strenge_straffe. pdf.

14 For more detailed offence-specific data, see Lappi-Seppälä, 2015 and, for a more detailed trend analysis for Norway, see Lid, 2015.

15 For more detailed analysis, see Lappi-Seppälä, 2015.

References

Andenæs, J. (2004) *Alminnelig strafferett. 5. Utgave ved Magnus Matningsdal og Georg Fredrik Rieber-Mohn*. Oslo: Universitetsforlage.

Anttila, I. (1952) *Nuori lainrikkoja*. Suomalaisen lakimiesyhdistyksen julkaisuja B-sarja no. 53. Helsinki.

Betænkning. (1972/667) Betænkning om de strafferetlige særforanstaltninger. No. 667, 1972.

Borgeke, M. and Månsson, C. (2007) Den nya lagstiftningen om påföljder för unga lagöverträdare, in *Svensk Juristtidning 2007/2*. Stockholm.

Borgeke, M. (2008) *Att bestämma påföljd för brott*. Norstedts Juridik.

Dünkel, F., Grzywa-Holte, J., and Horshfeld, P. (2015) *Restorative justice and mediation in penal matters*. Schriften zum Strafvollzug, Jugendstrafrecht und zur Kriminologie. Band 50. Godesberg: MG Forum Verlag. pp. 246–267

Egge, M. (2004) Forsøk med ungdomskontrakter –en alternativ reaksjonsform rettet mot unge lovbrytere. PHS-forskning:1, http://brage.bibsys.no/xmlui/handle/11250/175048 (Accessed 15 May 2018).

Greve, V. (1996) *Straffene*. Copenhagen: Jurist- og Økonomforbundets Forlag.

Holmboe, M. (2016a) Ytring: om «samfunnsnyttige oppgaver» i ungdomsplaner. Behov for reform? *Tidsskrift for Strafferett*, 16(1), 3–7.

Holmboe, M. (2016b) *Fengsel eller frihet*. Oslo: Gyldendal.

Justitsministeriets Forskningsenhed Marts 2006. *Udviklingen i strenge straffe til unge lovovertrædere 1990–2004*. http://justitsministeriet.dk/sites/default/files/media/Arbejdsomraader/ Forskning/Forskningsrapporter/2006/udviklingen_i_strenge_straffe.pdf (Accessed 15 May 2018).

Justitsministeriets Forskningskontor, (2010) Redegørelse om ungdomssanktioner og ubetingede fængselsstraffe til unge lovovertrædere, 1. Januar til 31. December 2009.

http://justitsministeriet.dk/sites/default/files/media/Arbejdsomraader/Forskning/Forskningsrapporter/2010/Redegorelse_om_US_2010.pdf. (Accessed 15 May 2018).

Justitsministeriets Forskningskontor, (2016) Kriminalitet og alder Udviklingen i strafferetlige afgørelser 2006–2015. www.justitsministeriet.dk/sites/default/files/media/Arbejdsomraader/Forskning/Forskningsrapporter/2016/Kriminalitet%20og%20alder%202006–2015%2009–2016.pdf.

Kriminalomsorgens Årsstatistikk (2015) www.kriminalomsorgen.no/publikasjoner.242465. no.html.

Kühlhorn, E. (2002) Sluten ungdomsvård'(Youth Custody), in *Rättsliga reaktioner på de ungas brott fore och efter införandet 1999*. Report no. 5. Stockholm: SiS.

Kyvsgaard, B. (2004) Youth justice in Denmark, in M. Tonry and A. N. Doob (eds), *Youth crime and justice comparative and cross-national perspectives* 31. The University of Chicago Press, Chicago 2004.

Lappi-Seppälä, T. (2009) Imprisonment and penal policy in Finland, in P. Wahlgren (ed.), *Scandinavian studies in law* 54. Stockholm: Stockholm Institute for Scandinavian Law.

Lappi-Seppälä, T. (2011) Nordic youth justice, in M. Tonry and T. Lappi-Seppälä (eds.), *Crime and justice: a review of research* 40. Chicago: University of Chicago Press.

Lappi-Seppälä, T. (2015) Youth justice without a juvenile court: a note on Scandinavian exceptionalism, in F. E. Zimring, M. Langer, and D. S. Tanenhaus (eds.), *Juvenile justice in global perspective*. New York: New York University Press.

Lappi-Seppälä, T. (2016) Nordic sentencing, in M. Tonry (ed.), *Crime and justice: a review of research*, 45. Chicago: University of Chicago Press.

Lappi-Seppälä, T. and Storgaard, A. (2015) Nordic mediation: comparing Denmark and Finland. *Neue Kriminalpolitik*, vol. 27, 2.

Lid, S. (2015) Utvikling i straffereaksjoner 2002–2013. SSB, Samfunnsspeilet 2/2015. www.ssb.no/sosiale-forhold-og-kriminalitet/artikler-og-publikasjoner/_attachment/232063?_ts=14e1ae2b530 (Accessed 15 May 2018).

Marttunen, M. (2008) *Nuorisorikosoikeus* (Juvenile Criminal Justice). Research reports 236/2008. Helsinki: National Research Institute of Legal Policy.

Nordlöf, K. (2005) Unga lagöverträdare i social-, straff- och processrätt. Printed in Sweden Studentlitteratur, Lund.

NOU (2008) Barn og straff – utviklingstötte og kontroll. Norgens offentlige utredningar 2008:15.

Ot.prp.nr.5 (2000–2001) Om lov om gjennomføring av straff mv.(straffegjennomføringsloven) www.regjeringen.no/no/dokumenter/otprp-nr-5-2000-2001-/id162307/ (Accessed 15 May 2018).

Palm, J. (2003) *Ungdomarnas upplevelse av sluten ungdomsvård. En jämförelse med LVU-placeringar och fängelse*. Rapporter Nr 2/2003. Vastervik: Statens Institutionsstyrelse.

Prop 135 (2010/11) Proposisjon til Stortinget (forslag til lovvedtak) Endringer i straffeloven, straffeprosessloven, straffegjennomføringsloven, konfliktrådsloven m.fl. (barn og straff) www.regjeringen.no/contentassets/6a695fd6f906408eb9af0e699da16db3/no/pdfs/prp201020110135000dddpdfs.pdf (Accessed 15 May 2018).

Sarnecki, J. and Estrada, F. (2006) Keeping the balance between humanism and penal punitivism: recent trends in juvenile justice in Sweden, in J. Junger-Tas and S. H. Decker (eds.) *International Handbook of Juvenile Justice*. Switzerland: Springer.

SOU (1977) (Statens offentliga utredningar 1977:83 Justitiedepartementet.) *Tillsynsdom*. Ungdomsfängelseutredningens förslag till ändringar i påföljdssystemet. Betänkande av ungdomsfängelseutredningen Stockholm 1977.

SOU (1986) (Statens offentliga utredningar 1986:13–15 Justitiedepartementet). *Påföljd för brott*. Betänkande av Fängelsestraffkommittén.

SOU (1993) (Statens offentliga utredningar 1993:35 Justitiedepartementet). *Reaktion mot ungdomsbrott*. Betänkande av Undomsbrottskommittén Del A. Malmö.

St.meld.nr.20 (2005–2006) *Alternative straffereaksjonar overfor unge lovbrytarar*. Det Kongelege Justis- og Politidepartement. Publikasjonen finst på internet: www.odin.dep.no/

Storgaard, A. (2009) The youth sanction: a punishment in disguise, in P. Wahlgren, (ed) *Scandinavian Studies in Law*, vol. 54. Stockholm: Stockholm Institute for Scandinavian Law.

Storgaard, A. (2013) Alternatives to custody for young offenders. National Report On Juvenile Justice Trends. Denmark. www.oijj.org/sites/default/files/baaf_denmark1.pdf (Accessed 15 May 2018).

Strahl, I. et al. (1955) *Om påföljder för brott*. Stockholm: Åhlén & Åkerlunds Boktryckeri.

Tärnfalk, M. (2007) *Barn och straff. En studie om socialtjänstens yttranden i straffprcessen för unga lagöverträdare.Rapportisocialtarbeitenr 122. 2007.*Doktorsavhandling.Stockholmsuniversitet. http://su.diva-portal.org/smash/get/diva2:197156/FULLTEXT01.pdf (Accessed 15 May 2018).

Vestergaard, J. (2004) A special youth sanction. *Journal of Scandinavian Studies in Criminology and Crime Prevention*, 5(1).

Vinnerljung, B. and Sallnäs, M. (2008) Into adulthood: a follow-up study of 718 young people who were placed in out-of-home care during their teens. *Child and Family Social Work*. 13(2), 144–155.

von Hofer, H. and Lappi-Seppälä, T. (2013) The development of crime in light of Finnish and Swedish criminal justice statistics, ca. 1750–2010. *European Journal of Criminology*.

7

JUVENILE (IN)JUSTICE AND NEOLIBERAL AUSTERITY IN THE EUROPEAN UNION

Emma Bell

Introduction

Analysing trends in juvenile justice at a European level is an extraordinarily difficult task. There are two principal reasons for this. First, there is the non-negligible problem of data collection. Despite the best efforts of researchers to compile comprehensive statistics on cross-national trends, the failure of individual states to keep up-to-date data 'frustrates meaningful analysis and makes it difficult, if not impossible, to track trends or compare jurisdictions' (Kilkelly, 2011: 42). One researcher has gone so far as to assert that the collection of data across member states 'is often totally deficient' (Pruin, 2011: 18). Data collection is not facilitated by the lack of common terminology or different understandings of key terms (such as the basic meaning of the word 'child') relating to juvenile justice across Europe (Pruin, ibid.; Muncie, 2008: 114). Furthermore, any attempt to identify trends across different jurisdictions is likely to be frustrated by the fact that juvenile justice systems 'assume multitudinous and widely varying forms' (Goldson, 2014: 47).

Regardless of these difficulties, it is of increasing importance to understand common trends, rather than focussing on differences. As Tom Daems has pointed out, the emergence of a common European penology suggests that European states are no longer fully in control of their own penal policies (Daems, 2013). For him, European-wide convergence is much more relevant than exceptionalism. The Council of Europe explicitly notes that its aim is 'to achieve a greater unity between the member states, in particular by promoting the adoption of common rules in legal matters' (Council of Europe, 2010: 13), whilst the European Commission aims to achieve 'a European area of justice' in order 'to move beyond the current fragmentation' (European Commission, 2009). With regard to juvenile justice, this has led to a focus on 'child-friendly justice' which purportedly aims to promote the rights and welfare of children. This is widely regarded as framing a more progressive approach to juvenile justice (Hammarberg, 2008; Goldson and Muncie, 2012). Yet, contemporaneous with this push for legal convergence, has been a push towards ideological and political convergence that threatens to undermine apparently progressive trends. It is argued here that the embedding of neoliberalism at the heart of European Union institutions (Hermann, 2007; Bugaric, 2013) is one major factor that can help to explain the contradictory nature of juvenile justice trends. Neoliberal austerity in particular is regarded as having had a negative impact on welfarist approaches to juvenile justice, despite claims that it may have a 'softening' impact on more punitive policies (Bateman, 2012; Goldson, 2015). This is not to suggest that macro-level trends have pushed juvenile justice policies in a uniformly punitive direction; rather to argue that these trends may help to explain the failure of European member states to match their practices to the dominant human rights rhetoric of European institutions.

This chapter begins by discussing several key aspects of juvenile justice policy, briefly assessing to what extent they live up to the principles of 'child-friendly justice'. It then attempts to situate these policies in the context of macro-level trends, notably those related to neoliberalism. It shows how the embedding of neoliberalism at the level of EU institutions leads to a limited conception of human rights that is incapable of realising social justice for young people, thus undermining welfarist approaches to juvenile justice. It then explores the current context of neoliberal austerity, exploring its potential to attenuate punitive trends in both practical and political terms. In conclusion, it offers some tentative suggestions regarding how genuine child-friendly justice policies might be implemented.

Child-friendly justice: rhetoric and reality

The notion of child-friendly justice builds on international guidelines on children's rights, notably the United Nations Convention on the Rights of the Child adopted by the UN General Assembly on 20 November 1989. It is defined by the Council of Europe as:

> Justice systems which guarantee the respect and the effective implementation of all children's rights at the highest attainable level... giving due consideration to the child's level of maturity and understanding and the circumstances of the case. It is, in particular, justice that is accessible, age appropriate, speedy, diligent, adapted to and focused on the needs and rights of the child, respecting the rights of the child including the rights to due process, to participate in and to understand the proceedings, to respect for private and family life and to integrity and dignity.
>
> *Council of Europe, 2010: 17*

For reasons of economy, it is obviously not possible to discuss whether or not all aspects of this comprehensive statement of child-friendly justice are upheld, but several key principles merit immediate attention.

Age-appropriate justice

One of the principal means of ensuring that justice is 'age-appropriate' is to guarantee that children under a certain age cannot be subject to penal measures. A whole host of European and international guidelines exist regarding the minimum age of criminal responsibility (MACR) (Goldson, 2013). The Council of Europe, in accordance with Rule 4 of the 'Beijing Rules',[1] has declared that the MACR 'should not be too low' (Council of Europe, 2008a: 3; Council of Europe, 2010: 25), which might be taken to mean under 14 years old, without exception (Schennach, 2014: 2). The Council has also expressed concerns about the upper age limit with regard to young adults aged under 21 in order to reflect 'the extended transition to adulthood' which means that 'the age of legal majority does not necessarily coincide with the age of maturity' (Council of Europe, 2003). It therefore recommends that 'young adult offenders may, where appropriate, be regarded as juveniles and dealt with accordingly' (Council of Europe, 2008b).

In practice, the average MACR in Europe is 14 years (Goldson, 2013) although, exceptionally, Lithuania and Portugal set their MACR at 16, whilst Scotland sets its MACR at 8, and England, Wales and Northern Ireland, along with Switzerland, set theirs at 10 (HEUNI, 2014: 404). Eleven EU nations conform to recommendations regarding the adoption of specific rules for the treatment of young adults, notably Portugal and Croatia, which may allow special rules to apply to young adults aged up to 22 and 23 respectively (ibid.). Yet, as Schennach (2014: 6) has pointed out, these figures can be misleading. In Scotland, for example, although children as young as 8 may be found guilty of a criminal offence, they can never appear before a court of law. Under section 52 of the Criminal Justice and Licensing (Scotland) Act, only children aged 12 or over may actually be prosecuted for a criminal offence. In France, whilst criminal sanctions cannot be imposed on children aged under 13, children as young as seven may be held criminally responsible provided the prosecution is satisfied that the child is capable of judging the gravity of his/her acts (in which case s/he will be subject to lesser sanctions than those of his/her elders). Furthermore, contrary to the recommendations of the Council of Europe, a number of exceptions for serious crimes apply to the MACR in countries such as Belgium, Hungary, Ireland, Lithuania, Luxembourg and Poland (ibid.). In addition, we should not assume that these MACRs are fixed. A small minority of countries have recently lowered or considered lowering their MACR. Denmark, for example, lowered its MACR from 15 to 14 in 2010 only to raise it again in 2012 (CRIN, 2013). In France in 2008, an official report on juvenile offending recommended fixing the age of criminal responsibility at 12 (Varinard, 2008), although this proposal was never implemented.

Whatever the MACR, the Council of Europe has made it clear that *all* young people are to be held responsible for their actions, if not *criminally* responsible:

> It is possible to argue that youth crime is essentially a welfare, not a delinquent, issue: the depraved are also the deprived. Although this perspective

carried some persuasion during the 1960s and 1970s (in some countries), it no longer holds sway. Young offenders have to take some responsibility for their actions.

Williamson, 2002: 85

Whilst the aim is to avoid criminalisation, it is hard to foster non-penal responses when the focus is on individual responsibility rather than on the wider social context in which offending occurs. 'Age-appropriate justice', even when applied as recommended by the Council of Europe is, therefore, not necessarily 'child-friendly' if it fails to address the wider problems that young offenders may suffer from. A focus on responsibilisation may distract from a 'focus on the needs and the rights of the child' (Council of Europe, 2010: 17).

Punishment as a last resort

A focus on the needs of the child necessarily implies using punishment as a last resort, particularly deprivation of liberty. The failure of detention to address the needs of both adults and children is well-documented (for example, Goldson, 2005; Scott, 2013). Echoing article 37(b) of the UN Convention on the Rights of the Child (1989), the Council of Europe states, 'any form of deprivation of liberty of children should be a measure of last resort and be for the shortest appropriate period of time' (Council of Europe, 2010: 24).

For the first decade of this century, there were concerns that many European nations were failing to respect these guidelines. The former European Commissioner for Human Rights noted that 'too many children are detained throughout Europe' (Hammarberg, 2009: 27) and singled out the United Kingdom for condemnation: 'over three thousand minors are kept in detention at any one time which means that about five thousand youngsters are given that experience during one year. This is hardly consistent with the norm of detention as a "last resort"' (Hammarberg, 2008: 195). Indeed, in the UK, there was a massive 550 per cent increase in the number of minors aged between 10 and 14 held in custody over a ten-year period from 1996 to 2006 (Barnardo's, 2008: 3). Yet, since 2010/11, official statistics have recorded a 51 per cent drop in the number of young people (under 18) coming into the criminal justice system and a 40 per cent drop in the number of young people in custody (Goldson, 2015; Ministry of Justice, 2015). This trend appears to have been replicated (although not so dramatically) across Europe, but most particularly in Central and Eastern European countries such as Croatia, the Czech Republic, Hungary, Latvia and Slovenia (Dunkel, 2014: 37). Trends do exist in the other direction, notably in Lithuania and Slovakia, but in general custody rates have been declining (ibid.).

Declining custody rates do not, however, indicate unequivocally that detention is being used as a 'last resort'. In general, rates of youth imprisonment in Europe are still described as 'worryingly high' (Moore, 2013: 27). The percentage of prisoners aged under 18 varies between 0 per cent (e.g. Italy, Spain and the Netherlands) and 1.5 per cent (Romania) of the total carceral population within member states

(Aebi and Dalgrande, 2014: 79). These rates increase quite considerably regarding prisoners aged between 18 and under 21, ranging from 1.3 per cent (Spain) to 9.6 per cent (Denmark) (ibid.). The absolute number of children detained suggests that the use of custody is not exceptional. Despite the number of children in detention having significantly declined, there are still 980 children detained in England and Wales (World Prison Brief, 2016). France detains the next highest number of children under 18: 701; a figure which rises to 5,446 for young adults aged over 18 but under 21 (Aebi and Dalgrande, 2014: 79).

Furthermore, these statistics hide certain realities. For example, they ignore the fact that some categories of children are more likely to be detained than others, notably children from BME groups (see, for example, Ministry of Justice, 2015: 28; Cunneen *et al.*, 2017), children of foreign origin and Roma children (Kilkelly, 2011: 34). They also ignore the large numbers of children detained pre-trial (ibid.) in contravention of European Council recommendations that 'special efforts must be undertaken to avoid pre-trial detention' (Council of Europe, 2008b). Some statistics do not include detention in welfare-oriented institutions (Pruin, 2011: 24). In addition, statistics on detention are generally limited to young offenders sentenced for criminal offences. They ignore the detention of minors due to their lack of residence status despite the UN Committee on the Rights of the Child (2013) and the Council of Europe condemning such practices (Council of Europe, 2010: 24). There is 'a paucity of reliable information' in this respect (Hamilton *et al.*, 2011: 63) but available data suggests that 15 EU countries detain unaccompanied migrants aged under 18, whilst 19 detain families with children (Keith and Levoy, 2015: 24–25).

Furthermore, it is questionable whether the 'best interests of the child' are really respected with regard to the children who do find themselves held in penal detention. Council of Europe (2008b) guidelines state that detention should be imposed 'for the shortest period possible'. Whilst 22 EU member states have explicitly abolished life imprisonment (Schennach, 2014: 8), and most countries fix the maximum youth prison sentence at ten years (Pruin, 2011: 22), extremely long maximum sentences remain legal (Schennach, 2014: 8; Cunneen *et al.*, 2017).

The conditions in which children are detained often breach their basic rights, as highlighted by the Committee on the Rights of the Child and the Committee for the Prevention of Torture. They have expressed concerns about: the failure to separate adults from juveniles in contravention of European and international guidelines; cases of abuse by prison staff; inhuman and degrading treatment in police detention; poor regimes; and lack of provision of meaningful activities (Kilkelly, 2011: 36–38; Goldson and Kilkelly, 2013).

Alternatives to detention

The adoption of alternative non-custodial measures is regarded as a principal means of ensuring that penal detention is only used as a last resort. As the former

Commissioner on Human Rights noted, 'making a clear commitment to the last-resort principle in legislation and policy will not in itself reduce the numbers of children in detention unless alternative community-based responses are also provided for by law' (Hammarberg, 2009: 28). He applauded the fact that 'many states now provide a range of community sanctions for young offenders... including welfare approaches involving the social services and restorative justice/family conferencing' (Hammarberg, 2009: 26). Restorative justice and other mediation measures have been expressly encouraged by the Council of Europe (2008b). This follows United Nations recommendations 'that the traditional objectives of criminal justice, such as repression/retribution, must give way to rehabilitation and restorative justice objectives in dealing with child offenders' (United Nations, 2007). Available sanctions vary widely across Europe, from more interventionist educational measures to suspended prison sentences (Pruin, 2011: 21–24), but it seems that elements of restorative justice have been incorporated in juvenile justice systems across Europe (Dunkel, 2014: 38).

Non-custodial measures do have diversionary potential but only so long as they remain genuine *alternatives* to custody (Shapland et al., 2006). If this is not the case, they may have the opposite effect, leading to net-widening (Aebi *et al.*, 2015). The UK provides a particularly striking example in this respect. The use of restorative justice embedded within the existing criminal justice system simply led to more young people being drawn into the juvenile justice system at an earlier age (Muncie, 2006: 779; Cunneen and Goldson, 2015), especially as these measures tended to be used to target low-level offending that would previously have escaped the attention of the courts altogether (Morgan, 2009). Even explicitly welfarist measures have punitive potential, leading in many instances to 'repressive welfarism' (Phoenix, 2009). Under successive New Labour governments in the UK, ostensibly welfarist measures designed to tackle problems such as drug abuse, educational failure and family breakdown led to the criminalisation of young people as failure to respond appropriately to these measures often led to penal sanctions. Rather than being regarded as indicators of structural vulnerability, such problems are commonly framed in terms of 'risk' and seen to result from individual deficiencies rather than from wider structural factors (White, 2015). Instead of being welfarist measures, they become in practice what Garland (1985) described as 'welfare sanctions' (see also, Bell, 2011). The genuine welfare potential of such measures is indeed limited if their focus is confined to the 'offender' rather than on the wider context in which that offending occurred. The Council of Europe's own focus on offender responsibility, highlighted above, may paradoxically limit the capacity of these measures to become genuine alternatives to custody.

Non-discrimination

Child-friendly justice should ensure that all children are treated equally by juvenile justice systems. The Council of Europe clearly states:

> Sanctions or measures shall be imposed and implemented without discrimination on any ground such as sex, race, colour, language, religion, sexual orientation, political or other opinion, national or social origin, association with a national minority, property, birth or other status (principle of non-discrimination).
>
> *Council of Europe, 2008b, para. 11*

Yet, as has just been suggested above, the tendency of social and juvenile justice services to regard certain structural vulnerabilities as 'risk factors' means that children who suffer from such problems are likely to be disproportionately targeted (White, 2015). Indeed, the Council of Europe itself recommends that 'some categories of juvenile offenders, such as members of ethnic minorities, young women and those offending in groups', 'may need special intervention programmes' (Council of Europe, 2003).

There is some evidence that specific groups of young people are targeted by the police and the courts across Europe, although international comparisons are limited. Stop and search is a case in point. A report on practice in Paris, France, for example, found that young people as a whole were 'overstopped', especially those wearing 'youth clothing' associated with hip-hop, goth, punk or tecktonic youth cultures who were 2.9 times more likely to be stopped than young people wearing 'casual' or 'business' clothing. Yet, the same report found that ethnicity mattered more, with non-White young people being 3.5 times more likely to be stopped than White young people. It concluded, 'it is probable that the police consider both belonging to an ethnic minority and wearing youth clothing to be closely tied to a propensity to commit crimes' (Open Society Institute, 2009: 31). Similarly, Amnesty International (2013) has expressed concern that young BME men are more likely to be stopped and searched than all other groups in the Netherlands. In the UK, the then Home Secretary, Theresa May, declared that stop and search powers are 'unfair, especially to young, black men' in a speech to the House of Commons (May, 2014) yet the Supreme Court recently declared that random searches (under section 60 of the Criminal Justice and Public Order Act 1994), particularly of BME groups, are compatible with the European Convention of Human Rights and may even help to protect such young people from crime (R v Commissioner of Police of the Metropolis and another [2015] UKSC 79).

Groups of BME young people have been further disproportionately targeted by the criminal justice system in the context of recent concerns about 'radicalisation'. In the UK, under the Counter-Terrorism and Security Act 2015, a specific duty has been imposed on local authorities, schools, nurseries and social services to refer 'vulnerable' young people – those who they think may be susceptible to radicalisation – to the police. The police will then decide whether or not the same young people should be referred on to a multi-agency panel (Channel) which will tailor an individual 'support plan' for them. In extreme cases, this may lead to children being removed from their homes if their family environment is thought to be encouraging radicalisation. Almost 37 per cent of all referrals to Channel between 2007 and 2014 involved young people aged under 18 whilst 56 per cent of all referrals between 2012 and 2014 involved Muslims (NPCC, 2015). This would suggest that young Muslims are disproportionately targeted by these measures. Whilst the aim of the Prevent programme is to address 'vulnerabilities', these are often interpreted as 'risks'. Indeed, the UK Government's official guidance notes:

> Risk is a theme that runs through the entire Channel process, i.e. risk to the individual; risk to the public; and risk to partners or organisations providing support to the individual, including any intervention providers. The panel is responsible for managing the risk in relation to the vulnerable individual.
>
> *HM Government, 2015: 16*

The danger is that Muslim children and young people will be *policed* rather than *supported* by these measures. As a result, their rights to freedom of thought, expression and association and non-discrimination – provided by the UN Convention on the Rights of the Child – face the prospect of being severely undermined (Institute for Race Relations, 2016). Whilst the UK's response appears to be unique regarding the statutory duty to report potential 'radicals' to the police, almost every European country has its own potentially discriminatory anti-radicalisation programme (Terra, 2014) and, since 2011, there has been a concerted EU-wide effort to develop a common strategy which, like the UK initiative, is to focus on multi-agency interventions to tackle the 'problem' (RAN, 2016).

Migrant children also appear to be disproportionately targeted by certain practices. The European Commission has expressed concern that the rights and needs of undocumented and stateless children in particular 'may be ignored' (European Commission, 2015: 4). As noted above, such children and young people may find themselves detained by simple reason of their immigration status. Worse, when detained, they may find that they are exempt from 'normal' legal protections. This is certainly the case when they are detained in extra-territorial zones such as at Roissy Charles de Gaulle airport near Paris, France. Given that they are considered not to have entered France, they are subject to an entirely separate legal regime which deprives them of certain rights (Troller, 2010). Human Rights Watch estimates that over 1,000 unaccompanied migrant children are held in such zones in France each year (ibid). At a 2015 meeting organised by the international children's rights NGO, *Terre des Hommes*, a representative from the French Ministry of Justice acknowledged that the principal way that vulnerable children on the move tend to come to the attention of the French authorities is via the criminal justice system when they commit petty crimes, whilst many of these children are in need of protection as victims of exploitation and trafficking (Terre des Hommes, 2015).

In summary then, the examples above suggest that key aspects of 'child-friendly justice' are not currently being upheld. Researchers have highlighted the 'considerable and continuing dissonance between the rhetoric of human rights discourse and the reality of juvenile justice interventions' (Goldson and Kilkelly, 2013; Schennach, 2014: 2; Cunneen *et al.*, 2017) and suggested that 'Governments cling to punishment over progress' (Moore, 2013: 6). Punitive responses are certainly evident: in the reluctance to raise lower minimum ages of responsibility; in the continued use of both administrative and penal detention; in the failure to develop genuine alternatives to penal responses; and in the continued, even increased, police bias against certain groups of children and young people (Cunneen *et al.*, 2017). This is not, however, to suggest that juvenile justice is moving in a uniformly 'dystopian' direction across Europe, simply to highlight that there are considerable obstacles to the development of coherent 'utopian' trends. In practice, juvenile justice in Europe is increasingly 'mixed', moving neither in a purely welfarist nor a purely punitive direction (Dunkel, 2014). As Goldson has pointed out, trends are complex and contingent upon a multitude of local factors (Goldson, 2014: 46). These factors are indeed important and can help to explain both subtle and more blatant differences in approaches to youth problems and offending but the focus here is on the macro-level factors which may act as a break on the implementation of a more uniformly progressive vision, despite the existence of a multitude of documents published by European institutions which appear to explicitly encourage a move in this direction. It is argued here that the overriding macro-level trend is defined by expanding and consolidating forms of neoliberalism.

Neoliberalism and the limits to child-friendly justice

Neoliberalism has frequently been held up as a key macro-level factor influencing penal trends across the global north (Wacquant, 2009; Bell, 2011). With regard to juvenile justice in particular, it has been suggested that it has been responsible for the erosion of the welfarist model across Europe, leading to an increased focus on risk and the responsibilisation of young offenders (Bailleau and Cartuyvels, 2007). Whilst local factors may be important, the institutionalisation of neoliberalism at the level of the European Union means that this is a macro-level trend that cannot be ignored. Indeed, the embedding of neoliberalism at this supranational level, symbolised by the adoption of 'free' trade policies, budgetary austerity, privatisation and the flexibilisation of labour markets, has severely limited the extent to which nation states may pursue their own 'sovereign' policies in a multitude of fields. This was the stated intention of key thinkers such as Hayek who regarded neoliberalism as a transnational project designed specifically to undermine nation-state autonomy (Hermann, 2007: 2, 8; Bugaric, 2013: 3).

Institutional neoliberalism and the limited view of human rights

Whilst the European Union has been seeking to apply a human rights model across member states, its simultaneous pursuit of neoliberalism has arguably fatally undermined such initiatives, principally by undermining the welfarist agenda of individual nation states which is essential for the development of a more progressive approach to justice generally and juvenile justice in particular.

The European Union, in its early forms as the European Coal and Steel Community and the European Economic Community, did not start out with a neoliberal agenda. Indeed, although the Treaty of Rome laid the foundations for a single European market free from impediments to competition, there were still considerable restrictions placed on the free movement of capital, individuals and services (Hermann, 2007: 8). It was not until the passing of the Single European Act in 1986 and the Maastricht Treaty of 1992 that the Union began to take a distinctly neoliberal turn, moving from embedded liberalism to embedded neoliberalism (Bugaric, 2013: 9–16). Neoliberalism became firmly rooted in dominant discourses and institutions and the liberal compromise between capital and welfare became firmly tilted in favour of the former. Indeed, EU nation states' capacity to adopt redistributive social policies was severely limited by their new commitment to pursue non-tariff barriers to trade, the budgetary constraints forced upon states via membership of the European Monetary Union and its Stability and Growth Pact and, more recently, via the recent legislative measures adopted in response to the eurozone crisis[2] (Bugaric, 2010: 23–29). Neoliberal goals became paramount over the social.

At the same time as the EU was moving towards embedded neoliberalism, it was also seeking to implement a human rights culture as the European Court of Justice became increasingly active and institutions such as the European Council issued a large volume of guidelines, not least in the field of juvenile justice. Yet, the emphasis on human rights masked the failure of European institutions to focus on social rights, which were increasingly subordinated to economic rights. European Institutions such as the European Central Bank tended to focus on enforcing economic policy (Clarke and Newman, 2012: 301) whilst the European Court of Justice's 'early case law paved the way for a future reconfiguration of the original balance between the economic freedoms and social rights in the EU legal order' (Bugaric, 2013: 10). The European Court of Justice has so far refused to address the issue of whether EU institutions are bound to the European Social Charter when they act in accordance with the demands of international institutions placed outwith the EU such as the European Stability Mechanism[3] (*Pringle v. Government of Ireland*). The European Council's Social Rights Committee did condemn Greece for failing to respect the right to social security enshrined in the European Social Charter in the context of its obligations to introduce severe pension cuts as part of its agreement with international creditors, but this decision was non-binding (Federation of Employed Pensioners of Greece [IKA-ETAM] v Greece). For Solomon (2015) this demonstrates that the extent to which nation states can be held responsible for upholding social and human rights enshrined in European treaties is questionable. Indeed, with regard to social and employment issues, a 'soft law' approach has been adopted which leaves much discretion to member states and contrasts sharply with the 'hard law' approach adopted when it comes to ensuring that EU member states uphold neoliberal policies such as budgetary retraction. As Hermann (2007: 23) has pointed out, 'whilst member states that fail to meet the convergence criteria are threatened with financial penalties, there are no sanctions in the case of a member state falling short of employment targets'.

This 'soft law' approach also applies to juvenile justice, which may help to explain the difficulty in upholding the principles laid down by international and

European organisations. As Muncie has pointed out, this is a key problem with the United Nations Convention on the Rights of the Child, breach of which attracts no formal sanction (Muncie, 2008: 111). Although legally binding, it has no formal system of petition allowing individuals to complain about breach (Pruin, 2011: 15). Hence, 'it may be the most ratified of all international human rights instruments but it is also the most violated' (Muncie, 2008: 111). The same is true of Council of Europe recommendations which simply 'encourage' member states to adopt key principles such as 'child-friendly justice'. This does not mean that 'soft law' provisions are meaningless – they 'are an expression of the behaviour which the respective Member States expect from each other' and they 'at the very least morally oblige themselves to fulfil the expectations that they have of others' (Pruin, 2011: 16). Nonetheless, when it comes to upholding other social rights, 'soft law' obligations can easily be set aside when they conflict with other obligations, namely those relating to the pursuit of a coordinated neoliberal agenda. Honouring the Council of Europe's recommendations concerning the adoption of alternative sanctions for children and young people in conflict with the law has the potential to contradict such an agenda in so far as this objective may encourage a focus on child welfare. Yet, as highlighted above, these recommendations are actually themselves framed in such a way that they focus on the rights and welfare of children at the individual rather than at the social level. The focus on individual responsibility ensures that there will be no obligation on member states to address the wider social context in which problem behaviour may arise. Furthermore, whilst member states may be formally sanctioned for failure to respect human rights with regard to juvenile justice, this is unlikely to lead to the development of a substantially new approach in this area. As Nolan (2014: 11) has pointed out, human rights are individual, political and legal; they do not concern social and economic rights, whether individual or collective. As such, they are incapable of addressing the main social problems facing young people today, especially those resulting from neoliberalism:

> Precisely because the human rights revolution has at its most ambitious dedicated itself to establishing a normative and actual floor for protection, it has failed to respond to—or even allowed for recognizing— neoliberalism's obliteration of the ceiling on inequality.
>
> *Moyn, 2014: 149*

In the context of neoliberal austerity, it is young people who have been hardest hit by the rise in inequality and the erosion of social rights, not least those who find themselves in conflict with the law.

Neoliberal austerity and welfare retrenchment

Contrary to popular political and macromedia discourse, current austerity measures are not a response to government profligacy (Wren-Lewis, 2015) but instead represent an attempt to shore up a neoliberal agenda of welfare state retrenchment and private sector expansion (Clarke and Newman, 2012). In continuity with the previous neoliberal period running from the late 1970s up until the financial crisis of 2008, the focus is on individual rather than state responsibility for social problems, yet the move towards an 'austerity union' at an EU level (Bugaric, 2013) is making it even more difficult than before to develop welfarist approaches to juvenile justice.

The social rights of children and young people and their families are being further eroded. According to a report by Eurochild, the European network working for children's rights:

> Despite greater recognition of children as independent rights holders in recent political statements of the European Union, the downward trend, jeopardising the respect of children's human rights is evident in all three pillar areas of the forthcoming European Commission 'Recommendation on Child Poverty and Child Well-being': access to adequate resources; access to quality services; and children's participation.
>
> *Ruxton, 2012: 3*

Unemployment in particular is stubbornly high, with youth unemployment rates (for under 25s) often being twice, or more than twice, as high as those in the general population. Despite a small drop after reaching a peak in 2013, the European youth unemployment rate stands at over 23 per cent, rising to as high as over 52 per cent in Greece and Spain (Eurostat, 2014). According to Goldson (2014: 42), these crisis conditions may fuel unrest and 'create social and economic environments that are known to give rise to youth crime and the disproportionate criminalisation of identifiable groups of young people'.

More directly, austerity has led to cuts to juvenile justice services, particularly in countries worst affected by austerity measures. In Greece, for example, the principal cuts have been targeted at 'additional activities' such as 'psychological support' and 'organisational specific activities' directed at particular children (Moore, 2013: 20). In such a context, member states may be more tempted to turn to traditional punitive measures or, alternatively, to adopt 'repressive welfarism' focussed on addressing risk rather than addressing the social needs of children (Squires, 2015).

However, some experts have suggested that the context of austerity has the capacity to influence trends in the opposite direction. Goldson (2014: 47–49), for example, proposes that the 'wasteful' nature of an over-reliance on expensive repressive correctional solutions to youth offending may be one factor allowing 'humane pragmatism' to win out over 'harsh punitiveness'. Similarly, Moore (2013: 9), in a report for the International Juvenile Justice Observatory, has suggested that although it is far from inevitable, 'economic crisis should be a time for societies to move forward' in terms of encouraging reflection and dialogue about more cost-effective ways than detention of reducing youth offending. For Schennach (2014: 10) too, 'the current financial crisis provides a positive incentive to reduce incarceration and allocate resources to invest in diversion, reintegration and restorative justice'. Loader (2010: 355) also suggests that the public may be particularly receptive to arguments highlighting the excessive costs of punitiveness in times of economic crisis. The case of Ireland appears to provide a recent example where the onset of economic crisis coincided with a fall in the number of children in detention as the government made the conscious decision to spend less money on detention facilities (Moore, 2013: 67; Rogan, 2013). In the UK too, austerity has coincided with a fall in the number of young people held in custody (Goldson, 2015). It is noteworthy that this does not appear to be the first time that the two trends have coincided. Bateman (2012: 40) argues that the decision of the Thatcher governments, through the 1980s committed to reducing state spending, to develop alternatives to youth custody 'can be viewed as a crude economic calculation' (Bateman, 2012: 40; see also Goldson, 1997; Goldson, 2015).

Yet, as highlighted above, a simple reduction in the use of custody and the development of alternatives to detention, although welcome, are not in themselves sufficient to ensure that the social and human rights of children and young people are respected (Cunneen et al., 2017). Governments seeking to transform juvenile justice systems need to focus on cost efficiency, not just on cost reduction. This might entail substantial justice reinvestment (JR), using funds previously allocated to detention to develop genuine community alternatives to incarceration and tackle the broader social context in which crime occurs, notably by investing in housing, healthcare, education and employment (Tucker and Cadora, 2003; Brown et al., 2016). There does not appear to be any official support for justice reinvestment at a European level but there has been some interest in the concept within individual states. The UK, for example, has developed some projects which 'have implemented discreet elements [of the JR model] which could be said to be in line with the principles of JR' but in general the approach has been limited to a narrow economic perspective (Fox et al., 2013: 39). In the context of neoliberal austerity there has been little effort to integrate the original social justice aspect of the concept. In such a context, it is likely that any efforts to refocus criminal justice spending will be limited to shifting responsibility from the State to individuals and communities. There is also the risk that the communities that are to be targeted by such measures might find themselves further stigmatised, portrayed as 'dysfunctional and deviant' (White, 2015: 73–74).

Furthermore, arguments in favour of moving away from repressive responses to offending based on cost considerations alone cannot hope to provoke long-term transformative change in juvenile justice as they fail to flag up the problem of social and human waste that punitive responses entail. They generally do not highlight the moral failure of such policies and the ways in which they may exacerbate the social problems that lead to problematic behaviour in the first place (Bell, 2014: 500). As a result, they do nothing to foster alternative approaches that may secure the social rights of young people. Just as individuals are responsibilised for the austerity measures they are subject to, they are also responsibilised for the social and crime problems which affect them.

This is the context of *neoliberal* austerity. The focus of governments across Europe is not just on saving money but also on ensuring that it is individuals who are responsibilised rather than the State and the economic elites (Clarke and

Newman, 2012; Bell, 2015). The context of economic and social crisis has made this imperative all the more pressing as suitable scapegoats must be found. Young people have often been apt to fill this role given the particularly visible nature of the forms of offending in which they tend to engage. Yet, as highlighted above, in the context of the current crisis, in many countries across Europe, it seems that there are fewer young people being responsibilised via the juvenile justice system. This poses something of a conundrum. Even if budget cuts to ministries of justice have led to short-term reductions in imprisonment, we might expect that governments' failure to invest in social services to lead to longer-term increases as adverse social conditions produce increased offending rates. This has yet to be the case. Nonetheless, as highlighted above, this does not mean that juvenile justice has been transformed or that a genuinely child-friendly approach has been adopted which is respectful of children's social and human rights. It may be that the focus has simply shifted as certain categories of youths are more likely than ever to find themselves targeted by juvenile justice systems.

Young people engaged in protest are, for example, likely to find themselves targeted by increasingly repressive measures. In Spain, the Basic Law for the Protection of Public Security (*Ley Orgánica para la Protección de la Seguridad Ciudadana*) adopted in 2015 introduces heavy fines for individuals who organise public meetings or demonstrations without prior notification. It has been widely criticised by human rights and civil society organisations on account of the severe limitations it places on the right to protest (Hudig, 2012; Joint Letter to EU Members of Parliament, 2015). Amnesty International (2012) has highlighted the excessive use of force and 'less lethal' weapons by police against protesters, many of them very young, in Greece, Spain and Romania. Furthermore, as noted above, young people thought to be at risk of radicalisation are also more likely to be policed.

Obviously, with regard to the latter issue, macro-level trends other than neoliberalism play a role, namely the context of the heightened threat from terrorism. Yet, the context of neoliberalism in general and of neoliberal austerity in particular can help to explain the adoption of increasingly authoritarian policies. The highly visible policing methods adopted in response to anti-austerity protests and the criminalisation of protesters serve as effective political means of deflecting attention from the social causes of such protests and the role played by European states in exacerbating these problems through austerity responses and their failure to address the inequalities resulting from neoliberal policies. Similarly, the focus on the behaviour of young people at risk of radicalisation allows states to appear to be doing something useful to address the threat from terrorism whilst failing to address the wider social context in which such radicalisation might occur. In both cases, it is communities and young people themselves who are responsibilised rather than the State.

Conclusion: beyond injustice?

Whilst there have been contradictory trends at play regarding juvenile justice across Europe in recent years, it seems that it can at least be affirmed that there has been no unidirectional trend towards creating 'child-friendly justice' that 'guarantee[s] the respect and the effective implementation of all children's rights at the highest attainable level' (Council of Europe, 2010: 17). Despite some positive trends, notably a reduction in the youth prison population in some European states, children and young people across Europe, but particularly those from minority groups, continue to experience social and penal injustice. The publication of numerous guidelines from European institutions such as the Council of Europe regarding the adoption of policies that uphold the human rights of children have not been sufficient to prevent injustice. Indeed, the human rights emphasis fails to challenge the wider neoliberal political response which has become entrenched in European institutions and has served to exacerbate inequalities, undermining social rights, especially those of young people. It is this neoliberal convergence across Europe that has been much more powerful than a child-friendly justice model.

This is not to suggest that neoliberalism is applied uniformly across Europe or in the same way at the same time. Nor is it to suggest that neoliberalism is the only macro-level explanatory factor worth analysing. Elsewhere, I have highlighted the importance of how local factors such as the electoral needs of specific political parties at certain historical moments can influence penal trends (Bell, 2011). We should heed Peck (2013: 139–140):

> Neoliberalism should never be taken at face value as an omnibus 'first cause', since it will always be found among other causes, not to say other culprits, while both its form and consequences can only be revealed in conjuncturally specific ways.

Yet, the institutionalisation of neoliberalism at the level of European institutions means that there is now unprecedented pressure on member states to accept its key tenets regardless of local resistance. The imposition of neoliberal austerity policies across Europe has undermined the capacity of national governments to implement policies capable of promoting the social rights of their citizens. This has profound implications for juvenile justice. Not only does it mean that it is increasingly difficult for nation states to implement genuine alternative policies to detention that are capable of addressing the social context of youth offending and promoting youth welfare. But, politically, it may even be desirable to adopt repressive policies towards young people, particularly those who revolt against the dominant order. Using heavy-handed policing tactics to police the current crisis of neoliberal capitalism serves to focus responsibility on disenfranchised youth whilst appearing to address the insecurity that affects the population at large (Hall et al., 1978).

Even in states such as the UK, where fewer young people overall now find themselves embroiled in the criminal justice system than ten years ago (Goldson, 2015), it is not at all unlikely that trends could easily shift in the opposite direction. Whilst at present it is migrants who seem to be the perfect scapegoats for both economic and physical insecurities, failure to adequately address those insecurities at root means that young people will remain reserve scapegoats to fall back upon should political expediency demand it. Trends against punitive practice will always be fragile so long as a welfarist approach is not firmly entrenched in culture and practice. Yet, as we have seen, countertrends at a European level make it extremely difficult to embed a welfarist model. So, although some European states may have witnessed an attenuation of certain punitive trends, there is little indication that there can be genuine *transformation* of juvenile justice systems in line with the lofty principles set out by European institutions.

If European states genuinely wish to develop 'child-friendly justice', it is necessary to move beyond a narrow legalistic notion of justice towards one that is capable of addressing injustice of all kinds, whether 'penal' or 'social' in nature. This is particularly necessary in a context in which Europe's youth are bearing the brunt of the injustice of selective austerity policies. It is necessary to recognise not just the economic wastefulness of repressive policies but also the human and social waste that plagues contemporary societies. Only a social justice approach can point the way forward.

Notes

1 This shorthand term is widely used to refer to the United Nations Standard Minimum Rules for the Administration of Juvenile Justice regarding the treatment of juvenile offenders in member states, adopted by the United Nations General Assembly in 1985.
2 These include the European Semester (2010), the European Financial Stability Facility (2010), the Euro-Plus Pact (2011), the Six-Pack (2011), European Stability Mechanism (2012) and Treaty on Stability, Co-ordination and Governance in the Economic and Monetary Union, also known as 'the Fiscal Treaty' (2012).
3 The ESM is the crisis resolution mechanism for eurozone countries. It is an intergovernmental organisation that operates under public international law rather than under EU law.

References

Aebi, M. F. and Dalgrande, N. (2014) *Council of Europe Annual Penal Statistics: Space I – Prison Populations, Survey 2013*. Strasbourg: Council of Europe.
Aebi, M. F., Dalgrande, N. and Marguet, Y. (2015) 'Have Community Sanctions and Measures Widened the Net of the European Criminal Justice Systems?' *Punishment & Society* 17(5): 575–597.
Amnesty International (2012) *Policing Demonstrations in the European Union* www.amnesty. org/en/documents/EUR01/022/2012/en/ (consulted 8 April 2016).
Amnesty International (2013) *Stop and Search Powers Pose a Risk to Human Rights. Acknowledging and Tackling Ethnic Profiling in the Netherlands*, www.amnesty.nl/sites/default/files/public/ amnesty_stopandsearchpowersposearisktohumanrights.pdf (consulted 8 April 2016).
Bailleau, F. and Cartuyvels, Y. (eds) (2007) *La Justice Pénale des Mineurs en Europe – Entre Modèle Welfare et Infléxions Néo-libérales*. Paris: L'Harmattan.
Barnardo's (2008) *Locking Up or Giving In: Is Custody for Children Always the Right Answer?* London: Barnardo's.
Bateman, T. (2012) 'Who Pulled the Plug? Towards an Explanation of the Fall in Child Imprisonment in England and Wales' *Youth Justice* 12(1): 36–52.

Bell, E. (2011) *Criminal Justice and Neoliberalism*. Basingstoke: Palgrave Macmillan.

Bell, E. (2014) 'There is an Alternative: Challenging the Logic of Neoliberal Penality' *Theoretical Criminology* 18(4).

Bugaric, B. (2013) 'Europe Against the Left? On Legal Limits to Progressive Politics' LEQS Paper No. 61/2013. (London: LSE). www.lse.ac.uk/europeanInstitute/LEQS%20Discuss ion%20Paper%20Series/LEQSPaper61.pdf (consulted 8 April 2016).

Clarke, J. and Newman, J. (2012) 'The Alchemy of Austerity' *Critical Social Policy* 32(3): 299–319.

Cunneen, C. and Goldson, B. (2015) 'Restorative Justice: A Critical Analysis', in Goldson, B. and Muncie, J. (eds) *Youth Crime and Justice*, 2nd edition. London: Sage.

Cunneen, C., Brown, D., Schwartz, M., Stubbs, J. and Young, C. (eds) (2016) *Justice Reinvestment: Winding Back Imprisonment* (Basingstoke: Palgrave).

Cunneen, C. Goldson, B. and Russell, S. (2017) 'Human Rights and Youth Justice Reform in England and Wales: A Systemic Analysis' *Criminology and Criminal Justice*. http://journals. sagepub.com/doi/abs/10.1177/1748895817721957?journalCode=crjb

Committee on the Rights of the Child (2012) *The Rights of All Children in the Context of International Migration*, www2.ohchr.org/english/bodies/crc/docs/ discussion2012/Rep ortDGDChildrenAndMigration2012.pdf (consulted 8 April 2016).

Council of Europe (2003) *Recommendation Rec(2003)20 of the Committee of Ministers to Member States Concerning New Ways of Dealing with Juvenile Delinquency and the Role of Juvenile Justice*, https://search.coe.int/cm/Pages/result_details.aspx?ObjectID=09000016805df0b3 (consulted 8 April 2016).

Council of Europe (2008a) *Commentary to the European Rules for Juvenile Offenders Subject to Sanctions or Measures*, www.coe.int/t/dghl/standardsetting/ prisons/Commentary_Rec_ 2008_11E.pdf (consulted 8 April 2016).

Council of Europe (2008b) *Recommendation CM/Rec(2008)11 of the Committee of Ministers to Member States on the European Rules for Juvenile Offenders Subject to Sanctions or Measures*, www.refworld.org/pdfid/4a7058c02.pdf (consulted 8 April 2016).

Council of Europe (2010) *Guidelines of the Committee of Ministers of the Council of Europe on Child-friendly Justice*, www.coe.int/t/dghl/standardsetting /cdcj/CDCJ%20 Recommendations/GuidelinesChild-FriendlyJusticeE.pdf (consulted 8 April 2016).

CRIN (Child Rights International Network) (2013) *Juvenile Justice: States Lowering the Minimum Age of Criminal Responsibility*, www.crin.org/en/library/pub lications/juve-nile-justice-states-lowering-minimum-age-criminal-responsibility (consulted 8 April 2016).

Daems, T. (2013) 'Punishment and the Question of Europe', in Daems, T., van Zyl Smit, D. and Snacken, S. (eds) *European Penology*. Oxford: Hart.

Dunkel, F. (2014) 'Juvenile Justice Systems in Europe: Reform Developments Between Justice, Welfare and "New Punitiveness"' *Kriminologijos Studijos* 1: 31–76.

European Commission (2009) *Communication from the Commission to the European Parliament and the Council: An Area of Freedom, Security and Justice Serving the Citizen*, http://eur-lex.europa. eu/legal-content/EN/TXT/?uri=CELEX%3A52009 DC0262 (consulted 8 April 2016).

European Commission (2015) *9th European Forum on the Rights of the Child: Coordination and Cooperation in Integrated Child Protection Systems*, http://ec.europa.eu/justice/funda-mental-rights/files/rights_child/9th_forum_report_en.pdf (consulted 8 April 2016).

Eurostat (2014) Unemployment Rates by Age and Gender, http://ec.europa.eu/eurostat/ statistics-explained/index.php/File:Unemployment_rates_by_age_and_gender.PNG (consulted 8 April 2016).

Fox, C., Albertson, K., and Wong, K. (2013) 'Justice Reinvestment and its Potential Contribution to Criminal Justice Reform' *Prison Service Journal* 207: 34–46.

Garland, D. (1985) *Punishment and Welfare: A History of Penal Strategies.* London: Gower.

Goldson, B. (1997) 'Children in Trouble: State Responses to Juvenile Crime', in Scraton, P. (ed.) *'Childhood' in 'Crisis'?* London: UCL Press.

Goldson, B. (2005) 'Child Imprisonment: the Case for Abolition' *Youth Justice: An International Journal*, 5(2): 77–90.

Goldson, B. (2013) '"Unsafe, Unjust and Harmful to Wider Society": Grounds for Raising the Minimum Age of Criminal Responsibility in England and Wales' *Youth Justice: An International Journal*, 13(2): 111–130.

Goldson, B. (2014) 'Youth Justice in a Changing Europe: Crisis Conditions and Alternative Visions', in Council of Europe and European Commission, *Perspectives on Youth: 2020: What Do You See?* Strasbourg: Council of Europe Publishing.

Goldson, B. (2015) 'The Circular Motions of Penal Politics and the Pervasive Irrationalities of Child Imprisonment', in Goldson, B. and Muncie, J. (eds) *Youth Crime and Justice*, 2nd edition. London: Sage.

Goldson, B. and Kilkelly, U. (2013) 'International Human Rights Standards and Child Imprisonment: Potentialities and Limitations', *International Journal of Children's Rights*, 21(2): 345–371.

Goldson, B. and Muncie J. (2012) 'Towards a Global "Child friendly" Juvenile Justice?' *International Journal of Law, Crime and Justice* 40(1): 47–64.

Hall, S., Critcher, C., Jefferson, T., Clarke, J. and Roberts, B. (1978) *Policing the Crisis: Mugging, the State and Law and Order.* London: Macmillan.

Hamilton, C., Anderson, K., Barnes, R. and Dorling, K. (2011) *Administrative Detention of Children: a Global Report*, UNICEF, www.unicef.org/protection/Administrative_detention_discussion_paper_April2011.pdf (consulted 8 April 2016).

Hammarberg, T. (2008) 'A Juvenile Justice Approach Built on Human Rights Principles' *Juvenile Justice* 8(3): 193–196.

Hammarberg, T. (2009) *Children and Juvenile Justice: Proposals for improvements.* Brussels: Council of Europe.

Hermann, C. (2007) 'Neoliberalism in the European Union' FORBA Discussion Paper 3/ 2007, *Studies in Political Economy* 79, www.forschungsnetzwerk.at/downloadpub/neoliberalism_eu_SR%2003–07.pdf (consulted 8 April 2016).

HEUNI (2014) *European Institute for Crime Prevention and Control, 'Publication Series No. 8: European Sourcebook of Crime and Criminal Justice Statistics'* www.heuni.fi/material/attachments/heuni/reports/qrMWoCVTF/HEUNI_report_80_European_Sourcebook.pdf (consulted 8 April 2016).

HM Government (2015) *Channel Duty Guidance: Protecting Vulnerable People from being Drawn into Terrorism*, www.gov.uk/government/uploads/system/ uploads/attachment_data/file/ 425189/Channel_Duty_Guidance_April_2015.pdf (consulted 8 April 2016).

Hudig, K. (2012) 'European Governments Step up Repression of Anti-austerity Activists' *Statewatch* 22(1): 1–3.

Institute for Race Relations (2016) *Prevent and the Children's Rights Convention*, www.irr. org.uk/wp-content/uploads/2016/01/IRR_Prevent_Submission.pdf (consulted 8 April 2016).

Joint letter to EU Members of Parliament (2015) 'Spain's Basic Law for the Protection of Public Security, a Threat to the Rights of Assembly and Asylum' /www.omct.org/human-rights-defenders/urgent-interventions/spain/2015/02/d22992/ (consulted 8 April 2016).

Keith, L. and Levoy, M. (2015) *Protecting Undocumented Children: Promising Policies and Practices from Governments.* Brussels: Platform for International Cooperation on Undocumented Migrants.

Kilkelly, U. (2011) *Measures of Deprivation of Liberty for Young Offenders: How to Enrich International Standards in Juvenile Justice and Promote Alternatives to Detention in Europe?* Brussels: International Juvenile Justice Observatory.

Loader, I. (2010) 'For Penal Moderation: Notes towards a Public Philosophy of Punishment', *Theoretical Criminology* 14(3): 349–367.

May, T. (2014) 30 Apr 2014: Column 833 Oral Answers to Questions, *Hansard*, www.publications.parliament.uk/pa/cm201314/cmhansrd/cm140430/debtext/140430-0001.htm (consulted 8 April 2016).

Ministry of Justice (2015) 'Youth Justice Statistics 2013/14: England and Wales'. London: Ministry of Justice.

Moore, M. (2013) *Save Money, Protect Society and Realise Youth Potential: Improving Youth Justice Systems during a Time of Economic Crisis.* Brussels: International Juvenile Justice Observatory.

Morgan, R. (2009) 'First-time Youth Offender Entrants: More Smoke and Mirrors' *Criminal Justice Matters* 76(1): 10–12.

Moyn, S. (2014) 'A Powerless Companion: Human Rights in the Age of Neoliberalism' *Law and Contemporary Problems* 77(4): 147–169.

Muncie, J. (2006) 'Governing Young People: Coherence and Contradiction in Contemporary Youth Justice' *Critical Social Policy* 26: 770–793.

Muncie, J. (2008) 'The "Punitive Turn" in Juvenile Justice: Cultures of Control and Rights Compliance in Western Europe and the USA' *Youth Justice* 8(2): 107–121.

Nolan, M. (2014) *'Human Rights and Market Fundamentalism', Max Weber Lecture Series 2014/2.* San Domenico di Fiesole: European University Institute.

NPCC (2015) *National Police Chiefs' Council National Channel Referral Figure'*, www.npcc.police.uk/FreedomofInformation/NationalChannelReferralFigures.aspx (consulted 8 April 2016).

Open Society Institute (2009) *Profiling Minorities: A Study of Stop-and-Search Practices in Paris.* New York: Open Society Institute.

Peck, J. (2013) 'Explaining (with) Neoliberalism, Territory, Politics' *Governance* 1(2): 132–157.

Phoenix, J. (2009) 'Beyond Risk Assessment: The Return of Repressive Welfarism', in Barry, M. and O'Neill, F. (eds) *Youth Offending and Youth Justice.* London: Jessica Kingsley.

Pruin, I. (2011) *The Evaluation of the Implementation of International Standards in European Juvenile Justice Systems.* Brussels: International Juvenile Justice Observatory.

RAN (2016) 'Radicalisation Awareness Network', http://ec.europa.eu/dgs/home-affairs/what-we-do/networks/radicalisation_awareness_network/index_en.htm (consulted 8 April 2016).

Rogan, M. (2013) 'Prison Policy in Times of Austerity: Reflections from Ireland' *Prison Service Journal* 207: 9–15.

Ruxton, S. (2012) How the Economic and Financial Crisis is Affecting Children & Young People in Europe, Eurochild, www.eurochild.org/fileadmin/public/ 05_Library/Thematic_priorities/02_Child_Poverty/Eurochild/Eurochild_Crisis_Update_Report_2012.pdf (consulted 8 April 2016).

Salomon, M. (2015) 'Of Austerity, Human Rights and International Institutions' LSE Law, Society and Economy Working Papers 2/2015. London: LSE.

Schennach, S. (2014) Child-friendly Juvenile Justice: from Rhetoric to Reality, Council of Europe, http://assembly.coe.int/nw/xml/XRef/Xref-DocDetails-EN.asp?fileid=20914&lang=EN (consulted 8 April 2016).

Scott, D. (2013) (ed.) *Why Prison?* Cambridge: Cambridge University Press.

Shapland, J., Atkinson, A., Atkinson, H., Colledge, E., Dignan, J., Howes, M., Johnstone, J., Robinson, G. and Sorsby, A. (2006) 'Situating Restorative Justice within Criminal Justice' *Theoretical Criminology* 10(4): 505–532.

Squires, P. (2015) 'Youth Justice Policy is Undergoing an Important Transition from "Costly Criminalisation" to "Precautionary Risk Management"' LSE Blog, http://blogs.lse. ac.uk/politicsandpolicy/the-austerity-of-youth-justice/ (consulted 8 April 2016).

Terra (2014) 'Inventory of the Best Practices on De-radicalisation from the Different Member States of the EU', www.terra-net.eu/files/nice_to_know/ 20140722134422CVERLTdef. pdf (consulted 8 April 2016).

Terre des Hommes (2015) 'Communiqué de Presse: Protecting European Children on the Move in Europe Needs a European Response', www.terredes hommes.hu/news/european-conference-focused-on-invisible-and-unprotected-european-children-on-the-move/7235 (consulted 8 April 2016).

Troller, S. (2010) *In the Migration Trap: Unaccompanied Migrant Children in Europe*, Human Rights Watch, www.hrw.org/world-report/2010/country-chapters/europe/central-asia-0 (consulted 8 April 2016).

Tucker, S. and Cadora, E. (2003) 'Justice Reinvestment' *Ideas for an Open Society* 3(3) www. opensocietyfoundations.org/sites/default/files/ideas_reinvestment.pdf (consulted 8 April 2016).

United Nations (2007) Committee on the Rights of the Child: General comment n°10 – Children's Rights and Juvenile Justice, www2.ohchr.org/english/bodies/crc/docs/ CRC.C.GC.10.pdf (consulted 8 April 2016).

Varinard, A. (2008) Commission de Propositions de Réforme de l'Ordonnance du 2 février 1945 Relative aux Mineurs Délinquants, www.premier-ministre.gouv.fr/chantiers/justice_856/rapport_varinard_sur_reforme_61850.html (consulted 8 April 2016).

Wacquant, L. (2009) *Punishing the Poor: The Neoliberal Government of Social Insecurity*. Durham, NC: Duke University Press.

White, R. (2015) 'Juvenile Justice and Youth Vulnerabilities' in te Riele, K. and Radhika, G. (eds) *Interrogating Conceptions of 'Vulnerable Youth' in Theory, Policy and Practice*. Rotterdam: Sense Publishers.

Williamson, H. (2002) *Supporting Young People in Europe: Principles, Policy and Practice, The Council of Europe International Reviews of National Youth Policy 1997–2001 – a Synthesis Report*, www.coe.int/t/dg4/youth/Source/IG_Coop/YP_Supporting_young_people_ Vol_I_en.pdf (consulted 8 April 2016).

World Prison Brief (2016) www.prisonstudies.org/country/united-kingdom-england-wales (consulted 8 April 2016).

Wren-Lewis, S. (2015) 'The Austerity Con' *London Review of Books* 37(4): 9–11.

8

'RACE', ETHNICITY, SOCIAL CLASS AND JUVENILE JUSTICE IN EUROPE

Colin Webster

Introduction

This chapter first emphasises the difficulty of presenting a systematic analysis of race, ethnicity and juvenile justice in Europe in the absence of comprehensive pan-European data. The discussion, then, relies largely on proxies for race and ethnicity such as 'foreign-born parents' and 'migrant' status. Moreover, the core line of argument emphasises the importance of taking account of the substantial over-representation of minority and migrant children and young people within conditions of persistent, long-term poverty and exclusion from education, employment or training (NEET), in order to explain the likelihood of their coming into contact with the police and juvenile justice systems across Europe. The central thesis is that welfare and justice mixes and clusters – the balance between welfare state provision and criminal (juvenile) justice system responses – among European countries best explain links between ethnicity, poverty, delinquency and juvenile justice. The chapter concludes that some children and young people in Europe are doubly punished for their minority/migrant status *and* for being poor.

What we know and don't know

Most European countries do not systematically gather data on race or ethnicity. Indeed, in many countries it is actually illegal to do so for historical reasons that render monitoring itself a form of discrimination. This chapter, then, faces the not inconsequential problem of a paucity of readily available, up-to-date, consistent and comparable data about the presence of minority ethnic children and young people in European juvenile and youth justice systems, alongside their treatment and experiences. The situation in the 'Anglo-Saxon' countries of the United Kingdom is unsatisfactory in an opposite way. In England and Wales, Scotland and Northern

Ireland, data pertaining to race and ethnicity and juvenile justice has been systematically collected and collated (locally and nationally) for some time but, arguably, to little positive effect in respect of reforming the system and ensuring equality before the law (Webster, 2012; Webster, 2015). The most recent and comprehensive analysis of race and ethnicity in juvenile justice processes in England and Wales, for example, reveals a persistent pattern of disproportionate black and minority ethnic (BAME) contact with the juvenile justice system (Uhrig, 2016).

The data presented and analysed by Uhrig (2016) is consistent with the findings of numerous other studies in the UK – and elsewhere – over many years. Although self-reported offending surveys generally reveal that BAME children and young people are no more likely to commit crime than their white counterparts (Sharp and Budd, 2003), BAME groups are:

- more likely to be arrested;
- more likely to be charged by the Crown Prosecution Service (CPS);
- more likely, once charged, to have their cases proceeded against at magistrates' courts;
- more likely to be committed for trial at the Crown Court (Uhrig, 2016).

Within such general patterning, more specific outcomes are also troubling. For example, although BAME children and young people are more likely to have their cases proceeded against at magistrates' courts, they are ultimately either 'as likely' or 'less likely' than white children and young people to be convicted. Equally, despite their over-representation within the number of young people being committed for trial at Crown Court, conviction rates for BAME groups are either proportionate to, or lower than, those pertaining to the white group (Uhrig, 2016). This implies that BAME children and young people are being both unduly processed into the lower courts *and* unnecessarily elevated to the higher courts. Moreover, BAME children and young people who are convicted – especially black and mixed ethnic young males – are normally more likely than their white counterparts to receive custodial sentences.

For many years, racist stereotyping has had the effect of distorting the criminalisation of BAME children and young people – again especially black and mixed ethnic young males – particularly in respect of robbery charges (Hall et al., 1978). Uhrig (2016) demonstrates that this phenomenon both persists today and that it amounts to unwarranted and excessive intervention. Even though black young males are ten times more likely than white young males to be arrested for robbery, therefore, they are only marginally more likely than white young males to be proceeded against at magistrates' courts, significantly less likely to be committed to the Crown Court for trial, no more likely to be convicted at either magistrates or Crown court and, even when convicted, no more likely to receive a custodial sentence. The picture is similar for mixed ethnic young males arrested for robbery. So, although robbery arrest rates for black and mixed ethnic males are high, outcomes pertaining to trials, convictions and sentences appear to be similar to the white group. This implies that *disproportionality* in child and youth imprisonment for the offence of robbery can be traced primarily to disproportionate arrest rates. Similarly, although the imposition of custodial sentences in respect of children and young people convicted of drug offences is relatively low, there is striking disproportionality in penal detention for BAME young people (males and females) convicted of such offences. This too can be traced back to a combination of disproportionate arrest and disproportionate custodial sentencing at the Crown Court (Uhrig, 2016).

If this known different, disproportionate and discriminatory treatment of BAME children and young people in England and Wales is replicated in the rest of Europe, the implications are profound for Europe's claims to uphold human rights and disallow discrimination. The European Union's adoption of rules for juvenile offenders based on human rights and the unanimous endorsement of the United Nations Convention on the Rights of the Child (UNCRC) in every country of Europe censures the illegitimate and unnecessarily harsh treatment and punishment of children. But the International Juvenile Justice Observatory (2008) report *Freedom, Security and Justice: What will be the future? – Consultation on priorities of the European Union for the next five years (2010–2014)* is silent about migrant and minority children.

This chapter argues that, given the paucity of systematic data pertaining to the treatment of minority ethnic children and young people in Europe's juvenile justice systems, we have to be creative in building a picture of what is happening. There are different ways of addressing this. The first, of course, is to use the data that is available and to attempt to extrapolate from it. Another indirect way is to seek to identify and analyse particular social and criminogenic conditions – and changes in these conditions – that may impact on minority ethnic children and young people in Europe, using proxies for race and ethnicity. That is, to examine critically the factors and risks experienced by minority ethnic children and young people that make it more likely that they – as an individual or as a group – will come into contact with the juvenile justice system.

Child poverty, parenting and class

The social scientifically powerful British Cohort Studies that were introduced in 1946 and subsequently tracked cohorts born in 1958, 1970, 1991 and 2000 – a total of over 70,000 people spread across successive generations – reveal, more than anything else, that the material conditions within which childhood is lived impose powerful and enduring influences and legacies that carry over into adulthood (Pearson, 2016). The general rule is that children who are born into wealthier families are more likely to do well in education, employment/occupation and health (including longevity). Those born into disadvantage, on the other hand, are more likely to struggle on every score. The impacts of social class and material conditions are also vitally important in shaping how children and young people are parented and supported as they grow up, develop and mature. Right from the outset, British

Cohort Studies have shown that *both* material conditions (wealth or poverty) and parenting matter. Moreover, contrary to popular belief, parenting cannot readily compensate for the deleterious impacts of poverty and material disadvantage. Parenting and other forms of support can foster resilience in the face of adversity but the capacity to parent and offer such support is itself contingent on material resources that are often persistently denied (Savage, 2009). Children living in enduring poverty are more likely than others to suffer psychological and social problems (including delinquency and criminality) as they grow up. Influenced by the British Cohort Studies, similar cohort studies – including whole population studies in the cases of Norway and Sweden – have been carried out in several European countries and the correlations between child and youth poverty and criminalisation/delinquency/offending will be discussed later.

At this point it is worth pausing to reflect upon why it is particularly timely to consider child poverty as a vital dimension of any analysis of juvenile justice in Europe. Poverty and the adverse socialisation effects that it can impose on children and young people, have deepened in recent years and continue to do so. According to the Institute for Fiscal Studies a 50 per cent increase in UK child poverty can be expected by 2020 (CPAG, 2016). Similarly, the OECD (2016) has shown that in recent years income inequality in Europe has remained at historically high levels, increasing significantly between 2010 and 2014. In fact, in 2014 income inequality reached the highest recorded level since the mid-1980s. Amongst the EU member states, the most unequal are the UK, the Baltic States, Spain, Greece and Portugal, whilst the least unequal are the Nordic States.

Returning to our theme of childhood poverty, parenting and social class, albeit using US studies, Putnam (2015) has shown that the class-based divide and socio-economic polarisation among young people has greatly widened in recent decades and it is linked to parental social class. Moreover, operating through education, the 'poverty deficit' for black children in the US is greater than anywhere else. An influential study focussing on parenting and socialisation found 'that higher social class provides parents with more resources to intervene in schooling and to bind families into tighter connections with social institutions than are available to working-class families' (Lareau, 2000: 173). A follow-up study showed that middle-class children's activities (where parents closely monitor, intervene and align with institutional and professional expectations), schooling and parent's occupation, impact crucially in influencing subsequent life experiences and outcomes. The study also revealed that for working-class and poor black and white young people their neighbourhood contact with the police was largely negative but for their white middle-class counterparts it was almost exclusively positive (Lareau, 2011).

These findings are unlikely to be significantly different in any European context. Serafino and Tonkin (2014), for example, have examined the extent to which the circumstances children grow up in affect their future life chances in selected European countries. They found that educational attainment and living in a workless household at aged 14 years, have the greatest impact on the likelihood of being in poverty as an adult in all of the countries considered. Household income mainly impacts on future life chances through the educational attainment of the child. However, childhood poverty alone predicts later poverty in the Southern and Eastern European countries, even after controlling for educational attainment. Parental education levels also impose a significant effect on the likelihood of low educational attainment for children and young people across many of the EU countries. Although the extent of this transmission varies it is highest for the Southern European countries and some Eastern European countries and Baltic States.

Migrant and minority child and youth poverty and the Eurozone crisis

Since the global recession of 2008 and the crisis of the Eurozone after 2010, the Eurozone's jobless total has risen whilst that of the US has fallen. American unemployment is back to its pre-recession levels of 5 per cent whilst Eurozone unemployment stands at just under 11 per cent (Elliot and Atkinson, 2016). The worsening of some European child and youth poverty rates (aged 0 to 17 years), especially among children and young people of foreign-born parents, is significant for our overall thesis about poverty, delinquency and criminalisation. According to Eurostat (2017a), the 'at-risk-of poverty' rate among children of *foreign-born* parents across the European Union, rose from 30 per cent in 2007 to 33 per cent in 2015. The corresponding rate in 2015 for children whose parents are *foreign citizens* was 38 per cent across the EU and 40 per cent in the Eurozone (Eurostat, 2017b). Furthermore, for children of foreign-born parents ('children with a migrant background', a proxy for minority ethnic children), substantial leaps in poverty rates began from 2007 onwards in Belgium, the Czech Republic, Greece, Spain and Italy. By 2015, almost a third of children across the entire EU suffered poverty risks, with significantly higher levels showing in specific countries including Belgium, Greece, Spain, France, Croatia, Italy and Lithuania (Eurostat, 2015).

Indeed, all children face a disproportionately high risk of poverty and social exclusion, and children with a migrant background and many minority ethnic young people face a higher risk still (Eurostat, 2016). Although 27.8 per cent of children in the EU are at risk of poverty or social exclusion, children with a migrant background face a greater risk of poverty than children whose parents are native-born. The highest 'at risk of poverty' rates for children with at least one foreign-born parent are in Belgium (37.2%), Greece (48.9%) and Spain (55.1%). Comparing 'risk of poverty' rates between the children of native-born parents and those of foreign-born parents across different countries in the EU reveals startling contrasts. The greatest differences are in Spain and Greece, whereas for other EU Member States including Croatia, the UK, Luxembourg, France, Czech Republic, Belgium, Slovenia, Netherlands, Austria, Cyprus – and especially the Nordic countries of Finland, Sweden, Denmark and Norway – the poverty rates among the children of foreign-born parents are approaching twice that of the children of native-born parents. (Eurostat, 2016).

Putting European child poverty levels in a wider political-economic context, Stiglitz (2016) has convincingly argued that the euro has led to an increase in inequality by deepening the divide *between* the weaker and stronger Eurozone members. But increasing inequality has also deepened and widened *within* specific Eurozone countries, especially those most negatively impacted by the financial crisis. The costs of such processes are especially high for children and young people 'whose future is being put in jeopardy [and] whose aspirations are being destroyed' (ibid: xx). Elliot and Atkinson (2016: 27) similarly argue that Europe's single currency has imposed an economic straightjacket – a 'machine for destroying rather than creating jobs' – and is serving to severely constrain social provision. By drawing attention to the fiscal politics of the single currency they argue that economic inflexibility has resulted in high levels of unemployment and underemployment, weak growth and a sense of semi-permanent crisis. Similarly, Gillingham (2016) has noted that the European financial crisis has been coming for a long time and radical reform is imperative. Whatever the merits of the respective arguments and critiques, however, the consequences of the Eurozone crisis for children and young people in many EU countries – particularly minority and migrant children – have been, and remain, dire.

As stated, austerity conditions and economic insecurities in Europe have fallen particularly heavily on children and young people in general and migrant children and young people in particular. The detrimental short-term – and possibly long-term – effects of the European Recession and Eurozone Crisis on children and young people are now on a new scale. The impact of such conditions on child-youth-adult transitions, and the extent to which different welfare state configurations serve to alleviate or compound such conditions, is vital (Walther and Plug, 2006). Fahmy (2014) has examined the nature, extent and distribution of vulnerability and disadvantage among 16–29-year-olds in Europe and concludes that although low income is endemic amongst young people across Europe, poverty appears to be higher in 'post-communist' and 'Mediterranean' (South European) welfare systems. In other words, particular systems can serve to perpetuate or deepen inequality whilst others have a mitigating effect. Here Antonucci et al. (2014) employ the concept of 'welfare mixes' to examine the interplay between the state, the family, schooling and labour market opportunities in shaping young people's transitions into adulthood. The case studies of Greece, Spain and the UK each reveal that the distribution of social risks (and ultimately the likelihood of criminalisation) is linked to the changing shape of 'welfare mixes' or a reconfiguration in the balance between family, state (and we might add 'criminal justice') and labour market as key sources of welfare support. Principally, this has included the substantial retrenchment of the welfare state and a corresponding increasing reliance on family as a source of welfare. Again, for migrant and minority children and young people the deleterious effects of such processes are amplified.

NEET: child and youth transitions across European countries

Many children and young people in conflict with the law are not in education, employment or training (NEET); excluded from the mainstream institutions that define social and economic life. According to Fergusson (2016: 5), such young people are 'living and surviving out of sight of systems which record all recognised forms of economic and educational participation'. Not unlike child poverty, NEET status is proliferating amongst young people in Europe and, also not unlike child poverty, the patterning of such status varies between countries/regimes. Pemberton (2015) first emphasises the importance of the international ratio of youth to adult unemployment rates (which has continued to increase across much of Europe), before differentiating between discrete regimes including 'Neoliberal', 'Liberal' and 'Social Democratic':

> The… Neoliberal regimes… have by far the highest NEET levels in both 15–19 and 20–24 age groups. The… Social Democratic regimes… have by far the lowest. The … Liberal regimes have NEET levels closer to those of the Social Democratic regimes particularly for 15 to 19-year-olds… it is important to note that the highest NEET levels are statistically significantly associated with regimes characterised as having the weakest forms of social solidarity… while those with the lowest NEET rates have the strongest social solidarity… In all, these findings suggest that high NEET levels are closely associated with other manifestations of social and economic inequality
>
> *Fergusson, 2016: 64–65*

Despite important differences between countries, however, young people's transitions across Europe have become more extended, non-linear, fragmented and precarious (Walther and Plug, 2006; Furlong, 2009; Antonucci et al., 2014). Such processes are accompanied by increasing tendencies to hold young people individually responsible for reconstructing their own biographies and transitions with all the risks that entails within precarious and unpredictable conditions (Pohl and Walther, 2007). Such responsibilising impositions and the risks that ensue are exacerbated by the general European crisis of youth unemployment and stagnant economic/labour market growth. In stark contrast to the demands placed on vulnerable young people – especially the demand for versatility and flexibility – national welfare and employment systems, policies and programs designed to support young people's transitions to work and integrate them into society have become more inflexible. Seemingly unable to adapt to crisis conditions and incapable of engaging with the complexity of young people's transitions, policies and institutional practices are increasingly lagging behind or misunderstanding the formidable realities experienced by identifiable sections of children and young people (including many BAME young people). There is little doubt that in respect of these children and young people the Eurozone appears to be failing (Elliot and Atkinson, 2016; Stiglitz, 2016).

Maestripieri and Sabatinelli (2014) show how increased work precariousness across European cities, together with scant welfare protection, has had particularly severe effects on young people, who face situations of acute instability that serve to compound their social vulnerability. As noted, the conditions that can facilitate or obstruct children's and young people's transitions vary according to national context. Of decisive importance have been different countries' reactions to the financial and Eurozone crises (Clasen, Clegg and Kvist 2012). Governments in many countries have reduced social spending and welfare investment in a decisive move towards less state-interventionist economic management. For example, the 'sub-protective transition regime' primarily found in the southern European countries, such as Greece, Italy, Spain and Portugal, is characterised by a high rate of unprotected living conditions and a 'dualistic' welfare regime in which the family and informal work play a significant role (Walther and Plug 2006). Young people are not entitled to welfare benefits and therefore engage in precarious jobs either in the informal economy, such as in Italy, or in casualised and often short fixed-term contracts, which are extremely prevalent in Spain. The cumulative effect of such processes compounds insecurities and vulnerabilities and, as ever, it is the poorest and most disadvantaged children and young people – including many minority ethnic young people – who suffer most.

Poverty, juvenile crime and criminalisation in Europe

A volume of recent evidence points (once again) to the underlying social structural foundations of crime and criminalisation in contexts of increasing poverty and extreme economic inequality. The underlying message is that inequality, poverty, relative and absolute deprivation and social exclusion are all linked to acquisitive offending and violence (see for example: Reiner, 2012a, 2012b; Webster and Kingston, 2014; Kingston and Webster, 2015; Fergusson, 2016; Reiner, 2016; Webster, 2017). But it is the long-term effects of persistent and recurrent poverty and inequality on childhood, adolescence, young adulthood and parenthood, unearthed by longitudinal studies, that provide the most vital insights into the links between poverty, juvenile crime and criminalisation. Savage (2009: Part I), for example, shows how the effects of enduring poverty on family, together with stressful life events over time, increase the likelihood of persistent offending.

Similarly, Hay and Forrest (2009) report that persistent offending between the ages of 10 and 14 years is significantly affected by both recent experience of poverty and long-term patterns of poverty experienced during the first decade of a child's life. They have calculated that the chances of being a persistent young offender increased by approximately 45 per cent for those experiencing poverty at age 9 years and by approximately 80 per cent for those experiencing enduring poverty throughout the first decade of life. The over-representation of minority ethnic children and young people within populations most likely to endure the corrosive effects of long-term poverty are particularly significant in this regard. A study by Hällsten et al. (2013) following two cohorts of children in Stockholm – native Swedes and the children of immigrants – up to their thirties, explained the differences in recorded crime between the two groups by reference to their parents socioeconomic resources and patterns of neighbourhood segregation (itself an expression of economic disadvantage) rather than by ethnicity or culture.

Hällsten et al.'s (2013) study is particularly pertinent to the question of the racialisation of juvenile justice, therefore. In Europe, as discussed earlier, the registered or recorded crime rates of immigrants far exceeds those of native populations. Although studies of self-reported crime present a mixed picture, the evidence generally implies that self-reported differences in rates of crime between immigrants and natives, if they exist at all, are too insignificant to explain the substantial variations in recorded crime rates. So, whilst parents' socioeconomic resources and patterns of neighbourhood segregation may go some way to explaining differences in recorded crime between native children and the children of immigrants as Hällsten et al. (2013) conclude, the researchers also report that selection processes in the juvenile justice system, or outright discrimination (selective criminalisation), may also explain such variations.

As Hay et al. (2007) point out, the effects of poverty on juvenile crime are apparently most evident in respect of serious rather than lower-level offending. This relationship holds between and within countries. However, the theorising that often emanates from such empirical data normally fails to explain why the majority of young people living in poverty and enduring multiple deprivation do not come to the attention of juvenile justice systems. Hay and Forrest (2009) suggest that the data can be read in such a way as to suggest that poor young people are more likely to be persistent offenders or, alternatively, that the same young people (perhaps especially immigrant and minority ethnic young people) may simply be more likely to be apprehended, arrested, charged, convicted and severely sanctioned. Here the distinction between the differential likelihood of committing crime on one hand, and the varying prospect of being formally criminalised on the other, is vital.

Scottish research that has focused on poverty-inequality-crime relations raises similar questions. The Edinburgh Study of Youth Transitions and Crime (ESYTC) (McAra and McVie, 2010) has found that youth offending is correlated to a broad range of social-structural vulnerabilities and adverse social conditions that are endured by children and young people. But the researchers have also argued very persuasively, that targeting the 'usual suspects' serves to label and stigmatize the most disadvantaged children and young people and expose them to increased prospects of criminalisation.

Welfare retreat, punitiveness and the increasing racialisation of juvenile justice in Europe

Whilst it is true to say that systematic up-to-date studies of race, ethnicity and juvenile justice in Europe are not readily available, we can begin to piece together a picture of the contemporary landscape by drawing upon the research that is to hand. The evidence implies that a hardening policy and practice context – perhaps most conspicuous in countries that have conventionally been known for their progressive penal tolerance – is bearing down particularly heavily on minority ethnic and immigrant children and young people. For example, the Belgium juvenile justice system – traditionally deeply embedded in welfarist priorities – has, more recently, been increasingly animated by the dramatisation of violent youth crime leading to political pressure to introduce repressive reforms and toughen-up what had perhaps previously been the most progressive system in Europe (Put and Walgrave, 2006; Cartuyvels et al., 2010; Christiaens, 2016). This pressure for tougher penalties and more repression has fallen heavily on minority – especially Moroccan, Immigrant or Eastern European – children and young people.

Similarly, Weenink (2009) has shown that one of the ways in which ethnic minority juveniles are punished more harshly in the Dutch juvenile justice system is through prosecutorial decision making, in which ethnic minorities are more often summoned to juvenile court. Further, the significant over-representation of ethnic minority children and young people in the Dutch juvenile justice system is, at least in part, a product of recent repressive reforms that have shifted the system from a welfare to a significantly more punitive approach. Ethnic minorities are very significantly over represented in police, court, prison and offending figures in the Netherlands. Well over half of the population of youth detention centres are foreign-born, and such disproportionality is further magnified when the number of juvenile prisoners whose parents are foreign–born are included (Beijerse and Swaaningen, 2006). As is the case all over Europe, this situation has been greatly exacerbated with the influx and growth of non-EU migrant children and young people.

The more progressive elements of juvenile justice law, policy and practice in Germany are also fraying at the edges, primarily induced by panics about young immigrant offenders (Cavadino and Dignan, 2006). Equally, juvenile justice in Italy is characterised by a high degree of specialisation on the part of all the agencies concerned, including police officers and prosecutors. Although custody is very rare, penal detention is used more extensively as a preventive measure with regard to foreign juveniles, who are not eligible for local authority social assistance and other welfare-based measures, since these are conditional on having a fixed address and a residence permit (Cavadino and Dignan, 2006). The French juvenile justice system has been – ostensibly at least – welfare-orientated like Belgium, the Netherlands, Germany and Italy. But the reality is somewhat different as growing public concern over the extent of youth crime has driven a shift towards a more neo-correctionalist approach. This harsher and more repressive climate has had a particularly adverse impact on immigrant children (Cavadino and Dignan, 2006; Grendot, 2006). In France there are very high levels of minority ethnic male youth poverty and unemployment accompanied by disproportionate arrests, prosecutions and convictions. In particular, immigrant children and young people suffer under French juvenile justice because they are less likely to enjoy residential and familial stability (Grendot, 2006).

In tandem with the burgeoning punitivity of some of the more traditionally progressive juvenile justice systems in Europe, others have retained their longstanding retributive approaches. The juvenile justice systems in Slovakia and Hungary, for example, although in flux, retain elements that directly flout international standards relating to the human rights of children and young people (Winterdyke, 2014). As previously noted, like most EU Member States, by law there is no systematic monitoring of ethnicity, but indirect data suggests that Roma children and young people are sorely over-represented in both arrests and incarceration.

For Muncie (2015) the 'globalization of juvenile justice' means the decline of social democratic approaches and the incursion of increasing punitiveness. There is certainly good evidence that juvenile justice systems in an increasing number of European countries are targeting young immigrants, children seeking asylum, young people of foreign descent and other children from minority ethnic communities, especially in respect of arrest and penal detention. This is particularly the case with regard to Roma and traveller children and young people across the entire EU (Muncie, 2015).

Conclusion

In the absence of systematically collected and collated comparative data we are simply denied a clear sense of the racialisation of juvenile justice in Europe. But we do know that child and youth poverty is deepening and widening across whole swathes of Europe and this imposes particularly negative impacts on (working-class) children and young people and, even more acute impacts, on minority and migrant children and young people. Equally, growing numbers of NEET young people, increasingly disfigured child-youth-adult transitions and a hardening of attitudes, laws, policies and practices within many juvenile justice systems, combine to disproportionately disadvantage minority ethnic children and young people and growing numbers of young migrants. Whilst crude forms of deterministic aetiology are deeply problematic there is manifest correlative evidence that such conditions give rise both to juvenile crime and to differentiated modes of criminalisation. As a consequence, profound forms of social and economic marginalisation and child and youth poverty effectively become criminalised (Fergusson, 2016).

Applying this perspective to the racialisation of juvenile justice in Europe, migrant and minority ethnic children and young people are more likely than any other group to be 'turned into' juvenile offenders. This is especially the case for growing numbers of child migrants. Because of their status as 'legal' or 'illegal' migrants – and also because of perceptions commonly held by the police and other juvenile justice agencies that such young people belong to supposed criminogenic ethnic groups – migrant and minority ethnic children and young people in Europe are particularly vulnerable to criminalisation through racialisation. Racialisation is the process of attributing meaning to national, religious or cultural characteristics, as a result of which individuals may be assigned to a social group deemed inferior, troublesome or criminal (Miles and Brown, 2003). There are a number of reasons for this including the correlations between poverty, structural exclusion, crime and criminalisation to which we have referred. But also, because in certain instances being 'foreign' or having migratory status may itself comprise a crime and actually be rendered illegal. Injustice is compounded in such cases and children and young people face double punishment: for being migrant/foreign *and* for being poor.

References

Antonucci, L. and Hamilton, M. (2014) 'Youth Transitions, Precarity and Inequality and the Future of Social Policy in Europe', in Antonucci, L., Hamilton, M. and Roberts, S. (eds.) *Young People and Social Policy in Europe: Dealing with Risk, Inequality and Precarity in Times of Crisis*. Basingstoke: Palgrave.

Antonucci, L., Hamilton, M. and Roberts, S. (eds.) (2014) *Young People and Social Policy in Europe: Dealing with Risk, Inequality and Precarity in Times of Crisis*. Basingstoke: Palgrave.

Beijerse, J. and Swaaningen, R. (2006) 'The Netherlands: Penal Welfarism and Risk Management', in Muncie, J. and Goldson, B. (eds.) *Comparative Youth Justice*. London: Sage.

Cartuyvels, Y., Christiaens, J., De Fraene, D. and Dumortier, E. (2010) 'Juvenile Justice in Belgium Seen Through the Sanctions Looking Glass', in Bailleau, F. and Cartuyvels, Y. (eds.) *The Criminalisation of Youth: Juvenile Justice in Europe, Turkey and Canada*. Brussels: VUB Press.

Cavadino, M. and Dignan, J. (2006) *Penal Systems: A Comparative Approach*. London: Sage.

Child Poverty Action Group (2016) 'Child poverty facts and figures', CPAG, available at www.cpag.org.uk/child-poverty-facts-and-figures (accessed 19 May 2018).

Christiaens, J. (ed.) (2016) *It's For Your own Good: Researching Youth Justice Practices*. Brussels: VUB Press.

Clasen, J., Clegg, D. and Kvist, J. (2012) *European Labour Market Policies in (the) Crisis*, Working Paper 2012.12. Brussels: European Trade Union Institute.

Elliot, L. and Atkinson, D. (2016) *Europe Isn't Working*. London: Yale University Press.

Eurostat (2015) Children at Risk of Poverty Rate by Country of Birth of Their Parents (population aged 0–17), 2014 (%), available http://ec.europa.eu/eurostat/statistics-explained/index.php/File:Children_at_risk_of_poverty_rate_by_country_of_birth_of_their_parents_(population_aged_0%E2%80%9317),_2014_(%25).png

Eurostat (2016) 'Children at Risk of Poverty or Social Exclusion', available http://ec.europa.eu/eurostat/statistics-explained/index.php/Children_at_risk_of_poverty_or_social_exclusion) (accessed 19 May 2018).

Eurostat (2017a) At-Risk-of Poverty Rate for Children by Citizenship of their Parents (population aged 0 to 17 years), available http://appsso.eurostat.ec.europa.eu/nui/show.do?dataset=ilc_li33&lang=en (accessed 19 May 2018).

Eurostat (2017b) At-Risk-of Poverty Rate for Children by Country of Birth of Their Parents (population aged 0 to 17 years) http://appsso.eurostat.ec.europa.eu/nui/show.do?dataset=ilc_li34&lang=en# (accessed 19 May 2018).

Fahmy, E. (2014) 'The Complex Nature of Youth Poverty and Deprivation in Europe', in Antonucci, L., Hamilton, M. and Roberts, S. (eds.) *Young People and Social Policy in Europe: Dealing with Risk, Inequality and Precarity in Times of Crisis*. Basingstoke: Palgrave.

Fergusson, R. (2016) *Young People, Welfare and Crime: Governing Non-participation*. Bristol: Policy Press.

Furlong, A. (ed.) (2009) *Handbook of Youth and Young Adulthood: New Perspectives and Agendas*. London: Routledge.

Gillingham, J. R. (2016) *The EU: An Obituary*. London: Verso.

Grendot, S. (2006) 'The Politicization of Youth Justice', in Muncie, J. and Goldson, B. (eds.) *Comparative Youth Justice*. London: Sage.

Hall, S., Critcher, C., Jefferson, T., Clarke, J. and Roberts, B. (1978) *Policing the Crisis: Mugging, the State and Law and Order*. Basingstoke: MacMillan.

Hällsten, M., Szulkin, R. and Sarnecki, J. (2013) 'Crime as a Price of Inequality? The Gap in Registered Crime between Childhood Immigrants, Children of Immigrants and Children of Native Swedes,' *British Journal of Criminology*, 53(3): 456–481.

Hay, C. and Forrest, W. (2009) 'The Implications of Family Poverty for a Pattern of Persistent Offending', in Savage, J. (ed.) *The Development of Persistent Criminality*. Oxford: Oxford University Press.

Hay, C., Fortson, E.N., Hollist, D.R., Altheimer, I. and Schaible, L.M. (2007) 'Compounded Risk: The Implications for Delinquency of Coming from a Poor Family that Lives in a Poor Community', *Journal of Youth and Adolescence*, 36(5): 593–605.

Kingston, S. and Webster, C. (2015) 'The Most "Undeserving" of All? How Poverty Drives Young Men to Victimisation and Crime', *Journal of Poverty and Social Justice*, 23(3): 215–227.

Lareau, A. (2000) *Home Advantage: Social Class and Parental Intervention in Elementary Education*. Updated Edition, Oxford: Roman & Littlefield.

Lareau, A. (2011) *Unequal Childhoods: Class, Race, and Family Life*. Oakland, CA: University of California Press.

Maestripieri, L. and Sabatinelli, S. (2014) 'Labour Market Risks and Sources of Welfare Among European Youth in Times of Crisis', in Antonucci, L., Hamilton, M. and Roberts, S. (eds.) *Young People and Social Policy in Europe: Dealing with Risk, Inequality and Precarity in Times of Crisis*. Basingstoke: Palgrave Macmillan.

McAra, L. and McVie, S. (2010) 'Youth Crime and Justice: Key Messages from the Edinburgh Study of Youth Transitions and Crime', *Criminology and Criminal Justice*, 10(2): 179–209.

Miles, R. and Brown, M. (2003) *Racism*, 2nd Edition. London: Routledge.

Muncie, J. (2015) *Youth & Crime*, 4th Edition. London: Sage.

OECD (2016) 'Inequality', www.oecd.org/social/inequality.htm (accessed 19 May, 2018).

Pearson, H. (2016) *The Life Project: The Extraordinary Story of Our Ordinary Lives*. London: Allen Lane.

Pemberton, S. (2015) *Harmful Societies: Understanding Social Harm*. Bristol: Policy Press.

Pohl, A. and Walther, A. (2007) 'Activating the Disadvantaged: Variations in Addressing Youth Transitions across Europe', *International Journal of Lifelong Education*, 26(5): 533–553.

Put, J. and Walgrave, L. (2006) 'Belgium: From Protection Towards Accountability?', in Muncie, J. and Goldson, B. (eds.) *Comparative Youth Justice*. London: Sage.

Putnam, R. D. (2015) *Our Kids: The American Dream in Crisis*. London: Simon & Schuster.

Reiner, R. (2012a) 'Casino Capital's Crimes: Political Economy, Crime, and Criminal Justice', in Maguire, M., Morgan, R. and Reiner, R. (eds.) *The Oxford Handbook of Criminology*, 5th edition. Oxford: Oxford University Press.

Reiner, R. (2012b) 'Political Economy and Criminology: The Return of the Repressed', in Hall, S. and Winlow, S. (eds.) *New Directions in Criminological Theory*, Abingdon: Routledge.

Reiner, R. (2016) *Crime*. Cambridge: Polity.

Savage, J. (ed.) (2009) *The Development of Persistent Criminality*. Oxford: Oxford University Press.

Serafino, P. and Tonkin, R. (2014) *Intergenerational Transmission of Disadvantage in the UK & EU*, London: Office for National Statistics.

Sharp, C. and Budd, T. (2003) *Minority Ethnic Groups and Crime: Findings from the Offending, Crime and Justice Survey 2003*. London: Home Office.

Stiglitz, J. E. (2016) *The Euro and Its Threat to The Future of Europe*. London: Allen Lane.

The International Juvenile Justice Observatory (2008) *Freedom, Security and Justice: What will be the Future? – Consultation on Priorities of the European Union for the Next Five Years (2010–2014)*, available at https://ec.europa.eu/home-affairs/sites/homeaffairs/files/what-is-new/public-consultation/2008/pdf/contributions/international_juvenile_justice_observatory_en.pdf (accessed 19 May, 2018).

The International Juvenile Justice Observatory (2017) website is available at www.oijj. org/en/european-policies-on-juvenile-justice/european-policies-on-juvenile-justice (accessed 19 May 2018).

Uhrig, N. (2016) *Black, Asian and Minority Ethnic Disproportionality in the Criminal Justice System in England and Wales*, London: Ministry of Justice, available at www.gov.uk/government/ uploads/system/uploads/attachment_data/file/568680/bame-disproportionality-in-the-cjs.pdf (accessed 19 May 2018).

Walther, A. and Plug, W. (2006) 'Transitions from School to Work in Europe: Destandardization and Policy Trends', *New Directions for Child and Adolescent Development*, 113: 77–90.

Webster, C. (2012) 'The Discourse on "Race" in Criminological Theory', in Hall, S. and Winlow, S. (eds.) *New Directions in Criminological Theory*. London: Routledge.

Webster, C. (2015) 'Race, Youth Crime and Youth Justice', in Goldson, B. and Muncie, J. (eds.) *Youth Crime and Justice*. 2nd edition, London: Sage.

Webster, C. (2017) 'Diversity and The Criminal Justice Process', in Harding, J., Davies, P. and Mair, G. (eds.) *An Introduction to Criminal Justice*. London: Sage.

Webster, C. and Kingston, S. (2014) 'Poverty and Crime', in *Reducing Poverty in the UK: A Collection of Evidence Reviews*, pp. 148–152, York: Joseph Rowntree Foundation, available, www.jrf.org.uk/report/reducing-poverty-uk-collection-evidence-reviews (accessed 19 May 2018).

Weenink, D. (2009) 'Explaining Ethnic Inequality in the Juvenile Justice System: An Analysis of the Outcomes of Dutch Prosecutorial Decision Making', *British Journal of Criminology*, 49: 220–242.

Winterdyke, J.A. (ed.) (2014) *Juvenile Justice: International Perspectives, Models, and Trends*. Boca Raton: CRC Press.

9

ILLEGAL YOUNG BODIES AND THE FAILINGS OF LIBERAL DEMOCRACY

Some reflections on the European Union's 'refugee crisis' and its implications for juvenile justice

Maria Pisani

Introduction

We live in an era of globalization: what happens in Aleppo today affects our lives within the European Union tomorrow. An image of the lifeless body of a child on a beach can go global within minutes, viewed around the world, although of course, not in every part of the world. We also live in an era that is defined by the intensification of interconnectedness and interdependence between people and nations. The processes of globalization, however, are not equal: inequalities are (re)produced and reinforced discursively, materially, symbolically and legally.

The global economic crisis and slow recovery continues to have a disproportionately negative impact on children and young people and their quality of life throughout the world, including within the European Union. The 'minorization of poverty' (Mai, 2010: 71) refers, not only to the increase in the number of children and young people living in poverty but, also, to the increasing number of people who are poor because they are young. The effects on children and young people in the poorest countries and regions in the world, however, were, and continue to be – again – disproportionate. In this era of globalization, with its intimate relationship with neoliberalism and increased interconnectivity (including access to social media), it comes as no surprise that, around the world, many children and young people are increasingly looking to migrate in search of better employment and economic opportunities and the hope of a better life (Mai, 2010). Massaged by *inter alia* age, 'race', gender and socioeconomic status, young people's chances to migrate in a safe and legal manner, are determined by where, and to whom, they happen to be born in the world – for some, the obstacles may be great, but then, often, the reasons for leaving, and the dreams of what awaits, are even greater.

For more than a decade the European Union has been witnessing the arrival of refugees and other forced migrants at its borders – this is nothing 'new'. In the summer of 2015 the external borders of the European Union were no longer able to contain the new arrivals, and countries who had, up until that point, remained relatively sheltered from forced migrant and refugee arrivals from the North of Africa suddenly had to deal with unprecedented arrivals. Represented as a 'threat' to the region, the (barely) functioning European Union asylum system imploded fast, human rights rhetoric and obligations were hastily replaced with national security rhetoric and bitter fighting between neighbouring States. Borders that were previously open started to close, razor fences demarcated lines of political space, delineating not only the sovereign state, but also those who belong and do not belong, those who are welcome and those who are not, those who are 'equal' and those who are not, those who have the right to rights, and those who do not (Arendt, 1968).

In 2015, 85,482 unaccompanied minors[1] (UAMs) applied for asylum in the EU+[2] (European Asylum Support Office, 2016), a 6% increase on the previous year. The reasons why children and young people choose/feel forced[3] to leave their home are as diverse as their reasons for choosing Europe as their destination. The decision to migrate is taken at the micro level (encapsulating the multifaceted individual and family resources available), interacting at a meso level (including informal social networks, often mediated through social media and, at times, including access to smugglers), and massaged by the broader geopolitical economic order (which will include the possibility of migrating in a legal manner and access to documentation). It is worth highlighting that in 2015 most UAMs crossing the Mediterranean were nationals of Afghanistan (54%), followed by Syrians (13%), Eritreans (7%), Iraqis (5%) and Somalis (4%), and thus children and young people coming from conflict-affected countries. The precise number of UAMs cannot be known since some countries within the European Union do not allow for their identification, and some unaccompanied minors will avoid being registered so as not to be held back by traditional protection mechanisms (International Organisation for Migration and Unicef, 2015). For the purposes of this chapter, my focus turns to those children and young people who, at the time of arrival, were under the age of 18, and who have either been refused protection or who remain within the European Union in an undocumented manner.

Reflecting on my own practice in Malta, and the broader European Union context, and drawing on the literature developed by forced migration studies and securitization literature, I demonstrate how apparently unrelated trends, namely containment and securitization discourse and practices, feed in to the illegalization and crimmigration of forced child migrants. I explore how the arrival of refugees and other irregular migrants, including unaccompanied minors, at the European Union external borders is socially constructed as a threat to national sovereignty and identity. In response to this 'threat' nation states justify a state of exception wherein the normal rules are suspended, and rights can be violated (Miggiano, 2009). An illegalization process is activated: a discursive, social, political and legal process, embodied in the term 'illegal immigrant', a course of action that must be framed within the securitization process, the strengthening of external and internal border controls, and the 'crimmigration' trend that positions migrants – perhaps especially children and young people – in spaces of precarity and illegality (Bauder, 2013: 2), strengthening the associations between 'illegal' status, crime and criminalization (Parkin, 2013). This process is juxtaposed with the State's legal obligations to protect the 'child', wherein a conflicting discourse emerges: the 'illegal threat' is also a 'vulnerable child', exposed to exploitation and at the mercy of criminal gangs. I look at how 'race' intersects with *inter alia* age and legal status, producing poverty, social marginalization and increased exposure to juvenile justice systems. I will argue that the prevalent, uncritical stance towards notions of human rights, the nation state and liberal democracy, alongside ambiguous and often opportunistic Western hegemonic representations of childhood and youth, are out of touch with the lived realities experienced by a growing number of 'illegal' children and young people within the European Union. An interrogation of these core concepts is central in understanding the experiences of undocumented youth in juvenile justice systems and informing advocacy strategies and service provision.

Forced migration and the denial of rights

By the end of 2014 global forced displacement reached the highest number ever recorded: 59.5 million people forced to flee their homes, defining an era 'dwarfing anything seen before' (United Nations High Commissioner for Refugees, 2015a). It is certainly undeniable that the number of forced migrants and refugees crossing the Mediterranean route has increased drastically: in 2015 more than one million people made the crossing, and more than 3,700 lost their lives in their efforts to reach safety. The images of refugees in camps in Greece, the columns of people crossing central Europe, the 'jungle' in Calais are, by now, familiar to us all. Their presence is felt in the European Union. The images of millions of refugees living in exile in camps in the global South, however, are somehow not so present: out of sight, they remain, out of mind.

Contrary to political and popular rhetoric within the European Union, the clear majority of the worlds' refugees are hosted in the poorest countries in the world; the so called 'developing countries' host 86% of the world's refugees (United Nations High Commissioner for Refugees, 2015b). To consider and understand the European Union context, it is important to reflect on the broader geopolitical perspective. Protracted refugee status – referring to people living in exile for more than five years – has become the invisible norm for too many children and young people in the global South. Child refugees who are born into this reality are quite literally warehoused in limbo. Contained in remote camps, they are denied the most basic rights to further education, work, residence and mobility, not to mention security and a life of dignity (Hyndman, 2011). Such children and young people are, in effect, imprisoned and the international community has thus far failed to provide any long-term political solutions.[4] So, in the absence of legal routes and opportunities, irregular movements have become an alternative strategy, for some, a rite of passage, whereby children and young people actively search for a way to overcome obstacles in search of their own 'durable solutions' and what is often perceived as the promise of utopia (Mai, 2010).

The 'illegalization' of young bodies

The disproportionate responsibilities placed on the poorest countries in the world do not occur in a vacuum, but rather, go to the core of the global North-South relationship. The past few decades have witnessed the strengthening of the external borders and the construction of Fortress Europe: the development of progressively restrictive migration and asylum policies intent on making it increasingly difficult for those in need to access protection within the European Union in a safe and legal manner. Such processes produce 'illegalization': 'the systematic process that renders people "illegal"' (Bauder, 2013: 4) (including visa restrictions and carrier sanctions). This approach includes an arsenal of tools, including increased cooperation with third countries, ensuring the externalization of European[5] border controls; detention and asylum processing and maritime patrols and militarized anti-smuggling operations,[6] and the construction of fences on the external land borders. These are just some examples of the increasingly militarized, ever more convoluted technologies of control the European Union has adopted to prevent unwanted migration and more importantly, to avoid its international obligations as enshrined within the 1951 Geneva Convention. For example, the EU-Turkey statement of March 2016 allows the forced return of all 'irregularly arriving migrants' back to Turkey (a country that, at the time, was already hosting three million Syrian refugees). The statement includes extensive financial and diplomatic concessions, including visa liberalization for Turkish nationals and re-energizing Turkish accession to the European Union (European Commission, 2016a). Aware of increasing racist sentiments and the rise of the Far Right within the European Union, the Turkish government has essentially used what Greenhill (2010) refers to as a 'weapon of mass migration' to apply coercive pressure on the European Union Member States – with extensive political and humanitarian consequences.[7]

At a financial cost of Euros 6 billion, criticism of the agreement has been scathing, including accusations of violating international human rights law;[8] contributing to, and increasing untold human suffering, putting more lives at risk as migrants and refugees seek alternative and more precarious alternative routes in search of protection;[9] further deterioration of the conditions in Greece and the Balkans, including violence, mandatory detention (including unaccompanied minors) and inhumane reception conditions;[10] pandering to right-wing populist discourse[11].

In short, the European Union Member States will apparently do whatever it takes to prevent asylum seekers from accessing protection within its borders, including the violation of international human rights law. Far from being in the best interest of arguably the most disenfranchised people in the world – including unaccompanied minors and other children – actions are rationalized and justified by appeals to self-defence. Sovereignty constructs the arrival of refugees and other forced migrants – the illegalized bodies – as a security threat: exceptional circumstances that demand an exceptional response, a shift from every day politics, to an emergency response that calls for militarization and the use of force against the migrant (read Muslim/terrorist) 'threat'.[12] Terms such as 'migrants', 'refugees', 'terrorists' and 'Muslims' morph,[13] propagated by alarmist media, authorizing 'racial hysteria in which fear is directed anywhere and nowhere... The result is that an amorphous racism abounds, rationalized by the claim of "self-defence"' (Butler, 2004: 39). An 'illegal' border crossing is constructed as a threat to sovereignty and the nation state – particularly in the case of young males (see for example United Nations High Commissioner for Refugees, 2016a), wherein representations of the young dark male criminal are recognizable (Clark, 2013). Reinforced by panic, the border demarking the line between 'them' and 'us' is reinforced, and liberal demo-cratic 'norms', including human rights, can be suspended. The 'illegalized' embody a depoliticized space wherein, by virtue of their political–and ontological–exclusion, lives are suspended, reduced to 'bare life' located outside the reach of law (see Agamben, 1998). And herein lies the toxic space in relation to children and young people. At the border, the young body is illegal first, child second, the enforcement of border patrols is prioritized over the States' international and national legal obligations vis-à-vis the rights of the child (Kanics, Hernandez, & Touzenis, 2010).

Fortress Europe: a state of exception?

The situation in the Mediterranean is constantly shifting. Whilst the number of arrivals into Greece dropped significantly in the Spring of 2016 because of the EU–Turkey statement, if we shift towards the Central Mediterranean, arrivals to Italy have remained consistent (almost 96,000 in the first seven months of 2017) whilst arrivals to Spain tripled in the first seven months of 2017 (8183 arrivals) (Missing Migrants, 2017). The European Union external borders, then, remain porous – tes-timony perhaps, above all else, to the agency and resilience of forced migrants and refugees fleeing persecution, conflict and existential threats. Whilst the Mediterranean crossings have been going on for more than a decade, 2015 marked the year the European Union faced the so called 'refugee crisis'. By the end of 2015 almost 1 million refugees crossed the maritime borders into the European Union and, in the first four months of 2016, 184,415 persons had crossed the Mediterranean, 82% of them coming from the world's top ten refugee-producing countries (United Nations High Commissioner for Refugees, 2016b). The external border states could no longer cope, and chaos ensued as migrants crossed internal borders. States clashed over border security and who should shoulder responsibilty for refugees, fences were errected, refugees were teargassed, and detention once again became normalized (see also Pisani, 2016).

The Greek context is particularly challenging. As European Union and other European states closed their borders, the situation within the country deteriorated rapidly. Thousands upon thousands of young refugees remained essentially stranded in limbo, in detention, in camps, and in the streets, awaiting either deportation to Turkey, relocation to another European Union Member State, or another way out.[14] As of the beginning of May 2016, 38% of the arrivals in Greece were minors (United Nations High Commissioner for Refugees, 2016c). Mandatory detention for new arrivals – including unaccompanied minors[15] – was introduced in Greece (United Nations High Commissioner for Refugees, 2016c). The harmful effects of detention – a practice that is not limited to Greece – is well documented (see for example Jesuit Refugee Service Malta, 2007, United Nations High Commissioner for Refugees and Integra Foundation, 2015; Bordermonitoring Bulgaria, 2016). The situation for children and young people is particularly disturbing, including exposure to violence, isolation and mental health problems, as described in the following extract taken from research conducted in Malta;[16]

> Some who spent more than a year, you can imagine how the person is feeling psychologically stressed, that is why they fight or do something worse. The soldiers tried to stop but they couldn't do anything about it. They never came between the people fighting. One day there was a very small boy, very thin, less than 50kg, and he was beaten by an older man, from Ghana… Many minors are being beaten severely, but what can the soldiers do?
> *United Nations High Commissioner for Refugees and Integra Foundation, 2015: 22*

The European Committee for the Prevention of Torture and Inhuman or Degrading Treatment or Punishment report a similar state of affairs in Greece, including deprivation of liberty for months on end, sometimes in conditions akin to solitary confinement, exposure to violence and abuse by police officers, limited access to outdoor recreation 'other than the possibility to kick a ball around within a small concrete yard fully sheltered and enclosed with metal bars' (Council of Europe, 2016: 63). A reminder, should it be necessary, that these children and young people *have not committed a crime* and that many will have claimed asylum. The report goes on to state that despite this, the children and young people are being treated as criminal suspects within a securitized approach (ibid: 8).

Human rights, and the liberal democratic norms otherwise taken for granted, are suspended by the sovereign power, justified by an 'exceptional' emergency (Agamben, 1998). As Bhaba (2009: 410) highlights, whether or not such children and young people have legal nationality, they are 'functionally stateless', and the 'fundamental rights to protection, family life, education and healthcare that these children have, in theory, under international law are unenforceable in practice. Moreover, their access to state entities willing and able to protect them is tenuous at best'. Within this scenario, 'crimmigration' also sets in, as outlined by Parkin (2013: 2), we can identify discursive criminalisation; the blurring of criminal law and migration law and the increased use of detention.

Welcome to dystopia

Throughout the European Union, unaccompanied minors are also warehoused in centres – sometimes for months and years on end, lacking basic access to healthcare, education, and decent housing conditions. In Malta, for example, particularly during the time of increased arrivals, younger unaccompanied minors (generally up to the age of 16) were placed in residential settings, whilst the older minors (17-year-olds) were generally housed in 'containers' in camps.[17] The physical conditions of the camps, limited access to material and non-material resources and protection (including *inter alia* access to welfare, employment, education) and an ongoing state of insecurity and/or fear of return, all contribute to a breakdown in social and cultural cohesion, social norms and regulations, producing an environment that is far from conducive to any sense of wellbeing:

> When the office is closed, it gets bad, people drink, fight…at night it is dangerous. There is no respect, people drink alcohol, beer and when the police come and find people drunk they tell us 'what can we do?' You go to your container and you lock your door, if they break your window you don't say anything…At night you don't sleep because people drink and shout. There are minors living there at the Open Centre, there is a space for minors, they are living together but it is an open space but even the minors drink, everyone drinks.
>
> *United Nations High Commissioner for Refugees and*
> *Integra Foundation, 2015: 27*

Such realities are being replicated in various countries within the European Union, particularly at the external borders. In February 2016, the Greek border with Macedonia was closed and, as the situation deteriorated rapidly, the Greek Interior Minister compared conditions in Idomeni to Nazi concentration camps (*The Independent*, 2016):

> Conditions at the makeshift camp – which lacks official structures and sanitation facilities – were not good to begin with. But in recent weeks, heavy rains have swept through the camp, turning the green fields into a mud-soaked bog… There are now about 11,500 people at the camp, grappling with the limited sanitation; many of the estimated 4,000 children at the camp wash in the cold, open air…Health workers have reported cases of pneumonia, septicaemia, complications of pregnancy and mental health issues. There have been at least two cases of hepatitis A, and more than 70 cases of respiratory infections among children.
>
> *Refugees Deeply, 2016*

Build a wall, erect a fence, remove the threat: European Union solidarity remains elusive

Efforts to develop and build a Common European Asylum System (CEAS) remain, at this point, a lost cause. Far from harmonized, differences between the Member

States exist in the number of asylum claims and, indeed, in the difference in refugee recognition rates – an asylum seeker's chances of being granted protection (and the quality of protection received) depend very much on where in the European Union they apply. The Dublin Regulation specifies which state is responsible for examining an asylum application determined by the point of entry, which, given the asylum restrictions described above, will generally be one of the external border states. For almost two decades the European Union countries of the north have pushed for humane asylum policies, but have simultaneously argued that asylum seekers remain in the country in which they first sought asylum, whilst the countries of southern Europe – and increasingly also eastern Europe – are arguing that the Dublin Regulation puts a disproportionate 'burden' on the external borders (Pisani, 2016). Following ongoing discussions, in May 2016 the European Commission put forward new proposals to reform the CEAS by

> creating a fairer, more efficient and more sustainable system for allocating asylum applications among Member States. The basic principle will remain the same – asylum seekers should, unless they have family elsewhere, apply for asylum in the first country they enter – but a new fairness mechanism will ensure no Member State is left with a disproportionate pressure on its asylum system.
>
> *European Commission, 2016b: 1*

The announcement was met with resistance from several Central European Member States, including accusations of 'blackmail' (Hungary) and comparisons with 'April Fool's Day' (Poland) (*The Washington Post*, 2016).

The relocation exercise, to date, can be described as nothing short of abysmal. In September 2015, the European Commission committed to relocating 160,000 people from the most affected member states. The number for relocation stands in stark contrast to – and falls far below – the number of people who arrived in 2015 alone. In the meantime, between 16 March and 11 April 2016, only 208 persons were actually relocated: 46 from Greece (to Estonia, Portugal and Finland) and 162 from Italy (to Portugal, France, Finland and Romania), bringing the total number of persons relocated to 1,145 (615 from Greece and 530 from Italy) (European Commission 2016c: para. 2.1). The obvious exception to this minimalist approach has been Germany,[18] whilst the UK, in the meantime, is exempted from this decision and will continue to expel asylum seekers arriving from other EUMS.[19] The absence of solidarity between the member states speaks volumes and makes a mockery of so-called European values. Paradoxically, all this is couched within a discourse that is steeped in the racialization of 'Muslims' represented as the unwanted 'cultural' other, excluded and criminalized and caricatured as hostile to 'European' values.

As right-wing populist movements have risen, so too have walls – border controls and fences replace the passport-free travel zone as individual states flex their sovereign muscle, reinforcing the boundary between 'us' and 'them'. Norway, Sweden and Denmark have reinstated border controls with neighbouring countries and Hungary, Austria, Croatia, Serbia and Macedonia have followed suit, a domino effect – in reverse (*Business Insider*, 2016). Calls such as those by the Hungarian Prime Minister to defend 'European Christianity against a Muslim influx' (*The Guardian*, 2015), or to 'protect our borders…against the swarm of migrants' by the British Prime Minister (BBC, 2015) have, apparently, become part of mainstream political discourse. Just as scenes of violence, police brutality, use of water cannons and tear gas have been used as a line of defence. The border provides the symbolic construction of the political community, demarcating the citizen and the non-citizen – there is no 'child', age is of no consequence and the border will always be defended against the threat of the illegal other.

The disappeared: protecting an illegal child?

Crossing the border and entering the fortress presents a number of possible outcomes, and consequent scenarios for unaccompanied minors, summarized as follows:

1. The child applies for asylum in the first country (more than likely Greece, Italy or Malta[20]). The young person will be located in a detention centre, camp or residence, sometimes subjected to invasive age assessment procedures, a process often cast in suspicion and doubt,[21] wherein, contrary to the 'best interests of the child' the burden of proof is placed on the minor. Relocation or family reunification might also be a possibility; however, this process can take months. In Greece, where the majority of unaccompanied minors have arrived, the situation has been described as 'near breaking point' and children and young people risk 'falling through the cracks' of the asylum system, their precarious rights placed in even more jeopardy (Migration Policy Institute, 2016).

2. The child is returned to Turkey as a 'safe' third country. On this possibility the Migrant Policy Institute reports that the capacity to meet procedural guarantees in 'the overburdened and underdeveloped asylum systems of Greece and Turkey is already legally difficult' and access to a fair hearing 'will be impossible to guarantee' (Migration Policy Institute, 2016).[22]

3. The child does not apply for asylum, and either remains in the country of arrival or continues his/her journey in an irregular manner.

It is the third scenario that lends itself to an increasing number of 'disappeared' children and young people. The absence of legal migration routes and the closure of borders make for a lucrative business for smugglers, criminal networks and other intermediaries to provide a number of services including *inter alia* recruitment, documentation and transport. According to a Europol report:

> An entire [criminal] infrastructure has developed over the past 18 months around exploiting the migrant flow. There are prisons in Germany and

Hungary where the clear majority of people arrested and placed there are in relation to criminal activity surrounding the migrant crisis.

The Observer, 2016

Research has demonstrated how irregular migration exposes children and young people to exploitation, smuggling and trafficking (Dimitriadi, 2016; REACH, 2015). In January 2016 Europol announced that 10,000 registered refugee children were missing (*The Guardian*, 2016a), speculating that many may have 'fallen into the hands' of traffickers.[23] The report represented the first attempt to quantify a long-standing concern. That said, this new evidence beholds an interesting shift in discourse: the emphasis on 'threat' can be juxtaposed with this focus on 'vulnerability' whereby 'illegal immigrants' now morph into 'child refugees' (see for example *The Observer*, 2016). The contradictions between these two representations, the criminalized threat and the vulnerable child in need of protection (ergo, stripped of agency and the complex contexualized realities that feed into forced migration at a micro/meso/macro level), are more than evident. Certainly, such 'victim'-'threat' contradictions are inherent to contemporary juvenile justice (Goldson, 2004), from the traditional welfare vs justice/welfare vs punishment debates, to the contemporary 'amalgam of rationales' shaping juvenile justice (Muncie, 2006: 2). However, there is an ontological shift in the case of the illegalized child, whereby reminding the State of its responsibilities towards its citizenry simply fails to cut it: the child is neither a citizen, nor a citizen 'in the making' (Pisani, 2016). In light of this, the implications in relation to policy and service provision also require some unpacking.

To be clear, children and young people including asylum seekers and those who remain undocumented have been disappearing for years. However, and as argued by Sigona and Allsopp (2016), the link between the disappearance of thousands (upon thousands) and trafficking is highly speculative at best, and simply is not borne out by research. As acknowledged by the European Commission, in truth, very little is known about the lives of the disappeared, but their reasons for disappearing are well documented, and can be linked to the consequences of securitization practices including surveillance practices, and external and internal border controls:

> ...some UAMs, in particular those who do not seek asylum may avoid registration by authorities in the country they first enter, to continue their journey to another state. Thus, very little is known about this group of unaccompanied migrant children who manage to stay off the radar of authorities in the (Member) States.
>
> *European Commission, 2015*

Over the past ten years I have worked with many unaccompanied minors who have expressed their intentions to leave Malta, and to continue their journey through Europe – and leave they did. Often, they have to make their 'escape' more than once: identified by their fingerprints, they would be returned to Malta as the first country of asylum (Pisani, 2011). Arguably an act of resistance against the control of the state, in the absence of a legal route, the intention is to continue their journey under the radar and in irregular status in order to reach their chosen country of destination:

> After leaving detention a good number manage to move on to a clandestine life on the continent, a few being identified and returned to Malta in line with Dublin 2 specifications, some of them going through this experience more than once
>
> *Pace et al., 2009*

In Malta, a young persons' decision – and it is a decision, there is agency, albeit constrained by structural conditions – to leave, often also reflects a disconnect with how state authorities fail to address their 'needs' within a 'child protection' approach that, paradoxically, reproduces vulnerability. For example, research conducted by the National Commission for Child Policy and Strategy (2014: 45) in Malta documents how unaccompanied minors perceive the Care Order as a 'punishment' whereby their 'independence is stifled'. Limited financial resources (children under the age of 16 years are given seven Euros a week, which barely covers the telephone expenses required to maintain contact with their families), racism, a lack of employment opportunities, an education system that fails to meet their needs, and the constraints of living on a small island (that is not, after all, their chosen destination but simply a staging post) are just some of the factors that interact, pushing young migrants to continue their journey to 'Europe' in the hope of improving their life opportunities (see also Pace et al., 2009; Sigona and Allsopp, 2016).

What emerges over and over again is this disconnect – grounded in different institutional, cultural, socioeconomic and legal experiences and realities – whereby the focus on control and vulnerability jars with constructions of independence and responsibility (see also Mai, 2010). I recall a conversation I had some years ago with a 15 year old who made the journey from Gambia to Malta – let's call him 'Daniel'. In response to his feelings of frustration, I explained that, in Malta, children and young people aged 15 years are not regarded as 'adults' and, as such, are not allowed to work to which he replied,

> I left home when I was 14, I travelled across the Sahara alone, I crossed the Mediterranean alone, and I was in detention alone. I am responsible for my sister's education back home, she is relying on me. I am not a child and I can look after myself.

Daniel's response draws attention to alternative constructions of the 'child' and 'adult' and the cultural narrative that, to borrow from Burman (2008: 67) defines 'who he is', 'why he is the way he is' and 'where he is going'. His 'maturity' is evidenced in his taking responsibility for another person. Far from providing 'care', however, the institutional response was experienced as controlling, simply not providing the support Daniel requested according to his needs and priorities. Within a month

Daniel had left Malta and now presumably makes up one of the 10,000 invisible, hidden and socially excluded child migrants in Europe. Daniel was also aware that his window of opportunity was limited. At the age of 18 years he would no longer be entitled to protection and, as such, the decision to move was also driven by the imperative to avoid deportation[24] (European Commission, 2015; Pisani, 2011).

Similarly, efforts to be reunited with family members through family reunification are often drawn out. A lack of trust in the asylum system on the part of unaccompanied minors, combined with prolonged delays and lack of cooperation between Member States, leads to many children and young people being urged to take control of the situation themselves and to continue their journeys in irregular ways (European Commission, 2016d).[25] Even as the internal European Union borders are reinforced, migration through irregular routes continues as children and young people tap in to their own networks to arrange their journeys. The process may also be facilitated by 'smugglers' or 'agents' and the use of falsified documents (REACH, 2015). Depending on the route and conditions of travel, smart phones can also provide updated information including maps, GPS, news on changing routes and new border restrictions and contact with family and friends. In my own experience, it is often Facebook that is used to communicate. Far from passive, such children and young people exercise agency in their efforts to defy the structural obstacles and immigration/asylum systems that often intensify their vulnerability (see also Sigona and Hughes, 2012). With new border controls, for example, the conditions at the external borders have deteriorated rapidly and thousands of refugees are left stranded at the borders, as noted by Save the Children:

> It is likely that there are 400 unaccompanied children aged up to 17 years in Idomeni, maybe more, who are waiting to pass the border and continue their journey to northern countries of Europe. But, the exact number is not clear, no one knows how many unaccompanied children are in Idomeni due to the lack of coordination, legislative gaps and closed borders.
>
> *themanews.com, 2016*

'Missing': the systematic exclusion of young undocumented migrants

Given the above, it is fair to surmise that the rough calculation of 10,000 unaccompanied minors who are living within the European Union in an irregular manner – 'missing' (*The Guardian*, 2016a) – is likely to be substantially underestimated. Furthermore, this figure refers to those unaccompanied minors who are actually registered in the asylum system and, as such, takes no account of unregistered children and young people. If we turn attention to the broader group of undocumented minors living within the European Union the numbers are little more than guestimates: reliable and systematic data mechanisms are essentially non-existant and, even where statistics exist, they are often not disaggragated according to age (Platform for International Cooperation on Undocumented Migrants, 2015: 7). By way of example though, an estimated 120,000 undocumented migrant minors are living in the UK alone (Sigona and Hughes, 2012: vii).

Certainly, what emerges over and over again in research is the systematic exclusion of young undocumented migrants (see, for example, Mai, 2010; UNESCO, 2010; Sigona and Hughes, 2012; United Nations High Commissioner for Refugees and Integra Foundation, 2015). The situation is nothing short of toxic, restrictive and punitive immigration policies mean that children and young people are forced to endure: increased risk of human rights violations; heightened exposure to labour market exploitation and homelessness; restricted access to healthcare, education and basic public services; disproportionate exposure to crime and criminalisation and; deeply problematic immigration enforcement practices, including raids, detention and identity checks (UN General Assembly, 2014; Global Migration Group, UNICEF and OHCRH, 2013).

Access to education is a legal requirement in all of the European Union member states and this, in principle, applies equally to unaccompanied child migrants. In reality, however, language barriers, administrative obstacles, fear of surveillance and exposure to immigration authorities, official examinations and adversarial certification processes combine to close-off access to education (PICUM, 2015; aditus Foundation, 2014; UN General Assembly, 2014). This is often compounded by the young person's compelling need to obtain an income, both to survive and, in many cases, to send remittances back home (UNESCO, 2010). It is not that education is not valued but, rather, that circumstances compel children and young people to secure subsistence. In stark contrast to dominant European trends wherein young people's economic dependence on parents is increasingly protracted (Goldson and Jamieson: 2002: 91), 'dependence' in this context is inverted as one young person explains:

> For me it is better to get an education but for now I cannot get an education and I cannot learn something because my family are waiting for me... I am ready to get a job and help my family.
> *Cited in United Nations High Commissioner for Refugees and Integra Foundation,*
> *2015: 45*

Beyond this, attending to other more immediate concerns and practical necessities – including eating and finding accommodation (Pisani and Azzopardi, 2009) – is imperative.

Lack of legal status and the ever-present fear of deportation also serve to compromise young people's access to safe and secure accommodation whereby, in their efforts to remain 'hidden', young undocumented migrants necessarily experience high levels of housing mobility (Sigona and Hughes, 2012). This is further aggravated by random evictions, little or no access to public housing and unduly restricted access to private accommodation due to the penalties landlords may face if they house 'illegal young bodies'. And all of this is further massaged by racism and discrimination, leading to overcrowding, substandard living conditions and homelessness (UN General Assembly, 2014). Low achievement in education, inse-cure accommodation and forced patterns of mobility, 'race', age and a lack of legal status interact and often negatively impact upon employment prospects. It is not unusual, therefore, for young undocumented migrants to be forced into the 'black economy' where they endure further violations and face disproportionate expo-sure to exploitation. It is a vicious circle and, despite encountering a multitude of illegal employment practices, young people's needs for basic subsistence, combined with fear of the authorities and lack of rights awareness (such as it is), render them unable to report such abuses (European Network Against Racism, 2013; Sigona and Hughes, 2012).

Clark (2013) argues convincingly that whilst males, ethnic minorities and working-class children and young people are commonly over-represented in juve-nile justice systems across Europe and beyond, establishing correlations should not be taken to imply causality. Indeed, such patterning tells us as much, if not more, about targeted surveillance, concentrated policing, processes of criminalization and the myriad injustices of the 'justice' process, than they do about the distribution of actual youth offending (Goldson and Muncie, 2015). As such, whilst being male, ethnically minoritized and poor may not necessarily predispose a young person to commit an offence, the likelihood of their becoming a 'youth crime statistic' is significantly increased (Clark, 2013: 128). In the case of young undocumented migrants, we must also factor in how legal status plays in to this scenario. Indeed, such phenomena are intensified when immigration law and criminal/juvenile jus-tice law merge. In light of systematic exclusion, many undocumented children and young people are cast into the shadows, both metaphorically and ontologically. The means by which the same children and young people are recruited as drug couriers and/or sex workers, come to depend on other illegal activities in order to survive (Mai, 2010), or turn to people smugglers and traffickers as a source of support 'by choice, through desperation, or through exploitation and abuse' (House of Lords, 2016: 53), are fast becoming an increasingly potent concern for juvenile justice research, law, policy and practice.

Illegalization and criminalization

Research has demonstrated how chronic poverty, social exclusion, unemployment and political alienation, intensified as a result of ongoing economic crises, austerity measures and uncertainty, are just some of the conditions that produce a fertile context for juvenile crime (Goldson, 2014). Whilst unaccompanied and separated children and young people are both disproportionately and acutely exposed to such phenomena (and their intersections), the very processes that 'illegalize' them, necessarily also expose them to heightened prospects of criminalisation. By defi-nition, they 'transgress the law' (Arendt, 1968: 288) and the presence of 'foreign' children and young people – including unaccompanied minors and young undocu-mented migrants – is already being felt within the juvenile justice systems of various European Union Member States. Certainly, juvenile justice systems across Europe face complex and diverse challenges and, as the number of irregularly residing young migrants and asylum seekers increases within the European Union, so too will their contact with the law.

As unaccompanied minors continue to make their way to the European Union, the number of children and young people denied protection and access to rights will increase. Whilst procedures and the quality of service provision vary throughout the European Union Member States (often according to the number of arrivals), the challenges are both common and recurrent. A recent report published by the House of Lords in the UK Parliament captures some of the key issues:

> The implementation of existing EU measures to protect unaccompanied migrant children has been poor, and the European Commission has not renewed its 2010–2014 Action Plan on unaccompanied minors. We are concerned that the EU and its Member States—including the UK—may have lost sight of the plight of unaccompanied migrant children. We have, therefore, sought to assess the nature and scale of the challenges they face across the EU. We have asked whether existing EU provisions are sufficiently clear and enforceable, and what further measures are needed to address the needs of unaccompanied migrant children. We received a wealth of evidence suggesting that a number of underlying, cross-cutting, problems affect unaccompanied migrant children. They face a culture of disbelief and suspicion. Authorities try to avoid taking responsibility for their care and protection. Existing EU and national measures are poorly implemented. Unsurprisingly, many children have lost trust in the institutions and measures intended to guarantee their rights, safety and well-being.
>
> *House of Lords, 2016: 3*

This contrasts sharply with the undertaking expressed by the European Union Agency for Fundamental Rights:

> European Union institutions are particularly concerned about the *rights of children, and in particular, those who are in a vulnerable situation, such as separated, asylum-seeking children*... the European Commission [has] identified the respect, protection, promotion and fulfilment of the rights of the child as one of its main priorities... *to ensure that the rights of children as immigrants, asylum seekers and refugees are fully respected in the EU and in Member States' legislation and policies.*
>
> *Fundamental Rights Agency, 2010: 18, emphases added*

Moreover, in the juvenile justice context, the lived experiences of many young unaccompanied migrants expose the profound limitations of the European 'child-friendly justice' project as articulated in the Guidelines of the Committee of Ministers of the Council of Europe:

Children should be treated with care, sensitivity, fairness and respect throughout any procedure or case, with special attention for their personal situation, well-being and specific needs, and with full respect for their physical and psychological integrity. This treatment should be given to them, in *whichever way they have come into contact with judicial or non-judicial proceedings or other interventions, and regardless of their legal status* and capacity in any procedure or case.

Council of Europe, 2011: 18, emphases added

Indeed, to take a single example, given the core values we would normally associate with a 'liberal democracy' – justice, rights, equality – one would think it inconceivable that a State can effectively 'imprison' thousands of children and young people where no crime has been committed, and where the notions of 'guilt' or 'innocence' are not brought into the equation. But illegalized children and young people are not, of course, citizens of the State and, as such, they appear to fall outside of such protections. As Dembour (2015) has argued, even the European Court of Human Rights treats migrants as 'aliens' first, and as human beings second. There is no 'social contract' here and claims to citizenship are profoundly compromised. It follows that in the case of the illegalized young body – the non-citizen – the 'right to rights' cannot be assumed (Pisani, 2016). In short, illegalized bodies are excluded from the democratic process, since democracy is ultimately limited to citizenship, and as such it is inherently exclusionary (Pisani, 2016). Instead, illegalized bodies, are constructed as a threat to the state, rather than the responsibility of the state. These children and young people embody contemporary structural changes and shifts in global governance and, as Weber, Fishwick and Marmo (2014: 233) point out, the challenge (not least for juvenile justice) is to move beyond the hegemony of the nation state and sovereign structures, and to 'consider how security may be achieved for all, and not only for those who are formally recognized as citizens or legal residents'.

Conclusion

The vast majority of children and young people crossing the Mediterranean are fleeing war, conflict, persecution and poverty. They also come in search of safety, protection, employment: a better life. In order to understand the needs and realities of irregularly residing children and young people living in the European Union, it is imperative that we position the discussion within its geopolitical contexts. Whilst international borders are increasingly open to the movement of finance, services, commodities and ideas, this is not the case for people. The arrival of refugees has been positioned as a threat to the labour market, to the welfare state, to social cohesion, to cultural identity and to national/regional security, producing a toxic space that is embodied in the illegalized and racialized young body. At the border, the child is an illegal immigrant first, and a vulnerable minor second: embodying the reconstituted and yet still very recognizable 'wretched of the earth' (Fanon, 1963).

Global, historical, economic, regional and national forces are colliding: unaccompanied minors in an irregular status embody this nexus, wherein human rights, as enshrined in the United Nations Convention on the Rights of the Child, are seemingly at odds with the interests of the nation state. Throughout Europe, irregularly residing unaccompanied minors face profound obstacles to accessing basic services, protection and justice (PICUM, 2015). The precise number of 'missing' children and young people living within the European Union is not known, yet certainly, the foundational needs of thousands of unaccompanied asylum seekers are simply not being met.

In their efforts to avoid detection, many children and young people are being compelled to live out their lives beyond the State and, in many cases, outside the law. Ironically, it is when an 'offence' has been committed that the child/young person becomes visible. And herein lies the paradox of the nation state and the notions of equality and inalienable human rights. As Arendt (1968) argued so pursuasively, rights are inextricably linked to the nation state, sovereignty and territory: the rights of the illegalized body cannot be upheld. Whilst far from being a new phenomenon, the growing presence of young undocumented/irregularly residing migrants within the European Union may force us to recognize and address this truth. Certainly, it is not a reality that juvenile justice systems can continue to ignore.

Notes

1 Directive 2013/33/EU of the European Parliament and of the Council of 26 June 2013 laying down standards for the reception of applicants for international protection (recast) defines 'unaccompanied minor' as

> a minor who arrives on the territory of the Member States unaccompanied by an adult responsible for him or her whether by law or by the practice of the Member State concerned, and for as long as he or she is not effectively taken into the care of such a person; it includes a minor who is left unaccompanied after he or she has entered the territory of the Member States.

2 At the time of writing, the EU+ is composed of EU-28 plus Norway and Switzerland.
3 This dichotomy does not work and the practical reality is often much more complex.
4 This ongoing scenario also continues to put pressure on the host and neighbouring states, which, all too often, also face economic and governance challenges. In May 2016, the Government of Kenya announced that it would be closing Dadaab and Kakuma refugee camps. The camps have been hosting hundreds of thousands of refugees from Somalia, South Sudan and the Democratic Republic of Congo for more than two decades. The decision is a violation of international law, and the negative impact on the lives of refugees will be considerable (see Refugees International, 2016) This is just one example of how the international community has failed to support host countries and to address the causes and realities of protracted refugee status.
5 The EU is not alone in this approach. Similar practices have been implemented in the US, Australia and beyond, wherein orders have shifted from territorial boundaries beyond and within, justified by the manipulation of national and international law. These

so called 'smart' borders are established to ensure that 'security threats' are blocked, whilst the 'trusted' are free to cross (see Heiskanen, 2014:70).

6 The absence of legal safe means of travel has witnessed the proliferation of ever more dangerous and unscrupulous smuggling networks. The UN Special Rapporteur on the human rights of migrants refers to the 2000 Palermo Protocol against the smuggling of migrants as a repressive tool used to serve State interests. He argues that the tool demonstrates a simplistic understanding of the phenomenon that is not only dangerous, but also dismisses the rights of refugees (Crépeau, 2003).

7 Muammar Gaddafi famously adopted similar threats in 2010, see for example the headline 'Gaddafi: Europe will "turn black" unless EU pays Libya £4bn a year' (*The Telegraph*, 2010).

8 See for example the Council of Europe report which states:

> [The agreement] raises several serious human rights issues relating to the deten-
> tion of asylum seekers in the "hotspots" on the Greek Aegean islands, the return
> of asylum seekers to Turkey as a "first country of asylum" or "safe third country",
> the Greek asylum system's inadequate capacity to administer the asylum process in
> the hotspots and delays in the provision of EU support to Greece, the likely low
> level of resettlement of refugees from Turkey, and delays in the disbursement of
> EU financial assistance to Turkey's efforts to support Syrian refugees.
>
> *Council of Europe, 2016*

9 Attempts to close the Eastern Mediterranean route through the EU-Turkey deals have witnessed a shift in smugglers' operations back to the Central Mediterranean route. 500 refugees drowned attempting the journey in the second week of April 2016 (see, for example, *New Europe*, 2016). Over the past four years an estimated 8,100 refugees and forced migrants lost their lives in the Mediterranean (Missing Migrants Project, 2016).

10 See for example Médecins sans Frontières, 2016; UNHCR, 2016.

11 The UN Special Rapporteur on the human rights of migrants stated:

> The only objective of European leaders is thus clearly stopping migrants. At any
> cost. At any financial cost. At any political cost resulting from endorsing an increas-
> ingly undemocratic regime. At any human cost to the migrants. All this to assuage
> the European electorates who are fired up against migrants by nationalist populist
> discourses. Thus, European leaders are actually vindicating the nationalist populist
> representation of migrants and refugees as a threat to the labour markets, the secu-
> rity, the health and the values of Europeans.
>
> *Crépeau, 2016*

12 See for example, newspaper headlines such as 'EU border agency warned of migrant terror threat 18 months ago – but nothing was done' (*The Telegraph*, 2015).

13 Following the Brussels terrorist attacks of 22 March 2016, anti-immigrant hate speech and acts were reported in Bulgaria, Hungary and Sweden. Hate crime incidents were also reported in Austria, Germany, Finland and Greece (Fundamental Rights Agency, 2016).

14 To get some perspective, arrivals on the island of Lesbos amounted to more than 70,000 people in the first two months of 2016 and there is space to shelter 6,000 (*Huffington Post*, 2016).

15 Article 3 of Directive 2013/33/EU of the European Parliament and of the Council of 26 June 2013 laying down standards for the reception of applicants for international protection (recast) states: 'Unaccompanied minors shall be detained only in exceptional circumstances. All efforts shall be made to release the detained unaccompanied minor as soon as possible'.

16 The Government of Malta had asserted its sovereignty in implementing a mandatory detention policy for all asylum seekers, extending to an 18-month duration for rejected asylum seekers. This is despite the fact that:

> The mandatory detention legal regime applied to unauthorized arrivals and asylum seekers does not seem to be in line with international human rights law. Migrants in an irregular situation are subjected to mandatory detention without genuine and effective recourse to a court of law. The length of their detention has not been clearly defined under law.
>
> *UN Working Group on Arbitrary Detention, 2010, pp. 1–2*

In 2014, the Prime Minister of Malta announced that unaccompanied minors would no longer be detained in Malta – this coincided with the cessation of boat arrivals. As such, whilst welcome, it is impossible to ascertain the consequence of this decision at this time.

17 The prefabricated one-room containers housed up to six individuals. Toilets, washing and cooking facilities were shared within a common area.

18 In 2015, more than a million asylum seekers crossed into Germany.

19 Interestingly, the UK government eventually conceded to relocating 3,000 UAMs, representing a U-turn in its original policy. That said, the amount undercuts the calculation considered to be the UKs 'fair share' of 10,000 (*The Guardian*, 2016b).

20 Since 2014, the number of boat arrivals to Malta has diminished significantly because of 'close collaboration' with the Italian Government – in 2015 arrivals dropped by 71.7% (*Times of Malta*, 2015).

21 'Age assessment' refers to the procedures through which authorities seek to establish the chronological age of a person to determine which immigration procedures and rules need to be followed. There is no common approach as to how these procedures are conducted, and there are different margins of error and disparities in how UAMs are treated in different European Union Members States. The various methods adopted have consistently been questioned on the grounds of ethics and determinative accuracy, and perhaps most worryingly, decisions are not always open to legal challenge (aida, 2015).

22 The situation in Turkey is even more grave: 'The Turkish law on asylum does not foresee the protection standards provided for in EU law, and only affords the rights foreseen in the 1951 Refugee Convention to those refugees fleeing "events occurring in Europe". Even where these rights apply, the day-to-day experience for children is still one characterized by economic deprivation, legal uncertainty and poor prospects for education and personal development. Among Syrian children enjoying the relatively privileged status of temporary protection in Turkey, three out of four of those outside of official camps are unable to access education, one in ten face economic pressures that force them into work, and one in three are unable to access healthcare services' (Migration Policy Institute, 2016).

23 In Hungary, children disappear at an estimated rate of 90–95%; in Slovenia, about 80% of children went missing; and in Sweden about 7 in 10 children are reported missing each week. One hundred children went missing from one centre in Austria and 4,700 unaccompanied children were recorded as missing in Germany as at January 1, 2016 (Fundamental Rights Agency, 2016).

24 Some Member States may enforce return prior to turning 18 years of age (European Commission, 2015).

25 For example, in February 2016, as conditions within the notorious 'Jungle' located in Calais worsened, UNHCR called for Member States to be proactive in applying the Dublin III regulation, and expediting procedures for unaccompanied minors to be reunited with their families.

References

aditus Foundation (2014) *Unaccompanied Minor Asylum-Seekers in Malta*. Valletta: aditus Foundation.

Agamben, G. (1998) *Homo Sacer.* Stanford: Stanford University Press.

aida (2015) *Detriment of the Doubt: Age Assessment of Unaccompanied Asylum-Seeking Children*. Brussels: European Council on Refugees and Exiles.

Arendt, H. (1968) *The Origins of Totalitarianism*. New York: Harcourt.

Bauder, H. (2013) *Why We Should Use the Term Illegalized Immigrant*, Research Brief No. 2013/1. Toronto: Ryerson Centre for Immigration and Settlement.

BBC (2015) 'David Cameron Criticised Over Migrant "Swarm" Language'. Retrieved 2016, 10 May from BBC News: www.bbc.com/news/uk-politics-33716501

Bhaba, J. (2009) 'Arendt's Children: Do Today's Migrant Children Have a Right to Have Rights?', *Human Rights Quarterly*, 31: 410–437.

Bordermonitoring Bulgaria (2016) 'Unaccompanied Minors inside Bulgaria's Detention Centers/Drills at the Border to Greece'. Retrieved 2016, 6 May from: http://bulgaria. bordermonitoring.eu/2016/03/09/unaccompanied-minor-refugees-inside-bulgarias-detention-centers-drills-at-the-border-to-greece/

Burman, E. (2008) *Deconstructing Developmental Psychology.* Hove: Routledge.

Business Insider (2016) 'This Map Shows how Much the Refugee Crisis is Dividing Europe'. Retrieved 2016, 9 May from: uk.businessinsider.com/map-refugees-europe-migrants-2016-2

Butler, J. (2004) *Precarious Life: The Powers of Mourning and Violence.* London: Verso.

Clark, M. (2013) 'Young People, Crime and Society: Some Critical Insights', in J. Azzopardi, S. Formosa, S. Scicluna, and A. Willis (eds) *Key Issues in Criminology*. Zejtun: University of Malta.

Council of Europe (2011) *Guidelines of the Committee of Ministers of the Council of Europe on Child-friendly Justice*. Strasbourg: Council of Europe.

Council of Europe (2016) *Report to the Greek Government on the Visit to Greece Carried out by the European Committee for the Prevention of Torture and Inhuman or Degrading Treatment or Punishment from 14 to 23 April 2015*. Strasbourg: Council of Europe.

Crépeau, F. (2003) 'The Fight Against Migrant Smuggling: Migration Containment Over Refugee Protection', in J. van Selm, K. Kamanga, J. Morrison, A. Nadig, S. Spoljar-Vrizna, and L. van Willegen (eds) *The Refugee Convention at Fifty: A View from Forced Migrant Studies*. Lanham: Lexington Books.

Crépeau, F. (2016) *The Costs of the EU's Deal with Turkey*. Retrieved 2016, 23 April from: http://francoiscrepeau.com/fr/the-costs-of-the-eus-deal-with-turkey/

Dimitriadi, A. (2016) 'The Interrelationship Between Trafficking and Irregular Migration', in S. Carrera and E. Guild (eds) *Irregular Migration, Trafficking and Smuggling of Human Beings: Policy Dilemmas in the EU*. Brussels: Centre for European Policy Studies. (pp. 64–69).

European Asylum Support Office (2016). *Latest Asylum Trends: 2015 Overview.* Retrieved 2016, 16 April from: https://easo.europa.eu/wp-content/uploads/LatestAsylumTrends 20151.pdf

European Commission (2015) Policies, Practices and Data on Unaccompanied Minors in the EU Member States and Norway. Retrieved 2016, 13 May from: http://ec.europa.eu/ dgs/home-affairs/what-we-do/networks/european_migration_network/reports/docs/ emn-studies/emn_study_policies_practices_and_data_on_unaccompanied_minors_in_ the_eu_member_states_and_norway_synthesis_report_final_eu_2015.pdf

European Commission (2016a) *EU-Turkey Agreement: Questions and Answers*. Retrieved 2016, 22 April from: http://europa.eu/rapid/press-release_MEMO-16-963_en.htm

European Commission (2016b) *Towards a Sustainable and Fair Common European Asylum System*. Retrieved 2016, 9 May from: http://europa.eu/rapid/press-release_IP-16-1620_en.htm

European Commission (2016c) *Report from the Commission to the European Parliament, the European Council and the Council: Second Report on Relocation and Resettlement*. Retrieved 2016, 29 April from: https://ec.europa.eu/home-affairs/sites/homeaffairs/files/what-we-do/policies/european-agenda-migration/proposal-implementation-package/docs/20160412/communication_second_report_relocation_resettlement_en.pdf

European Commission (2016d) *Evaluation of the Implementation of the Dublin III Regulation*. Brussels: European Commission.

European Network Against Racism (2013) *Racism and Discrimination in Employment in Europe*. Brussels: European Network Against Racism.

Fanon, F. (1963) *The Wretched of the Earth*. New York: Gove Press.

Fundamental Rights Agency (2010) *Separated, Asylum-seeking Children in European Union Member States: Comparative Report*. Vienna: European Union Agency for Fundamental Rights.

Fundamental Rights Agency (2016) *Monthly Data Collection on the Current Migration Situation in the EU*. Retrieved 2016, 15 May from: http://fra.europa.eu/sites/default/files/fra_uploads/fra-2016-monthly-compilation-com-update-4-0_en.pdf

Global Migration Group, UNICEF and OHCRH (2013) *Human Rights of Undocumented Adolescents and Youth*. Brussels: Global Migration Group, UNICEF and OHCRH.

Goldson, B. (2004) 'Victims or Threats? Children, Care and Control', in J. Fink (ed) *Care: Personal Lives and Social Policy*. Bristol: The Policy Press in association with The Open University.

Goldson, B. (2014) 'Youth Justice in a Changing Europe: Crisis Conditions and Alternative Visions', *Perspectives on Youth*, 1: 39–52.

Goldson, B., and Jamieson, J. (2002) 'Youth Crime, the "Parenting Deficit" and State Intervention: A Contextual Critique', *Youth Justice*, 2(2): 82–99.

Goldson, B. and J. Muncie (eds) (2015) *Youth Crime and Justice*, 2nd edition. London: Sage.

Greenhill, K. (2010) 'Weapons of Mass Migration: Forced Displacement as an Instrument of Coercion', *Strategic Insights*, 9(1): 116–159.

The Guardian (2015) 'Migration Crisis: Hungary PM says Europe in Grip of Madness'. Retrieved 2016, 10 May from: www.theguardian.com/world/2015/sep/03/migration-crisis-hungary-pm-victor-orban-europe-response-madness

The Guardian (2016a) '10,000 Refugee Children are Missing, says Europol'. Retrieved 2016, 16 April from: www.theguardian.com/world/2016/jan/30/fears-for-missing-child-refugees

The Guardian (2016b) 'Should David Cameron's U-turn on Unaccompanied Child Refugees be Celebrated?' Retrieved 2016, 1 August from: www.theguardian.com/world/2016/may/07/should-david-camerons-u-turn-on-unaccompanied-child-refugees-be-celebrated

Heiskanen, H. (2014) 'Border Games: From Dual to Russian Roulette at the Border', in E. Vallet (ed) *Borders, Fences and Walls: State of Insecurity?* Farnham: Ashgate.

House of Lords (2016) *Children in Crisis: Unaccompanied Migrant Children in the EU*. London: Authority of the House of Lords. Retrieved 2108, 22 May from: https://publications.parliament.uk/pa/ld201617/ldselect/ldeucom/34/34.pdf

Huffington Post (2016) *More And More Refugees Stranded In Greece After Other Countries Close Borders*. Retrieved 2016, 2 May from: www.huffingtonpost.com/entry/greece-refugee-numbers-borders-closed_us_56d5e0bee4b03260bf783f3e

Hyndman, J. (2011) 'A Refugee Camp Conundrum: Geopolitics, Liberal Democracy and Protracted Refugee Situations', *Refuge*, 28(2): 7–15.

The Independent (2016) 'Greek Refugee Camp is "As Bad as a Nazi Concentration Camp", Says Minister.' Retrieved 2016, 9 May from: www.independent.co.uk/news/world/europe/idomeni-refugee-dachau-nazi-concentration-camp-greek-minister-a6938826.html

International Organisation for Migration and UNICEF (2015, November) *IOM and UNICEF Data Brief: Migration of Children to Europe.* Retrieved 2016, 14 April from: www.iom.int/sites/default/files/press_release/file/IOM-UNICEF-Data-Brief-Refugee-and-Migrant-Crisis-in-Europe-30.11.15.pdf

Jesuit Refugee Service Malta (2007) *Becoming Vulnerable in Detention.* Malta: Jesuit Refugee Service.

Kanics, J., Hernandez, D. S. and Touzenis, K. (2010) *Migrating Alone: Unaccompanied and Separated Children's Migration to Europe.* Paris: UNESCO.

Mai, N. (2010) 'Marginalized Young (Male) Migrants in the European Union', in J. Kanics, J. Senovilla Hernández, and K. Touzenis (eds) *Migrating Alone: Unaccompanied and Separated Children's Migration to Europe.* Paris: UNESCO.

themanews.com. (2016) '"It is so easy a child to go missing here in Idomeni", a volunteer of Save the Children said.' Retrieved 2016, 13 May from: http://en.protothema.gr/at-least-400-unaccompanied-children-stranded-in-idomeni/

Médecins sans Frontières (2016) *Migration: Why the EU's Deal with Turkey is No Solution to the 'Crisis' Affecting Europe.* Retrieved 2016, 23 April from: www.msf.org/article/migration-why-eu%E2%80%99s-deal-turkey-no-solution-%E2%80%9Ccrisis%E2%80%9D-affecting-europe

Miggiano, L. (2009) *States of Exception: Securitisation and Irregular Migration in the Mediterranean.* Geneva: United Nations High Commissioner for Refugees.

Migration Policy Institute (2016) *Children: The Forgotten Aspect of the EU-Turkey Deal.* Retrieved 2016, 15 May from: httwww.migrationpolicy.org/news/children-forgotten-aspect-eu-turkey-deal

Missing Migrants Project (2016) *Mediterranean Migrant Arrivals in 2016: 160,547; Deaths: 488.* Retrieved 2016, 25 April from: https://missingmigrants.iom.int/mediterranean-migrant-arrivals-2016-160547-deaths-488

Muncie, J. (2006) 'Governing Young People: Coherence and Contradiction in Contemporary Youth Justice', *Critical Social Policy,* 26(4): 770–793.

National Commission for Child Policy and Strategy (2014) *The Voice of the Child in Care.* Valletta: Ministry for the Family and Social Solidarity.

New Europe (2016) *EU-Turkey Refugee Pact Leads to Fatal Libya Crossings.* Retrieved 2016, 23 April from: https://neurope.eu/article/eu-turkey-refugee-pact-leads-fatal-libya-crossings/

The Observer (2016) '10,000 Refugee Children are Missing, says Europol'. Retrieved 2016, 13 May from: www.theguardian.com/world/2016/jan/30/fears-for-missing-child-refugees

Pace, C., Carabott, J., Micallef, E. and Dibben, A. (2009) *Unaccompanied Minors in Malta: Their Numbers and the Policies and Arrangements for their Reception, Return and Integration.* Malta: European Migration Network.

Parkin, J. (2013) *The Criminalisation of Migration in Europe, A State-of-the-Art of the Academic Literature and Research.* Brussels: Centre for European Policy Studies.

Pisani, M. (2011) 'There's an Elephant in the Room and She's "Rejected" and Black: Observations on Rejected Female Asylum Seekers from Sub-Saharan Africa in Malta', *Open Citizenship,* 2: 24–51.

Pisani, M. (2016) '"Illegal Bodies" on the Move: A Critical Look at Forced Migration towards Social Justice for Young Asylum-seekers', *Perspectives on Youth,* 3: 83–98.

Pisani, M. and Azzopardi, A. (2009) 'The Odyssey of the Young Female Asylum Seeker: Engaging Critically on Gendered Forced Migration', *Forum 21 [Research] European Journal on Child and Youth Research*, 3: 128–135.

Platform for International Cooperation on Undocumented Migrants (2015) *Protecting Undocumented Children: Promising Policies and Practices from Governments*. Brussels: Platform for International Cooperation on Undocumented Migrants.

REACH (2015) *Situation Overview: European Migration Crisis, Western Balkans.*Retrieved 2018, 22 May from: www.reachresourcecentre.info/system/files/resource-documents/reach_eu_situation_overview_european_migration_trends_december_2015_5.pdf

Refugees Deeply (2016) *Documenting Daily Life at Idomeni Camp*. Retrieved 2016, 9 May from: www.newsdeeply.com/refugees/articles/2016/04/06/documenting-daily-life-at-idomeni-camp

Refugees International (2016) *Kenyan Decision to Close Refugee Camps Potentially Puts Hundreds of Thousands at Risk*. Retrieved 2016, 9 May from: http://reliefweb.int/report/kenya/kenyan-decision-close-refugee-camps-potentially-puts-hundreds-thousands-risk

Sigona, N. and Allsopp, J. (2016) *Mind the Gap: Why are Unaccompanied Children Disappearing in their Thousands?* Retrieved 2016, 13 May from: www.opendemocracy.net/5050/nando-sigona-and-jennifer-allsopp/mind-gap-why-are-unaccompanied-children-disappearing-in-thous

Sigona, N. and Hughes, V. (2012) *No Way Out, No Way In: Irregular Migrant Children and Families in the UK*. Oxford: ESRC Centre on Migration, Policy and Society, University of Oxford. https://www.compas.ox.ac.uk/media/PR-2012-Undocumented_Migrant_Children.pdf

The Telegraph (2010) 'Gaddafi: Europe will "turn black" unless EU pays Libya £4bn a year'. Retrieved 2016, 3 May from: www.telegraph.co.uk/news/worldnews/africaandindianocean/libya/7973649/Gaddafi-Europe-will-turn-black-unless-EU-pays-Libya-4bn-a-year.html

The Telegraph (2015) 'EU Border Agency Warned of Migrant Terror Threat 18 Months Ago – But Nothing was Done.' Retrieved 2016, 25 April from: www.telegraph.co.uk/news/worldnews/europe/12009710/EU-border-

Times of Malta (2015) *Minister Confirms 'Close Collaboration' with Italy to Take Migrants*. Retrieved 2016, 15 May from: www.timesofmalta.com/articles/view/20150915/local/minister-confirms-close-collaboration-with-italy-to-take-migrants.584563

UNESCO (2010) *Migrating Alone: Unaccompanied and Separated Children's Migration to Europe*. Paris: UNESCO.

United Nations High Commissioner for Refugees (2015a) *Worldwide Displacement Hits All-time High as War and Persecution Increase*. Retrieved 2015, 26 December from: www.unhcr.org/558193896.html

United Nations High Commissioner for Refugees (2015b) *UNHCR Report Shows World's Poorest Countries Host Most Refugees*. Retrieved 2015, 11 March from: www.unhcr-centraleurope.org/: www.unhcr-centraleurope.org/en/news/2015/unhcr-report-shows-worlds-poorest-countries-host-most-refugees.html

United Nations High Commissioner for Refugees (2016a) *Protection of Adolescents and Youth – Thematic Paper*. Retrieved 2016, 29 April from: www.unhcr.org/ngo-consultations/ngo-consultations-2016/thematic-protection-of-adolescents-youth.pdf

United Nations High Commissioner for Refugees (2016b) *Refugee/Migrants Emergency Response – Mediterranean*. Retrieved 2016, 4 May from: http://data.unhcr.org/mediterranean/regional.php

United Nations High Commissioner for Refugees (2016c) *UNHCR Redefines Role in Greece as EU-Turkey Deal Comes into Effect*. Retrieved 2016, 23 April from: www.unhcr.org/56f10d049.html

United Nations High Commissioner for Refugees and Integra Foundation (2015) *My Diversity: Age, Gender and Diversity Perspectives in the Maltese Refugee Context.* Valletta: United Nations High Commissioner for Refugees.

The Washington Post (2016) *Central European Countries Resist New E.U. Refugee Quota Proposal.* Retrieved 2016, 9 May from: www.washingtonpost.com/world/europe/central-european-countries-resist-new-eu-refugee-quota-proposal/2016/05/04/5be5a32c-120e-11e6-a9b5-bf703a5a7191_story.html

Weber, L., Fishwick, E. and Marmo, M. (2014) *Crime, Justice and Human Rights.* Hampshire: Palgrave Macmillan.

10

UNDERSTANDING AND LEARNING FROM OTHER SYSTEMS OF JUVENILE JUSTICE IN EUROPE

Describing, explaining and interpreting

David Nelken

Introduction

Can we learn from other ways of doing juvenile justice?[1] Certainly, in one sense we can *only* learn from other societies as this is the best way to see how often reforms that are proposed from within the same culture bear in themselves the seeds of the problem they are trying to solve. But what is it exactly that those of us doing comparative work need to know about other places and how can we find it out (Nelken, 2010)? In this chapter we begin with a general discussion about the purposes of studying juvenile justice comparatively. We shall then discuss descriptive, explanatory and interpretative enquiries and their relation to the challenges of finding equivalence, discovering what is salient and thinking reflexively. As an illustrative case study we will be examining whether Italy has an especially lenient system of juvenile justice. What could that mean? What are the conditions that make it possible? What are the implications for those who want to learn from it?

Why study juvenile justice comparatively?

The reasons for making comparisons depend on whom we are trying to learn from as well as whom we are trying to persuade; policymakers, practitioners, activists, colleagues, students or the general public. Policy-oriented and activist ways of learning, including action-research and the 'Delphi method' for bringing experts together, can all be important. But the most common approach to producing policy-relevant work is to compare the legal processes or socio-educational measures and projects used for prevention, diversion, rehabilitation and punishment by different systems and to try and 'cherry-pick' the ones that seem most promising.

Some writers may also seek to promote legal harmonisation, or the application of international standards or other 'best practices'. In some situations 'academic' work can leave practitioners unsatisfied.[2] On the other hand, scholars who are more interested in contributing to academic debates – so as to understand why different systems of juvenile justice take the form that they do – may want to resist the constraints of policy relevance.

Michael Tonry, a leading penologist, has recently offered some reflections on the variety of goals that comparative criminal justice may be used to pursue. It can seek, he tells us, to learn about 'better ways of dealing with familiar problems' and 'it can help in 'examining conditions under which countries successfully import ideas from elsewhere'. 'Most important', he says, it can 'put national policies and practices into cross-national contexts in order to know what differences they make in national patterns of crime and punishment' (Tonry, 2015: 506–507). The question that will concern us, however, here is how these goals relate. Can we combine learning *from* another system with learning *about* another system?

Tonry gives a hint of this problem too, saying that a 'precondition to figuring out how to do comparative research effectively is to be clear about why something is to be studied and what is hoped to be learned', but, on the other hand, also implying that it may be better to let such insights emerge by themselves, writing that 'the best social scientists can do is try to understand culturally and historically contingent things in hopes that what they think they learn is useful' (Tonry, 2015: 507). At the extreme, reports about other places that are driven too directly by the desire to learn useful lessons can end up producing 'foil comparisons' that do little more than reinforce what we already think we know (Nelken, 2015). Tonry warns us that we need to be especially cautious about thinking that studying other systems of criminal justice will provide us with the key to reducing crime rates. 'Crime rates and patterns', he tells us,

> appear largely oblivious to criminal justice policies and appear to be shaped by deep cross-national forces. Punishment policies and practices to the contrary are products of distinctive national histories and political cultures and have little effect on crime rates and patterns.
>
> *Tonry, 2015: 511–512*

This claim may be a little overstated,[3] after all. If, according to Tonry, punishment policies and practices can have 'little effect' on crime rates, how can he also recommend comparative criminal justice as a way to help us find 'better ways of dealing with problems' and the 'successful' importation of ideas? Certainly, we can try to learn from elsewhere how not to make things worse! When Tonry tells us that 'mass imprisonment' in the USA was not the inexorable product of rising or high crime rates, but the consequential result of conscious policy choices' (Tonry, 2015: 507) he implies that a policy choice to be less punitive would have had different – and better – results.

Description and equivalence

The usual starting point for comparison, especially common in textbooks used for teaching, is to insert legal systems into established classifications of comparative law, such as common law and civil law systems.[4] But those who write about juvenile justice more typically try to capture the specificity of parts of the larger systems by describing the various goals that they pursue. Tonry and Chambers (2011), for example, contrast what they call the English juvenile court model with its heavy emphasis on crime reduction, the German youth criminal court model with its emphasis on social integration of young offenders and the Scandinavian non-juvenile-court model. Pratt (1989: 16) suggests that England and Wales adopted a 'corporatist' third model of juvenile justice so as to go beyond and synthesise the welfare and justice models. Often the goals in question are also matched to asserted underlying ideas about crime: a result of pathology; free will; normality; unsocialisation; conflict; or, alternatively, in terms of the key personnel involved: 'psy' and social work professions; lawyers; non-specialised experts in juvenile justice; or mediators (see, for example, Reichel, 2013 or Winterdyk, 2002). Sometimes, however, their purpose may be heuristic; serving as ideal types or models pointing, for example, to the problems, if any, that arise when systems try to achieve contradictory goals. Uberto Gatti, a leading academic commentator and psychologist in the Italian system, offers a good illustration of this approach:

> [t]he new juvenile justice system represents the results of a compromise between various ideologies. It represents an attempt to pursue a whole range of objectives that are difficult to reconcile: safeguarding the rights of the minor, increasing the minor's responsibility by means of punishment, obtaining rehabilitation through personalised approaches to social problems, pursuing de-penalising options, and release from imprisonment by reducing the terms of preventive detention. Clearly, there are many points of contrast between the treatment-oriented view, for instance, and the position based on depenalisation.
>
> *Gatti and Verde, 2002: 310; see also Gatti 2002*

In addition, however, many of those who create descriptive taxonomies are interested in highlighting the differences between more or less interventionist approaches or (what is not necessarily the same thing) ones that lead to more or to less punitiveness. Frieder Dunkel (2013), in his recent overview of what he calls 'Youth justice policy in Europe', distinguishes 34 countries on a continuum of 'minimum intervention, welfare and new punitiveness'. He tells us *inter alia* that English youth justice is characterised by an emphasis on responsibility, restitution (reparation), restorative justice and (occasionally openly publicised) retribution, whereas juvenile justice in Italy is characterised as prioritising diversion, decriminalisation, deinstitutionalisation and due process.

Gatti and Verde too have increasingly come to see minimal intervention and leniency as the guiding mission of the 1988 reform.[5]

> Juvenile justice in Italy was reshaped at the end of the 1980s through the introduction of measures that brought educational features to penal procedure. The guidelines of the new code openly envision the possibility to remove the minor promptly from the penal procedure ... and to prohibit publicity of the fact in order to avoid stigmatization. Moreover, they recommend detention, whether preventive or punitive, as a residual measure to be used as little as possible. The objective is to reduce the institutionalization of minors as far as possible through the provision of support for the individual's family, as envisaged by international conventions. A mainstay of the new system is the option to suspend the penal procedure and to put the minor on probation, the aim being to avoid the untoward effects inherent in the penal response and to favour support and education.
>
> *Gatti and Verde, 2016*

But it is important to distinguish leniency as a characteristic of the system from leniency as a description of how individual cases are handled. Glauco Giostra, a leading Left-leaning legal academic, edits an important textbook on juvenile justice procedure that has long criticised the Italian system for being overly compromised by the aims of rehabilitation and reform. In language reminiscent of the 'justice versus welfare' critique of the 1970s, he tells us:

> a procedural system conceived and 'lived' with its institutional compass broken means that too often evidence of crime is taken as indicator of social unease and the accused is treated as someone needing re-education and preventive measures which represent appropriate means of correcting behaviour. As a result, the presumption of innocence is often displaced by the idea that the person can be improved, and the search to find the facts of the case translated instead into the search to discover the personal characteristics of the accused.
>
> *Giostra, 2001: 3, my translation*

Any serious effort at description has to go beyond such generalisations so as to provide extensive historical and contemporary detail about the relevant rules, institutions and practices in the systems being studied. We need to know about the various stages of the criminal process; the writing of the laws, reporting offences, police enforcement, prosecution decision-making, judicial sentencing, the use of prison, the cancelling of convictions, and so on. Matters get more complicated when we try to take into account the 'law in action'.[6]

We cannot safely 'read out' from the law or its aims what actually happens on the ground. For example, many authors treat the age when criminal responsibility begins as a proxy for leniency (see, for example, Cavadino and Dignan, 2006; Tonry and Chambers, 2011) and urge action to raise the age level. But Dunkel,

(2013), argues that the age of criminal responsibility has no necessary relationship to leniency in the handling of cases. Furthermore, he claims that political rhetoric in Germany about the need for more punishment of juveniles is not necessarily matched by what is actually done by officials in practice (nor, we may add, was it in the case of Thatcher's Britain). Comparing discretionary decision-making in different systems also shows the importance of this point. Italy is a country where prosecutors are constitutionally obliged to prosecute all cases for which there is evidence. In England and Wales, by contrast, there is more recognition of the need to make pragmatic choices. But just because of that, as well as because so many legal and lay actors are allocated important decision-making responsibilities, discretion there is more carefully and tightly structured by administrative and managerial requirements.

In any comparative exercise special attention has to be paid to telling similarities and differences.[7] But which of these matters? This issue is simply avoided when experts from different countries are invited to write about developments in juvenile justice in their own countries. Because such authors tend to keep close to unfolding the local politics of criminal justice this can make it hard to tell which of the larger similarities and differences count. Dunkel (2013) informs us both about similarities across Europe (informal diversion, prison as a last resort, restitution being used to greater or lesser extent) and also differences (as in the age of onset of criminal responsibility and when juveniles become adults and leave the system). In Italy, we could add that there are many fewer options for non-custodial sentences than are found in most other European juvenile justice systems.

One-to-one comparisons may also offer some advantages. In comparing England and Wales with Italy, for example, we could note that while in the former jurisdiction legislative and administrative changes in the system follow each other at a breathless rate, Italy has witnessed stable legislative and policy-making since the 1988 New Code of Criminal Procedure for Minors, even if the higher courts have played a role in clarifying the meaning of the Code's provisions. Only now is there a currently controversial proposal for the juvenile justice tribunal to become part of an all-embracing family court. Critics of the reform say that would put at risk the advantages of specialisation that undergird the high standards of the Tribunal. The issue of punitiveness or leniency has not been discussed.

The most challenging problem in descriptive comparison is deciding whether we are 'comparing like with like'. How far can we assume that we are talking about the same things and that the terms we use apply in the same way to all the places being compared? Should we count those (as in Italy) who have been convicted once but have the right to an automatic appeal on the facts, as examples of convictions or not? There is no lack of puzzling equivalents in juvenile justice. Some commentators have taken the sanction of *perdono giudiziale* (literally, 'judicial pardon') in Italy to be another example of a means for diversion introduced by the 1988 New Code. In fact, it is a long-standing penalty dating back to the Fascist Rocco Code, and is available to dispose of first-time offences where prison sentences would have been less than two years. Interestingly, even though it leaves a criminal record, it does not involve social services intervention and lawyers acting for youngsters in the south of Italy – who are on the margins of organised crime – prefer to accept that penalty rather than recommend that their clients agree to *messa alla prova* (pre-trial probation) which does not leave a record but does involve far more interference with their lifestyle.

All places are somewhat different or there would be nothing to compare. But can differences be so great as to render a comparison pointless? Assume that, as compared to England and Wales, Italy has a much stronger family structure, with less family breakdown, and it is a place where it is not unusual for children to live at home until their late thirties. Does that count as a valuable finding of our comparative exercise – or does it suggest that the comparison was inappropriate to begin with? Arguably, it is worthwhile comparing places that we take to be similar if such comparison is able to disclose unexpected differences, and conversely, it is worth comparing places that we have reason to think are likely to be different if we can show that there are in fact surprising similarities (Nelken, 2010). In practice this can be tricky. How are we to read the significance of the over-representation of (the often unaccompanied) migrant children and those from Roma (gypsy) backgrounds throughout the system and especially in prison? While the foreign-born make up less than 5 per cent of the population, the site of the Italian department of juvenile justice for 2007 reported that they made up 27 per cent of the minors reported to the authorities, 54 per cent of admissions to reception centres and 52 per cent of admissions to juvenile prisons. Similarly, foreigners are less likely to have their cases dismissed or to be placed on probation; in 2007 only 16 per cent of these provisions were granted to foreign minors (cited in Gatti and Verde, 2016).

Is this an example of the familiar 'bifurcation' in penal responses to different groups of offenders? As Gatti and Verde put it:

> the old methods, which are not abandoned completely in that they are the expression of the intrinsically punitive nature of the system as a whole, end up as a receptacle for those individuals who are less fortunate, like foreign juveniles. Added to this is the fact that foreign juveniles are not eligible for local authority assistance programs for prevention that now seem chiefly oriented towards containing the phenomenon of drug addiction and its related pathologies. The welfare of young offenders of Italy would appear to be caught in-between the chaos.
>
> *Gatti and Verde, 1997: 203*

Similarly, Duccio Scatolera, another academic commentator, speaks of 'the "benevolent tolerance" that often accompanies the view taken of small-scale criminality by young Italians' (Scatolera 2004: 400, *my translation*). He argues that the willingness to show such tolerance has increased in recent times because the authors of such behaviour no longer belong exclusively to the marginalised classes at risk (ibid).

It is certainly plausible to argue that migrants, at least in the North of Italy, have become the new marginal class. But should this apparent structural discrimination be taken as evidence that the Italian system in the end is no different from the system in English and Wales once we have shown that it too directs its sanctions at marginal groups (Hudson 2006)? It would be a mistake to lose sight entirely of the way the Italian system manages to be relatively lenient with home-born Italian youth. And to do this we need to understand better the 'working logic' of the Italian courts, which, unlike those in England and Wales, are less likely to see the behaviour of Italian young people as 'out of control'.

Explanation and salience

A second approach towards understanding differences in (juvenile) criminal justice systems involves trying to explain the social, economic political and cultural factors that help shape them. Such an approach aims to reveal the connections between independent and dependent variables (in our case with special reference to punitiveness and leniency) and thereby provide guidance as to the likely effects of changes in policy. Where a large number of cases are being compared this will usually involve using deliberately simplified contrasts – such as modes of political economy – whilst sometimes adding 'idiosyncratic detail' (Cavadino and Dignan, 2006.) But the line between explanation and description is, of course, not hard and fast. For example, once we are clear about the different goals that each system claims to pursue we may also be able to predict its dynamic over time. For Thomas Bernard (2010), punitiveness in the USA juvenile justice system is followed cyclically by a renewed call for leniency, as the limits and downsides of trying to reduce crime through punishment become increasingly obvious. It should be noted, however, that whatever may be true in the USA, the current, supposedly lenient system in Italy, did *not* emerge as a direct reaction to a previously punitive period. Indeed, the contemporary juvenile justice system in Italy evolved as a means of imposing greater responsibilisation on offenders. The previous system – that constructed juvenile offending as a welfare problem to be delegated to local government social services – was judged to be a failure as services lacked the resources, and sometimes the will, to address 'the problem' effectively.

What gets explained depends on what is thought to need explanation. Why is leniency a salient issue and why is it seen as connected to certain factors rather than others? It may seem 'natural' to Anglo-American, or even to some European scholars, to contrast what happens in Italy with systems that have been affected by the 'new punitiveness' connected with the supposed rise of what Garland (2000) famously called the 'culture of control' (see, for example, Bailleau and Cartuyvels 2007; Goldson, 2002; Muncie, 2008; Pratt *et al.*, 2005). Dunkel too (2013) discusses the resistance to punitiveness in Southern Europe. But whereas it makes sense to speak of adopting, or resisting, blueprints or fashions such as 'rehabilitation' or the 'justice model', it is less obvious that 'punitiveness' circulates in the same way. Rather than the leniency of Italy needing to be accounted for, it could be the severity of places such as the USA and England and Wales that needs explaining. Importantly, there is no reason to think that explanations of harshness and leniency are necessarily symmetrical. Leniency needs explaining as more than just the absence of harshness.

What makes us so sure that Italy is more lenient? If we were to compare the Italian system to Scandinavian jurisdictions we would find that it would not stand out anything like as much, and even in Scotland the Children's Hearings system aims to avoid punishment for most youth crime. But surely it is lenient when compared with England and Wales? In very broad terms, with roughly similar national populations only between 500 and 1,000 young Italians are sent yearly to prisons, and another 1,000 to non-secure homes or reception centres, whereas the rate in England and Wales has varied over the past 30 years from three to two times as many. But matters look different if we focus on the proportion of cases brought into the system that end up being given custodial sentences. In England and Wales in this period, more than one hundred thousand cases enter the system; but in Italy only forty thousand cases were reported annually, and action was taken in around twenty thousand. So, the numbers of children and young people who end up in prison in each country, as a proportion of those who enter the respective juvenile justice systems, are not that dissimilar.

The question then shifts to asking why so many more young offender cases are brought into the system in England and Wales than in Italy. Could this be just because young people in England and Wales commit more crimes? Gatti and Verde (2016) provide evidence – from an earlier self-report study of various European sites – that shows that young people in Italy report similar levels of offending to those in other countries and that Italy has the second highest level of property crime (after Ireland) amongst the 25 countries surveyed (including Russia, Poland and the Netherlands). On the other hand, it is unclear whether or not we can assume from this that the crime levels are as reported. Self-report studies of schoolchildren tend to be less reliable in measuring repeated offending than similar studies involving more serious offenders, so it remains possible that there is a real difference between the level of youth crime in Italy as compared to England and Wales. In addition, some part of the reason for the greater number of children and young people being processed in England and Wales is the younger minimum age of criminal responsibility that obtains.[8] If we are to truly compare like with like, therefore, we would have to take only those in England in the 14–18 years age group. On the other hand, if we take a broader view of the two systems we could see the inclusion of the younger age group in England as evidence of greater severity. As this suggests, even more than with adult justice, reliance on the conventional measure of prison rates alone is a misleading criterion if what we are interested in is the more general harshness of the systems being compared (see Whitman, 2003).

Could the explanation lie in the different national rates of reporting alleged offenders to the authorities? The tendency to report crime is something that varies even within Italy. Gatti and Verde (2016) explain:

> Proportionately more crimes are reported in the North and Centre of Italy than in the South even though youth crimes are more serious in the South…

This can be explained by the greater number of immigrants (and gypsies) in the North, as well as by the fact that in the South families are more jealous of their autonomy and more suspicious of the state.

But, as the above comment makes clear, it is far from obvious that these kind of motives for non-reporting count as signs of leniency in the sense that is meant by those debating comparative levels of punitiveness. Even if we assume, for argument sake, that proportionately fewer offenders are being punished in Italy than in England and Wales this does not itself necessarily signal a commitment to lenience. Could they be responding less punitively to a lesser threat? Offences by 14–18-year-olds in Italy may be taken to represent less of a risk to 'social order' because Italians feel they can rely on other means, especially the family and the Church, in dealing with such problems. As stated above, it is not uncommon for young people to remain living at home until well into their thirties. In addition, there is less of the excessive drinking culture that plays such a role in youth crime and disorder in city centres in Northern Europe.[9] This means that the severity of a case is not an intrinsically determining quality. Even at the granular level, in reading case reports about offenders and the actions taken in responding to them in Italy and in England and Wales (as we have been doing in our research), it is difficult to disentangle the response from the behaviour. When families are described as problematic, this can be as much a result as a cause of the decision taken in relation to their child. Even the level of recidivism in a sample of cases can turn out to be an aspect of how quickly a case is dealt with and what is 'made' of continued offending (Cicourel, 1968).

Assuming, however, that there were differences in response that need to be explained, what are the independent variables that need to be considered? Most arguments about punitiveness link it to shifts towards neo-liberalism as this affects choices made by politicians, and public demands for more punishment (although the extent to which what politicians do is driven by popular pressure or, more likely, vice versa, is a matter of debate.) In Italy national elections are rarely won or lost over the crime issue in itself although, that said, immigration has become a major concern and immigrants are often accused of being a source of crime. Italy also experiences much less central direction or target-setting for juvenile courts than is found in England and Wales. Judges (and judicial prosecutors) play a much larger role in 'defining' the crime problem in Italy as compared to common law countries; the police, by contrast, have significantly less influence. The juvenile justice system has been remarkably free of governmental interference, except for an ill-thought out 'reform' proposal in 2003 sponsored by Roberto Castelli – the Northern League Minister of Justice in one of Berlusconi's governments – which was designed to make the system less benevolent, but which failed to gather sufficient support even from his own party.

Linked to all of this is the role the media. Tabloid newspapers in England and Wales have no real equivalent in Italy. But some Italian newspapers do carry regular stories about offending by young people, focussing on bullying, drug taking and prostitution. In the South of the country there are regular reports of robbery as well as so-called 'baby killers', who are supposedly recruited by organised crime groups such as the Mafia and the Camorra. There have also been some recent high-profile cases[10] – especially the famous case involving Erika and Omar in which a teenager, from a good family in Nuove Liguri in Northern Italy, killed her mother, and younger brother, aided by her boyfriend. Indeed, it was on the back of public concern over this case that Castelli tried – and failed – to tighten up the Italian juvenile system and make it more punitive.

On the other hand, taking Italy as a case study also illustrates the need to look for explanatory factors that are less emphasised in the mainstream debates about the 'punitive turn'. Of key importance in Italy is the role played by family and religion. The strength of Italian family life (with the relatively low level of 'broken homes') is key. The family serves as a surveillance mechanism, as a key distributor of resources and as a major influence in helping young people to find work in a society where most employment is in small firms. Italian society is characterised by low trust in the state, a daily diet of political corruption scandals and a succession of weak governments. In difficult times much is delegated to families in terms of keeping society going and their role in bringing up their children is much less likely to be challenged than it would in many other places.[11] Catholic culture also helps shape a large part of Italian thinking and behaviour even amongst those who see themselves as lay or anti-clerical. Catholic thinking may also help tone down the significance of 'actions', as compared to confession and undertakings to make a new start. The relative insignificance of concern for victims can be linked to religious expectations concerning forgiveness and pardon.

Care is needed in identifying the dependent variable that our independent variables are supposed to explain. Is the legal process the cause or consequence of what we are explaining? Are we trying to explain intentions or (unintended) outcomes (a distinction that has obvious implications for learning and borrowing from other places)? We have noted how few Italian offenders end up being convicted. This has much to do with lengthy procedures (characteristic of legal processes and bureaucratic requirements in Italy generally) and organisational and court delays. More, the Italian 1988 juvenile reform was only a procedural one (necessitated by the move to the overall procedural reform for adults) no substantive change in punishments could be or were introduced. Even for young people, therefore, prison remains the 'standard' post-trial sentence (albeit still reduced by a third from that of adults). Arguably, the lack of post-sentence sanctions other than prison in Italy means that young offenders are less at risk of failing a series of official social interventions and thereby moving up the tariff of penal severity. In England and Wales, on the other hand, by running through alternatives to prison, offenders can eventually ratchet up the severity of sanctions so that prison comes to be seen as the 'inevitable' next step. The role of the legal process comes up again in relation to another issue. How far in seeking to explain differences in *juvenile justice* comparatively should we be focusing specifically of attitudes towards young people and provisions for young offenders? Differences in juvenile justice are also a reflection of larger contrasts in the wider adult criminal justice system (Zimring, Langer and Tannenhaus, 2014). Thus, it is worth noting that there are many less 'young adults' in the 18–21 and 21–25 age ranges in prison in Italy than in England and Wales or Scotland (Aebi and Delgrande, 2008). Hence arguments which focus exclusively on special consideration of children in Italy, or the effects of 1988 New Code of Criminal Procedure for Minors, are likely to be wide of the mark.

Interpretation and reflexivity

There is a limit to how far we can get by mechanically relating independent variables to different levels of punishment. What we are really trying to understand is the meaning of variables for the social actors we are studying. Differences in religious culture, for example, do not determine any given outcomes. Everything depends on what parts of which cultural traditions are drawn on, and how they are lived and fought over in given societies.[12] 'Punitiveness' and 'leniency' too are not terms that have standard or stable cross or inter cultural meanings.[13] What one society (or group within it) might see as praiseworthy examples of forbearance or benevolence, others might regard as examples of formalism, indulgence or neglect. But the interpretative approach can itself lead us astray if it amounts to essentialising a single viewpoint within each society. Claire Hamilton for example, one of the most acute of current comparative writers – in her comparison of Ireland, Scotland and New Zealand – quotes one of her informants as suggesting that Scotland's relatively lenient approach to young offenders is:

> based upon Presbyterianism or indeed Calvinism. It's part of the egalitarian interest of Scotland: We're all Jock Tamson's bairns; these are our kids. These kids who are misbehaving, there's some right bad people who have to go to prison but the rest of them, they're our laddies... they're our folk. We can't send them to the colonies.
>
> *Hamilton, 2014: 162*

Endorsing her informant's views Hamilton (ibid) adds: 'the roots of this culture... may be related to the higher levels of poverty in certain Scottish cities such as Glasgow, its history of trade unionism or, indeed, democratic traditions within the Church'.

But the comparativist must be cautious in deciding what credit to give to informants (Nelken, 2000) and cannot assume that any given informant speaks on behalf of her entire culture. In the particular case above, a claim alleging long-standing reasons for leniency overlooks the radical and relatively recent reform that was introduced in the 1970s comprising the establishment of the Children's Hearing system based on welfare principles and representation of the community in decision-making. Before the Hearings system was introduced children were processed in ways that barely distinguished them from adults.

Grasping the meaning of punitiveness and leniency in different systems means immersing ourselves in local debates. It requires us to explore and to deconstruct the varying discourses of politicians, youth justice practitioners, the media and others, about the criminal law, crime data, the crime problem and so on, and show how these interpret and (thereby) shape their cultures. Our core task involves making sense of a variety of competing interpretations. In an increasingly interconnected world we also need to understand the way 'insiders' go about comparing their own systems with others – even when they misunderstand the others – insofar as their interpretations of comparative contexts shape what they do at the domestic level (Nelken, 2014). In Italy, for example, some leading practitioners do their best to 'talk down' the problem of youth crime. Melitta Cavallo, for example, a senior juvenile court judge in Rome, and past president of the Association of Juvenile Court Judges, begins her book about juvenile justice by stating:

> I am one of those judges who think it more correct and right to speak of young people and crime rather than juvenile crime because, as we will have the chance to show in this book, *there are no young delinquents but only young people in difficulty in their process of growing up* and a criminality that, like an octopus, wraps them in its tentacles, at first caressing them with flattery then squeezing them mercilessly. The expression 'juvenile crime' will nonetheless be used in this text, given that is commonly used.
>
> *Cavallo 2002: 11, my translation and emphasis*

Significantly, however, others working in the same system promoted a different view. An experienced judge and head of the Youth Court Prosecution Office (and declared man of the Right), Romano Ricciotti, authored an established textbook on juvenile justice procedure that was organised in terms of the different types of leniency that the system incorporates. He was very critical of the 1988 New Code of Criminal Procedure for Minors. According to him:

> in simple terms, with respect to crimes when committed by youngsters it is now thought appropriate to respond no longer with the penal sanction or a thought-through exercise of mercy but only with an offer of help which the subject may even refuse.
>
> *Ricciotti 2001: 56, my translation*

In his view:

> the legislator of the 1988 code had in mind certain fundamental choices: only one type of criminal actor, the occasional deviant under the influence of adolescent swings of mood, the sort of person who really

would be damaged by being exposed to prison. He did not take account of the perverse delinquent whose freedom of movement represents a threat to the collectivity and especially for the persons most at risk and weakest sectors of the population.

Ricciotti 2001:56 my translation

Clues to difference can often be found by parsing the words used in public discussions about crime and punishment.[14] In Italy, well into the 1990s, offences as serious as robbery, burglary and even rape were referred to as 'micro-crimes' (or sometimes 'street crimes' or 'diffuse crimes') so as to distinguish them from the type of crimes that threatened to undermine the state such as political corruption, terrorism and organised crime (Nelken, 2000). Key terms used to criticise those in favour of stronger penalties in Italy include *'giustizialismo'* (those using criminal processes as an instrument of political battle against adversaries without giving them a chance to defend themselves) or the related term *'forcaiolo'* ('To the gallows!'). By contrast, we find the attribution *'buonismo'* meaning 'wanting to be too kind without attending to the possibly negative consequences' (being a do-gooder?), and, crucially, *'perdonismo'*, which is used as a label to signify being too willing to forgive offenders. *'Le garanzie'* is an all-important term. It translates roughly as what Anglo-American commentators would call 'due process' or 'fair procedure'. More generally, *'garantismo'* points to the struggle to ensure that state -pursued crime control projects do not trample on fundamental rights. But where such rights begin and end, a controversial matter in most modern societies, is especially complicated in Italy. Politicians of both the Right and the Left speak strongly in favour of more rights for the accused (for different kinds of offenders). But the danger that this can lead them to – that favour legal procedures that have no purpose other than to make conviction near impossible – is captured in the untranslatable *'garanzie pelose'* or 'hairy guarantees'.

Records and other data can appear to constitute more 'objective' evidence of what goes on in a given society. But they too inevitably enshrine controversial local understandings and interpretations. Take the key issue of how far a given system succeeds in reducing levels of repeat offending or recidivism. The Italian Ministry of Justice website speaks proudly of a near 80% success rate in the application of its *messa alla prova* (pre-trial probation) measure. And most of the welfare resources of the Ministry social workers working within the juvenile justice system are expended on this procedure, even though we are speaking of no more than two to three thousand carefully chosen cases a year. But two senses of 'success' are being (deliberately?) confused here (Nelken 2006; Scardaccione 1997). The one used by the Ministry of Justice only refers to the decision of the pre-trial judge to treat the requirements of the order as having been met sufficiently so that there is no need to go on and stage a trial. The evidence of the case files sampled from different courts for the purpose of comparing Italy to England and Wales that I have examined, however, shows that compliance with *messa alla prova* requirements by such youngsters is often far from perfect – in some cases even relapses into offending are evident. But, when the judge comes to decide what to do, he or she knows that the only possible sentence after trial on conviction is prison (or suspended prison) and this is assumed not to have any reformative potential. So, in practice the young person's compliance has to be really poor for judges to decide that pre-trial probation has 'failed' and that the case should be sent for trial and a potential prison sentence.

The Ministry of Justice site, therefore, is not talking about the success rate in the conventional criminological sense of desistance from crime for one or two years after the end of the measure. And it is very difficult to find out such information because it often requires collating the (confidential) records from the juvenile court with that of adult courts. The few academic studies that have tried to estimate the recidivism rate in the more conventional sense of levels of reconviction in fact found much higher figures of around 30% or even 40% (see, for example, Colamussi and Mestitz, 2012; Gili and Pieroni, 2013; Mastropasqua *et al.*, 2013; Scivoletto, 1999).

Other artefacts may also conceal their meanings. Take for example the legend '*lavorare stanca*' ('working makes you tired') that used to be placed over the street door of the laboratory that forms part of the juvenile prison in Bologna. For some time I was convinced that this phrase was an ironic and jesting way of referring to the attitude to work of this group of young offenders in Italy. Here was clear evidence, if any more was needed, of light-hearted 'lenient' attitudes. It was only after further research that I discovered that there was nothing ironic about this phrase at all. It is taken from the title of a collection of poems by Cesare Pavese written during the Fascist period (1936) which describes the isolation of 'young people in the world of adults, (a man) without a woman in the world of love and family, without defence in a world of cruel politics and demanding social duties', and also includes denunciation of those who end up in prison in that regime.[15] The citation at Bologna prison thus expresses much more than meets the eye – and reminds us of the richness of literary background which participants may draw on in creating meaning. But we may also wonder what, if anything, is made of it by the largely immigrant youngsters now incarcerated there.

A final word on the limits of interpretation. The need for continuing reflexive questioning about what we think we understand about the other does not provide any warrant for cultural relativism, whether cognitive or normative. We need to probe the significance of local nuance, not abandon the task in the name of indemonstrable incommensurability. Recognising the difficulty of grasping difference is precisely an attempt to get nearer to understanding it. The goals and values that are debated by commentators on Italian juvenile justice for example are, to a large degree, shared and intelligible throughout Europe (and beyond). Indeed, greater knowledge of the different contexts in which such values are debated can help us to see why the same values may need to be realised differently in different contexts.

Conclusion: learning about leniency

Many policymakers will no doubt continue to treat criminal justice in general, and juvenile justice in particular, as a field in which it is possible to adopt 'best practice', or evaluate 'what works', on the basis of evidence-based social experimentation that deliberately ignores deeper causes and the larger social context (Lipsey *et al.*, 2010). But what we have been arguing is that this sort of 'scientific' approach will often prove illusory insofar as what we are trying to understand is the way societies go about *distributing stigma* not just how they arrange technical 'fixes'. Rather than persist with context-light approaches we have suggested that learning *from* other places is inextricably bound with learning *about* other places and that using descriptive, explanatory and interpretative approaches can help us in this task.

What have we learnt? In the first place, that it would be a mistake to understand Italian leniency, inasmuch as it exists, as a singular product of the success of its welfare approaches to reducing juvenile crime.[16] There is something too good to be true in the description of Italian legal procedures as ones that manage to bring few cases for processing, and then, through resolving causes of delinquency, help those few to quickly find their way out. For Frances Cook of the Howard League for Penal Reform:

> 'The judge can recommend that social services conduct an investigation of the child's background and the circumstances that have led to the offence and ensure that a package of support is put in place for the child and also for the parents if necessary. This is expensive but it is recognised that if you tackle the social and welfare problems you save in the long term as the child will not end up in the adult penal system.
>
> *Crook, 2012: np*

In practice, however, with the possible exception of pre-trial probation, the Italian system gives little (too little?) attention to measuring the consequences for recidivism of the range of sanctions it has available (Maggiolini, Ciceri, Macchi, Marchesi and Pisa, 2008). It would be just as possible to point to the Italian system as support for the virtues of minimal and late intervention, reflecting a legislative mandate to avoid the stigmatising effects of criminalisation. But the system's ability to make cases 'disappear' often depends on doing little, through delay (deliberate or otherwise), and this often produces arbitrary and unjustifiable differences between the ways in which similar cases are sanctioned. And its structure of pre-trial dispositions may sometimes lead youngsters to sacrifice legal rights, as where *messa alla prova* is imposed even though the youngster has neither accepted that he did the offence nor expressed clear willingness to accept probation. The lack of alternatives to prison within the community and the shortage of social workers and residential institutions means that the system often fails youngsters, especially non-Italian-born ones. As noted, the low rate of children in prison may have more to do with the limited availability of post-trial sentences, less proof of the success of its rehabilitative philosophy and more an unintended outcome of the 1988 reforms.

We can certainly point to a variety of positive features of Italian law and society that help explain its relative leniency (and this includes much to envy). But what

we may consider to be 'good' characteristics of another society and its juvenile justice system are not always necessarily linked to other 'good' characteristics.[17] Lower
levels of punitiveness may often be correlated with high levels of welfare, greater
economic equality, or more public participation in political life. But there may also
be other less obvious connections, for example, that have more to do with having
less trust in the state and relying more on informal sanctions. Nor should we assume
that 'informal justice' is always better than state punishment. It has been claimed, for
example, that some Italian magistrates rely on the assumption that young offenders
in parts of Sicily are deterred by organised criminals who guarantee 'protection'
against street crime (Scalia and Mannoia, 2008).

Italian youngsters live at home until a relatively late age, but even some Italians
concede that this can make children overdependent on families, living in a gilded
prison. This leads to the fear that, as one commentator has entitled his book,
'Children never grow up' (Crepet, 2005) There is currently a very high (over 40%)
unemployment rate amongst young people,[18] which reliance on family helps to
cushion. But 'family-like' methods also underlie the embedded nepotism that
blocks development in public and private life. The Catholic Church may in some
important respects help promote a culture of forgiveness. But, on some views, its
approach to confession, and historical rivalry with the lay state may also encourage
a certain acceptance of malfeasance.

The high level of constitutionally guaranteed judicial independence from government helps explain the lack of political interference in Italian juvenile justice.
But it also goes together with a political abdication from policy making that
leaves the judges alone to respond to social problems such as those linked to
the environment or unplanned immigration. Politicians then criticise judges for
getting involved in politics, or for using their autonomy to advance their own
individual or collective interests (Nelken, 2013). Likewise, the fact that judges and
prosecutors try not to be swayed by populist pressure ('*allarme sociale*') does indeed
provide an important bulwark against politically driven popular punitivism. But
the exclusion of public participation from legal decision-making may also have
its downside. It may, for example, go together with a failure to give much heed to
the victims of juvenile crime – including other youngsters.

But the problem is not only that even if 'we' might like a given outcome we
may not like the conditions that make it possible. Our own conditions may be
even more unsuitable for any borrowing of different procedures. Indeed, some
of the central features of Italian juvenile justice have already been tried and
explicitly rejected in England and Wales, as when the previously extensive use of
diversion via repeated cautions was repudiated in the name of 'no more excuses'
(Audit Commission 1996). Rightly or wrongly, some magistrates we interviewed
in Wales were convinced that too much use of diversion could leave young people
vulnerable to (even) more social marginalisation.

Comparison is too often embraced to use other places to (re)discover a 'truth'
that is already known or a politics that is valued for its own sake. On the other hand,
learning from other places does not have to involve borrowing. There is much to

be gained by discovering that things can be done differently and thereby understanding more about one's own starting point. As T.S. Eliot put it:

> the end of all our exploring
> Will be to arrive where we started
> And know the place for the first time.
> *Eliot, 1943*

Comparison may often mean no more (but also no less) than learning to see one's own society in a new light (Balvig, 1988). But for that light to be illuminating it needs to be more than just a projection of our existing prejudices.

Notes

1 This chapter draws largely on my earlier work on Italian juvenile justice (see e.g. Nelken, 2006, 2006a, 2015) and the comparison with England and Wales which I have been pursuing together with Stewart Field (see, for example, Field and Nelken, 2007, 2010). Although I limit my discussion to two of the European countries of which I have first-hand experience, the points being made here are intended also to have some more general application beyond the countries considered and the specific topic of punitiveness and leniency.

2 I remember from my time as a member of the Scottish Children's Hearings system the exasperated reaction at our annual conference to a critique offered by a visiting academic from England. It was not so much that we objected to what was being said as such, but we were put off by his failure to address the limited choices that were the only matters that we could actually address through our decision-making.

3 See Nelken (2017) for further discussion.

4 Greater leniency at the system level does not always coincide with that at the level of the individual offender. Common law systems arguably provide more protections for the accused at trial – protections that are increasingly becoming the new standard for procedural justice (Vogler, 2005). But in Western Europe, courts in common law countries send more people to prison than courts in Continental Europe.

5 Though they do add, 'nevertheless, the system is not free from ambiguity ... this seems to be inevitable when the educational design is located within a framework that is globally constrictive' (Gatti and Verde, 2016).

6 This is all the more necessary because some countries produce more information about the law in action than others, so if we are not careful there is a risk that we compare an idealised picture with one that 'tells it like it is, warts and all'.

7 It is also important to note the extent of internal differences, for example in Italy, between North and South and even from one court to another.

8 The MACR in England and Wales is 10 years whereas in Italy it is 14 years (see Goldson, 2013).

9 A senior policymaker in the Irish youth justice system asked to meet me as part of his exploratory tour to learn lessons from the Italian youth justice system. As we stood in one of the largest of the Florence Piazzas he marvelled at the way interactions amongst young people were not fuelled by alcohol.

10 See Green 2008 for an excellent comparison of the influence of the media in England and Wales in the Bulger case as compared to Norway in a roughly comparable case. But it is important not to look only at high-profile cases. In Italy, murder cases that hit the news are likely to end with a prison sentence, but the majority of cases are dealt with through *messa alla prova*.

11 This is the key factor for Gatti, who writes 'North American and Anglo-Saxon northern European systems are more punitive, whilst Scandinavian and Southern European countries are less so. How does Italy fit into this context?... the importance of family ties and the strength of informal systems of control explain why juvenile justice in Italy is mild' (Gatti and Verde, 2016).

12 Melossi (2004) explains that he abandoned the attempt to argue that 'Protestantism' in America connected to harsh punishment whereas Catholicism in Italy leads to leniency, once he saw that Protestantism has very different effects in the Netherlands.

13 The Dutch form of tolerance, for example, may take the form of being pragmatic about morals offences, as in the way prostitutes are expected to pay tax; the English, on the other hand, are thought to be tolerant in their welcoming of different ideas including those which are unpopular, and in their valuing of idiosyncratic individuality. Italian practices (in any comparison with these countries) would be less likely to be characterised by these aspects of tolerance. They have more to do with the ability to live with a large number of laws to which lip service is paid but which are only enforced erratically.

14 When trying to unpack such terms so as to make them intelligible and accessible for those in a different culture it is inevitable, as the pun in French (and Italian) has it, that 'to translate is to betray'. For an interesting recent collection on this theme, see Glanert, 2014.

15 See https://it.wikipedia.org/wiki/Lavorare_stanca.

16 The blog also implied that the Italian approach could serve as a model to imitate because of its success in reducing recidivism (in Lombardy). Ironically, when followed up, it turned out that such success was attributed by the person in charge not to the employment of a more lenient Italian approach to young people in difficulty but to the application of the theories of the (English) psychologist Donald Winnicot! (Chessa, Gasparini and Poli, 2008; See also Nelken, 2015).

17 Whitman (2003) seeks to explain the relative harshness of the treatment of criminals in the USA in comparison to that reserved for them in the countries of Continental Europe. His argument is that whereas France and Germany 'levelled up' their treatment of criminals, on the basis of long-standing more respectful treatment for higher-status prisoners, in America criminals suffered from a general levelling-down process that presupposed status equality (Whitman, 2003). Some of the best recent analyses of the dark side of otherwise good systems come not surprisingly from those with first-hand knowledge of the Scandinavian justice systems that are now seen as the leading models for others to follow. See, for example, Ugelvik, 2012 and Barker, 2013.

18 www.ilsole24ore.com/art/notizie/2017-01-31/istat-disoccupazione-giovani-risale-40,1 percento-100915.shtml?uuid=AEVOdGL.

References

Aebi, M. F. and Delgrande N. (2010) *Council of Europe Annual Penal Statistics* – SPACE I. Survey 2008. Strasbourg: Council of Europe and University of Lausanne.

Audit Commission. (1996) *Misspent Youth: The Challenge for Youth Justice*. London: Audit Commission.

Bailleau, F. and Y. Cartuyvels (eds.) (2007) *La Justice Pénale des Mineurs en Europe. Entre Modèle Welfare et Inflexions Néo-libérales.* Paris: L'Harmattan.

Balvig, F. (1988) *The Snow White Image: The Hidden Reality of Crime in Switzerland.* Scandinavian Studies in Criminology, 17. Oslo: Norwegian University Press, Scandinavian Research Council for Criminology.

Barker, V. (2013) 'Nordic Exceptionalism Revisited: Explaining the Paradox of a Janus-faced Penal Regime' *Theoretical Criminology*, 17(1): 5–25.

Cavadino M. and Dignan J. (2006) *Penal Systems: A Comparative Approach.* London: Sage.

Cavallo, M. (2002) *Ragazzi Senza: Disagio, Devianza e Delinquenza.* Milan: Mondadori.

Chessa, M. Gasparini, M. and Poli, A. (2008) 'La Messa alla Prova nella Esperienza del Giudice per l'Udienza Preliminare presso il Tribunale per i Minorenni di Milano' *Minori Giustizia*, 4: 102–118.

Cicourel A. V. (1968) *The Social Organisation of Juvenile Justice.* New York: Wiley.

Colamussi, M. and Mestitz, A. (2012) *Devianza Minorile e Recidiva. Prosciogliere, Punire o Responsabilizzare?* Rome: Franco Angeli.

Crepet, P. (2005) *I Figli non Crescono Più.* Einaudi: Torino.

Crook, F. (2012) *Howard League Blog.* April 2.

Dünkel, F. (2013) 'Youth Justice Policy in Europe: Between Minimum Intervention, Welfare and New Punitiveness' in *European Penology?* edited by T. Daems, D. van Zyl Smit, and S. Snacken, 145–170. Oxford: Hart.

Eliot, T. S. (1943) *Little Gidding*: section V. London: Faber.

Field, S. and Nelken, D. (2007) 'Youth Justice: A Comparison of Italy and Wales' in *European Ways of Law*, edited by V. Gessner and D. Nelken, 349–374. Oxford: Hart:

Field, S. and Nelken, D. (2010) 'Reading and Writing Youth Justice in Italy and Wales' *Punishment and Society*, 12: 287–308.

Garland, D. (2000) *The Culture of Control.* New York: Oxford University Press.

Gatti, U. (2002) 'La Delinquenza Giovanile' in *La Criminalità in Italia*, edited by M. Barbagli and U. Gatti, 159–170. Bologna: Il Mulino.

Gatti, U. and Verde, A. (1997) 'Comparative Juvenile Justice: An Overview on Italy' in *Juvenile Justice Systems: International Perspectives*, edited by J. Winterdyk, 177–203. Toronto: Canadian Scholars Press.

Gatti, U. and Verde, A. (2002) 'Comparative Juvenile Justice: An Overview on Italy' in *Juvenile Justice Systems: International Perspectives*, edited by J. Winterdyk, 297–320. Toronto: Canadian Scholars Press (2nd edn).

Gatti, U and Verde, A. (2016) 'Juvenile Justice in Italy' in Oxford Handbooks online. www.oxfordhandbooks.com/view/10.1093/oxfordhb/9780199935383.001.0001/oxfordhb-9780199935383-e-66

Gili, A. and Pieroni, L. (2013) 'L'Applicazione della Messa alla Prova nella Riduzione del Tasso di Recidiva: Primi Risultati' in *La Recidiva nei Percorsi Penali dei Minori Autori di Reato. Report di Ricerca*, edited by I. Mastropasqua, M. S. Totaro, A. Gili, M. M. Leogrande, C. Zanghi, and L. Pieroni, 89. Rome: Gangemi.

Glanert S. (2014) *Comparative Law: Engaging Translation.* London: Routledge.

Giostra, G. (ed.) (2001) *Il Processo Penale Minorile.* Milano: Giuffrè.

Goldson, B. (2002) 'New Punitiveness: The Politics of Child Incarceration' in *Youth Justice: Critical Readings*, edited by J. Muncie, G. Hughes and E. McLaughlin. London, Sage.

Goldson, B. (2013) '"Unsafe, Unjust and Harmful to Wider Society": Grounds for Raising the Minimum Age of Criminal Responsibility in England and Wales' *Youth Justice: An International Journal*, 13(2): 111–130.

Green, D. A. (2008) *When Children Kill Children: Penal Populism and Political Culture.* Oxford: Oxford University Press.

Hamilton, C. (2014) *Reconceptualising Penality: A Comparative Perspective on Punitiveness in Ireland, Scotland and New Zealand.* Aldershot: Ashgate.

Hudson, B. (2006) Book Review, 'The New Punitiveness: Trends, Theories, Perspectives' *Criminology and Criminal Justice*, 6(3): 354–356.

Lipsey, M. W., Howell J. C., Kelly, M. R, Chapman, G. and Carver, D. (2010) *Improving the Effectiveness of Juvenile Justice Programs: A New Perspective on Evidence-based Practice.* Centre for Juvenile Justice Reform. Washington: Georgetown University.

Maggiolini, A., Ciceri, A. Macchi, F. Marchesi, M., Pisa, C. (2008) 'La Valutazione del Rischio di Recidiva nei Servizi della Giustizia Minorile' *Rassegna Italiana di Criminologia*, 3: 481–495.

Mastropasqua, I., M. S. Totaro, A. Gili, M. M. Leogrande, L. Zanghi and C. Pieroni (eds.) (2013) *La Recidiva nei Percorsi Penali dei Minori Autori di Reato. Report di Ricerca.* Rome: Gangemi.

McAra, L. and McVie, S. (2007) 'Youth Justice? The Impact of System Contact on Patterns of Desistance from Offending' *European Journal of Criminology*, 4: 315–345.

Melossi, D. (2004) 'The Cultural Embeddedness of Social Control: Reflections on a Comparison of Italian and North American Cultures' in *Criminal Justice and Political Cultures: National and International Dimensions of Crime Control*, edited by T. Newburn and R. Sparks, 80–102. Cullompton, Devon: Willan.

Muncie, J. (2008) 'The "Punitive Turn" in Juvenile Justice: Cultures of Control and Rights Compliance in Western Europe and the USA' *Youth Justice*, 8: 107–121.

Nelken, D. (ed.) (2000) *Contrasting Criminal Justice.* Aldershot: Dartmouth.

Nelken, D. (2005) 'When is a Society Non-punitive? A Case Study of Italy' in *The New Punitiveness: Current Trends, Theories, Perspectives*, edited by J. Pratt, D. Brown, S. Hallsworth, M. Brown, and W. Morrison, 218–238. Cullompton, Devon: Willan.

Nelken, D. (2006) 'Italy: A Lesson in Tolerance?' in *Comparative Youth Justice: Critical Issues?* edited by J. Muncie and B. Goldson, 159–176. London: Sage.

Nelken, D. (2006a) 'Italian Juvenile Justice: Tolerance, Leniency or Indulgence?' *Youth Justice*, 6: 107–128.

Nelken, D. (2009) 'Comparative Criminal Justice: Beyond Ethnocentrism and Relativism' *European Journal of Criminology*, 6(4): 291–311.

Nelken, D. (2010) *Comparative Criminal Justice: Making Sense of Difference.* London: Sage.

Nelken, D. (2013) 'Can Prosecutors be too Independent? An Italian Case Study' in European Penology?, edited by T. Daems. D. van Zyl Smit and S. Snacken, 249–270. Oxford: Hart.

Nelken, D. (2014) 'The Changing Roles of Social Indicators: From Explanation to Governance' in *Globalisation, Criminal Law and Criminal Justice: Theoretical, Comparative and Transnational Perspectives*, edited by P. Alldridge, L. Cheliotis, and V. Mitsilegas, 25–44. Oxford: Hart.

Nelken, D. (2015) 'Foil Comparisons or Foiled Comparisons? Learning from Italian Juvenile Justice' *European Journal of Criminology*, 12: 519–534.

Nelken, D. (2017) 'Rethinking Comparative Criminal Justice' in *Oxford Handbook of Criminology*, edited by M. Bosworth, A. Liebling and L. McAra, 6th edn. Forthcoming.

Pratt J. (1989) 'Corporatism: The Third Model of Juvenile Justice' *British Journal of Criminology*, 29(3): 236–254.

Pratt, J., D. Brown, M. Brown, S. Hallsworth, W. Morrison (eds.) (2005) *The New Punitiveness.* London: Routledge.

Reichel, P. (2013) *Comparative Criminal Justice Systems: A Topical Approach*, 6th edn. London: Pearson.

Ricciotti, R. (2007) *La Giustizia Penale Minorile*, 3rd edn. Milano: CEDAM.

Scalia, V. and Mannoia, M. (2008) 'I Minori sono Cosa Nostra? Criminalità Organizzata, Devianza Minorile e Sistema Giudiziario a Palermo e Catania' *Sociologia del Diritto*, 35(3): 113–138.

Scardaccione G. (1997) 'Gli Studi sul Recidivismo: Vecchi e Nuovi Modelli' *Rassegna Penitenziaria e Criminologica*, 1(1–2): 9–28.

Scatolera, D. (2004) 'Devianza Minorile e Coercizione Personale' *Questione Giustizia*, 2–3: 397–411.

Scivoletto, C. (1999) *C'è Tempo per Punire. Percorsi di Probation*. Milano: Franco Angeli.

Tonry, M. (2015) 'Is Cross-national and Comparative Research on the Criminal Justice System Useful?' *European Journal of Criminology*, 12(4): 505–516.

Tonry, M. and C. Chambers (2011) 'Juvenile Justice Cross-Nationally Considered' in *The Oxford Handbook of Juvenile Crime and Juvenile Justice*, edited by D. M. Bishop and B. C. Feld, chapter 34. Oxford: Oxford University Press.

Ugelvik, T. (2012) 'The Dark Side of a Culture of Equality: Reimagining Communities in a Norwegian Remand Prison' in *Penal Exceptionalism? Nordic Prison Policy and Practice*, edited by T. Ugelvik and J. Dullum, 121–138. London: Routledge

Vogler R. (2005) *A World View of Criminal Justice*. Aldershot: Ashgate.

Whitman J. (2003) *Harsh Justice: Criminal Punishment and the Widening Divide between America and Europe*. Oxford: Oxford University Press.

Winterdyk J. (ed.) (2002) *Juvenile Justice Systems: International Perspectives*, 2nd edn. Toronto: Canadian Scholars Press.

Zimring, F. E., Langer M. and Tannenhaus D. S. (2015) *Juvenile Justice in Global Perspective*. New York: New York University Press.

PART III

Future

11

READING THE PRESENT AND MAPPING THE FUTURE(S) OF JUVENILE JUSTICE IN EUROPE

Complexities and challenges

Barry Goldson

> 'The future is not inevitable'.
>
> Garland, 2001: 201

> 'It is never too late to notice that things could have turned out differently – and hence that they still could. All that is needed is a little of that opposing power that one might have possessed in earlier times, and to think not of the youth past, but of that to come'.
>
> Fassin, 2013: 229

> 'We are all time travelers, journeying together into the future. But let us work together to make that future a place we want to visit'.
>
> Hawking, 2015: np

Introduction

This extended chapter is presented in two interrelated sections. The first section engages with a range of complexities that pertain to reading the present state of juvenile justice in Europe. Three levels of analysis are engaged: transnational/pan-European, inter-national and intra-national/sub-national. It is argued that high narratives (transnational/pan-European accounts) are theoretically/conceptually flawed and that finer-grained (inter-national and intra-national/sub-national) critical inquiry is necessary to comprehend the differentiated nature of European juvenile justice systems. The second section maps a series of key transformations bracketed as the 'changing state of Europe', the 'changing state of childhood and youth in Europe' and the 'changing state of juvenile justice'. Such transformations impose formidable challenges and, taken together, they will almost certainly shape the future(s) of juvenile justice in Europe.

Reading the present: high narratives

Both historically and contemporaneously, juvenile justice systems in Europe – as elsewhere – have been, and are, beset by ambiguities, paradoxes, tensions and contradictions. Fundamentally, the question as to whether children and young people in conflict with the law should be conceptualized as vulnerable *becomings* (in need of special protection, help, guidance and support), or as undisciplined and threatening *beings* (necessitating regulation, control, correction and ultimately punishment) is a central and recurring concern. Moreover, if it can be said that throughout the twentieth century evolving welfare imperatives defined juvenile justice systems in most European countries, it might also be argued that in the opening decades of the twenty-first century the underpinning logics of juvenile justice have become more contested and uncertain. In simple terms, high narratives have come to assume a binary form. On one hand, many commentators envision a steadily developing emphasis on human rights and a maturing sense of penal tolerance as representing standard European responses to children and young people in conflict with the law. On the other hand, others argue that various conditions of late modernity including, but not limited to, wrenching social and economic transformations, unprecedented patterns of population mobility and migrations, heightened insecurities and neo-liberal politics are combining to give rise to increasingly harsh forms of penality and punitivity. Although such high narratives derive from strikingly different readings of the present they both appear to offer, at face value at least, seductive explanatory accounts of pan-European trends.

Human rights and penal tolerance

This narrative conceptualizes juvenile justice as embracing human rights priorities and progressing incrementally towards a state of penal tolerance, where the 'best interests' of children and young people prevail and where recourse to juvenile justice intervention – particularly custodial detention – is only ever mobilized as a 'last resort'. It is underpinned by both *global* and *European* human rights standards.

The formalization of global human rights standards consolidated with the creation of the United Nations and the adoption of the Universal Declaration of Human Rights in 1948. Subsequently, the United Nations General Assembly adopted five further core human rights treaties: the International Convention on the Elimination of All Forms of Racial Discrimination (1965); the International Covenant on Economic, Social and Cultural Rights (1966); the International Covenant on Civil and Political Rights (1966); the Convention on the Elimination of All Forms of Discrimination against Women (1979) and the Convention Against Torture and Other Cruel, Inhuman or Degrading Treatment or Punishment (1984). Each of the treaties apply to children, young people and adults, but it was not until 1989 when the United Nations Convention on the Rights of the Child (UNCRC) was adopted by the United Nations General Assembly – and 1990 when the Convention came into force – that a global human rights instrument focused exclusively and comprehensively on protecting and promoting a broad range of children's interests.

Article 1 of the UNCRC provides that the term 'child' refers to 'every human being below the age of eighteen years'. The Convention comprises 54 articles bringing together children's economic, social, cultural, civil and political rights. General measures incorporated within the UNCRC include a fundamental obligation on governments (referred to as 'States Parties') to develop and sustain a children's human rights infrastructure within their jurisdictional spheres comprising, for example: the right to non-discrimination (Article 2); the primacy of the child's best interests (Article 3); the right to life and maximum development (Article 6); and the right of children and young people to have their views given due weight in all matters affecting them (Article 12). The UNCRC also provides a range of 'civil rights' including: the child's right to freedom of expression and association; the right to receive information; and the right to protection from all forms of violence, abuse, neglect and mistreatment. The Convention further provides for every child's right to an adequate standard of living and the right to the best possible healthcare and educational services.

The Universal Declaration of Human Rights (1948), the UNCRC (1989) and each of the intervening human rights instruments signalled above, have a bearing on juvenile justice law, policy and practice, be it direct or indirect. Indeed, economic, social and cultural rights; civil and political rights; the elimination of all forms of discrimination; safeguards against torture and other cruel, inhuman or degrading treatment or punishment; protection from violence, abuse, neglect and mistreatment; a recognition of the 'special status' of childhood; 'best interest' principles; the right to life and maximum development; the right to be informed and the right to be heard, all have salience regarding the treatment of children and young people in conflict with the law. Furthermore, provisions of these instruments, together with an additional range of more specific global and European human rights standards, treaties, rules, conventions and guidelines, relate more explicitly still to juvenile justice.

At the *global* level, three key instruments are especially important. First, the 'United Nations Standard Minimum Rules for the Administration of Juvenile Justice' (the 'Beijing Rules') were adopted by the United Nations General Assembly in 1985. The Rules provide guidance for the protection of children's human rights in the development of separate and specialist juvenile justice systems. Rule 4.1 provides: 'juvenile justice shall be conceived as an integral part of the national development process of each country, within a comprehensive framework of social justice for all juveniles' (United Nations General Assembly, 1985). Second, the United Nations Guidelines on the Prevention of Delinquency (the 'Riyadh Guidelines') were adopted by the United Nations General Assembly in 1990. The Guidelines are underpinned by diversionary and non-punitive imperatives: 'the successful prevention of juvenile delinquency requires efforts on the part of the entire society to ensure the harmonious development of adolescents' (para. 2); 'formal agencies of social control should only be utilized as a means of last resort' (para. 5) and 'no child or young person should be subjected to harsh or degrading correction or punishment measures at home, in schools or in any other institutions' (para. 54) (United Nations General Assembly, 1990a). Third, the United Nations Rules for the Protection of Juveniles Deprived of their Liberty (the 'Havana Rules') were adopted by the United Nations General Assembly in 1990. The 'Rules' provide core principles including: deprivation of liberty should be a disposition of 'last resort' and used only 'for the minimum necessary period' and, in cases where children are deprived of their liberty, the principles, procedures and safeguards provided by international human rights law, standards, treaties, rules, guidelines and conventions must be seen to apply (United Nations General Assembly, 1990b).

In addition to the above, various Articles of the UNCRC distinctly resonate with juvenile justice including:

- In all actions concerning children… the best interests of the child shall be a primary consideration (Article 3)
- No child shall be subjected to torture or other cruel, inhuman or degrading treatment or punishment (Article 37a)
- No child shall be deprived of his or her liberty unlawfully or arbitrarily. The arrest, detention or imprisonment of a child shall be in conformity with the law and shall be used only as a measure of last resort and for the shortest appropriate period of time (Article 37b)
- Every child deprived of liberty shall be treated with humanity and respect for the inherent dignity of the human person, and in a manner that takes into account the needs of persons of his or her age. In particular, every child deprived of liberty shall be separated from adults unless it is considered in the child's best interest not to do so (Article 37c)
- Every child deprived of his or her liberty shall have the right to prompt access to legal and other appropriate assistance, as well as the right to challenge the legality of the deprivation of his or her liberty before a court or other competent, independent and impartial authority, and to a prompt decision on any such action (Article 37d)
- States parties recognize the right of every child alleged as, accused of, or recognized as having infringed the penal law to be treated in a manner consistent with the promotion of the child's sense of dignity and worth, which reinforces the child's respect for the human rights and fundamental freedoms of others and which takes into account the child's age and the desirability of promoting the child's reintegration and the child's assuming a constructive role in society (Article 40(1))
- States parties shall seek to promote the establishment of laws, procedures, authorities and institutions specifically applicable to children alleged as, accused of, or recognized as having infringed the penal law, and, in particular: (a) The establishment of a minimum age below which children shall be presumed not to have the capacity to infringe the penal law; (b) Whenever appropriate and desirable, measures for dealing with such children without resorting to

judicial proceedings, providing that human rights and legal safeguards are fully respected (Article 40(3)) (United Nations General Assembly, 1989)

Shifting from the global to the *European* level, the concept of 'child-friendly justice' is pivotal. By extending the human rights principles that inform the 'European Rules for Juvenile Offenders Subject to Sanctions or Measures' (Council of Europe, 2009), the Council of Europe Committee of Ministers has adopted specific 'Guidelines for Child Friendly Justice' (Council of Europe, 2010). The 'Guidelines' echo *general provisions* of the UNCRC in stating that 'a "child" means any person under the age of 18 years' (Council of Europe, 2010: section II(a)) and that they apply 'to all ways in which children are likely to be, for whatever reason and in whatever capacity, brought into contact with... bodies and services involved in implementing criminal, civil or administrative law' (ibid: section I: para. 2). The Guidelines also reiterate more *specific juvenile justice provisions* that are found within United Nations instruments including: 'the minimum age of criminal responsibility should not be too low and should be determined by law'; 'alternatives to judicial proceedings... should be encouraged whenever these may serve the child's best interests'; 'respect for children's rights as described in these guidelines and in all relevant legal instruments on the rights of the child should be guaranteed to the same extent in both in-court and out-of-court proceedings' (ibid: section IV(B): paras. 23–26); and, 'any form of deprivation of liberty of children should be a measure of last resort and be for the shortest appropriate period of time' (ibid: section IV(A): para. 19).

The Council of Europe has also emphasized the pan-European unifying objective of the Guidelines by explaining that they apply to its 47 Member States[1] and are intended to:

> achieve a greater unity between the member states... by promoting the adoption of common rules in legal matters... [and] ensuring the effective implementation of... binding universal and European standards protecting and promoting children's rights.
>
> *ibid: Preamble*

Similarly, Stalford (2012: 1) has drawn attention to parallel developments within the European Commission and the 28 Member States[2] of the European Union (EU) including:

> the significant changes that have taken place over the past 20 years, not only in relation to the institutional and constitutional architecture of the EU, but also against the readiness of the EU legal and policy actors to engage more boldly with children's rights issues... [providing] a supra-national response to a range of children's rights concerns that transcend national boundaries... [and] offering a platform for political dialogue, best practice exchange and resource pooling between the member States in relation to children's rights issues of common concern.

Indeed, in 2011 the European Commission issued a key 'Communication', 'An Agenda for the Rights of the Child' with the overarching purpose to:

> reaffirm the strong commitment of *all EU institutions* and of *all Member States* to promoting, protecting and fulfilling the rights of the child in *all relevant EU policies* and to turn it into concrete results. In the future, EU policies that directly or indirectly affect children should be designed, implemented, and monitored taking into account the principle of the best interests of the child enshrined in the EU Charter of Fundamental Rights and in the UNCRC...
>
> *European Commission, 2011: 3, emphases added*

The 'Agenda' also explicitly connected European and global human rights imperatives and undertook to 'ensure that EU action is exemplary in ensuring the respect of the provisions of the Charter and of the UNCRC with regard to the rights of children' and, more explicitly within the juvenile justice context, to focus on 'a number of concrete actions in areas where the EU can bring real added value, such as child-friendly justice, protecting children in vulnerable situations and fighting violence against children both inside the European Union and externally' (ibid: 4).

Penality and punitivity

In stark contrast to the contention that contemporary developments in juvenile justice in Europe are characterized by evolving human rights sensibilities, a burgeoning mood of penal tolerance, 'best interest' principles and 'last resort' imperatives, an alternative high narrative emphasizes a conspicuous recourse to penality and punitivity, represented by an increasingly harsh 'culture of control' (Garland, 2001). This reading of the present detects a 'weakening of the founding principles of juvenile justice' in a 'majority of countries in Europe' (Bailleau *et al.*, 2010: 13). It is argued that the protected status conventionally provided for children and young people within European juvenile justice systems is diminishing, traditional and long-established welfare-based responses are dissolving, children and young people are increasingly exposed to forms of 'responsibilization' and 'adultification' and both global and European human rights standards are routinely breached. Penal tolerance – rather than being in the ascendancy – is progressively displaced by what Muncie (1999) terms 'institutionalized intolerance', as juvenile justice forms a distinctive component of the State's wider strategy for managing 'urban outcasts' within conditions of 'advanced marginality' (Wacquant, 2008).

Developing and consolidating waves of penality and punitivity, it is argued, are characterized by both quantitative and qualitative dimensions. A deepening and widening reliance on penal detention – both more and longer custodial episodes – is said to reflect a 'logic of prisonisation' (Bailleau *et al.*, 2010: 21). Moreover, this is accompanied by the increasing mobilization of 'immigration detention' and practices 'in more and more countries [where] juvenile... justice systems are tending to focus more on young foreigners or young people of foreign descent' (Bailleau *et al.*, 2010: 9–10). Taken together, such processes are said to signify the key quantitative dimensions of burgeoning penality and punitivity. Corresponding qualitative dimensions are seemingly evidenced by 'a decline in rehabilitative ideals, harsher prison conditions, more emotional and expressive forms of punishment emphasizing shaming and degradation… or increased attention to victim's rights as opposed to the rights of offenders' (Snacken and Dumortier, 2012: 2–3). Indeed, Bailleau *et al.* (2010: 7) claim that a 'neo-conservative paradigm [has] become dominant within the European Union' and, consequently, juvenile justice 'has undergone major changes in recent years in Europe' (ibid: 8):

> Social intolerance in various States is rising against a backdrop of a drift to hard-line law-and-order policies and practices. The deviant youth is perceived first and foremost as a social problem… to the detriment of a vision that saw the "child in danger" as someone whom society also had to protect… a greater tendency to hold the youth's "entourage" accountable for his/her actions by shifting responsibility to his or her family and the local community (either the geographic community or cultural or ethnic community) … There has also been a shift in the State's orientations and strategies in the public management of youth deviance… The main consequence of this new orientation is the increased surveillance of young people and families by a host of entities and the extension of criminalization to include certain types of behaviour that used to be considered to be mere deviations from the norm and/or petty delinquency.
>
> *ibid: 8–9*

This alternative high narrative conveys a decidedly 'bleak', if not 'dystopian', outlook (Zedner, 2002); a 'criminology of catastrophe' even (O'Malley, 2000). Human rights, penal tolerance and 'best interest' principles are replaced with notions of impatience, censure, condemnation, reprobation, retribution and punishment. The argument implies that social cohesion, equilibrium and stability can only be achieved by excluding 'undesirable' sections of the population (including children and young people in conflict with the law) in a way that is approved of, and instils confidence in, the majority community (Durkheim 1893/2014; see also, Reiner, 2007; Pratt and Eriksson, 2013).

Such reactionary punitive responses are said to be part of wider transformations in the political economy of Europe (and elsewhere), where the rise of neo-liberalism and the restructuring of the liberal democratic (welfare) state facilitates mass imprisonment as a preferred strategy for managing the poor (Beckett and Western, 2001). Perhaps the most prominent protagonist of this 'dystopian' high narrative is Wacquant (2009: 1) who maps the development and diffusion of what he terms a 'new punitive common sense', initially incubated in the USA before being 'exported to Western Europe and the rest of the world'. Wacquant argues that we are witnessing a transmogrification from the 'social state' to the 'penal state';

the 'downsizing of the welfare sector' and the 'upsizing of the penal sector' characterized, ultimately, by the 'iron fist' of a diversifying, expanding and increasingly intrusive penal apparatus. For Wacquant (2009: 167), this 'generalized technique for managing rampant social insecurity' means that the spaces created by processes of economic deregulation and welfare retrenchment are filled by an architecture of neo-liberal penality and the aggressive advances of punitivity. Five overlapping processes are said to be at play: first, 'vertical expansion' (swelling prison populations); second, 'horizontal expansion' (the proliferation and diversification of technologies of regulation, control and surveillance – net-widening); third, simultaneous, yet contradictory, modes of system expansion and contraction (penal and welfare respectively); fourth, the burgeoning privatization of the criminal (including juvenile) justice apparatus and, fifth, a policy of 'carceral affirmative action' (the manifest racialization of penality and punitivity).

The seductions and the limitations of high narratives

At face value, each of the high narratives might appear to provide conceivable conceptual typologies for comprehending pan-European (perhaps even global) trends in juvenile justice. Paradoxically – given their analytical incongruity – both seem plausible but, ultimately, each is singularly inadequate. Whatever the respective seductions of the contrasting visions, therefore, neither provides a tenable comprehensive account of the complexity, contradictory nature and inherent inconsistencies of transnational juvenile justice.

On one hand, despite the adoption of the global and European human rights standards considered above – including the United Nations Convention on the Rights of the Child, perhaps the most widely adopted human rights instrument in the world – the 'potentialities' for such standards to drive and sustain progressive juvenile justice reform in Europe are compromised repeatedly by a series of operational and implementational 'limitations' (Goldson and Kilkelly, 2013. See also, Goldson and Muncie, 2012; Goldson and Muncie, 2015). Indeed, just as Doob and Tonry (2004: 3) refer to the 'contrasts between law in books and law in action' and remind us that 'the distinction between law as it is written and law as it is administered… is crucial in understanding a youth justice system' (ibid: 17), so it is with human rights standards. In other words, translational discrepancies between human rights standards 'as written' and the operational realities of juvenile justice policies and practices 'as administered', are not uncommon. Three key illustrations of this phenomenon are particularly revealing. First, the muted purchase that human rights standards appear to have imposed in the juvenile justice sphere through the processes of European enlargement. Second, the persistent failings of many European juvenile justice systems to conform to the provisions of international human rights standards evidenced, not least, by reports and 'concluding observations' issued by the United Nations Committee on the Rights of the Child. Third, the intrinsic unenforceability of the United Nations Convention on the Rights of the Child (and other human rights standards) within the wider corpora of domestic statute in individual nation states.

Turning first to the question of EU enlargement, 2004 witnessed the accession of 10 new Member States to the European Union: Cyprus; the Czech Republic; Estonia; Hungary; Latvia; Lithuania; Malta; Poland; Slovakia and Slovenia and, in 2007, membership of the EU was further extended to Bulgaria and Romania. Stalford (2012: 197) contends that:

> the extent to which children's rights are articulated in the accession negotiations and… EU membership affects children's rights and experiences… [through] the enlargement process [provide] a valuable context for assessing the currency of children's rights at EU level since it lays bare the legal, economic and political standards to be achieved by a candidate country to gain EU membership. In that sense, we can interrogate whether children's rights are sufficiently valued by the EU to warrant inclusion within pre-accession criteria. Carrying this analysis through to post-accession experience, we can explore how the process of social and political adjustment applied by accession – for the acceding state, the Member States and for the EU institutions – manifests itself in relation to children. In short, EU enlargement offers a lens through which to explore how domestic children's rights regimes respond to the dynamics of EU integration and how children are really affected on the ground.

Stalford (ibid: 211) also notes that the negotiations and expectations that frame such accession processes often 'centre on some core priorities, notably the integration of Roma children, the plight of children in institutionalized care and juvenile justice'. By taking a cursory look at two of the states that gained accession to the EU in 2004 (Hungary and Poland), and two that were granted similar status in 2007 (Bulgaria and Romania), therefore, we can offer some preliminary judgments concerning the relation between children's human rights as 'they are written' and the same rights 'as they are administered' or, to put it another way, between the rhetorical constructions of children's rights (as they might appear in the formal mechanisms for approving accession) and the operational realities of children's experiences (in post-accession settlements).

Perhaps the most reliable data available – regarding the purchase of international human rights standards over the juvenile justice systems in each of the four selected accession states – is offered by Baeva (2014: 17) who notes that 'in Central and Eastern Europe… depriving children of liberty continues to be used extensively' and provides:

> a systematic overview of the closed institutions… including those for children with imposed criminal sanctions and children placed in institutions for other purposes (educational supervision, medical treatment, immigration control etc.) in Bulgaria, Hungary, Poland and Romania… [and] an up-to-date picture regarding… [the] compliance of national legislation with international standards both in law and in practice.

The discordance between the provisions of international human rights standards and the operational realities of juvenile justice policies and practices, is striking in each of the four countries. In Bulgaria, 'unlawful and arbitrary deprivation of liberty', 'institutionalized discrimination', the over-representation of 'children from vulnerable groups… in closed institutions… children from ethnic minorities (Roma), poor children and children with special needs', 'unacceptable material conditions', 'a lack of effective separation by age and profile' and a 'frightening record of violence and abuse' characterize the realities of child detention (Furtunova *et al.*, 2014: 292–294). In Hungary, the 'petty offence confinement of juveniles is particularly problematic' (Kádár *et al.*, 2014: 393) alongside multiple 'problems related to detention conditions' (ibid: 407). In Poland, 'legislative dispersion in the field of juvenile justice results in lack of detention standards [and] there is no systematic framework regarding comprehensive legislation in the area' (Wiśniewska *et al.*, 2014: 535). And, in Romania, 'facilities fall short of international standards or offer inappropriate detention conditions for children' (Buzatu *et al.*, 2014: 654).

Furthermore, it is not only processes of EU enlargement – and the conditions that can be found within the recently acceded states – that reveal discrepancies between the provisions of international human rights standards and the practices of juvenile justice. Neither are the practical mutations of children's human rights the sole preserve of Central and Eastern European states. Indeed, this takes us to the second illustration – signaled above – of the divergence between rights 'as written' and rights 'as administered', that is amply evidenced by reports published by the United Nations Committee on the Rights of the Child. For now, we might focus on reports published by the UN Committee, over the period 2016–17, that specifically concern countries in Northern and Western Europe. Each and all the reports imply that such countries are failing to observe core aspects of their human rights obligations to children and young people in conflict with the law. In respect of France, the report of the UN Committee, published in February 2016, recommends:

> that the State party adopt all measures necessary to address those previous recommendations that have been partly or insufficiently implemented, or not implemented at all… such as those relating to corporal punishment, the minimum age of responsibility, the juvenile justice system and unaccompanied migrant children
> *United Nations Committee on the Rights of the Child, 2016a: para. 6*

In its report on Ireland, published the following month, the Committee similarly recommends:

> that the State party take all necessary measures to address its previous recommendations of 2006… that have not been sufficiently implemented… those relating to… refugee and asylum-seeking children, the administration of juvenile justice and children belonging to minorities.
> *United Nations Committee on the Rights of the Child, 2016b: para. 7*

In July 2016, the Committee turned its attention to the UK and recommended that the State Party:

> raise the minimum age of criminal responsibility in accordance with acceptable international standards; ensure that children in conflict with the law are always dealt with within the juvenile justice system up to the age of 18 years, and that diversion measures do not appear in children's criminal records; abolish the mandatory imposition of life imprisonment for children for offences committed while they are under the age of 18; establish the statutory principle that detention should be used as a measure of last resort and for the shortest possible period of time and ensure that detention is not used discriminatorily against certain groups of children; ensure that child detainees are separated from adults in all detention settings [and]; immediately remove all children from solitary confinement, prohibit the use of solitary confinement in all circumstances and regularly inspect the use of segregation and isolation in child detention facilities.
>
> *United Nations Committee on the Rights of the Child, 2016c: para. 79 a–f*

In March 2017, the UN Committee published its report on Estonia in which it:

> urges the State party to bring its juvenile justice system fully into line with the Convention and other relevant standards… [such as implementing] as soon as possible, its proposals to promote alternative measures to detention, such as diversion, probation, mediation, counselling or community service… and [ensuring] that detention is used as a last resort and for the shortest possible period of time and that it is reviewed on a regular basis with a view to withdrawing it… [and to] ensure that detention conditions are compliant with international standards [and] the provision of qualified and independent legal aid to children in conflict with the law at an early stage of the procedure and throughout the legal proceedings.
>
> *United Nations Committee on the Rights of the Child, 2017a: para. 49a–d*

And, finally, in October 2017 the Committee reported on Denmark – often regarded as one of Europe's most tolerant and rights-compliant juvenile justice jurisdictions – and felt obliged to 'urge':

> the State Party to bring its juvenile justice system fully into line with the Convention and other relevant standards… place emphasis on prevention policies… [and] in view of the current lack of any juvenile courts, expeditiously establish specialized juvenile courts and procedures… designate specialized judges for children and ensure that such judges receive appropriate education and training; promote non-judicial measures in the case of children accused of criminal offences… ensuring that detention is used as a measure of last resort and for the shortest possible period of time and that it is reviewed

on a regular basis with a view to its withdrawal; take the steps necessary to reduce the maximum prison sentence for children… [and] in the light of the abundant evidence that the placement of children in adult prisons or jails compromises their basic safety, well-being and their future ability to remain free of crime and to reintegrate, amend section 78 (2) of the Sentence Enforcement Act in order for children not to be placed in prison together with adults.

United Nations Committee on the Rights of the Child, 2017b: para. 44 a–g

So, although there may be questions of degree, human rights violations not entirely dissimilar to those found in recently acceded states in Central and Eastern Europe are also produced, and reproduced, in juvenile justice systems in Northern and Western Europe. Ultimately, this invites consideration of the third key limitation of the human rights narrative; the intrinsic unenforceability of international standards (and European 'Guidelines') within individual nation states and their national jurisdictions.

Taken together, the body of United Nations, Council of Europe and European Commission standards, treaties, rules, guidelines and conventions provide a well-established 'unifying framework' for encouraging legislative reform, modelling juvenile justice systems, formulating policies and developing practices in all nation states to which they apply (Goldson and Hughes, 2010; Hamilton, 2011). There is, however, a vital caveat. As Fortin (2008: 60) has observed, the United Nations Convention on the Rights of the Child has 'not been made part of domestic law' in many countries where it has been ratified and, as such, it essentially remains 'unincorporated'. What this means in practice is that although – following ratification – nation states might be morally obliged to implement the provisions of the Convention (and other international standards and European Guidelines), they are not legally compelled to do so. In short, the international standards ultimately 'lack teeth' (Fortin, 2008: 60) and:

there are no sanctions imposed on states who fail to comply with the obligations to which they have agreed… This begs the question as to whether the UNCRC can hope to hold any persuasive force at EU level when its enforceability by the very Member States that have ratified it remains so fragile and inconsistent.

Stalford, 2012: 34

Returning to the alternative high narrative and the privileging of penality and punitivity, this too is burdened by crucial limitations. Although 'many worrying developments' concerning 'punitiveness in Europe' (Snacken and Dumortier, 2012: 2) are plain to see – excesses characterized by Garland (2005: 814) as being symptomatic of a 'deliberate flouting of the norms of modern and civilized penology' – there is also evidence to imply that the 'new punitive common sense', as imagined by Wacquant (2009: 1), is being 'resisted'. Variants of penality and punitivity, therefore, are distributed asymmetrically in both their breadth (geographical reach) and their depth (the severity of penetration). As Wacquant (2009: 173) himself concedes, whilst processes of diffusion and regressive policy transfer might be apparent in Europe, and elsewhere, 'neo-liberalism is from its inception a multi-sited, polycentric, and geographically uneven formation'. In other words, there are many discernible sites – both juvenile and adult justice systems – where 'neo-liberalism has been thwarted… and the push towards penalization has been blunted or diverted' (ibid: 172–173. See also: Goldson and Muncie, 2006; Muncie and Goldson, 2006; Pratt, 2008a; Pratt, 2008b; Lappi-Seppälä, 2012; Pratt and Eriksson, 2013; Ruggiero and Ryan, 2013; Baldry *et al.*, forthcoming, 2019).

If juvenile prison rates are taken to signify the relative punitivity, or otherwise, of a given jurisdiction, we know – despite problems regarding the availability of truly comparable and reliable data (see below) – that significant variations are evident across both temporal and spatial comparative axes. Certain jurisdictions are susceptible to 'circular motions', as the stock and flow of child and youth imprisonment ebbs and flows over time (Goldson, 2015). Equally, at any given moment spatial differences are evident as 'prison rates vary greatly, both in western and eastern European countries' (Snacken and Dumortier, 2012: 3). The temporal fluctuations that impact upon the presence, or otherwise, of overtly penal and punitive juvenile justice settlements – and determine the size and shape of juvenile prison populations – are often determined by political contingencies and transient moments of 'moral panic'. Typical manifestations of such phenomena are expressed by way of 'get tough' impulses and periodic 'clampdowns'. The spatial differentiations of penality and punitivity – and corresponding inter-jurisdictional differences in juvenile prison rates – are more likely embedded in historical, cultural, social, economic and political traditions and complexes. Cavadino, Dignan and Mair (2013), for example, argue that the nature and form of penality and punitivity and, more particularly, rates of imprisonment, are closely correlated with specific political-economic formations.[3] Drawing on the earlier work of Lash and Urry (1987; 1994) and Esping-Andersen (1990), they contend that 'it is possible to relate some important characteristics of a country's political economy – and in particular its welfare system – to the severity of its penal practices' (Cavadino, Dignan and Mair, 2013: 80). Further, they establish a typology principally comprising three categories of political economy: 'neo-liberal' (including England and Wales); 'conservative corporatist' (including France, Germany, Italy and the Netherlands); and, 'social democratic' (including Finland and Sweden) (ibid: 80–83). The argument follows that neo-liberal political economies tend to be the most punitive and social democratic formations are normally the least punitive:

> in these different kinds of political economy, we find different cultural attitudes towards [the] deviant and marginalized… The neo-liberal society tends to exclude both those who fail in the economic marketplace and those who fail to abide by the law… both types of exclusion are associated with a highly individualistic social ethos… economic failure is seen as the fault of

the individual, not the responsibility of society – hence the minimal, safety-net welfare state. Crime is likewise seen as entirely the responsibility of the offending individual. The social soil is fertile ground for a harsh law and order ideology. On the other hand, corporatist societies... and to an even greater extent social democratic ones... have traditionally had a different culture and a different attitude towards the failing or deviant... [offering] a far greater degree of protection... to ensure all citizens are looked after... the offender is regarded not as an isolated culpable individual who must be rejected and excluded... but as a social being who is still the responsibility of the community as a whole. A more developed welfare state goes along with a less punitive penal culture. The most developed welfare states... have the lowest imprisonment rates.

ibid: 82

In sum, whatever the value and the seduction of high narratives and binary visions – whether they appeal to evolving cultures of human rights and penal tolerance or, conversely, to consolidating forms of penality and punitivity – juvenile justice systems assume multitudinous and widely varying forms and it is simply not possible to identify an internationally unifying thrust or European norm. Such variability – temporal and spatial in nature – fatally inconveniences high narratives. On one hand, there is ample evidence of human rights violations within juvenile justice systems across Europe, such as to contend that children's rights as 'they are written' are rarely translated evenly and purely to the legal, administrative, operational and institutional realms of juvenile justice as they are practised and experienced. On the other hand, variations in the temporal and spatial patterning of penal detention – and the profound significance and impact of differentiated histories, cultures and social, political and economic formations in crafting such patterning – imply that 'there are real grounds for optimism that dystopian analyses have been overplayed' (Downes, 2012: 32). At its simplest, the march of human rights and penal tolerance may not be as strident and far-reaching as we might like to imagine but, just as readily, the corrosive impact of penality and punitivity is neither as rampant, nor as evenly distributed, as we might fear. To put it another way, the rights-punitivity binary is intrinsically flawed and more nuanced forms of analysis are necessary to read the present (and to begin to map the future(s)) of juvenile justice in Europe.

Reading the present: finer-grained analysis

Having completed an ambitious and detailed survey of 34 European jurisdictions,[4] Dünkel (2015: 49) reflects that 'juvenile justice systems in Europe have developed in various forms and with different orientations'. He further observes that:

in the past 25 years, [juvenile] justice systems in Europe have undergone considerable changes, particularly in the former socialist countries of central and eastern Europe… [and] differing and sometimes contradictory [juvenile] justice policies have also emerged in western Europe.

ibid: 9

The survey design employed by Dünkel and his colleagues comprised a standardized pro-forma/questionnaire – completed by each of the 34 participating jurisdictions – to provide a 'national report' (for each country/jurisdiction). Each national report is composed of 14 fields or sub-sections including: the historical development and overview of juvenile justice legislation; trends in reported delinquency/offending; the nature of the sanctions system (informal and formal); the defining characteristics of juvenile justice procedures and systems; sentencing practices since 1980 (including 'informal' practices and 'juvenile court dispositions'); regional patterns and differences in sentencing outcomes; the inter-face between juvenile justice and young adult (18–21yrs) justice systems; transfer and waiver arrangements between juvenile and adult justice systems; residential care and pre-trial detention policies, practices and procedures; penal detention policies, practices and procedures; vocational training and educational programmes for juvenile offenders; current and prospective reforms and a 'summary and outlook' (Dünkel *et al.*, 2010: 6–8). It is claimed that the published version of the research – extending over four volumes and consisting of almost 2,000 pages – amounts to what is 'probably the most comprehensive database on juvenile justice systems in Europe' (ibid: 8). In this sense, it builds upon and extends earlier comparative studies, both in Europe and elsewhere (see, for example: Bailleau and Cartuyvels, 2002; Bala *et al.*, 2002; Winterdyk, 2002; Doob and Tonry, 2004; Junger-Tas and Decker, 2006; Muncie and Goldson, 2006; Bailleau and Cartuyvels, 2010; Terrill, 2016). By illustrating the diverse and differentiated inter-national nature of juvenile justice in Europe, such finer-grained analysis points-up the singular inadequacy of the more monolithic transnational/pan-European high narratives reviewed above.

Indicators of inter-national difference? The minimum age of criminal responsibility and the rate of penal detention

Two apparent indicators of inter-national difference are especially noteworthy: the minimum age of criminal responsibility (the entry point at the 'front end' or the 'shallow end' of juvenile justice systems) and, as stated above, the rate of penal detention (at the 'back end' or the 'deep end' of the same systems). At face value at least, both appear to illustrate significantly differentiated legal constructions and practical outcomes within juvenile justice systems in Europe.

The most obvious point to make pertaining to the minimum age of criminal responsibility across the 47 Member States of the Council of Europe is that it extends from 10 years (in Switzerland and in two of the UK jurisdictions – England and Wales and Northern Ireland), to 18 years (in Belgium) (see Table 11.1). The minimum age of criminal responsibility stands at 14 years in most of the Member States, but ten countries 'responsibilize' children below the age of 14 years and 11

TABLE 11.1 Minimum Age of Criminal Responsibility (MACR) in the 47 Council of Europe Member States (CoEMS)

CoEMS	MACR
Switzerland, UK (England and Wales and Northern Ireland).	10 years
Ireland, Netherlands, Turkey, UK (Scotland).	12 years
France, Monaco, Poland.	13 years
Albania, Andorra, Armenia, Austria, Azerbaijan, Bosnia and Herzegovina, Bulgaria, Croatia, Cyprus, Estonia, Georgia, Germany, Hungary, Italy, Latvia, Liechtenstein, Lithuania, Macedonia, Malta, Moldova, Montenegro, Russia, San Marino, Serbia, Slovakia, Slovenia, Spain, Ukraine.	14 years
Czech Republic, Denmark, Finland, Greece, Iceland, Norway, Sweden.	15 years
Luxembourg, Portugal, Romania.	16 years
Belgium.	18 years

Source: Data derived from Aebi *et al.*, 2016.

jurisdictions refrain from imposing such responsibility until children reach the age of 15 years or beyond.

If we shift our attention to recorded rates of penal detention and narrow our focus to the 28 Member States of the European Union, similar diversity is again seemingly apparent (see Table 11.2).

The data implies that the rate of penal detention for children and young people aged 17 years or under, extends from less than 1: 100,000 (in Sweden) to 44: 100,000 (in Poland). At face value, Member States in the West and North of Europe appear to be less inclined to place children and young people in penal detention than their neighbouring States in the South and East of Europe. But the picture is more complicated than this might imply, and such *inter*-regional differences are also accompanied by *intra*-regional variations. In other words, there are also both relatively low and high rates of penal detention to be found *within* each of the regions of Europe. In the North, from 1: 100,000 or less (Sweden, Denmark and Ireland) to 14: 100,000 (Estonia) and 16: 100,000 (Lithuania). In the West, from 2: 100,000 (Luxembourg) to 14: 100,000 (the Netherlands). In the South, from 1: 100,000 (Slovenia) to 24: 100,000 (Portugal). And, in the East, from 5: 100,000 (Bulgaria) to 44: 100,000 (Poland). If manifest differences might appear obvious, therefore, how they are understood, interpreted and vested with meaning, requires care and analytical caution.

To turn first to differences in the minimum age of criminal responsibility. Although there is no categorical international or European standard regarding the age at which criminal responsibility can reasonably be imputed on a child, the provisions of specific human rights instruments are pertinent. For example, Article 4(1) of the 'United Nations Standard Minimum Rules for the Administration of Juvenile Justice' (the Beijing Rules) (United Nations General Assembly, 1985) states: 'in those legal systems recognizing the concept of the age of criminal responsibility for juveniles, the beginning of that age shall not be fixed at too low an age

TABLE 11.2 Minimum Age of Criminal Responsibility (MACR) and recorded rates of penal detention[a] (2014)[b] in the 28 European Union Member States (EUMS)

EUMS	MACR (years)	Recorded rate of detention in 2014
Austria	14	5
Belgium	18	No available data
Bulgaria	14	5
Croatia	14	9
Cyprus	14	No available data
Czech Republic	15	6
Denmark	15	1
Estonia	14	14
Finland	15	9
France	13	5
Germany	14	No available data
Greece	15	19
Hungary	14	24
Italy	14	11
Ireland	12	1
Latvia	14	11
Lithuania	14	16
Luxembourg	16	2
Malta	14	19
Netherlands	12	14
Poland	13	44
Portugal	16	24
Romania	16	9
Spain	14	9
Slovakia	14	9
Slovenia	14	1
Sweden	15	<1
United Kingdom (E&W)[c]	10	6

Source: Data derived from United Nations Office on Drugs and Crime (UNODC), 2017.

a Rate per 100,000 children and young people aged 17 years or under (rounded up or down) detained: 'persons held in prisons, penal institutions or correctional institutions'.

b The most complete up-to-date data available applies to 2014.

c The UK comprises three separate jurisdictions: England and Wales (E&W), Northern Ireland and Scotland. England and Wales is substantially the largest jurisdiction.

level'. A very similar statement is provided by Rule 4 of the 'European Rules for juvenile offenders subject to sanctions or measures' (Council of Europe, 2009). The presumption, therefore, is that the more progressive and human rights compliant juvenile justice systems are characterized by measures that serve to delay the imputation of criminal responsibility. But a low minimum age of criminal responsibility in any given jurisdiction is not necessarily a signifier of punitivity, just as a higher age of responsibility cannot, in and of itself, be taken to represent penal tolerance.

Returning to Table 11.2, for example, some European Union Member States with comparatively low minimum ages of criminal responsibility appear to also record relatively low rates of penal detention. Conversely, some of the higher rates of penal detention are recorded in countries where the minimum age of criminal responsibility is also at the higher end of the continuum. To put this another way, the relation between the minimum age of criminal responsibility and the rate of penal detention does not appear to be consistently determinative.

Indeed, in many countries with a low minimum age of criminal responsibility a rebuttable presumption of innocence – the principle of *doli incapax* – provides a vital safeguard in respect of children aged 10–14 years. Equally, in the same jurisdictions the most severe penal sanctions (detention) are normally reserved for children and young people aged 15 years plus. Conversely, in several jurisdictions where the age of criminal responsibility is markedly higher, juvenile justice systems nonetheless reserve powers to prosecute children – otherwise below the specified minimum age of criminal responsibility – who are deemed to have committed grave offences. In this way, Pruin (2010: 1546) explains:

> Further analysis demonstrates that the issue of age groups in juvenile justice is very complex. In some countries, a low age of criminal responsibility is relativized through much higher age thresholds for severe punishments. Many systems provide the doctrine of *doli incapax* or comparable regulations which in fact raise the age of criminal responsibility. On the other hand, there are countries that allow for the application of adult criminal law in cases of serious offences... Some questions remain. Can we rank the different systems by defining which system is better than another? Can we say... which kind of behavior should be covered by the juvenile justice system – and are we able to define the "best age thresholds"? Not surprisingly, the honest answer to these questions is predominantly negative.

Similar analytical complexities apply when attempting to comprehend the transnational and/or inter-national patterning of penal detention. We have drawn attention to both inter-regional and intra-regional variations in rates of juvenile penal detention and, to some extent at least, this inconveniences the interpretive purchase of the political-economy typologies that we considered above. At a conceptual/theoretical level, therefore, even though we are likely to find that countries at similar stages of historical, cultural, social, political and economic development will share identifiable penal trends in common, 'national *particularities* rather than across the board *commonalities*' (Ryan, 2013: 5) appear to provide more accurate signifiers of comparative analysis. At a more mundane level, the complexities of comparative analysis are further compounded by the quality and availability of data.

Rates of penal detention, as distinct from simple counts, provide better data for the purposes of comparative analysis. But many commentators have drawn attention either to the unavailability, or to the intrinsic inaccuracy, of recorded data amounting to 'a general lack of reliable comparative and longitudinal data' (Dünkel,

2015: 42). To take the data compiled and collated by the United Nations Office on Drugs and Crime as an example (see Table 11.2 above), every presented data set is accompanied by the caveat: 'data supplied by countries may not exactly reflect the definition [of prisons, penal institutions or correctional institutions] provided by UNODC'. Baeva (2014: 17) makes a similar point:

> Traditionally [research] projects on children deprived of liberty adopt an approach that limits monitoring to institutions pertaining formally or informally to the criminal justice system... [and exclude] other institutions that inherently replicate the placement and living conditions of criminal justice institutions (reformatories, pre-trial detention facilities, police stations), where children are placed by a judicial, administrative or other authority and from which they cannot leave at will... closed establishments such as institutions for the placement of children for educational supervision, welfare and protection purposes, migrants with irregular status, children with disabilities and institutions for active treatment of children with mental disabilities.

In other words, even when recorded data sets are available, those that pertain only to particularly narrow interpretations of 'penal detention', will necessarily fail to take account of, and count, children and young people who are detained in related forms of 'secure' institutions (see also Pitts and Kuula, 2005; Goldson and Muncie, 2006; Sykiotou, 2017). Furthermore, as Muncie (2015: 361) asserts, even when data are recorded it may only be of limited comparative value because:

> it is not always clear whether the data are based on statistics of "stock" (numbers on a given day) or "flow" (numbers admitted during a calendar year). We are never quite sure whether "juvenile" always refers to under-18s or to under-21s. Custody data may be of total custodial populations or might only include those under sentence (excluding remands)... the lack of uniform definitions... of common measuring instruments and of common methodology makes comparisons between countries extremely hazardous.

Finer-grained analysis helps us to understand further the limitations of transnational/pan-European high narratives and, what Nelken (2017: 421) has termed 'comparison by juxtaposition', reveals a range of inter-national differences in contemporary juvenile justice systems in Europe. The ways in which such variations might be interpreted, however, invoke extraordinary complexities and challenges both at conceptual/theoretical and empirical/practical levels. Even to take the 'national' as the primary unit of comparative analysis is itself problematic.

The significance of sub-national contexts

Thus far, we have centred our reading of the present at transnational/pan-European (high narrative) and at inter-national (finer-grained) levels. But if the high narratives fail to take account of finer-grained inter-national specificities and particularities, fixing the analytical gaze at the national level also risks concealing, or at least obfuscating, intra-national or sub-national, regional and/or local differences that might prevail within otherwise discrete juvenile justice jurisdictions. Indeed, in many countries it is difficult to prioritize *national* developments above widely divergent *sub-national* variance, perhaps most evident in sentencing disparities ('justice by geography') (Baldry *et al.*, forthcoming, 2019). Once it is recognized, therefore, that variations *within* national borders may be as great, or even greater, than some differences *across* and *between* them, then taking the national (let alone the pan-European) as the principal lens through which we read the present becomes more questionable (Hughes and Edwards, 2002; Muncie, 2005; Muncie and Goldson, 2006; Hughes, 2007; Goldson and Hughes, 2010; Edwards, 2016).

As stated above, it is important to recognize the significance of pan-European trends – including, for example, the impact of international human rights standards, alongside United Nations, European Commission and Council of Europe policy and practice concordats – but equally the national, sub-national and local governance of juvenile justice is also vitally important. Even highly centralized state agencies and national bodies are – at least in part – 'power-dependent' on sub-national, regional and local bodies through which they aim to govern and with whom they need to negotiate. The significance of looking beyond an exclusively state-centred and/or national reading of the present, therefore, is not to deny the power that transnational bodies (including the European Commission and the Council of Europe), alongside national government agencies (including Government Ministries, Departments and national services) bring to bear on sub-national, regional and local juvenile justice agencies, policies and practices, but rather to recognize the inter-relational and, ultimately, mutually dependent nature of political power that underpins juvenile justice policy and its codification, translation and operationalization (Fergusson, 2007).

Embracing the significance of sub-national contexts for the purposes of reading the present necessitates recognizing the political and professional agency of local juvenile justice managers and practitioners, key individuals, the complex 'partnerships' that they co-ordinate and the operationalization of professional discretion. As Christiaens (2015: 11) observes 'no model [of juvenile justice] remains completely pure' in its translation, implementation and practical operationalization:

> this is why it is important to grasp and understand the complexity of *doing juvenile justice…* dig[ging] into the way the police, social workers, magistrates and the courts are not only involved in juvenile justice practices, but also embody what juvenile justice, on a daily basis, does and is… [its] daily practices… although hierarchy, power and authority are clearly at play… justice practices cannot be understood as merely top down interventionism. Involved professionals but also non-professionals have their own *interests* and perspectives when engaging in the dynamics of juvenile justice procedures.
>
> *ibid: 12, original emphases*

Ultimately, it is only by adopting a sub-national 'area studies' (Nelken, 2017: 428) approach, that we might understand how higher-level national juvenile justice policy is 'visioned and reworked (or made to work) by those "on the ground"' (Muncie, 2015: 383). Crucially important to such understanding are the complex and myriad ways in which inter-personal and inter-agency interactions, organizational processes and institutional practices operate; including how top-down national policies are necessarily mediated and filtered 'from below'. It is by unravelling the complex dialectical relations and reciprocal exchanges between the transnational/pan-European, the inter-national and the intra-national/sub-national levels – including both 'top-down' and 'bottom-up' translations – that we might read the present in such a way to avoid the analytical errors of what Edwards *et al.* (2013: 152) term 'false universality' and 'false particularity'.

Mapping the future(s) (1): The changing state of Europe

Juvenile justice systems in Europe are normally embedded within the wider apparatus of welfare states and welfare settlements, whatever their precise configurations. Moreover, and without exception, the same systems – especially at their 'deeper ends' – typically 'sweep-up' children and young people from the most damaged, distressed and disadvantaged families, neighbourhoods and communities from within their given jurisdiction. No matter where we might care to pitch our gaze – temporally or spatially – police stations, juvenile courts, various residential facilities and penal institutions, are routinely populated by children and young people who suffer the most acute social and economic adversities and for whom the infrastructure of everyday life is disfigured by multiple deprivations and social harms. Furthermore, the intersections between structural disadvantage, ethnicity, 'race' and racism are also manifest. It is not unusual, therefore, for juvenile justice systems to be characterized by the disproportionate presence – often the striking over-representation – of children and young people from minority ethnic communities. With this is mind, any consideration of the future(s) of juvenile justice in Europe must necessarily take account of, and be informed by, the changing state of welfare settlements in Europe and other conditions that impact specifically upon minority ethnic communities.

The reformulation of welfare settlements and welfare state retrenchment

If post-war welfare state settlements – in Western Europe at least – were underpinned by broad-based working class-middle class accommodations and a general mood of consensus regarding the shape, form and principal objectives of 'welfare capitalism' (Esping-Andersen, 1990) – principally comprising support for a relatively high standard of social provision sustained by a 'politics of social solidarity' (Baldwin, 1990) – more recent social, economic and political developments appear to signify the incremental weakening and undermining of such consensual solidarities. Economic globalization, demographic changes, shifts in family structures and formations, contracting labour market opportunities, greater job insecurity, casualization and precarity (especially for the least well-paid) and widening and deepening inequalities in the distribution of income and wealth have consolidated (Piketty, 2014). Equally, key sources of political power and support for state welfare – trade unions and labour organizations – have weakened, in tandem with the decline of manufacturing industries and processes of de-industrialization. Of course, the precise nature, pace and impact of such changing conditions – that have served to disrupt welfare state settlements – have varied across European countries and regions, but their overall effects have been generally deleterious:

> the outcome is a move away from the old politics of welfare which… posited a major role for the state in redistribution from better to worse off. The structures that previously sustained the various welfare systems… are being dismantled. There is considerable uncertainty as to the form of welfare state that will emerge, or whether a transition to a different political economy with weaker provision for the most vulnerable… is under way… [but] the greater political influence of the rich [has] led to demands for tax cuts, imposed pressures on spending and on cost-efficiency and undermined… traditional welfare states.
>
> *Taylor-Gooby et al., 2017a: 8–9*

If such conditions have been steadily eroding traditional European welfare state settlements for some time, the so-called 'great recession' of 2007–09, the financial crash of 2008 and a further major dip into recession in 2011–12, accelerated and intensified them. Widespread austerity measures, severe cuts in public expenditure, welfare state retrenchment and a corrosive neo-liberal logic, have combined to deepen poverty, widen inequality and open-up new cleavages including, but not limited to, 'intergenerational and deserving/undeserving divisions' (Taylor-Gooby *et al.*, 2017a: 23). With specific regard to the spread of poverty, Ballas *et al.* (2014: 160) have noted that 'according to the latest data from the World Bank and Eurostat, the total number of people living in poverty… is 109,387,770, this is approximately 18% of the total population in Europe'. More generally, the International Federation of Red Cross and Red Crescent Societies (2013: 2) observes that 'as the economic crisis has planted its roots, millions of Europeans live with insecurity, uncertain about what the future holds'. If the future invokes a sense of uncertainty however, Europeans appear to be less unsure about the present. The 'Special Eurobarometer' survey – carried out between September 23 and October 2, 2017 in the 28 European Union Member States – invited respondents to identify up to three main challenges currently faced by the EU. The three most popular responses were 'unemployment', 'social inequalities' and 'migration issues' (European Commission, 2017a: 8). It is to a consideration of the latter that we now turn.

Migrations, immigration and reactionary responses

Throughout history, migration(s) has/have enriched Europe in innumerable ways; culturally, socially, economically. But the most recent patterns of migration and immigration have assumed unprecedented levels and have occurred at precisely the same time that welfare state retrenchment and conditions of austerity have bitten deepest. In the summer of 2015 alone, 1.5 million refugees arrived at Europe's borders and, in the same year, 1.3 million people applied for asylum in Norway, Switzerland and the 28 European Union Member States (Tyler, 2017). The combination of the conditions outlined above, together with exceptionally high levels of immigration, have been toxic; fueling an anti-immigration backlash and a series of reactionary political responses:

> Two types of immigration can be distinguished across Europe... First, non-EU migration, mostly consisting of asylum seekers and refugees from countries affected by military conflicts such as Afghanistan, Iraq, Somalia and Syria. These immigrants travel across the Mediterranean and into Greece, Italy and Spain, and overland from Turkey through Romania, Greece and Eastern Europe. Secondly, EU migration, as some EU citizens, particularly from the Central and Eastern European 2004 and 2007 accession states, used their mobility rights to seek better socio-economic conditions. Concerns over security and welfare abuse have strengthened demand for anti-immigration policies across Europe.
>
> *Taylor-Gooby et al., 2017b: 204*

The reactionary responses to such processes have included either the emergence, or the development and increased popularization, of Nationalist, Far-Right and crypto-Fascist movements and political parties including, but not limited to: Alternative for Germany; the Danish People's Party; Fidesz in Hungary; the Finns Party in Finland; the Front National in France; the *Moviment Patrijotti Maltin in Malta* (Maltese Patriots Movement); the National Popular Front in Cyprus; the National Movement in Poland, the Party for Freedom in the Netherlands, the Progress Party in Norway; the Swedish Democrats and the UK Independence Party (UKIP).

Such movements and political organizations have, in turn, provoked a range of different reactionary responses. In the UK, UKIP was instrumental in engineering the referendum that led to a vote to leave the European Union – Brexit – which has, alongside a range of other major implications, 'created severe tensions and strengthened exit movements elsewhere, notably in France, Italy and Denmark' (Taylor-Gooby *et al.*, 2017a: 3). In Greece – which, as stated, has become a major gateway into Europe for migrants and asylum seekers from Asia and Africa – a Fascist movement that goes under the name of Golden Dawn has been responsible for a substantial upturn in racist violence (Papageorgiou, 2017). Indeed, if forms of racism have long existed in both Eastern Europe (Nowicka, 2017) and Western

Europe (Lentin, 2017), the current wave of anti-immigration sentiment has had the effect of re-awakening and re-energizing it; of 'evoking ghosts of Europe's recent past' (Tyler, 2017: 15).

At a conceptual level, such reactionary responses have altered 'the experience of being in linear time' and forced a rethinking of the conventional ways in which we normally 'separate and sequence the past, the present and the future' (Gordon, 2011: 2). Instead, they beg questions of the ways that such responses might comprise representations and contemporary manifestations of an otherwise 'repressed or unresolved social violence' vested deeply in racism (ibid). For Tyler (2017: 4), 'different genealogies of racism [have] converged in responses to the "refugee crisis"' whereby the 'stigmatization of refugees' and the processes of 'degradation and dehumanization' to which they are exposed, serve to 'animate historical spectres of racism… through which humanity is classified and disciplined into humans, not-quite-humans and nonhumans'.

At a more immediate and practical level, the same reactionary responses have invoked questions concerning security and have inflated fears of insecurity. The conflation of immigration, 'radicalization', security and 'terror' are especially problematic and have started to seep into the juvenile justice realm.[5] More generally, discourses that centre the most recent waves of migration and immigration are serving to both *victimize* migrants on the street and to *criminalize* them in the public imagination. Van Kesteren (2016: 152) has reported that the 'top position of migrant status as an independent risk factor for hate crime victimization confirms that migrants are prime targets of hate crimes in Western Europe', with young males being disproportionately exposed to risk of victimization and the same risks being 'especially high among religious immigrants suggest[ing] that anti-Islam sentiments are at play'. At the same time, migrants are criminalized in the public imagination. Papageorgiou (2017: 1498), for example, notes that the results of a study conducted in Greece revealed that 71% of respondents considered immigration to be 'the cause of increased criminality'.

Key implications for juvenile justice

If the 'clientele' of juvenile justice systems typically comprise the most disadvantaged children and young people, then welfare state retrenchment, widening inequalities and deepening poverty across Europe have obvious implications. Similarly, if children and young people from minority ethnic communities are routinely over-represented in juvenile justice systems – a key signifier of racialized injustice – then unprecedented migrations and patterns of immigration, re-awakened Nationalist and Far-Right sensibilities, consolidating antipathy and developing fear of the 'other' (perhaps especially Islamophobia), and the increasing victimization and criminalization of migrants and immigrants, signal a range of equally obvious implications. Indeed, the adversarial conditions within which many children and young people are growing-up and, more particularly, the hostile environments endured by child migrants – especially 'unaccompanied minors' – pose serious challenges for the future(s) of juvenile justice systems in Europe.

Mapping the future(s) (2): The changing state of childhood and youth in Europe

According to the European Commission (2017b), there were 79,692,580 children under the age of 15 years living in the European Union at the beginning of 2017 and a further 88,029,366 young people aged 15–29 years. At the same time, 5.3% of the population of the European Union comprised young people aged between 15–19 years (European Commission, 2017c), and it is estimated that more than 25 million children and young people are over the minimum age of criminal responsibility (European Commission, 2017d: 6). The reformulation of welfare settlements and related processes of welfare state retrenchment that we considered above, have obviously impacted upon children and young people and since 2008, in the post-financial crash period, deleterious conditions have accelerated and intensified. Several high-level initiatives have been implemented and developed to address such conditions, including the 'European Union Youth Strategy 2010–18' and 'Europe 2020' (for a fuller discussion see Coyotte *et al.*, 2015). Such initiatives aim to 'promote equal opportunities so that all children can achieve their full potential, provid[e] a focus on children who face an increased risk due to multiple disadvantages and stress the need to develop integrated strategies' (ibid: 167). Notwithstanding such efforts however, the most recent 'Eurobarometer' survey – carried out between September 23 and October 2, 2017 in the 28 European Union Member States – reveals that a 'majority of respondents think the life of today's children in the EU will be more difficult than the life of those from their own generation' (European Commission, 2017a: 62). Perhaps more significantly, the available data suggests that such concerns are well-founded and that many children and young people are 'caught up in an age of increasing despair' (Giroux, 2012: xiv), comprising a 'generation that will remember the crash of 2008 most acutely' (Ballas *et al.*, 2014: 65), even a 'lost generation' (Malik, 2012: 13).

Poverty and impoverishment

Guio *et al.* (2017: 209) observe that 'the fight against child poverty and the importance of investing in children's well-being has been high on the EU political agenda for many years'. That said, and following a detailed analysis of the most up-to-date data, Atkinson *et al.* (2017: 46) conclude:

> we see no grounds for disagreeing with one of the Key Messages of the Social Protection Committee in its 2014 annual report, 'the EU is still not making any progress towards achieving its Europe 2020 poverty and social exclusion target'.

This has particularly acute implications for children and young people, as Coyotte *et al.* (2015: 190) report:

the current economic climate of austerity measures has done little to help policymakers face these widespread challenges... [and] has resulted in an increasing share of the EU's population suffering... monetary poverty and/ or social exclusion and material deprivation. The impact of the crisis has been proportionally greater across those households with children... the risk of poverty is more common among children than it is for the population as a whole.

Indeed, data derived and collated from various European Commission sources reveals that in 2013, 11.6% of all young people aged 15–19 years who were living in the European Union were enduring 'severe material deprivation' and, by 2016, 30.1% were deemed to be 'at risk of poverty and social exclusion' (see Table 11.3). Such EU-wide averages conceal striking disparities between specific countries and regions. For example, less than 5% of young people residing in Austria (2.9%), Denmark (3.7%), Finland (3.2%), Germany (4.8%), Luxembourg (2.0%), the Netherlands (2.9%) and Sweden (2.3%) were enduring 'severe material deprivation' in 2013, whereas more than 25% of their counterparts in Bulgaria (46.2%), Greece (25.4%), Hungary (35.2%), Latvia (29.7%) and Romania (30.6%) were severely deprived. Broadly speaking, young people in the North and West European states appear to enjoy significantly better material conditions to those living in the South and East of Europe.

Similar, differences apply to the proportions of young people judged to be 'at risk of poverty and social exclusion'; ranging from approximately 1-in-5 (or less) in Austria, the Czech Republic, Denmark, Finland, Germany, the Netherlands and Slovenia, to almost 1-in-2 (or more) in Bulgaria, Greece and Romania. Notwithstanding such inter-country and inter-region differences, however, overall rates of both 'severe material deprivation' and 'risk of poverty and social exclusion' amongst children and young people are high in an otherwise 'rich continent' (Atkinson *et al.*, 2017: 47).

The relatively high rates of poverty and 'severe material deprivation' amongst children and young people in Europe impose both immediate and longer-term negative effects. Immediate implications include living in families that are unable to afford to pay rent/mortgage or utility bills on time, to keep their home adequately warm, to face unexpected expenses and/or to eat meat, fish or a protein equivalent every second day (Coyotte *et al.*, 2015: 169). But such adverse conditions also have longitudinal ramifications. Bellani and Bia (2017: 449), for example, have noted that growing-up poor 'raises the probability of falling below the poverty threshold in adulthood' and – having pooled numerous national datasets together and applied sophisticated quantitative modelling – they conclude that: 'our estimates provide strong evidence that experiencing financial difficulties in childhood leads to lower levels of income later in life' (ibid: 460).

Unemployment and institutional exclusion

Growing rates of youth unemployment represent a particularly conspicuous aspect of the changing state of childhood and youth in Europe (and elsewhere).

TABLE 11.3 Severe material deprivation rate (2013) and at risk of poverty and social exclusion rate (2016) for young people aged 15–19 years in the 28 European Union Member States (EUMS)

EUMS	Enduring severe material deprivation in 2013 (%)	At risk of poverty and social exclusion in 2016 (%)
European Union (28 MS)	**11.6**	**30.1**
Austria	2.9	19.2
Belgium	6.8	26.1
Bulgaria	46.2	48.2
Croatia	18.2	34.3
Cyprus	22.3	31.2
Czech Republic	9.3	17.0
Denmark	3.7	15.9
Estonia	8.2	24.4
Finland	3.2	15.5
France	8.2	26.0
Germany	4.8	20.5
Greece	25.4	46.5
Hungary	35.2	39.2
Italy	15.6	36.4
Ireland	11.0	32.5
Latvia	29.7	32.8
Lithuania	16.4	34.6
Luxembourg	2.0	31.9
Malta	12.6	24.4
Netherlands	2.9	20.6
Poland	14.6	34.4
Portugal	15.4	33.9
Romania	30.6	51.4
Spain	7.6	42.3
Slovakia	14.7	24.0
Slovenia	7.6	19.1
Sweden	2.3	28.3
United Kingdom	11.0	28.3

Sources: Data derived from European Commission (2017e) and European Commission (2017f).

The United Nations (2012: 15) has observed: 'young people are disproportionately affected by unemployment, underemployment, vulnerable employment and working poverty… the financial and economic crisis has further hit young people particularly hard'. At the global level, the rate of youth unemployment – which has long exceeded that of other age groups – saw the 'largest annual increase over the 20 years of available global estimates' in 2009 (United Nations, 2012: 16. See also, International Labour Organization, 2011). At the European Union level, the average rate of youth (15–19 years) unemployment across the 28 Member States at the beginning of 2016, stood at 21.8% (see Table 11.4) – just over 2% higher

TABLE 11.4 Unemployment rate and long-term unemployment rate (2016) for young people aged 15–19 years in the 28 European Union Member States (EUMS)

EUMS	Unemployment (%)	Long-term unemployment (12 months or longer) %
European Union (28 MS)	**21.8**	**4.0**
Austria	12.8	2.5
Belgium	26.3	4.7
Bulgaria	29.9	No data available
Croatia	52.0	11.2
Cyprus	48.7	No data available
Czech Republic	24.7	4.3
Denmark	14.0	No data available
Estonia	24.9	No data available
Finland	30.1	No data available
France	31.2	7.4
Germany	7.3	1.3
Greece	55.5	22.5
Hungary	26.4	No data available
Italy	57.2	21.7
Ireland	21.9	4.9
Latvia	19.4	No data available
Lithuania	No data available	No data available
Luxembourg	27.7	No data available
Malta	19.5	No data available
Netherlands	13.7	1.8
Poland	32.2	No data available
Portugal	37.8	No data available
Romania	30.7	8.4
Spain	60.6	12.2
Slovakia	45.0	11.5
Slovenia	12.2	No data available
Sweden	29.3	No data available
United Kingdom	20.2	2.3

Sources: Data derived from European Commission (2017g) and European Commission (2017h).

than the corresponding rate in 2008 (19.7%) (European Commission, 2017g). Not unlike the data considered immediately above, the European Union-wide average conceals striking disparities between specific countries and regions. For example, the youth unemployment rate ranges from a low of 7.3% (in Germany) to a high of 60.6% (in Spain). In seven countries (Austria, Denmark, Germany, Latvia, Malta, the Netherlands and Slovenia) less than 2-in-10 young people are recorded as unemployed, whereas in six countries (Croatia, Cyprus, Greece, Italy, Spain and Slovakia) the rate ranges between 4-in-10 and 6-in-10.

Equally, although data for many countries are not available, the average recorded rate of long-term youth unemployment (12 months or more) across the European

Union has increased from 3.2% in 2008 to 4.0% in 2016 (European Commission, 2017h), and it currently ranges from 1.3% (in Germany) to a staggering 22.5% (in Greece). In fact, the absence of data may well conceal the real state of long-term youth unemployment in Europe. Mascherini *et al.* (2017: 3), for example, have argued that 'almost one-third of unemployed young people have been looking for a job for 12 months or more without success... [and] the majority have been out of work for more than two years, illustrating the risk of job-seekers becoming trapped in protracted spells of unemployment'. They also refer to the 'scarring effects' that long-term unemployment imposes on young people: 'in particular... it increases the risk of social exclusion, whilst also decreasing optimism about the future' (ibid: 1).

High rates of youth unemployment in Europe are accompanied by equally high numbers of children and young people who are institutionally excluded from education and training programmes. Indeed, according to the European Commission (2015: 3) approximately 13.7 million young people 'are neither in employment nor education or training (NEETs)' and such young people tend to 'have less trust in public institutions and participate less in social and civic activities than their peers' (ibid: 4). Although the average rate of young people (aged 15–19 years) afflicted by NEET status has declined – across the 28 European Union Member States – from 13.4% in 2008 to 10.6% in 2016 (European Commission, 2017i), the numbers remain high (see Table 11.5).

Just over 1-in-10 young people aged 15–19 years are literally institutionally excluded and are cut adrift from employment, education and training opportunities in the European Union. Significant national variations are again evident with the rate of NEETs ranging from a low of 3.2% (in Luxembourg) to a high of 23.9% (in Croatia). Indeed, 'inactivity, poverty and exclusion do not strike evenly' (European Commission, 2015: 4) and, as we have noted, there are manifest differences *between* both individual countries and regions across Europe. But just as importantly – perhaps more importantly from a juvenile justice perspective – there are also striking variations *within* individual countries, where identifiable groups of children and young people are more likely than others to experience adverse material conditions. It is the very children and young people who 'start life with fewer opportunities [who] tend to accumulate disadvantages' and, in this context, it is not surprising that 'young people with a migrant background... are more likely to become NEETs' (ibid: 4).

Migration, immigration and criminalization

At a global level, approximately 50% (or 30 million) of the world's involuntarily displaced people – including refugees, asylum seekers and internally displaced persons – are children (United Nations Secretary General, 2016: para. 18). At a European level, 'the current refugee crisis is the greatest humanitarian challenge to have faced the European Union since its foundation... in 2015 88,245 unaccompanied children applied for asylum in the EU' (House of Lords European Union Committee, 2016: 3). The terms 'unaccompanied children' or, more commonly,

TABLE 11.5 Neither in Education, Employment or Training NEET rate (2016) for young people aged 15–19 years in the 28 European Union Member States (EUMS)

EUMS	NEET (%)
European Union (28 MS)	**10.6**
Austria	10.8
Belgium	7.1
Bulgaria	15.7
Croatia	23.9
Cyprus	10.4
Czech Republic	5.8
Denmark	7.3
Estonia	6.9
Finland	9.0
France	10.0
Germany	7.2
Greece	10.8
Hungary	10.4
Italy	13.6
Ireland	15.7
Latvia	7.8
Lithuania	No data available
Luxembourg	3.2
Malta	22.1
Netherlands	6.0
Poland	5.6
Portugal	9.0
Romania	19.5
Spain	11.3
Slovakia	11.7
Slovenia	6.1
Sweden	9.4
United Kingdom	14.2

Source: Data derived from European Commission (2017i).

'unaccompanied minors', are widely used in the context of European Union migration law, to refer to all foreign nationals or stateless persons below the age of 18 years, who either arrive in Europe unaccompanied (without a responsible adult) or who are left unaccompanied after their arrival. Such children and young people comprise a profoundly vulnerable group and the number of unaccompanied minors applying for asylum in the European Union Member States has risen steeply in recent years (both in real terms and as a proportion of all asylum applications received) (see Table 11.6).

The vulnerabilities of such children and young people derive largely from their experiences of: separation from their parents, carers and families; traumatic episodes in their countries of origin; migrating via irregular means and through dangerous

TABLE 11.6 Unaccompanied minors applying for asylum in the 28 European Union Member States (EUMS) (2013–15)

Year	Total applications for asylum	Applications from unaccompanied minors	% of total applicants who were unaccompanied minors
2013	431,090	12,725	3.0
2014	626,960	23,150	3.7
2015	1,321,600	88,245	6.7

Source: House of Lords European Union Committee, 2016: para. 12.

routes and adversarial conditions in countries of transit/transition. Perhaps more telling, however:

> is the fact that when unaccompanied migrant children arrive in the EU, they face suspicion and disbelief. They are subjected to repeated interviews questioning their motivation, family relations and age. They may be subjected to invasive age assessments to test that they truly are under 18. Often, the authorities simply decline to accept responsibility for them as children, and allow them to continue their journeys across borders alone
>
> *House of Lords European Union Committee, 2016: para. 2*

Against this backdrop, Europol estimates that at least 10,000 unaccompanied minors – profoundly vulnerable children and young people – are now 'missing' in the European Union and are potentially victims of sexual exploitation, trafficking or other criminal activity (ibid: para 3). Other processes of criminalization are also at work, often meaning that such children 'end up in detention':

> Accompanied or unaccompanied, all children travelling without official documents, whether seeking asylum or as refugees or irregular migrants, are at risk of being detained, given that in many countries illegal entry and illegal residence are considered as criminal offences.
>
> *Sykiotou, 2017: 9*

Key implications for juvenile justice

Chronic social exclusion, impoverishment, unemployment, NEET status, deep-cutting and wide-ranging austerity measures, patterns of forced migration and the prospect of exploitation, trafficking and detention. These are the conditions that confront millions of young Europeans. The same conditions also create social and economic environments that are known to give rise to juvenile crime and the disproportionate criminalization of identifiable groups of children and young people. As previously stated, juvenile justice systems throughout Europe and beyond, typically process (and punish) the most disadvantaged, distressed and damaged children and young people. This is not to suggest that *all* impoverished children and young people commit crime, or that *only* impoverished children and young people offend, but the corollaries between poverty, institutional exclusion, ruptured child-youth-adult transitions, juvenile crime and criminalization are very well-established.

It is particularly at the intersection of class and 'race'/ethnicity where some of the most pressing challenges for juvenile justice in Europe – present and future – reside, and where the human rights of the most disadvantaged children and young people are most readily compromised. Muncie (2008) found that of the 18 European jurisdictions he studied, 15 were explicitly exposed to critique by the United Nations Committee on Rights of the Child for negatively discriminating against children from minority ethnic communities and migrant children seeking asylum. The over-representation of such children is particularly conspicuous at the polar ends of juvenile justice systems – arrest and penal detention. Similarly, Roma people – the largest minority ethnic group in the European Union – endure systematic discrimination, harassment, ghettoization, forced eviction, expulsion and detention. By collating data drawn from 22 country-specific reports, Gauci (2009: 6) notes: 'most… reports identify the Roma… as being particularly vulnerable to racism and discrimination… in virtually all areas of life'. Increased ghettoization of 'foreigner' communities in various European countries – whether because of institutional decisions or practical realities such as chronic unemployment – is serving to entrench institutional exclusion and systematic marginalization: 'the creation of spatial segregation and socially excluded localities where communities are effectively denied access to basic services such as water and electricity' (ibid: 10).

Welfare 'safety nets' are becoming increasingly strained whilst, at the same time, the 'justice' apparatus appears to offer minimal relief for minoritized communities – including children and young people – enduring a pan-European upsurge of hate crime and racist violence:

> Racist and xenophobic reactions to the arrival of refugees, asylum seekers and migrants in the EU that marked 2015 continued unabated in 2016. They included hate speech, threats, hate crime, and even murder.
> *European Union Agency for Fundamental Rights, 2017: 91*

Perhaps more problematically, 'members of ethnic minority groups continued to face discriminatory ethnic profiling by the police in 2016' (ibid: 92). An insidious process of double-victimization is apparent, therefore, whereby the very children and young people most vulnerable to structural exclusion, systematic discrimination, hate crime and racist violence are also conceptualized primarily as 'suspects' and disproportionately criminalized.

To put it another way, the contemporary social, economic and political conditions that frame what we have respectively referred to as the 'changing state of Europe' and the 'changing state of childhood and youth in Europe' raise big questions of, and pose formidable challenges for, the protectionist principles that have historically defined welfare states and juvenile justice systems in Europe. Bailleau *et al.* (2010: 13) observe that:

> These principles, or at least some of them, are currently being challenged to various extents in a majority of countries in Europe. This weakening of the founding principles of juvenile justice is going hand in hand with a deterioration of the conditions of access to jobs for the least schooled youths, changes in the social ties and relations between generations, and a change in our relationship with social norms.

Mapping the future(s) (3): The changing state of juvenile justice

The antecedents of juvenile justice in Europe can be traced back to the 'invention' of 'juvenile delinquency' in the early nineteenth century, and the subsequent inception of a specific corpus of legislation, court structures, policies, procedures and practices for the processing of children and young people in conflict with the law at the beginning of the twentieth. Thereafter, the development of juvenile justice has not followed an even or linear trajectory. Harris and Webb (1987: 7–9), for example, have noted that juvenile justice 'is riddled with paradox, irony, even contradiction ... [it] exists as a function of the child care and criminal justice systems on either side of it, a meeting place of two otherwise separate worlds'. Similarly, Muncie and Hughes (2002: 1) have reflected that juvenile justice has oscillated, and continues to oscillate, 'around and beyond the caring ethos of social services and the... legalistic ethos of responsibility and punishment'. The ways in which 'two otherwise separate worlds' are reconciled or, to put it another way, the balance that is struck between the 'caring ethos' and the 'ethos of responsibility and punishment', is contingent and subject to multiple vagaries.

As such, and as noted above, it is difficult – perhaps impossible – to conceptualize European juvenile justice systems by referring to any singular defining rationale, or even to compartmentalize them into discrete self-standing 'models'. Clearly, there are times and places when certain thematic priorities are more ascendant than others. But in the final analysis, such systems comprise dynamic and hybridized forms that are both temporally and spatially contingent and subject to widely divergent ideological imperatives, political calculations, cultural priorities, judicial conceptualizations and operational strategies. For sure, any attempt to map the future(s) must surely take account of the changing state of juvenile justice in Europe, but the fact of the matter is such that juvenile justice is ever-changing.

That said, we have mapped a series of macro-level conditions that are currently shaping juvenile justice in Europe and will almost certainly continue to do so into the foreseeable future. In this sense, Cartuyvels and Bailleau (2010: 263) note that:

> juvenile justice systems in Europe... [are] grappling with far reaching transformations... [and] reflect the uncertainties of political actors and

lawmakers about the place that should be given to young people in a changing world. In societies that are marked by the globalization of trade and the deficits and upheavals affecting the traditional institutions and tools for integrating young people in society, e.g. training, the labour market, the family, etc., juvenile justice is trying to find its way.

In 'trying to find its way', juvenile justice systems in Europe need to address and reconcile the challenges that have ensued, and will continue to ensue, from the changing conditions that we have considered including, but not limited to, radically reformulated welfare settlements and welfare states, adverse social and economic environments and increasingly diverse and heterogeneous child and youth populations (emanating not least from patterns of migration and immigration). Two further changing conditions merit passing mention, the first pertaining to youth-adult transitions and the second to 'new' forms and patterns of youth offending.

The entry point for juvenile justice systems in Europe is normally determined by the minimum age of criminal responsibility that pertains in any given country and we have noted significant inter-national variance in this regard (see above). There is similar variance in relation to the exit point from juvenile justice systems, that is the stage at which young people are exposed to adult criminal justice. This is normally activated at the age of majority which is conventionally fixed at 18 years. Traditionally this corresponds with the point in the life course when young people are perceived to have assumed greater independence as they transition into adulthood. However, it is now widely recognized that for identifiable groups of young people – including those engaged in juvenile/criminal justice systems – youth-adult transitions are becoming increasingly hazardous, precarious, distorted and stretched. Mascherini *et al.* (2014: 24) have noted that:

> … the economic crisis has meant young people all over Europe have been faced with significantly less favourable transitions than before the crisis… It is essential to acknowledge that school to work transitions are closely connected with other steps on young people's path to adulthood, such as moving out of the parental home, finding a partner and having children… there have been general trends of postponement and increased complexity of these transitions… Most importantly, it can be assumed that, in times of economic crisis, uncertainty increases among young people, which can lead to the further postponement of achieving their goals of adulthood. This implies that the economic crisis not only excludes young people economically from the European labour markets, but also hampers them in becoming independent citizens. This is a source of real concern…

Indeed, the average ages at which young men and women 'leave home' across the Member States of the European Union are 26.3 years and 23.8 years respectively. Furthermore, patterns of national and regional variance – not dissimilar to those that we considered earlier – also obtain. For example, the average age at which men leave home ranges from 20.6 years (in Denmark) to 34.5 years (in Bulgaria), and the corresponding ages for women are 19.6 years (in Denmark) and 28.0 years (in Slovakia) (ibid: 23). Considered alongside conditions of poverty, unemployment, NEET status and social exclusion, and framed within a broader context of welfare state retrenchment, the multiple vulnerabilities that normally characterize such extended transitions raise questions pertaining to the legitimacy of exporting many young adults from juvenile justice systems and exposing them to the conventionally less forgiving realms of adult criminal justice. To put this another way, there may well be a case for extending the jurisdiction of 'juvenile' justice systems in Europe in order that they better correspond with stretched youth-adult transitions. In precisely this way Dünkel (2015: 51) refers to 'an interesting initiative to increase the maximum age at which young offenders can be treated as if they were juveniles' as a means of 'protect[ing] a potentially vulnerable group'. He draws attention to a 'recent reform… in the Netherlands increasing the scope of juvenile justice up to the age of 23' and suggests that this 'may be seen as the forerunner in juvenile justice reform in this respect' (ibid).

So, what of 'new' forms and patterns of youth offending? In concluding a detailed comparative study, Cartuyvels and Bailleau (2010: 265) note that 'no explosion of youth delinquency statistics was found in any of the countries'. Moreover, several commentators have even referred to a 'crime drop' (see, for example, Farrell *et al.*, 2015). Notwithstanding this, there is evidence to suggests that 'new' forms and patterns of youth offending are emerging, and that such 'offences' are often committed by a constituency of children and young people occupying 'virtual worlds' and who are conventionally not associated with juvenile justice systems.

Cyberbullying, for example, is an emerging concern and it can often take the form of unlawful and criminal behaviour. Children and young people across Europe routinely communicate via social media and cyberbullying can occur on Facebook, Instagram, Snapchat, Twitter and through text and email messaging. In many respects cyberbullying is more corrosive than 'traditional bullying' given that it does not stop when a child/young victim reaches the relative safety of their own home. Equally, in cases where a child or young person is bullied at school, on the playground or on the street, they obviously know who their bully is. But the relative 'anonymity' associated with cyberbullying can leave victims feeling like they have no recourse or ways of resolving their victimization. In this sense cyberbullying can be relentless and may severely damage a child's/young person's mental health and self-esteem. A similar concern relates to the practices of 'sexting', including the digital recording of naked, semi-naked, sexually suggestive or explicit images and their distribution via social media. The practices, perceptions, regulation and legislation pertaining to cyberbullying and 'sexting' raise major issues for juvenile justice in Europe and elsewhere (Crofts *et al.*, 2015).

Other forms of cybercrime are equally troubling and the National Cyber Crime Unit Prevent Team (2017: 1) refers to 'teenagers who… [are] unlikely to be involved in traditional crime' but who increasingly engage with 'cybercrime', including 'offenders [who] begin to participate in gaming cheat websites and "modding" (game modification) forums and progress to criminal hacking forums'. Many young people convicted for such cybercrime offences are motivated by curiosity, wanting to learn, understanding how computer systems work, excitement at meeting challenges and earning the respect of their peers (ibid). But their activities can lead to serious offences including hacking government websites and fraud. The key issue here is that for many children and young people – including the well-educated and 'respectable' middle classes – the retreat from the public realm of the street to less visible virtual worlds invokes previously unknown challenges for juvenile justice systems.

The futures(s) of juvenile justice in Europe will be shaped by the macro-level conditions of late modernity that we have reviewed. More specifically, stretched and disfigured life course transitions and 'new' youth cultures and behaviours that play out in virtual worlds, present previously unknown challenges that will need to be addressed and accommodated.

Conclusions, reflections and speculations

We conclude by recalling the inadequate analytical and explanatory power of high-narratives and the intrinsic flaws embedded in conceptual and theoretical accounts that privilege transnational/pan-European foci. Juvenile justice in Europe is differentiated at inter-national and intra-national/sub-national levels necessitating finer-grained critical inquiry and detailed engagement with a range of daunting complexities. Only then might we be able to read, and to begin to comprehend, the present.

We have reflected upon a series of profound socioeconomic transformations – structural and institutional shifts – their intersecting tendencies and the changing conditions that have ensued. The combined effect of: reformulations of welfare settlements and welfare state retrenchment; unprecedented patterns of migration and immigration; reactionary political responses; deepening child and youth poverty and impoverishment; consolidating unemployment and institutional exclusion; the criminalization of 'unaccompanied minors'; disfigured and elongated youth-adult transitions; and, new forms and patterns of juvenile offending, pose extraordinary challenges for juvenile justice in Europe.

Informed by such conclusions and reflections, we might speculate about the future(s) (perhaps the most complex and challenging venture of all). Such speculation is timely not least because, as Snacken and Dumortier (2012: 17) note, '"Europe"' as an institutional structure and the separate European countries are currently facing fundamental choices as to the kind of society they want to build for the future'. Both certainties and uncertainties are at play. We can be sure that the adverse post-2008 socioeconomic and political conditions will not simply disappear. We also know that Europe is not a monolithic or homogeneous entity and the formidable challenges currently confronting her constituent nation-states are distributed unevenly and are experienced with varying levels of gravity. It seems likely, for example, that some countries (in the South and East) will endure more prolonged and intense hostile conditions than others (in the North and West), possibly giving rise to a spectrum of differentiated responses. But although such responses will almost certainly be structurally *related* they will not necessarily be structurally *determined*. As Garland (2001: 201–202) has observed, 'the same structural co-ordinates can support quite different political and cultural arrangements'. In other words, the future(s) of juvenile justice in Europe is/are not pre-ordained, it/they will be made, shaped and formed by choices, the exercise of individual and collective agency and particularized political and professional adaptations. Of all this we can be more-or-less certain, but it is far more difficult to speculate – with any degree of confidence – about the *precise* shape and form that European juvenile justice systems will assume in the future. But that said, three key foundational principles may well frame the various transnational/pan-European, inter-national and intra-national/sub-national deliberations.

The first is underpinned by questions of political legitimacy, social cohesion and trust. Based upon analyses of 25 countries, Lappi-Seppälä (2012: 53) contends:

> Trust is relevant also for social cohesion and (informal) social control. Generalized trust and trust in people is an indicator of social bonds and social solidarity… There is a link from trust solidarity and social cohesion to effective informal social control. Finally, trust in institutions and legitimacy is also conducive to norm compliance and behaviour… And the crucial condition for this to happen is that people perceive the system is fair and legitimate. A system which seeks to uphold norm compliance through trust and legitimacy, rather than fear and deterrence, should be able to manage with less severe sanctions, as the results also indicate… Associated with norm compliance based on legitimacy, this decreases the need to resort to formal social control and to the penal system.

The second foundational principle concerns the iatrogenic effects of overzealous juvenile justice intervention. Informed by their detailed longitudinal research on pathways into and out of offending for a cohort of 4,300 children and young people in Scotland – and drawing more broadly on a long-standing and ever-growing body of international experience and evidence – McAra and McVie (2007: 337 and 340) conclude that:

> Doing less rather than more in individual cases may mitigate the potential for damage that system contact brings… targeted early intervention strategies… are likely to widen the net… Greater numbers of children will be identified as at risk and early involvement will result in constant recycling into the system… As we have shown, forms of diversion… without recourse to formal intervention … are associated with desistance from serious offending. Such findings are supportive of a maximum diversion approach… Accepting that, in some cases, doing less is better than doing more requires both courage and vision on the part of policy makers… To the extent that systems appear

to damage young people and inhibit their capacity to change, then they do not, and never will, deliver justice.

The third and final foundational principle – for present purposes at least – relates to the 'dangerous', 'ineffective', 'unnecessary', 'wasteful' and 'inadequate' nature of penal detention. In summarizing a substantial body of international evidence Mendel (2011: 5–25 *passim*) reports that the practices of child and youth imprisonment are:

Dangerous: juvenile corrections institutions subject confined youth to intolerable levels of violence, abuse, and other forms of maltreatment.

Ineffective: the outcomes of correctional confinement are poor. Recidivism rates are uniformly high, and incarceration in juvenile facilities depresses youths' future success in education and employment.

Unnecessary: a substantial percentage of youth confined in youth corrections facilities pose minimal risk to public safety.

Wasteful: most states are spending vast sums of taxpayer money and devoting the bulk of their juvenile justice budgets to correctional institutions and other facility placements when non-residential programming options deliver equal or better results for a fraction of the cost.

Inadequate: Despite their exorbitant daily costs, most juvenile correctional facilities are ill-prepared to address the needs of many confined youth. Often, they fail to provide even the minimum services appropriate for the care and rehabilitation of youth in confinement.

So, the future shape and form of juvenile justice in Europe? Any attempt to prophesize detailed specificities is necessarily hampered by the uncertainties, contingencies, complexities and challenges that operate at each of the transnational/pan-European, inter-national and intra-national/sub-national levels. But if choices, the exercise of individual and collective agency and particularized political and professional adaptations take account of accumulated knowledge, evidence and experience, the combined effect will be to construct approaches that: foster social cohesion and facilitate informal mechanisms of social control (commanding trust and enjoying legitimacy); limit criminalizing modes of intervention by maximizing diversion (and community support); and, ultimately, avoid the calamitous practices of child and youth imprisonment.

Notes

1 The 47 Council of Europe Member States are: Albania, Andorra, Armenia, Austria, Azerbaijan, Belgium, Bosnia and Herzegovina, Bulgaria, Croatia, Cyprus, Czech Republic, Denmark, Estonia, Finland, France, Georgia, Germany, Greece, Hungary, Iceland, Ireland, Italy, Latvia, Liechtenstein, Lithuania, Luxembourg, Macedonia, Malta, Moldova, Monaco, Montenegro, Netherlands, Norway, Poland, Portugal, Romania, Russia, San Marino, Serbia, Slovakia, Slovenia, Spain, Sweden, Switzerland, Turkey, Ukraine and the United Kingdom.

2 The 28 European Union Member States are: Austria, Belgium, Bulgaria, Croatia, Cyprus, Czech Republic, Denmark, Estonia, Finland, France, Germany, Greece, Hungary, Italy, Ireland, Latvia, Lithuania, Luxembourg, Malta, the Netherlands, Poland, Portugal, Romania, Spain, Slovakia, Slovenia, Sweden and the United Kingdom.

3 For similar lines of analysis, see also the work of David Downes and Kirstene Hansen (2006), David Downes (2012) and Nicola Lacey (2008).

4 The jurisdictions surveyed comprise: Austria; Belgium; Bulgaria; Croatia; Cyprus; Czech Republic; Denmark; England and Wales; Estonia; Finland; France; Germany; Greece; Hungary; Ireland; Italy; Kosovo; Latvia; Lithuania; The Netherlands; Northern Ireland; Poland; Portugal; Romania; Russia; Scotland; Serbia; Slovakia; Slovenia; Spain; Sweden; Switzerland; Turkey and Ukraine. See Dünkel *et al.* 2010, Volumes 1–4.

5 In 2017, for example, the Brussels-based International Juvenile Justice Observatory announced a major programme entitled: 'Strengthening juvenile justice policies in the counter-terrorism context'. A key 'objective' of the programme is 'to gather information… concerning terrorism and violent extremism in juveniles within… European juvenile justice systems'. An anticipated stated 'result' of the initiative is the 'improvement of national criminal policies and programmes in juvenile justice systems and more efficient judicial counter-terrorism policies directed at juvenile suspects'. Accessed December 9, 2017: www.oijj.org/en/strengtheningjjs-introduction.

References

Aebi, M., Tiago, M. and Burkhardt, C. (2016) *Council of Europe Annual Penal Statistics: SPACE 1: Prison Populations Survey 2015*. Strasbourg: Council of Europe.

Atkinson, A., Guio, A. C. and Marlier, E. (2017) 'European Social Goals in the Global Perspective of 2030', in Atkinson, A., Guio, A. C. and Marlier, E. (eds.) *Monitoring Social Inclusion in Europe*. Luxembourg: Publications Office of the European Union.

Baeva, S. (ed.) (2014) *Children Deprived of Liberty in Central and Eastern Europe: Between Legacy and Reform*. Sofia: Bulgarian Helsinki Committee.

Bailleau, F. and Cartuyvels, Y. (eds.) (2002) 'La Justice Pénale des Mineurs en Europe', *Déviance et Société*, 26(3) (special issue).

Bailleau, F. and Cartuyvels, Y. (eds.) (2010) *The Criminalisation of Youth: Juvenile Justice in Europe, Turkey and Canada*. Brussels: VUB Press.

Bailleau, F., Cartuyvels, Y. and de Fraene, D. (2010) 'The Criminalisation of Youth and Current Trends: The Sentencing Game', in Bailleau, F. and Cartuyvels, Y. (eds.) *The Criminalisation of Youth: Juvenile Justice in Europe, Turkey and Canada*. Brussels: VUB Press.

Bala, N., Hornick, J., Snyder, H. and Paetsch, J. (eds.) (2002) *Juvenile Justice Systems: An International Comparison of Problems and Solutions*. Toronto: Thompson.

Baldry, E., Briggs, D., Brown, D., Cunneen, C., Goldson, B., Russell, S. and Schwartz, M. (forthcoming, 2019) *Youth Justice and Penality in Comparative Context*. Abingdon: Routledge.

Baldwin, P. (1990) *The Politics of Social Solidarity, 1875–1975*. Cambridge: Cambridge University Press.

Ballas, D., Dorling, D. and Hennig, B. (2014) *The Social Atlas of Europe*. Bristol: Policy Press.

Beckett, K. and Western, B. (2001) 'Governing Social Marginality: Welfare, Incarceration and the Transformation of State Policy', *Punishment and Society*, 3(1): 43–59.

Bellani, L. and Bia, M. (2017) 'The Impact of Growing up Poor in Europe', in Atkinson, A., Guio, A. C. and Marlier, E. (eds.) *Monitoring Social Inclusion in Europe*. Luxembourg: Publications Office of the European Union.

Buzatu, C., Mihai, D., Boboşatu, D-A., Benezic, D., Gheorghe, G., Andreescu, M-N. and Pascu, E-G. (2014) 'Country Report: Romania', in Baeva, S. (ed.) *Children Deprived of*

Liberty in Central and Eastern Europe: Between Legacy and Reform. Sofia: Bulgarian Helsinki Committee.

Cartuyvels, Y. and Bailleau, F. (2010) 'Youth Criminal Justice in Europe: At the Intersection of Protective Thinking, a Neo-liberal Turn and Neo-conservative Ideology', in Bailleau, F. and Cartuyvels, Y. (eds.) *The Criminalisation of Youth: Juvenile Justice in Europe, Turkey and Canada*. Brussels: VUB Press.

Cavadino, M. Dignan, J. and Mair, G. (2013) *The Penal System: An Introduction*, 5th edition. London: Sage.

Christiaens, J. (2015) 'It's For Your Own Good! Researching Youth Justice Practices', in Christiaens, J. (ed.) *It's For Your Own Good: Researching Youth Justice Practices*. Brussels: VUB Press.

Council of Europe (2009) *European Rules for Juvenile Offenders Subject to Sanctions or Measures*. Strasbourg: Council of Europe Publishing.

Council of Europe (2010) *Guidelines of the Committee of Ministers of the Council of Europe on Child Friendly Justice* (Adopted by the Committee of Ministers on 17 November 2010 at the 1098th meeting of the Ministers' Deputies). Strasbourg: Council of Europe.

Coyotte, C., Fiasse, I., Johansson, A., Montaigne, F. and Strandell, H. (2015) *Being Young in Europe Today*. Luxembourg: European Union Publications Office.

Crofts, T., Lee, M., McGovern, A. and Milivojevic (2015) *Sexting and Young People*. Basingstoke: Palgrave Macmillan.

Doob, A. and Tonry, M. (2004) 'Varieties of Youth Justice', *Crime and Justice*, 31: 1–20. Minnesota: Minnesota Law School.

Downes, D. (2012) 'Political Economy, Welfare and Punishment in Comparative Perspective', in Snacken, S. and Dumortier, E. (eds.) *Resisting Punitiveness in Europe? Welfare, Human Rights and Democracy*. London: Routledge.

Downes, D. and Hansen, K. (2006) *Welfare and Punishment: The Relationship Between Welfare Spending and Imprisonment*. London: Crime and Society Foundation.

Dünkel, F. (2015) 'Juvenile Justice and Crime Policy in Europe', in Zimring, F., Langer, M. and Tannenhaus, D. S. (eds.) *Juvenile Justice in Global Perspective*. New York: New York University Press.

Dünkel, F., Grzywa, J., Horsfiled, P. and Pruin, I. (eds.) (2010) *Juvenile Justice Systems in Europe: Current Situation and Reform Developments*, Volumes 1–4. Mönchengladbach: Forum Verlag Godesberg.

Durkheim, E. (1893/2014) *The Division of Labour in Society*. New York: The Free Press.

Edwards, A. (2016) 'Multi-centred Governance and Circuits of Power in Liberal Modes of Security', *Global Crime*, 17(3–4): 240–263.

Edwards, A., Hughes, G. and Lord, N. (2013) 'Urban Security in Europe: Translating a Concept in Public Criminology', *European Journal of Criminology*, 10(3): 260–283.

Esping-Andersen, G. (1990) *The Three Worlds of Welfare Capitalism*. Cambridge: Polity.

European Commission (2011) *An EU Agenda for the Rights of the Child: Communication from the Commission to the European Parliament, the Council, the European Economic and Social Committee and the Committee of the Regions*. Brussels: European Commission.

European Commission (2012) *EU Youth Report, Commission Staff Working Document: Status of the Situation of Young People in the European Union*, SWD(2012) 257. Brussels: European Commission.

European Commission (2015) 'Communication from the Commission to the European Parliament, the Council, the European Economic and Social Committee and the Committee of the Regions: Draft 2015 Joint Report of the Council and the Commission on the Implementation of the Renewed Framework for European Cooperation in the Youth Field (2010–2018)', 15.09.2015, *COM(2015)429*. Brussels: European Commission.

European Commission (2017a) *Special Eurobarometer 467: Future of Europe – Social Issues.* Brussels: European Commission.

European Commission (2017b) *Eurostat: Child and Youth Population on January 1 by Sex and Age.* Accessed October 3, 2017: http://ec.europa.eu/eurostat/web/youth/data/database

European Commission (2017c) *Eurostat: Ratio of Young People in the Total Population on January 1 by Sex and Age.* Accessed October 3, 2017: http://ec.europa.eu/eurostat/web/youth/data/database

European Commission (2017d) *11th European Forum on the Rights of the Child 7–8 November 2017, Data.* Accessed November 7, 2017: http://ec.europa.eu/newsroom/just/item-detail.cfm?item_id=128349

European Commission (2017e) *Eurostat: Severe Material Deprivation of Young People by Sex and Age.* Accessed October 3, 2017: http://ec.europa.eu/eurostat/web/youth/data/database

European Commission (2017f) *Eurostat: People at Risk of Poverty or Social Exclusion by Sex and Age.* Accessed October 3, 2017: http://ec.europa.eu/eurostat/web/youth/data/database

European Commission (2017g) *Eurostat: Youth Unemployment Rate by Sex, Age and Country of Birth.* Accessed October 3, 2017: http://ec.europa.eu/eurostat/web/youth/data/database

European Commission (2017h) *Eurostat: Youth Long-term Unemployment Rate (12 Months or Longer) by Sex and Age.* Accessed October 3, 2017: http://ec.europa.eu/eurostat/web/youth/data/database

European Commission (2017i) *Eurostat: Participation Rate of Young People in Education and Training by Sex, Age and Labour Status (incl.) NEET status.* Accessed October 3, 2017: http://ec.europa.eu/eurostat/web/youth/data/database

European Union Agency for Fundamental Rights (2017) *Fundamental Rights Report 2017.* Luxembourg: Publications Office of the European Union.

Farrell, G., Laycock, G. and Tilley, N. (2015) 'Debuts and Legacies: The Crime Drop and the Role of Adolescence-limited and Persistent Offenders', *Crime Science*, 4(16).

Fassin, D. (2013) *Enforcing Order: An Ethnography of Urban Policing.* Cambridge: Polity.

Fergusson, R. (2007) 'Making Sense of the Melting Pot: Multiple Discourses in Youth Justice Policy', *Youth Justice*, 7(3): 179–194.

Fortin, J. (2008) 'Children as Rights Holders: Awareness and Scepticism', in Invernizzi, A. and Williams, J. (eds.) *Children and Citizenship.* London: Sage.

Furtunova, D., Angelova, D., Stanev, K., Kanev, K., Baeva, S. and Ivanova, Z. (2014) 'Country Report: Bulgaria', in Baeva, S. (ed.) *Children Deprived of Liberty in Central and Eastern Europe: Between Legacy and Reform.* Sofia: Bulgarian Helsinki Committee.

Garland, D. (2001) *The Culture of Control: Crime and Social Order in Contemporary Society.* Oxford: Oxford University Press.

Garland, D. (2005) 'Penal Excess and Surplus Meaning: Public Torture Lynchings in Twentieth-century America', *Law and Society Review*, 39(4): 793–834.

Gauci, J-P. (2009) *Racism in Europe.* Brussels: European Network Against Racism (ENAR).

Giroux, H. A. (2012) *Disposable Youth: Racialised Memories and the Culture of Cruelty.* New York: Routledge.

Goldson, B. (2009) 'Child Incarceration: Institutional Abuse, the Violent State and the Politics of Impunity', in Scraton, P. and McCulloch, J. (eds.) *The Violence of Incarceration.* London: Routledge.

Goldson, B. (2015) 'The Circular Motions of Penal Politics and the Pervasive Irrationalities of Child Imprisonment', in Goldson, B. and Muncie, J. (eds) *Youth Crime and Justice*, 2nd edition. London, Sage.

Goldson, B. and Hughes, G. (2010) 'Sociological Criminology and Youth Justice: Comparative Policy Analysis *and* Academic Intervention', *Criminology and Criminal Justice*, 10(2): 211–230.

Goldson, B. and Kilkelly, U. (2013) 'International Human Rights Standards and Child Imprisonment: Potentialities and Limitations', *The International Journal of Children's Rights*, 21(2): 345–371.

Goldson, B. and Muncie, J. (2006) 'Rethinking Youth Justice: Comparative Analysis, International Human Rights and Research Evidence', *Youth Justice: An International Journal*, 6(2): 91–106.

Goldson, B. and Muncie, J. (2009) 'Editors Introduction', in Goldson, B. and Muncie, J. (eds.) *Youth Crime and Juvenile Justice, Volume 2, Juvenile Corrections*. London: Sage.

Goldson, B. and Muncie, J. (2012) 'Towards a Global 'Child friendly' Juvenile Justice?', *International Journal of Law, Crime and Justice*, 40(1): 47–64.

Goldson, B. and Muncie, J. (2015) 'Children's Human Rights and Youth Justice with Integrity', in Goldson, B. and Muncie, J. (eds.) *Youth Crime and Justice*, 2nd edition. London: Sage.

Gordon, A. (2011) 'Some Thoughts on Haunting and Futurity', *Borderlands*, 10(2): 1–21.

Guio, A. C., Gordon, D. and Marlier, E. (2017) 'Measuring Child Material Deprivation in the EU', in Atkinson, A., Guio, A. C. and Marlier, E. (eds.) *Monitoring Social Inclusion in Europe*. Luxembourg: Publications Office of the European Union.

Hamilton, C. (2011) *Guidance for Legislative Reform on Juvenile Justice*. New York: Children's Legal Centre and UNICEF.

Harris, R. and Webb, D. (1987) *Welfare, Power and Juvenile Justice*. London: Tavistock.

Hawking, S. (2015) *Message to World Economic Forum Annual Meeting*, 21–24 January. Davos-Klosters, Switzerland. Accessed September 9, 2017: www.weforum.org/agenda/2015/09/stephen-hawking-we-are-all-time-travellers/

House of Lords European Union Committee (2016) *Children in Crisis: Unaccompanied Migrant Children in the EU*. London: House of Lords.

Hughes, G. (2007) *The Politics of Crime and Community*. Basingstoke: Palgrave.

Hughes, G. and Edwards, A. (eds.) (2002) *Crime Control and Community: The New Politics of Public Safety*. Cullompton: Willan.

International Federation of Red Cross and Red Crescent Societies (2013) *Thinking Differently: Humanitarian Impacts of the Economic Crisis in Europe*. Geneva: IFRC.

International Labour Organization (2011) *Global Employment Trends for Youth: 2011 Update*. Geneva: International Labour Office.

Kádár, A., Nemes, A., Tóth, B., Kirs, E., Matevžič, G., Iván, J., Novoszádek, N., Somogyvári, Z., Zadori, Z., Moldova, Z. and Simon, Z. (2014) 'Country Report: Hungary', in Baeva, S. (ed.) *Children Deprived of Liberty in Central and Eastern Europe: Between Legacy and Reform*. Sofia: Bulgarian Helsinki Committee.

Lacey, N. (2008) *The Prisoners' Dilemma: Political Economy and Punishment in Contemporary Democracies*. Cambridge: Cambridge University Press.

Lappi-Seppälä, T. (2012) 'Explaining National Differences in the Use of Imprisonment', in Snacken, S. and Dumortier, E. (eds.) *Resisting Punitiveness in Europe? Welfare, Human Rights and Democracy*. London: Routledge.

Lash, S. and Urry, J. (1987) *The End of Organised Capitalism*. Cambridge: Polity.

Lash, S. and Urry, J. (1994) *Economies of Signs and Space*. London: Sage.

Lentin, A. (2016) 'Racism in Public or Public Racism: Doing Anti-Racism in "Post Racial" Times', *Ethnic and Racial Studies*, 39(1): 33–48.

Malik, S. (2012) 'Youth Unemployment – €153bn a Year: Price Europe is Paying for its Lost Generation of Young Adults', *The Guardian*, October 22: 13.

Mascherini, M., Ludwinek, A., Vacas, C. and Meierkord, A. (2014) *Mapping Youth Transitions in Europe*. Luxembourg: European Foundation for the Improvement of Living and Working Conditions (Eurofound)/Publications Office of the European Union.

Mascherini, M., Ledermaier, S.,Vacas-Soriano, C. and Jacobs, L. (2017) *Long-term Unemployed Youth: Characteristics and Policy Responses*. Luxembourg: European Foundation for the Improvement of Living and Working Conditions (Eurofound)/Publications Office of the European Union.

McAra, L. and McVie, S. (2007) 'Youth Justice? The Impact of System Contact on Patterns of Desistance from Offending', *European Journal of Criminology*, 4(3): 315–345.

Mendel, R. (2011) *No Place for Kids: The Case for Reducing Juvenile Incarceration*. Baltimore: Annie E. Casey Foundation.

Muncie, J. (1999) 'Institutionalised Intolerance: Youth Justice and the 1998 Crime and Disorder Act', *Critical Social Policy*, 19(2): 147–175.

Muncie, J. (2005) 'The Globalization of Crime Control – The Case of Youth and Juvenile Justice: Neo-liberalism, Policy Convergence and International Conventions', *Theoretical Criminology*, 9(1): 35–64.

Muncie, J. (2008) 'The Punitive Turn in Juvenile Justice: Cultures of Control and Rights Compliance in Western Europe and the USA', *Youth Justice: An International Journal*, 8(2): 107–121.

Muncie, J. (2015) *Youth and Crime*, 4th edition. London: Sage.

Muncie, J. and Goldson, B. (eds.) (2006) *Comparative Youth Justice: Critical Issues*. London: Sage.

Muncie, J. and Hughes, G. (2002) 'Modes of Youth Governance: Political Rationalities, Criminalisation and Resistance', in Muncie, J., Hughes, G. and McLaughlin, E. (eds.) *Youth Justice: Critical Readings*. London: Sage.

Nelken, D. (2017) 'Rethinking Comparative Criminal Justice', in Liebling, A., Maruna, S. and McAra, L. (eds.) *The Oxford Handbook of Criminology*. Oxford: Oxford University Press.

National Cyber Crime Unit Prevent Team (2017) *Pathways into Cyber Crime*. London: National Crime Agency.

Nowicka, M. (2017) '"I don't mean to sound racist but…" Transforming Racism in Transnational Europe', *Ethnic and Racial Studies*, online first.

O'Malley, P. (2000) 'Criminologies of Catastrophe? Understanding Criminal Justice on the Edge of the New Millennium', *Australian and New Zealand Journal of Criminology*, 33(2):153–167.

Papageorgiou, A. A. (2017) 'Racist Violence in Greece: Mistakes of the Past and Challenges for the Future', in Spinellis, C. D., Theodorakis, N., Billis, E. and Papadimitrakopoulos, G. (eds.) *Europe in Crisis: Crime, Criminal Justice, and the Way Forward. Essays in Honour of Nestor Courakis*. Volume 2. Athens: Ant. N. Sakkoulas Publishers.

Piketty, T. (2014) *Capital in the 21st Century*. Cambridge, MA: Harvard University Press.

Pitts, J. and Kuula, T. (2005) 'Incarcerating Young People: An Anglo-Finnish Comparison', *Youth Justice*, 5(3): 147–164.

Pratt, J. (2008a) 'Scandinavian Exceptionalism in an Era of Penal Excess: Part I: The Nature and Roots of Scandinavian Exceptionalism', *British Journal of Criminology*, 48(2): 119–137.

Pratt, J. (2008b) 'Scandinavian Exceptionalism in an Era of Penal Excess: Part II: Does Scandinavian Exceptionalism Have a Future?' *British Journal of Criminology*, 48(3): 275–292.

Pratt, J. and Eriksson, A. (2013) *Contrasts in Punishment: An Explanation of Anglophone Excess and Nordic Exceptionalism*. London: Routledge.

Pruin, I. (2010) 'The scope of juvenile justice system in Europe', in Dünkel, F., Grzywa, J., Horsfiled, P. and Pruin, I. (eds.) *Juvenile Justice Systems in Europe: Current Situation and Reform Developments*, Volume 4. Mönchengladbach: Forum Verlag Godesberg.

Reiner, R. (2007) *Law and Order: An Honest Citizen's Guide to Crime and Control*. Cambridge: Polity.

Ruggiero, V. and Ryan, M. (eds.) (2013) *Punishment in Europe: A Critical Anatomy of Penal Systems*. Basingstoke: Palgrave Macmillan.

Ryan, M. (2013) 'Introduction', in Ruggiero, V. and Ryan, M. (eds.) *Punishment in Europe: A Critical Anatomy of Penal Systems*. Basingstoke: Palgrave Macmillan.

Snacken, S. and Dumortier, E. (2012) 'Resisting Punitiveness in Europe? An Introduction', in S. Snacken and E. Dumortier (eds.) *Resisting Punitiveness in Europe? Welfare, Human Rights and Democracy*. London: Routledge.

Stalford, H. (2012) *Children and the European Union: Rights, Welfare and Accountability*. Oxford: Hart Publishing.

Sykiotou, A. P. (2017) *A Study of Detention Practices and the Use of Alternatives to Immigration Detention of Children*. Strasbourg: Council of Europe Publishing.

Taylor-Gooby, P., Leruth, B. and Chung, H. (2017a) 'The Context: How European Welfare States have Responded to Post-industrialism, Ageing Populations and Populist Nationalism', in Taylor-Gooby, P., Leruth, B. and Chung, H. (eds.) *After Austerity: Welfare State Transformation in Europe after the Great Recession*. Oxford: Oxford University Press.

Taylor-Gooby, P., Leruth, B. and Chung, H. (2017b) 'Liberalism, Social Investment, Protectionism and Chauvinism: New Directions for the European Welfare State', in Taylor-Gooby, P., Leruth, B. and Chung, H. (eds.) *After Austerity: Welfare State Transformation in Europe after the Great Recession*. Oxford: Oxford University Press.

Terrill, R. J. (2016) *World Criminal Justice Systems: A Comparative Survey*, 9th edition. Abingdon: Routledge.

Tyler, I. (2017) 'The Hieroglyphics of the Border: Racial Stigma in Neoliberal Europe', *Ethnic and Racial Studies*, online first: 1–19.

United Nations (2012) *United Nations World Youth Report 2011 – Youth Employment: Youth Perspectives on the Pursuit of Decent Work in Changing Times*. New York: United Nations Department of Economic and Social Affairs.

United Nations Committee on the Rights of the Child (2016a) *Concluding Observations on the Fifth Periodic Report of France*. CRC/C/FRA/CO/5. Geneva: United Nations Office of the High Commissioner for Human Rights.

United Nations Committee on the Rights of the Child (2016b) *Concluding Observations on the Third and Fourth Periodic Reports of Ireland*. CRC/C/IRL/CO/3–4. Geneva: United Nations Office of the High Commissioner for Human Rights.

United Nations Committee on the Rights of the Child (2016c) *Concluding Observations on the Fifth Periodic Report of the United Kingdom of Great Britain and Northern Ireland*. CRC/C/GBR/CO/5. Geneva: United Nations Office of the High Commissioner for Human Rights.

United Nations Committee on the Rights of the Child (2017a) *Concluding Observations on the Combined Second to Fourth Periodic Reports of Estonia*. CRC/C/EST/CO/2–4. Geneva: United Nations Office of the High Commissioner for Human Rights.

United Nations Committee on the Rights of the Child (2017b) *Concluding Observations on the Fifth Periodic Report of Denmark*. CRC/C/DNK/CO/5. Geneva: United Nations Office of the High Commissioner for Human Rights.

United Nations General Assembly (1985) *United Nations Standard Minimum Rules for the Administration of Juvenile Justice*. New York: United Nations.

United Nations General Assembly (1989) *United Nations Convention on the Rights of the Child*. New York: United Nations.

United Nations General Assembly (1990a) *United Nations Guidelines for the Prevention of Juvenile Delinquency*. New York, United Nations.

United Nations General Assembly (1990b) *United Nations Rules for the Protection of Juveniles Deprived of their Liberty*. New York: United Nations.

United Nations Office on Drugs and Crime (2017) *UNODC Statistics: Crime and Criminal Justice*. Vienna: UNODC. Accessed September 9, 2017: https://data.unodc.org/

United Nations Secretary General (2016) *Status of the Convention on the Rights of the Child: Report of the Secretary-General.* New York: United Nations.

Van Kesteren, J. (2016) 'Assessing the Risk and Prevalence of Hate Crime victimization in Western Europe', *International Review of Victimology,* 22(2): 139–160.

Wacquant, L. (2008) *Urban Outcasts: A Comparative Sociology of Advanced Marginality.* Cambridge: Polity Press.

Wacquant, L. (2009) *Prisons of Poverty.* Minneapolis: University of Minnesota Press.

Winterdyk, J. (ed.) (2002) *Juvenile Justice Systems: International Perspectives,* 2nd edition. Toronto: Canadian Scholars Press.

Wiśniewska, K., Wolny, M., Szwast, M., Bodnar, A., Pietryka, A., Kremplewski, A., Grochowska, A., Chmielewska, B., Przywara, D., Czyż, E., Pacho, I., Smętek, J., Szuleka, M. and Kubaszewski, P. (2014) 'Country report: Poland', in Baeva, S. (ed.) *Children Deprived of Liberty in Central and Eastern Europe: Between Legacy and Reform.* Sofia: Bulgarian Helsinki Committee.

Zedner, L. (2002) 'Dangers of Dystopias in Penal Theory', *Oxford Journal of Legal Studies,* 22(2): 341–366.

INDEX

Note: **bold** page numbers indicate tables, *italic* numbers indicate figures.

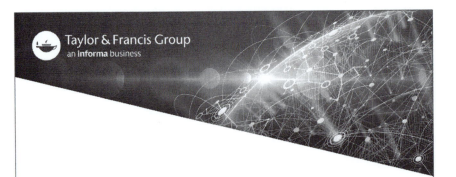